op in hardback

H/O
GN671 .S2 S54

BCL3 4.686

24-
AW
?

D1601122

SALA'ILUA
A Samoan Mystery

BRADD SHORE

GN
671
.52
S54
1982
West

New York   Columbia University Press   *1982*

This book has been published with the assistance of grants from
the National Endowment for the Humanities and
the National Science Foundation

Library of Congress Cataloging in Publication Data
Shore, Bradd, 1945–
Sala'ilua, a Samoan mystery.

Bibliography: p.
Includes index.
1. Ethnology—Western Samoa—Sala'ilua.
2. Sala'ilua (Western Samoa)—Social life and
customs.   I. Title.
GN671.S2S54   306'.0996'14   81-24188
ISBN 0-231-05382-7 (cloth)   AACR2
ISBN 0-231-05383-5 (paper)

Columbia University Press
New York *and* Guildford, Surrey

Copyright © 1982   Columbia University Press
All rights reserved
Printed in the United States of America

Clothbound editions of Columbia University Press books are Smyth-sewn
and printed on permanent and durable acid-free paper.

Maps and graphics are the work of Elaine Lorenz.

For
Pesetā Gatoloai Siaosi

Contents

Tables

Illustrations

Preface

An alien culture is inevitably a mystery and its comprehension can aptly be described as a piece of detective work. Baffling to begin with, at times intriguing (though more often merely annoying), a culture reveals itself to even the most careful observer as a network of clues, usually misleading at first, and as gradual disclosures at best only partly accurate. Such partial disclosure represents an inevitable limit to anthropological understanding both because of the peculiar route by which an anthropologist makes his way into a culture, and because of the nature of human life as it is manifested in a particular culture. The paradoxical stance of the anthropologist as participant–observer forces him to straddle two cultures—one his own, the other one which will change him and to some extent become his own as well. And there is the third perspective—usually implicit but nonetheless powerfully intuited by a fieldworker—which somehow includes both cultures and makes possible the act of translation between them. This is the intuition of the human situation itself, more powerfully apprehended in the erection of a cultural bridge than it might otherwise be. Roy Wagner (1975) has aptly characterized the construction of ethnography as an act of "symbolic mediation" in which the anthropologist "invents" the culture he studies through metaphorical bridges thrown out from his own culture.

There is also a second kind of bridging in an ethnography. This is the movement that transforms the flood of events that constitute fieldwork into a coherent account of the general symbolic patterns we call *culture* and the modes of social interaction we generalize and reify as *social structure*. The general propositons we frame are assumed to be more stable and somehow "deeper" than the particular events we observe and involve an inevitable freezing and framing of historical time. The creation of such general "structures" is not a simple mechanical task, but is inherently interpretive and thus at least partly subjective. Anthropological puzzles are not solved by any mechanical methodology that simply pieces together bits of data according to an explicit formula. Interpretation requires careful observation, a good deal of introspection, considerable doubt, and some courage as well. This is the courage of human insight and requires a tolerance for both empathy—the recognition that one can approach knowing the other—and objectivity—the awareness that in some important sense the other is profoundly different from oneself.

At its best, cultural interpretation does its bridgings between cultures and between events and structures with grace and care, illuminating rather than

swallowing up the idiosyncratic qualities of events in their local and historical contexts. Novelistic accounts, more closely married to the narrative
flow of events in time, will always have an impressionistic accuracy foreign
to standard anthropological accounts. By nature, the novel represents the
particular and only implies the general, while ethnography makes explicit
the general forms by which people live but often only sketches those events
and persons actually known and experienced by the ethnographer. Whatever
they may lack in experiential immediacy, interpretive accounts have a power
of their own, defining their own level of mystery.

For the past ten years my chief mystery has been Samoan. What follows
is an interpretive ethnography of Samoa cast as a mystery story. Whatever
disclosures of structure and meaning have been granted me unfold gradually, much as they do in the course of fieldwork itself. Obviously, there
is sleight-of-hand involved here, since a book is necessarily the product of
hindsight on predigested events, and structures already perceived through
them. But to approximate the anthropologist's own experience in understanding an unfamiliar culture, we begin with events, albeit somewhat
extraordinary events, and move gradually toward structure and meaning.

The first stage of our Samoan mystery is murder, violent death in high
places, and the sequence of events surrounding it. The mystery in this
Samoan tragedy is not that of the simple whodunit, however, for we quickly
come to know who did it and how and, even in a limited sense, why it
occurred. The mystery here is of a deeper sort, having to do with the
interplay of cultural and social structures that constitute an adequate general
context for understanding the crime and its consequences.

It is precisely this kind of understanding which comes so slowly to the
anthropologist, as to any alien observer. Unfamiliar notions of person,
place, and time, the moral context in which behavior is evaluated and made
meaningful, and the structure of social relations and its implications for
social control all constitute parts of the greater mystery which is the anthropologist's special domain of exploration. And it is with these mysteries,
so intimately bound up with a single act of homicide, that this study is
most properly concerned. On these cultural structures of social control in
Samoa the distinctively anthropological solution to the mystery at hand is
thus predicated.

In the process, we shall move well beyond the scene of the murder,
appearing at times to leave the village of Sala'ilua and its inhabitants well
in the background. In the end, we turn from death to other, perhaps greater,
mysteries—those of life and of the thinking of a people who had once been
for me a source of bafflement, and who gradually came to be a source of
atonishment.

Research Methods

This study is based on my ten years of active interest in Samoa, seven
of them as an anthropologist. In 1968 I first went to Western Samoa as a

Peace Corps volunteer teacher. I returned home after two years with a fair fluency in Samoan and a fascination with the intricacies of Samoan life and social organization. In 1971 I went back to Samoa as a graduate student in anthroplogy, and spent three months investigating Samoan adoption, incest prohibiton, and other aspects of Samoan kinship. A third trip to Samoa was made in 1972 under the auspices of the National Science Foundation and the Department of Anthropology at the University of Chicago. I undertook eighteen months of doctoral dissertation research under the primary supervision of David M. Schneider.

During almost five years of residence in Western Samoa, I lived in virtually every part of the archipelago and developed a wide network of friends and acquaintances. The case study material was collected for the most part in the village of Sala'ilua, in western Savai'i, over a period of six months. I was fortunate enough to live with the family of one of the two senior chiefs of the village, an extraordinarily canny and helpful teacher through whom I gained access to the other families of the village.

Aside from the general field notes based on observations and household surveys, my information is based on (a) a series of fifty-five two-hour interviews; (b) an extensive questionnaire distributed to approximately 140 schoolchildren on Savai'i; (c) materials written on Samoa, both published and unpublished; and (d) a series of recordings of Samoan village and district meetings, speech-making, popular songs, comedy plays, and other cultural performances, which I made during my stay in Samoa.

The final phase of my research was carried out in New Zealand at the University of Auckland and at the Alexander Turnbull Library in Wellington. I spent many weeks at the Turnbull Library working through the detailed *Reports of Evidence* of the Davidson Commission for the Study of Village and District Government, carried out in 1949 and 1950 in preparation for Western Samoa's independence. I also had the opportunity to examine the many manuscripts on Samoa that were available at the University of Auckland and, especially, at the Turnbull Library. Finally, my stay in New Zealand gave me the chance to get to know and talk with a large number of Oceanic specialists working there. These contacts were of great value in the formation of many ideas contained in this study.

Given the nature of this study, it has been difficult to maintain the anonymity of the village studied as is common practice in anthropology. The events associated with the murder of Tuatō Fatu made headlines in local Samoan papers, and are common knowledge throughout Samoa. Moreover, the particular nature of the village in which I worked turns out to be crucial to the study, and to mask the village beyond Samoan recognition while preserving the study's analytical power would by virtually impossible, given the distinctive political structure of Sala'ilua. I have tried to protect particular individuals, by using fictional personal names; the chiefly titles, however, are accurate. When I asked the chiefs and orators of Sala'ilua whether they felt I should try to mask the identity of their village when writing the book, I was urged to present the village as it was, making sure only to be as truthful and accurate as possible. I hope that my account justifies their trust, and does justice to this remarkable village and its inhabitants.

A Note on Samoan Orthography and Pronunciation

The orthography used throughout this book is the standard form used for written Samoan. The glottal stop is represented by the apostrophe ('), and vowel length is indicated by the presence or absence of the macron (ˉ).

Samoan pronunciation poses few problems for English speakers. The form written as "g" following standard orthography, is pronounced "ng" in all cases. The glottal stop is a break or constriction in the voice, such as that in the English "uh-oh!" or the Cockney pronunciation of "bottle." Otherwise, all consonants have approximately the same values as their English counterparts.

Vowels are pronounced with their "pure" values as in Spanish or Italian; there are no diphthongs. Vowel length is approxiamtely doubled when the vowel is marked by a macron. Stress is generally on the penultimate syllable.

Following Samoan practice, the plurals of Samoan words will omit the English -s. Thus such terms as *matai, ali'i,* or *tulāfale* may be either plural or singular depending on the context.

Acknowledgments

One does not come to terms with another society in a vacuum. Many voices hover behind these pages, voices from Samoa, from the United States, and from New Zealand. To give them all names and to give those names thanks here would be impossible. I would like, however, to acknowledge some of the more important of these debts.

First I would like to acknowledge the cooperation of the late Honorable Fiamē Matā'afa Mulinu'u, former Prime Minister of Western Samoa, who permitted me an extended stay in his country. Seumanatafa Pogai and Tuiletufuga Papāli'i Hunkin, chiefs of Apia Village, were kind enough to help me understand something of the social organization of an urban Samoan village. To the Ali'i and Faipule of Sala'ilua, Savai'i, I owe an enormous debt. For giving me a home, for taking me into their confidence and into their councils although I was untitled and thus out of place, for their patience with my microphones and cameras, with my endless questions and my ignorance, I owe them a debt that can only be repaid by a fair and accurate account of what they taught me. A very special note of recognition must be given to Tuatō Tualevao Fatu, whose sudden death while I resided in his family represents one of those tragic and illuminating ironies of field work, when the paradoxical stance of the field worker as participant–observer becomes most painfully apparent.

Uelese Petaia, Moana Matatumua, and Felix Wendt provided many hours of interesting and valuable discussion, as well as help and kindness in so many ways. The Samoan Commissioner of Police, the Honorable Lavea Onosā Lio, was kind enough to accord me access to Tafa'igata Prison, and to grant me interviews with several inmates. Mata'ina Te'o, Senior Librarian at the Nelson Memorial Library in Apia, has long been a friend and enthusiastic guide through the impressive holdings of the South Pacific Collection in her library. And finally, in Samoa, I owe a truly immense debt intellectually to Pesetā Gatoloai Siaosi, who constantly challenged my understandings of Samoa with his own extraordinary grasp of its culture and history, and dealt with remarkable patience and forbearance with my persistent questions and my insistent ignorances. This study bears throughtout the mark of his intellect.

My debts to scholars and friends in New Zealand are great, especially considering the relatively short time I spent there. David Pitt of the Sociology Department at the University of Auckland generously provided me with an office and a home in his department for the duration of my New Zealand stay. Cluny Macpherson has been a constant friend, intellectual adviser on matters Samoan, and perceptive critic.

My second home in Auckland was with the Anthropology Department at the University of Auckland. Special thanks must go to Tony Hooper, Judith Huntsman, and Garth Rogers for intellectual and moral support throughout my stay in New Zealand. Guy Powles, Jr. was kind enough to let me have copies of his publications on Samoan constitutional law, as well as the benefit of his long experience with and insights into the complex legal systems of Western Samoa, in both its Western and traditional aspects. The staff of the Turnbull Library in Wellington made my work there as pleasant as it was fruitful.

Parts of chapter 12 were originally published in an article printed in *Man*. Permission to reprint sections of that article is gratefully acknowledged. Sarah Lawrence College aided in the preparation of the manuscript with a small grant from its fund for faculty development.

This study has benefited from long discussions with Shelly Errington, Irving Goldman, Richard Goodman, and Penelope Meleiseā, and from critical readings by Marshall Sahlins, Bernd Lambert, Martin Silverman, and Raymond Fogelson. Marshall Sahlins also suggested the casting of the ethnography as a cultural mystery story, a suggestion quickly adopted and gratefully acknowledged. Above all the other voices which have converged behind these lined, one retains a special place. David M. Schneider, adviser, friend, adversary, and teacher, has taught me most of what I find valuable in anthropology. Where we have agreed should be clear throughout these pages. And where we have disagreed, it has been for the most part in relation to questions that he has taught me to ask. Needless to say, I alone bear final responsibility for the content of the work.

Sala'ilua: A Samoan Mystery

The Island Setting

On a map at least, the Samoan (or Navigators) Islands sit comfortably within our descriptive categories. The inhabited islands of the Samoan Archipelago lie in an area of the southwest Pacific Ocean between the latitudes 13° and 15° south and longitudes 168° and 173° west. Despite the travel-poster claim that Samoa is "the heart of Polynesia," geographically at least the Samoan Islands are found near the western edge of the Polynesian triangle, bearing close cultural and historical ties to peoples of the nearby Tongan Islands, Niue, Tokelau, and Ellice Islands.

Although there are about fourteen islands in the Samoa group (depending on how islands are to be distinguished from rocks), only nine are permanently inhabited. Only three are of any significant size, and these contain the great majority of the population. All are volcanic "high" islands of relatively recent origin. To the far west in the group lies Savai'i, the largest and highest of the islands, with Mt. Silisili rising 6,095 feet above the Pacific and six other mountains above 5,000 feet. Savai'i contains about 700 square miles and is vaguely diamond-shaped. Despite this great land area, however, the presence of two great lava fields to the north of the island (evidence of volcanic activity at the turn of the century), poor harbors, a generally stony soil, and relative scarcity of readily available fresh water have limited cultivation and population density on the island. The 1971 Census listed Savai'i's population as 40,572—close to the estimated population of the entire archipelago at the time of initial European contact.[1] This population is distributed among some eighty-five named villages,[2] of which all but thirteen are coastal settlements. Today Savai'i has two major harbors. Saleloga, in the southwest, is the major landing for the interisland launches and ferries which daily cross the twelve-mile Apolima Channel between Upolu and Savai'i. In recent years, the development of a timber industry in the north of Savai'i by an American company has led to the construction of a new deep-water wharf at Asau and the growth of an incipient urban area for Savai'i.

To the east of Savai'i lies Upolu island. Although considerably smaller in area than its neighbor, comprising 430 square miles, Upolu has the highest population in the archipelago. In 1971 Upolu's population was reported to be 106,063—just over 2.5 times that of Savai'i. Unlike Savai'i, Upolu has a fairly good natural harbor at Apia on the north coast, although a true deep-water wharf had to be dredged. The relatively favorable hydrological resources of Upolu, the fertility and arability of its soil, and the presence of a broad expanse of gently sloping coastal lowland in the north-west of the island have all contributed to the island's high population density.[3] The population of the island is distributed over about 165 named villages, the great majority of them fringing the coastline.

Demographically and economically, the island may be thought of as comprising three distinct regions.[4] The Apia urban area, the governmental seat of the independent state of Western Samoa, is actually a loose association of about fifty distinct villages, of which the traditional village of Apia is only one. This confederation of villages called Apia or "the urban area" has no legal existence and, indeed, the precise boundaries of the area are difficult to draw. The commercial life of the country is centered in this area, whose 1971 population was listed as between 26,000 and 40,000, depending on how its boundaries are defined.

The second demographic area of Upolu is composed of an almost continuous string of densely populated villages lying along the twenty-five miles of paved road between Apia and the international airport at Faleolo. These villages, numbering over thirty, may be termed "urbanizing" or "transitional" in that population density is considerably higher than in rural villages, and there is a greater dependence on a cash economy and Western material culture than in the more rural areas.

The third region is really a residual category, generally called rural or traditional villages. To Samoans they are "the back villages." They include the villages of the eastern or southern parts of Upolu which have only limited access to the urban area, and whose dependence on the traditional subsistence economy is greater than in other parts of the island.

In the middle of the Apolima strait, between Upolu and Savai'i, lie two smaller inhabited islands, Manono and Apolima. Together only about 1.5 square miles in area, these two islands, together with Upolu and Savai'i, make up the inhabited islands of Western Samoa. There is but a single village on Apolima, sitting within the partially eroded cone of an extinct volcano. The resident population of the island is about 250, and access to the village is through a small opening in the reef fringing the mouth of the volcano cone. Only the experienced rowers of the island's longboats attempt daily the perilous journey from Apolima to the Upolu "mainland." Although the island is watered by a freshwater stream, arable land on Apolima is scarce and poor. The national government has given the villagers of Apolima a section of arable land on the northwestern coast of Upolu, now named Apolima Fou (New Apolima), where many of the island's residents farm their gardens and some make their home.

Manono, about two miles in circumference, contains four villages, Its gently sloping interior does provide plantation land, although the island is devoid of natural sources of fresh water except for rain-catchment. As with Apolima, the island's main cash crop is copra, but the land of Manono has not proved adequate to support the more than one thousand villagers on the island. Like Apolima, Manono has been granted a parcel of land on Upolu, named Manono Uta (Manono Inland) for planting. Because it lies within the fringing reef that surrounds most of Upolu, access to Manono is relatively easy, and several small motor launches ferry passengers several times daily between Manono and Upolu.

Despite its small size, Manono has played an important role as a naval power in Samoan history. Within historical times, Manono contracted a military alliance with Malietoa, one of the four paramount chiefs of Western Samoa, and through him with parts of the island of Savai'i. Manono today is accorded general Samoan recognition as *'āiga i le tai* "family of the sea," one of Malietoa's families, and thus an important place in Samoan political life.[5]

Approximately eighty miles off the eastern tip of Upolu and slightly south lies the island of Tutuila, the main island of American Samoa, an "Unincorporated Territory" of the United States since 1900. Between eighty and one hundred miles due east of Tutuila lie the three tiny islets of Ofu, Ta'ū, and Olosega, known jointly as the Manu'a group of American Samoa. Tutuila and its tiny inhabited satellite island of Aunu'u together total only about fifty square miles, less than one eighth of the area of Upolu. Topographically, Manu'a and Tutuila are characterized by steep, rugged mountains falling off sharply to the sea, providing relatively little readily arable land. It is common today to see patches of taro appearing to hang from the steep lower slopes of the mountains of Tutuila, and for the most part Tutuilans today are dependent on imported produce from Western Samoa and the United States. Historically at least, the most significant geographic feature of Tutuila is the large natural deep-water harbor at Pago Pago, now the main port and capital town of the Territory of American Samoa. This harbor, one of the finest in the South Pacific, has featured prominently and militarily in the colonial history of the archipelago, and in the nineteenth century made Tutuila a strategic coaling station for European and American ships.[6]

Culturally and linguistically, the entire Samoan archipelago reveals a remarkably unified identity and striking homogeneity.[7] This homogeneity reflects, in part, the elaborate network of kinship and political alliances not only throughout any one island, but among the different islands as well. Samoans are avid travelers, both within and between islands.

One notable effect of Samoan mobility within the archipelago is the almost total absence of significant language dialects.[8] There appear to be slight lexical and intonational differences between the languages spoken in American Samoa, at least in part because of the influences of different degrees of colonization. Western Samoans also frequently assert that the pronunciation in both Manu'a and the remote Savai'i village of Faleālupo conserve in colloquial as well as formal speech a phonemically older and "purer" Samoan than that spoken in the rest of the archipelago.[9] This assertion appears, however, to have more ideological than factual status, since my own visit to Faleālupo revealed no significant difference in pronunciation from that found elsewhere in the islands. (For a closer look at some of the implications of this dual phonology in Samoan, see chapter 13.) With these possible exceptions noted, the lack of significant dialects in the Samoan language remains an important linguistic and cultural fact.

In the indigenous political macrostructure of the Samoan islands, Tutuila and Aunu'u Islands were incorporated with the Atua District in eastern Upolu.[10] Only the Manu'a islands had any degree of political autonomy from the western part of the archipelago, a political and historical autonomy symbolized by the office of Tui Manu'a, paramount chief of Manu'a. These traditional political divisions did not, however, play a significant part in the political status of the archipelago in the face of the political and economic ambitions of European and American colonial powers in the western Pacific during the second half of the nineteenth century, which culminated in the political division of the archipelago in 1900 between Germany and the United States (see Gilson 1970).

PART I

EVENTS

CHAPTER ONE

A Death in the Family

The heat grows steadily in Samoa throughout the late morning and early afternoon. It is hot and steamy, even in the "cool months" when the Trades lend a cooling breeze to the islands. On ordinary days, not much happens in Sala'ilua during these blazing hours.

Conversation among the women and older girls sitting or reclining in the open *fale* becomes more muted, only occasionally broken by shrill laughter at a piece of fresh gossip, or by the crying of an infant. The drone of soft music from the radio only adds to the general torpor. The weaving of mats slows in the heat and many simply sleep the afternoon out, occasionally lifting a hand to swat an annoying fly, or halfheartedly flick a fan to raise a transient breeze.

In the gardens, the sweep of bush knives clearing undergrowth for new planting, and the thud of the digging sticks preparing the way for new taro shoots, also give way to the sun. The men and boys and the occasional women who come to help there retire to the small temporary *fale* erected casually amid the baroque layers of enormous taro and ta'amū leaves. These huts serve as temporary shelters for the workers and lookout posts to protect the gardens from marauding pigs or, even worse, taro thieves who live, as the villagers complain, off the sweat of others.

It was in the late afternoon of one such hot and cloudless day in July of 1973 that I roused myself from an hour of sifting indecisively through a recent batch of field notes. Feeling vaguely guilty at my lack of energy and fighting off a powerful urge to stare blankly out to sea, I resolved to take a therapeutic run a mile or so down the main road. The winter sun was already sinking mercifully low in the western sky, but it was not yet dark and the dogs had not laid claim to the road.

Being well out of shape from too many months of slow movement and a diet heavy with toro, I jogged hesitantly from the large two-story *fale* where I was living with Tuatō Fatu and his large family. Carefully avoiding the stones and small holes that pocked the grassy area around Tuatō's compound, I made my way to the dirt road that lay some twenty-five yards from the main house and turned north, heading into the *'a'ai* or village center.

Sala'ilua is a large village by Samoan standards, comprising three sub-villages, three large churches, and a number of major trading stores. Tuatō's compound was near the outer edge of the *'a'ai*. The main government road running through the village winds along the rugged coastline, and I could just make out the thin white line of breakers washing over the reef about a mile out into the lagoon. A number of small fishing canoes were making their way slowly toward the shore, with the enormous bamboo bonito fishing poles trailing in a graceful arc at the rear. Perhaps there would be fresh fish tonight, a welcome break from the canned pilchards and mackerel that complemented the taro and bananas in most meals.

I lumbered past some of the larger buildings of the village, including the sizable wooden structure housing a branch of an Apia-based trading company and home of one of the few freezers in the district. Like most general stores, this was a place to meet neighbors, catch up on gossip, and (in this case) for dehydrated anthropologists to savor a cold and appallingly sweet soft drink imported from Apia. On the seaward side of the road lay the Apollo Club, a large clapboard building at present boarded up, but known throughout the district as the site of some lively dances, and which served now and then as a local movie theater. For an outsider, of course, the real entertainment at these showings is not so much the kung-fu or cowboy movie as it is the boisterous enthusiasm of the audience, as some of the local film buffs keep up a running public commentary on the film—a commentary unimpeded by any apparent comprehension of the plot or dialogue.

I was now in the very center of the village, and to my right lay one of the village's two *malae,* open areas empty of *fale,* and sacred political centers of the village. That this large sandy area, patched here and there with grass, was sacred is a matter of tradition, but aside from the presence of several large, round meeting houses on its periphery, there was nothing much to distinguish the *malae* from any other places in the village. Indeed, a concrete cricket pitch placed seemingly irreverently just inside the *malae* attested to the occasional nature of this sanctity, and to the fact that the village would gather at a *malae* only in rare times of great political celebration or a crisis affecting the whole community.

I jogged on, beginning to breathe heavily but determined to find my second wind. After passing by the freshwater spring that serves for both bathing and washing clothes, I suddenly decided to turn around and head back through the village center and toward the less populated fringes of the village. Farther north lay a contiguous string of smaller villages; there I was on less familiar ground, and would certainly be an object of great amusement and curiosity. After a busy morning, I suddenly felt the urge to be alone and headed south for the bush.

The great white concrete Congregational church is an unofficial boundary of the southern part of the main residential area of Sala'ilua, and as I approached it and the enormous two-story pastor's residence adjacent to it, I felt my pace quicken and my breathing ease. I was leaving the village, and felt happy at the prospect of a long, isolated stretch of unpopulated ground. Living in a Samoan village means unrelieved sociality, an experience with inevitable strains for even the accustomed Western visitor.

The household compounds began to thin out, with fewer, smaller houses, and much larger garden areas or bush between them. The frequent waves and hellos from others on the road and from occupants of the *fale* gave way to longer stretches of silence and solitude. These were treasured moments for me, for now I could indulge in the luxury of uninterrupted introspection, a withdrawal from the insistent civilities of Samoan social life into a private world of recollections and musings. It had been a long, busy week, and my stay in Sala'ilua was rapidly drawing to a close. There was much to think about. Gradually my body was finding its pace, and the steady rhythms of my breathing and the regular pounding of my feet on the sandy roadbed made the thoughts come more easily. Now and then I would meet a few men headed home from the gardens laden with baskets of taro and coconuts, and my attention would be briefly diverted in a breathy greeting. But there was less to distract me now, and the dense vegetation on both sides of the road provided little to draw me from my thoughts.

I had come to Sala'ilua six months before to live with Tuatō Fatu and his family. (See appendix C for a diagram of relationships among the major figures in the events to follow.) His elder sister, in whose family I had once lived for a year as a Peace Corps volunteer, had insisted that if I wanted to learn about the real Samoa I should go to distant Savai'i, to Sala'ilua, a "back village" and her own father's birthplace. Sala'ilua had a certain notoriety in its district, she had said, and would almost certainly prove to be an interesting place for someone like myself concerned with the intricacies of Samoan culture. Her brother, Tuatō, was one of the village's two senior *matai,* or chiefs, as well as a teacher in the local primary school. He would, I was assured, be able to look after my welfare properly and could teach me, moreover, whatever customs I wanted to learn about. Her arguments were persuasive. Besides, I had my own interests in this village. Five years earlier, while still a Peace Corps volunteer, I had circled Savai'i on a small motorbike. After a relatively uneventful two days clattering from village to village over the uneven stretches of road, I found myself in Sala'ilua, overwhelmed and a bit frightened by a crowd of perhaps a hundred very curious children, eager to climb onto the bike, and perhaps get to touch the *pālagi.* At that time, the Peace Corps was new to Samoa and few *pālagi,* other than missionaries and schoolteachers, had much contact with remote Samoan villages. Most villagers were initially quite shy in our presence, but not those from Sala'ilua. Here, I had thought, is an unusual village. Perhaps one day I would come back and find out more.

I had not been disappointed. There was, as it turned out, a great deal more to learn about Sala'ilua, and Tuatō had proved to be a valuable informant and an amusing guide through his village. Not yet fifty, he was nonetheless one of the "old men" of the village, wielding power and influence beyond his years. One of his two chiefly titles, Tuatō, although that of a *tulāfale* or orator, was nonetheless one of the two leading titles in the village. The Tuatō title had, in Sala'ilua, a supreme status, shared with another orator title, Tuitolova'a. Together these titles were known formally in ceremonial address as *igoa matua*—"senior names." In older published accounts of Sala'ilua the Tuatō and Tuitolova'a titles had been referred to as "demon-men," and even today these titles conferred upon their holders the attributes of being "tough" or "strong" men.

There was nothing in Fatu's appearance to suggest great power. Neither particularly tall nor of grand proportions, Fatu did not through sheer corporeal presence suggest the *mamalu* or dignity that Samoans associate with power. And yet there was in his eyes a distinct twinkle, lively and amiable, and a restless alertness which suggested a keen and curious observer and a capacity for fun and even mischief.

Power in Samoa does not bring with it inevitably the affection of those in its shadow. Respect is not confused with personal regard. In Fatu's case, his relatively recent arrival in the village and his rapid ascendancy to political preeminence through title, intelligence, and oratorical ability contributed to the ambivalent feelings with which villagers viewed him. And yet, while he had his detractors and even his enemies, Fatu was generally well liked in Sala'ilua. Admired for his vitality and appreciated for his wit, Fatu was a man who obviously knew how to live well. Quick to anger, he was also quick to laugh. He was a funny man, *tausua* as Samoans say, and in Samoa, humor is the perfect complement to power. Even his formal speeches were marked by wit, and the solemnity of the weekly chiefs' meetings was often broken by his joking.

Nonetheless, Fatu was a kind of pillar of morality in the community, responsible as a ranking *matai* for maintaining the good name and social harmony of Sala'ilua. With great seriousness he had recounted to me all of the important laws which he had helped formulate for the village and which he was now responsible for enforcing—laws concerning drinking of alcohol or bush beer, laws against gambling in the village, laws regulating the lives of the youth, all necessary to protect villagers not only from others but also from their own passions. And yet Fatu, no severe martinet, had a keen sense of human frailty. One could often find him at the schoolhouse engaging in a poker match after school, and a sly nip of beer now and then wouldn't after all damage the dignity of the laws. Solemnity was essential but life went on after hours too.

Tuatō Fatu wielded his power deftly, usually with a light touch. But he could be assertive—even rough when occasion warranted. One such occasion had presented itself a few years before my arrival when Fatu's neighbor, married to one of his distant cousins, had presumed to build a large *pālagi*-style house next to, and just in front of, his own. Fatu had been furious at what he saw as an act of pretension and a personal insult, placing the house of a lesser chief between his own official residence and the *malae*. The *mana* of the Tuatō title, Fatu had told me, was too strong to bear such an insult lightly. Retribution was certain. Indeed, Fatu had confided to me, the old man had recently taken ill. The local doctor could find nothing wrong. He had all but stopped eating, was growing weak and thin. One morning, Fatu had come to me and in a whisper had asked if I had heard the dogs howling in the taro patch during the night. I had. This was, Fatu told me, a sure omen of impending death. He had gone to the old man that morning to forgive him. But it was too late. The man's sons were already hammering together a coffin, as I could hear. The *mana* of the Tuatō title was powerful, said Fatu, and Fatu promised that before the week was out, we would have a death in the village.

I had slowed my jog to a rapid walk, my body both exhilarated and exhausted from the unaccustomed exercise. It was almost dusk and the day's heat had finally given way to the more benevolent coolness that comes with the evening. The heavy smell of smoke from the cookhouses was everywhere. Ribbons of smoke rose dreamily in the distance. Soon the conch would sound the curfew for evening prayers, and it would be embarrassing to be caught like this on the road. I turned back towards Sala'ilua, and walked quickly up the road again, anxious to get back to the village, but not quite ready to give up my stream of thoughts.

My mind moved around some of the more recent events in the village. The day before, I had been permitted to attend a noisy special meeting of the Women's Committee, convened to adjudicate a fight that had broken out the previous day between two girls. One, it was said, had made some uncomplimentary remarks about the other and her alleged affair with a young man from Apia who had come to help the Committee set up water-seal toilets in the village. Such slanderous remarks are not taken lightly, particularly when the two young ladies happen to come from the families of Tuitolova'a and Tuatō. A hair-pulling fight erupted between the girls who were in the same work party, and the Committee's work had been completely disrupted. Accusations, apologies, and impassioned defenses were heard, and many tears were shed.

Women were like this, some men had told me, and had less control over their feelings than did men. Neither of the two girls was ever called on to testify in the meeting, and despite all of the commotion, no real resolution to the conflict had been sought. Each of the girls' families was simply levied heavy fines in food, and the legal matter of slander and assault was left for the government courts. Such sensitive matters, I was assured, were better dealt with in the courts than in the village itself, where they would only serve to disrupt peaceful relations between the two senior descent groups in the village.

Earlier in the day, I had gone to the village school where Fatu was a teacher, to observe a few classes. I was particularly interested in the ways in which the Samoan teachers managed to transform a boisterous class into a regiment of attentive students through a combination of fear and cajoling. In some of the younger classes, a lesson was begun with a kind of simon-says routine, in which the students all imitated the teacher in making various hand motions. Gradually the tangle of small jumping bodies began to move together, at one with the teacher. Now it seemed they were ready to learn, to repeat again and again the teacher's words, committing them to memory. The teachers had asked me to give them a lesson, any kind of lesson, after school, and I complied with a lesson on English comprehension. Following

morning tea, I had left the schoolhouse, Fatu remaining behind with one
or two of the other teachers, presumably for an afternoon poker match.

In some Samoan villages events move slowly, and little breaks the regular
pace of things. Occasionally there is a death in the village, an important
title is bestowed, or the marriage of an important person is celebrated, and
frequently there are births to mark the passing of time. Then the village
swells with excitement as kin assemble from all over Samoa, and the place
vibrates with the excitement of significant events. It had long been clear
to me that Sala'ilua was not such a backwater. An unofficial district center,
Sala'ilua was a place where things just seemed to happen, and this fact was
apparent to the villagers themselves. *Apia Lua,* Second Apia, someone had
once dubbed the village, and the villagers were proud of their reputation.
"We of Sala'ilua—we know how to get things done," I was told repeatedly,
and for an anthropologist such a high pitch of village activity made life
continually interesting, if exhausting.

Fatu had assured me of my good fortune in choosing Sala'ilua. I was able
to see firsthand so many of the important Samoan institutions at work.
There had been a meeting of the entire district just at the time I had first
arrived in Sala'ilua: the district had gathered to discuss the recent closing
of the district hospital by the government Department of Health. Some
boys from one of the villages had stoned one of the hospital buildings, and
the staff nurse had complained to the Director of Health in Apia. Now it
was up to the district to punish the offending village. The boys themselves
had already been taken to jail.

There were also more pleasant occurrences. When an important traveling
party had arrived from Tutuila in American Samoa to visit affines in
Sala'ilua, the entire village had turned out for the festivities. There had been
an elaborate kava ceremony, performed this time not by the chiefs but by
the *aualuma,* the young girls' organization. (Kava, a drink made from the
root of the *piper methysticum* tree, is served ceremonially at all important
gatherings, especially meetings of chiefs.)[1] A lot of money, food, and mats
had changed hands. This had been expected. It was after all a visit from
wealthy relatives in American Samoa, relatives who would never come
empty handed. That night there was great festivity, exuberant singing and
dancing, and comedy routines performed by both hosts and guests.

When there was a lull in village activities, Fatu created significant events
for me. One day only a few weeks before he had taken me to see his
plantation, far from the village. We sat in the small plantation hut, and Fatu
let me record a formal Samoan speech. He said that he wanted to record
on my tape cassette a sample of his own oratory, and I was more than glad
to oblige. For a moment Fatu pondered over the various speeches in his
extensive repertory. Then suddenly he broke into a smile and said that he
had a wonderful speech that he wanted to record, a speech that had won
the day for him several years before, and had turned the ears of even the
most experienced orators present. It was, he said, an oration on the death
of a distinguished chief, and it was for this speech that he wanted to be
remembered in America.

And indeed it was a marvelous speech, so far as I could make out, full of biblical allusions, interwoven with traditional proverbs and a few colorful images of Tuatō's own making. The sky, we were told, had been rent asunder, the moon torn from its moorings because of the death of a great chief. The speech extolled the virtues of the departed and the greatness of his family, spelling out the terrifying consequences of this chief's having "left the government." I found myself deeply moved by the speech, although unable to follow the more obscure allusions and elevated language. Tuatō was clearly a skillful speaker, and his deep, resonant voice was affecting as the speech moved towards its conclusion.

When it was over, Fatu insisted on replaying the recording three or four times, evidently pleased at his own performance. His eyes gleamed; he was totally taken up with his words, as if they had a power and life of their own. "Now you have in your machine," Fatu said, "some great Samoan words to take back to America. You have seen many things here in Sala'ilua; there is much for you to take back to your university. But there is one thing which you have yet to witness, one great event which we need to cap off your study. That is the *fono tauati*, the great general convocation of the entire village on the *malae*. Only here will you see the greatest of Samoan meetings, where speeches are made outside on the *malae*, rather than inside the meeting house. But to see a general convocation we must have a great event—a crisis. And before you leave, perhaps we will be lucky. Perhaps we will find a way to convene such a meeting."

I was nearing the outskirts of Sala'ilua now. There was considerable activity around the cookhouses in each of the compounds, as the young men prepared the *saka*—the boiled taro, yams and bananas—which made up the staple of the evening meal. Some of the smaller children ran out to the road to watch me, and the by-now familiar cries of *Pālagi, Pālagi,* or Peleti (my Samoan name), followed me as I jogged up the road at a slightly quickening pace.

A young chief overtook me, walking quickly as if propelled by the weight of the taro he carried in baskets slung on a stick that rested firmly on his massive shoulder. "*Fa,*" he said, bidding me farewell as he made his way toward the village. This was Fotu'a'ava, a talented younger orator, and a distant relative of Tuatō Fatu whom, some said, Fatu was grooming for a place of power in Sala'ilua.

Fotu'a'ava's own mother was a distant cousin of Tuatō, and for some reason which was never made clear to me, old Ruta had taken up residence in a small hut in the rear of Tuatō's own compound, rather than with her own son. Not long before leaving for my run, I had completed an extensive interview with this garrulous old lady. It had been a strange interview, but interesting. Like many older ladies Ruta had lost many of the inhibitions of her youth; she was quick to provide me with village gossip and had ready opinions about almost everything.

Despite her great candor, and her enthusiasm for the more lurid aspects of village life, there was one part of Ruta's interview which stood out as an anomaly. In the course of the interview, I had asked for her assessment of the worst crimes she could think of, and the punishments appropriate for them. I was mainly interested here in the criteria used by informants for evaluating the relative seriousness of different offenses and the punishment appropriate for each. Ruta's assessment of human nature was hard, even cynical. She was quick to relate cases of theft, rape, and other serious crimes that she had heard about.

When I asked about her omission of murder, she looked at me, her expression changed, and replied: "Murder? Samoa today has nothing of that sort. We don't have any murders of our own people here." She stopped suddenly, her eyes avoiding mine briefly, lost in thought. Then she continued, "We don't have the kinds of wars here where if one person kills another person from another family, a person from that family tries to kill that person's relatives in revenge. Not here in Samoa." She looked at me intently. "Of course, we have minor skirmishes, and the fines take care of those matters. But nothing like murder. Nothing really serious like that."

I had let the incident pass, knowing that she was partly right—murder *was* extremely rare, at least in well-ordered villages, and traditional Samoan legal institutions were normally successful in keeping conflicts to relatively minor levels. But, of course, one did hear now and then of murders, and the *Samoa Times* rarely went a week without a report of a death resulting from a lovers' quarrel or a jealous husband, or a family feud. Ruta had not been completely candid in this case. Perhaps she was simply falling into the common Samoan practice of presenting an idealized account of what should be, and letting it pass for what is.

This made sense and, as I approached the village proper, other things caught my attention. Ahead, in the distance, was the roof of the Congregational church and just beyond, Tuatō's compound. Since it was now just before dinnertime, and most people are normally preparing for the evening meal or taking their evening showers, it struck me as strange to see so many people congregating on the road ahead. They seemed more animated than usual, and I unconsciously quickened my pace as I approached the crowd.

Suddenly a group of small children hurtled past me, running at a full clip toward the village, and I began to sense that something was not right. An old man, a holder of one of the lesser chiefly titles of the village, appeared at the side of the road from his house. "Go quickly," he said to me, with an urgency in his voice. Noting my surprise he asked, "Have you not heard what has happened?" I answered that I hadn't, and he suddenly looked away. "Go quickly; Elena needs you," he said. Elena was Tuatō's wife. I began to run towards the crowd.

As I approached the crowd, I heard a scream. "*'Ua maliu, 'ua maliu,* he's dead," one of the old women cried, and suddenly everyone was crying and running up the road, toward the far end of the village. "Who's dead?" I asked. "What's happened?" "Don't you know? Didn't you hear?" shouted old Ruta, calling down from the upper story of our *fale*. "We're cursed, we're cursed," she kept crying. "It's Tuatō. He's dead! They murdered him! They murdered the old man on the road!"

I was no longer running. Standing there in the middle of the road, I stared blankly ahead. Momentarily paralyzed by fear and confusion, a dozen thoughts and images washed through my mind. Flashes of my own father's death, several years earlier, gave way to images of Tuatō sitting at his desk at school, where I had left him a few hours earlier. All about me was panic and confusion, violent cries and people running. To the anthropologist, fieldwork is always partly drama, an impression fostered by the distance one is obliged to maintain. Here suddenly was real drama or, rather, no drama at all. Everything seemed trapped midway between fact and dream. I was slow to react. I found myself running with the others up the road past the Apollo Club and the *malae,* heading for the large crowd that had gathered near Nelson's Store, by the path leading down to the road from the schoolhouse. An old truck owned by one of the village shopkeepers suddenly lurched forward with a squeal from among the crowd and roared up the road. On the back of the truck, I could make out a group of men huddled around something. It was, I would soon find out, Fatu's body being taken to the hospital.

Pushing myself through the crowd of tensed bodies, I made my way to the spot where the old man had evidently fallen. All that was left now was a pool of blood and a spattered shirt which someone had torn from Tuatō's body. I felt a hand on my shoulder. It was old Tuiatua, a distinguished orator with whom I had become friendly over the past months. "Peleti," he said, his voice grim and urgent, "get back home. Or better, go to the pastor's house. You'll be safe there. There is much danger here; perhaps there will be war."

I turned to ask what had happened, but he was gone. Heeding Tuiatua's advice, I headed quickly back toward the compound to find Elena. Approaching the house, I heard moans coming from the top story of the house, moans followed by a slow, shrill wail. I found myself shivering, in a cold sweat, and a wave of nausea suddenly swelled from my gut. The cries, strange unearthly sounds, came from Ruta; sounds of fear and of grief, at once spontaneous and conventional. My eyes, I discovered, were wet with tears.

Elena had gone to the hospital to be with her husband. Her eldest son Galu, on hearing of his father's death, had uttered a strange cry, grabbed a machete, and run out of the house. I managed to calm Ruta enough to learn that Tuatō had been shot in the chest with a rifle—shot by Agafili Ioane. Gradually Tuiatua's warning to me began to make sense. The gravity of the crisis was becoming evident.

Agafili Ioane, some fifteen years Tuatō's junior, was also a Sala'ilua orator of considerable intelligence and skill. He and Fatu were both teachers in the village school. That the two did not get on well had been evident earlier in the day, when they had argued briefly over morning tea. Most significant, though, was the fact that Agafili was the son of Tuitolova'a Aleki, a ranking holder of the Tuitolova'a title from Sala'ilua and, along with Tuatō, one of the two senior chiefs of the village. The Agafili title held by Ioane was clearly subordinate in power and authority to both the Tuitolova'a and

Tuatō titles, so that from one point of view the murder constituted an act of extraordinary political insubordination and an offense to the rank and dignity of the family of Tuatō.

From another point of view, however, the murder was understood as a most serious rift and confrontation between the two most senior political titles of Sala'ilua. In Samoa, as elsewhere, murder is considered the most serious of crimes. Particularly awful is the murder of a senior chief. But when one of the two senior chiefs of a village is murdered by the son of the other, the two representing major families and political factions in a village, then that village is brought to the brink of war and its political integrity is undercut.

CHAPTER TWO

Repercussions

With the events surrounding the death of Tuatō Fatu still vividly before us, let us now take a step back, gaining some distance from the immediate events, and in so doing move closer into the heart of the murder as it touched the lives of the villagers. Fatu was dead, taken suddenly by a rifle shot. The man who pulled the trigger, it was quickly discovered, was a young teacher, a colleague of Fatu's and an up-and-coming member of the village council of chiefs. The death was obviously of considerable personal consequence to me, but it also had complex ramifications for the political and social life of the village itself.

Fatu and Agafili Ioane had a history of competition and overt conflict. Both taught in the local village school, both among the most intelligent and ambitious of the staff. Ioane, a graduate of Samoa College, was young, extremely intelligent, and skillful in both English and Samoan oratory. About a year earlier, Fatu and Ioane had come to blows after a card game, during which Fatu had called Ioane a "lapdog," a reference to the fact that the Agafili title traditionally "serves" the two senior titles of the village. The fight, I was told, had led to a general village meeting on the *malae,* which resulted in Fatu's banishment from the village and a fine of fifteen large sows. Later the banishment order was rescinded and the fine reduced to only five pigs. Fatu attempted to satisfy the fine by paying six forty-pound tins of cabin biscuits, but the chiefs refused to accept his offer, enforcing their demand for the five pigs.

It also appears that at the time of the murder Fatu and Ioane were engaged in a dispute over land boundaries in their gardens. In previously unplanted and unclaimed bushland within the recognized limits of village garden lands, a planter has the right to claim all the land he can work. His garden must, however, be developed straight inland toward the central highlands of the island rather than diagonally, since diagonal garden expansion would present difficulties in determining boundaries. Had Fatu lived, it is probable that the village plantation committee would have been called in to adjudicate the matter and, failing a satisfactory solution to the problem, the matter would have been taken to the Land and Titles Court for arbitration.

The immediate cause of the murder appears to have been a fight on the school compound over a late afternoon poker session among several of the teachers. It appears that Fatu had been winning and had accused Ioane of cheating. The accusations had led to an exchange of angry words and finally to blows. All the players had been drinking and tempers had grown short.

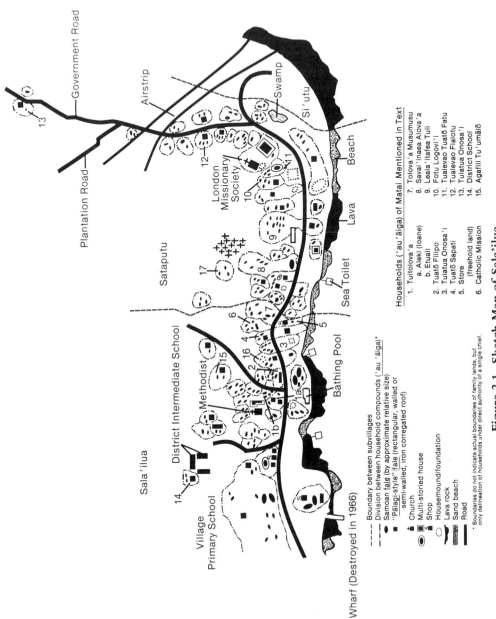

Figure 2.1. Sketch Map of Sala'ilua.

In this first encounter between Fatu and Ioane, the latter had been knocked to the ground and had received a minor injury to his head when he fell on a stone. Enraged, Ioane left the school compound and returned to his European-style house, which was situated on the main road near its intersection with the path to the school compound (household no. 1a, fig. 2.1). Grabbing his rifle, Ioane hid behind the louvered windows of his house, waiting for Fatu to pass by on his way home. When Fatu finally appeared, Ioane gave vent to his anger, killing Fatu with a single bullet in the chest.

The Second Day: Moves Toward Reconciliation

Very early on the morning of July 20, the day after the shooting, before sunrise and under the cover of darkness, two figures seated themselves on the ground just outside the large house where Fatu lay, surrounded by friends and relatives keeping an all-night vigil over the body. The two solitary figures sat quietly, their heads covered with fine mats. This was the *ifoga,* a ceremonial humiliation by members of the descent groups defined by the Agafili and Tuitolova'a titles (Tuitolova'a is commonly abridged to Tolova'a, a practice I shall follow here) who had come to apologize formally to the descent groups in which Fatu had held his two titles. Under the mats, in ceremonial disgrace, were neither Agafili Ioane, the murderer, nor his father, Tolova'a Aleki. The former was in police custody at the Tuasivi Government Hospital. He had been operated on the previous evening and was recovering from a machete attack by Tuatō's eldest son Galu. The local constable had been unable to prevent the feared attempt at revenge by Fatu's sons. Tolova'a Aleki had been in Apia at a church conference at the time of the murder and was not in the village to represent his family. At the time of the *ifoga* he was probably not even aware of what had occurred in the village or of the part his son had played in the affair. Representing the two political families were Aleki's cousin and co-titleholder, Tolova'a Etuali, and Etuali's younger brother Agafili Tu'umālō. Holding parallel political ranks to those of Aleki and Ioane, the two were the logical representatives for them.

At about 6:00 A.M., just at sunrise, Tualevao Fialotu, who had shared the Tualevao title with Fatu and who had informally taken over the affairs of Fatu's household for the moment, invited the two penitent chiefs into the house of Fotu'a'ava Logovi'i (household no. 10, fig. 2.1), adjoining Fatu's own household on a common piece of land. Ironically, this was the very house that had so angered Fatu in his lifetime because it blocked his own house from the *malae.* This invitation for the *ifoga* party to meet with the representatives of the murdered man's political families was the first move toward formal reconciliation, since it indicated a certain measure of goodwill on the part of the victim's kin.

Thus early on the morning following the murder the first of several formal meetings took place. Present at this all-important first confrontation of the antagonistic families were Tualevao Fialotu and his close friend, Fa'atoafe, senior orator from the Sala'ilua subvillage of Si'utu. Also present were the Congregational pastor and a group of chiefs from the village of Taga, a traditional political ally of Sala'ilua, who had come to pay their respects. Finally, there were Tolova'a Etuali and Agafili Tu'umālō representing the families of the murderer.

The meeting began with a long, dignified speech by the pastor, speaking in the controlled and gentle "t-pronunciation" (see chapter 13). The first part of his talk was filled liberally with *tatou* "we-plural-inclusive" forms, a common linguistic indication that there is fragmentation within a group which the speaker is trying to mask. The speech was intoned like a prayer and, indeed, represented a kind of prayer to those present to resist the temptations placed in their path by Satan, and to draw from God the will and the spirit to resist the desire for revenge. The plea was phrased in terms of an ongoing war between Satan and God within each person.

Addressing Tolova'a and Agafili, the pastor indicated by way of two proverbs that they had been reduced to humiliation and great suffering through the acts of one of their kinsmen. The emphasis was on both directing blame and deflecting it—softening the impact of the confrontation. The pastor admonished the families of the murderer to remain humble in the face of their actions so that God would show them mercy.

Faiumu, the senior chief present from Taga village, delivered a long speech congratulating all present on meeting in the spirit of love and reconciliation and assuring continued peace in this part of *tatou nu'u* (our district). The pastor then delivered a final speech thanking God for having brought peace and reconciliation on this terribly difficult day. Then he asked permission to leave and withdrew from the gathering.

Old Fa'atoafe of Si'utu addressed some concluding remarks to the chiefs from Taga, asking them to stay on and have a rest in the village. At this point, however, he was interrupted by Tolova'a Etuali, who had until this point remained silent. Barely able to speak, Tolova'a managed the appropriate honorific greetings. Then he stammered that he felt like a *pagotā* (prisoner), suggesting that the murder had placed him in a degraded position in which he, through his relation to the murderer, was at the mercy of those whom his family had victimized. Again, whatever the genuine feelings that lay behind these self-deprecatory expressions, they were also conventional and intended to elicit assurances of forgiveness. Indeed, Etuali was immediately interrupted here by Fa'atoafe, who reminded him that Tualevao, representing Tuatō's family, had already spoken and assured them all that the matter was finished so far as the family of the victim was concerned. Tolova'a then thanked Fa'atoafe for his assurances that he, the prisoner, had been resurrected. Another brief round of dignified thanks and mutual recognition of the ranks of all present brought the emotional meeting to a close. The fine mats under which Tolova'a and Agafili had sat were left with Tuatō's family as a blood payment.

Lagi: Funeral of a Ranking Chief

By law in Samoa, where there are no refrigeration facilities a corpse must be buried within twenty-four hours of death. On Friday morning, the day after Fatu died, a steady stream of visitors arrived in Sala'ilua from throughout the archipelago. Fatu's siblings were among the first to arrive, bringing food and money to aid in the feeding of the many guests who would follow them.

Representatives also arrived from the families of Fatu's wife Elena, her father's family from Tutuila, American Samoa, and her mother's family from Fagaloa on Upolu. Their "path" to the occasion was as *paolo* (affines), through Elena, and more specifically through her children. The most impressive presentations of fine mats were made by Elena's kin, one side of her *'āiga* bringing nine mats and the other, six. These included some of the finest and most valuable mats presented in the course of the funeral. These mats were presented on behalf of Elena's children, and among them one particularly fine mat was specified as the "mat of the parting," a special mat to bid farewell to the deceased and reclaim Elena for her own families. Elena's brother was among the delegation from Tutuila, and he announced that he had come on behalf of the family of Tuatō Fatu's wife to "open the covenant" of marriage and to reassert the brother–sister covenant in its place. This claim was made upon Elena, and also upon her children by the two *'āiga* of their mother. Elena in fact was now an outsider in Sala'ilua, her residual rights to remain in the village being only through her children. Sala'ilua was still their village, but now no longer hers.

In addition to numerous kin and affines of Fatu, parties of chiefs from neighboring, and in some cases distant, villages began to arrive. Formal mourning parties of chiefs are called *'auala* (paths). Normally, such *'auala* parties come in single file procession, each chief bearing a small branch, usually a palm frond, though other branches are customary in some villages. Announcing their arrival with the cry, "Tulou ma le lagi, ma le lagi tulou!" (May the heavens pardon us), these processions make their way one by one to the *malae,* near the place where the mourning family is receiving its guests. The branches are then laid in a pile before the main orator representing the host family, brief formal speeches are exchanged, and the visiting chiefs either depart or enter the guest house to sit and relax.

The village of the deceased chief makes the first *'auala,* and no other village may precede it. The Taga chiefs had come early with their palm leaves prepared for the *'auala,* but could not proceed until the Sala'ilua chiefs had made their own procession.

Aside from the chiefs from neighboring villages, there were in attendance some *matai* from more distant places, exploiting political connections with Sala'ilua. Most of these guests brought with them one or more fine mats. Frequently these mats were carried along the main road held open for public display before being brought into the guest house. Those watching the procession showed their approval of the mats with the conventional exclamations, "Sāō. Mālō lālelei!" (Wonderful. Just beautiful). There were 240 fine mats collected during the funeral. The number and quality of the mats presented by a guest reflected the relation of the donor to the deceased and his family, and the prestige he wished to accrue from the public gift. Orators connected with the family of the deceased accepted the mats and the gifts of food and money. All gifts were precisely recorded in a notebook, along with the names of their donors. Formal speeches of condolence and appreciation were exchanged at the time of presentation.

At the time of their departure, all guests who had brought something were presented with a reciprocal gift by orators representing the host group. These gifts are in the form of money, food, or fine mats, or some combination thereof. A person making an early departure would be given his gift before leaving. Most guests, however, waited until the general redistribution of goods took place, often the day after the burial. The redistribution is highly charged and, for many of the guests, the most important part of the funeral. Here prestige and political acumen are put on the line, and oratorical ability and political astuteness are frequently rewarded.

The types of food which were included in the redistribution were cooked pork, divided conventionally according to rank and status, cooked beef, baked fish, cases of canned fish, large tins of *pisupo* (canned cooked beef), kegs of salt beef, boxes of hard biscuits called *masi,* and, finally, loaves of fresh bread purchased from a local bakery.

The most important item of redistribution symbolically is the fine mat. An individual bringing one mat will rarely receive a mat in return, except in cases where the mat is a particularly fine or large one, in which case the donor may receive a smaller or less fine mat in return. Donors of mats will also receive baskets of food and sums of money ranging from fifty cents up to five or even ten dollars, the money being termed "bus fare."[1]

There is then, in terms of the exchange of mats, a "profit" accruing to the host family in a funeral. This profit is offset, however, by the enormous outlay of food and money to provision guests. Several hundred dollars may be collected by the bereaved family from their close kin. The funeral also puts a drain on the crop resources of the host family, particularly on taro, breadfruit (if in season), and yams, which constitute the staples of the guests' meals. At the end of Tuatō's funeral, several dozen mats were left over and were distributed internally, several of the best ones going to the orators who had conducted the formal affairs of the funeral on behalf of the family, others going to close kinsmen of the deceased who had contributed to the funeral with gifts and labor.

At times redistribution may proceed with some difficulty, and may be marked by dispute. Sometimes a guest will protest politically at the quantity and quality of a return gift he has received, citing his dignity and the reputation of the host family as reasons for receiving better treatment. Should the hosts remain firm in their original decision, the disgruntled guests may well become less polite, and angrily remind the orators of other times and places in which the bereaved family had been shown generous hospitality by the guests' own family or village.

One such dispute occurred at Tuatō's funeral. An orator from the village of Satupa'itea, an important center of traditional political power in Savai'i, protested vehemently when he was given no fine mat in return for the one he had brought to the funeral. A young Sala'ilua orator engaged him in an extended exchange of protest and polite refusal. When the young Sala'ilua orator refused to accede to the Satupa'itea chief's request for a fine mat, offering instead a far less desirable piece of tapa cloth, the guest became indignant, reminding the hosts of the dignity of Satupa'itea, and of the obligation on the part of Sala'ilua to treat him well. At this point old Fa'atoafe, who had been listening from the guest house with increasing annoyance, angrily stepped onto the *malae* where the exchange was taking place, took the orator's staff from the younger chief who was representing the bereaved family and village and, shaking his finger angrily at the chiefs from Satupa'itea, reminded him that Tuatō and Tolova'a had gone to his village some months earlier for a funeral and had returned empty-handed. Memories are long and sensitivity to insult is acute in Samoa, and reciprocity has its negative dimensions.

The interment itself took place in the late afternoon of July 20, the day after the murder. It was preceded by a church service at which three sermons were delivered by the Congregational pastors of Sala'ilua, Si'utu, and Taga, each of whom had been a student of Fatu's father. The Sala'ilua pastor, closest to Tuatō Fatu despite a history of friction between them, delivered the eulogy. It was a particularly candid sermon in which the congregation was reminded that Tuatō, like the rest of us, had his weaknesses. The stress in the speech was, however, on Fatu's strengths, which were his intelligence, his kindness and generosity, his energy and strong will, his patience, and his forgiving spirit. The theme of revenge was addressed several times, and the congregation was advised to put the evil in their hearts aside as well of all thoughts of vengeance.

After the service, Fatu was buried next to the grave of his father, beside the family's main house. While there is a common village burial ground, the preferred place for burial is in the immediate vicinity of the main house. Following the burial, Tuiatua, an elderly and respected orator of Sala'ilua, "opened the sky," declaring, "the heavens are clear," the restrictions that had been placed on normal village activities were rescinded. "To the east, to the west, from inland to the sea, all is now opened." With these words, the *lagi* of Tuatō Fatu came officially to an end.

Judgment and Reconciliation: Village Level

While Tuatō was buried officially on Friday evening, the day after he had been shot, and while an *ifoga* on the part of the guilty family had been carried out and accepted, the matter was far from settled. Publicly, and in the delicate "t-pronunciation," the pastor had spoken of the evils of revenge and the importance of forgiveness. Privately, however, and in the cruder and more intimate "k-pronunciation," the same man had remarked that Tuatō's sons were in fact duty-bound to avenge the murder of their father, to exact "blood for blood," and that if they did not try to do so they "were no sons of their father." Hence, the traditional value placed on the moral legitimacy of retaliation and the consequent balance in social life was in conflict with the value, both Samoan and Christian, placed on the need for forgiveness and harmony and the avoidance of further bloodshed. Despite the overt emphasis on reconciliation and harmony expressed in the *ifoga* and sermons, the village remained tense, a delicate balance disrupted.

Galu, the eldest son of Tuatō who had attacked and nearly killed his father's murderer, had voluntarily gone to stay at the government compound at Tuasivi, in the Fa'asaleleaga district. This was a precautionary measure to prevent further violence in Sala'ilua. Galu was now liable for prosecution for murder should Ioane die of his knife wounds, or for assault to kill, even if Ioane should live. Galu was treated not as a criminal but sympathetically by both villagers and constables, and as a sort of hero within his own family and by the other untitled men. Although he had clearly broken government law, Galu had acted admirably according to custom, and his actions were privately praised by those close to the family.

On the night of the murder, his close relatives, including his wife and children, had barricaded themselves within their *pālagi*-style house, the men standing guard throughout the night with rifles to protect the family from retaliation by Fatu's kin. A message had been sent to Tolova'a Aleki, the senior chief of the family and Ioane's father. On the day of the funeral, Ioane's immediate family had left the village to seek refuge with relatives elsewhere. By Sunday it was rumored that Ioane had survived the assault and was being kept in police custody in Tuasivi Prison.

After nightfall on the night of Sunday July 22, a secret meeting of senior orators from Sala'ilua was held. Such secret meetings are known as *fono māitu*. They are held at night, and only when the most serious problems threaten a village. In attendance were orators of the large political "family" known as Sālemuliaga, an important part of the political structure of Sala'ilua, including as it does all of the village's senior orator titles with the important exceptions of Tuatō and Tolova'a. At such a meeting, the blinds of the house are generally lowered, and the discussions take place in whispers, suggesting the sensitivity of the issues under discussion. I was not permitted to attend the session, but was informed that two senior orators of the Sālemuliaga had met with Fa'atoafe of Si'utu subvillage to discuss their strategy for the general meeting that would take place on the *malae* the following day, a meeting necessary to pass formal judgment on the murderer and his family. The purpose of this initial secret meeting was to have the senior orators of the village arrive at the *fono tauati* with a common "voice," any major disagreements having been worked out beforehand and in private. The emphasis had to be on formal unity of action on the part of the village council.

To understand the gravity of the murder's political implications, it is necessary to know something further about the place of the Tuatō and Tolova'a titles in Sala'ilua. As I have noted, Tuatō and Tolova'a have a special standing in Sala'ilua, greeted in the village *fa'alupega,* the formal roll call of the important political components of the village, as "senior titles." Within Sala'ilua, those bearing either title are accorded the deference that goes with such seniority, and their voices have great weight in council deliberations.

Tuatō and Tolova'a derive their seniority from their historical position as the founders of the village and its first settlers. In addition, the original Tuatō appears to have distinguished himself as a war hero. Turner (1884) and Kraemer (1902) both allude to a story in which a Tuatō rescued the settlement from Malietoa Tamafaigā, whose cannibalistic appetite demanded sacrifices as tribute from subservient villages.

One notable fact about Tuatō and Tolova'a is that they are both orator titles, rather than *ali'i.* Only in very few Samoan villages do orators hold senior rank in the village.[2] The Samoan system of chiefs and its implicit conceptions of rank and power are particularly rich and complex. They will be explored in detail in later chapters; at this point it is sufficient to suggest the central importance of the distinction between *ali'i* and *tulāfale* for our understanding of Sala'ilua village and to note that in this local polity the relations between these types of chief were quite different from those in other villages.

I began to suspect that the *tulāfale* status of the village's senior titles might be a significant factor in Sala'ilua's political and social climate. In Kraemer's version of the formal greeting for Sala'ilua, Tuatō and Tolova'a are addressed as *'oulua āitutagata,* "you two demon-men," a reference to their reputed power and ferocity. Today this term is never openly used, although it is still understood by informants. Tuatō and Tolova'a and their families pride themselves on being strong and tough men in the village, known for their cleverness and courage. There are also other orator titles in the village, as well as *'āiga ali'i* (families of *ali'i*), the *tamāli'i* or "noblemen" of the village; but still the undisputed leaders of Sala'ilua are holders of two orator titles, Tuatō and Tolova'a. As we shall see, the apparent irony of the highest respect and greatest deference in the village polity going to holders of orator titles is not unnoted by village *ali'i,* and is a source of some resentment.

While the *fono māitu* was taking place in whispers, a junior orator walked the length of the main road announcing publicly and in the conventional formal manner that the following morning the village would gather for a general meeting. The meeting, it was announced, would take place on the Vā-i-Paepae, the *malae* associated with *ali'i* title Leala'itafea.[3] There would be four houses used for it, corresponding with four divisions of the *fono*:

one for the 'Āiga Sā Tuatō, another for the 'Āiga Sā Tuitolova'a, a third for 'Āiga ma Sālemuliaga (general council of *ali'i* and orators of the village), and a special house for the *'autapua'i,* the group of well-wishers and on-lookers, consisting mainly of clergymen.

On Monday morning at eight o'clock, the village assembled for the general *fono tauati*. Tuatō's promise to me had with tragic irony, come to pass and I was able to witness and record the entire proceeding. Each of the relevant groups took its own house on the *malae*.

Figure 2.2 indicates the plan of the *malae* for the meeting and the relative positions of the different parties in the gathering. Note especially the po-sition of the pastor's house, directly between the houses of the Sā Tolova'ā and the Sā Tuatō, the two adversaries in the conflict. The pastors are called in polite speech *feagaiga* (bond or covenant), a word that is also used to refer to a sister and her bond of respect with her brothers. As we shall see, the place of the *feagaiga,* interposed directly between the two rival parties in a dispute, is symbolically significant for Samoans.

Since this was a village meeting, an in-house affair, rather than a meeting with strangers, there was no formal presentation of kava roots. Due to the extreme gravity of the situation formalities were, in fact, kept to a mini-mum. No oratorical debate was held, nor was any speech made in honor of the kava. The meeting began simply with the kava ceremony, which was carried out separately in each of the four houses about the *malae*. The effect was an impressive series of calls echoing each other around the *malae,* underscoring the dignity and seriousness of the occasion.

A characteristic of the *fono tauati* is the fact that the main speeches are all made outside the houses on the *malae* itself. In a *fono tauati* where participants are distributed over several meeting houses, preliminary discussion may be held separately within each house, but the main speeches are public and

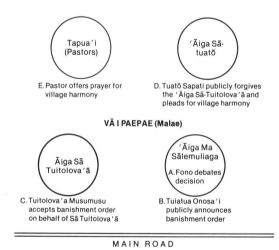

Figure 2.2. Plan of Sala'ilua *Fono Tauati* for a Banishment Order.

always made on the *malae*. Another special characteristic of this kind of meeting is the repetition of the kava ceremony after each major speech is delivered, in addition to the ceremony that begins the meeting.

Following the opening kava ceremony, a long discussion ensued among the chiefs within the main meeting house, where the *'ali'i* and orators were seated. Before announcing publicly the judgment of the village against the family of the murderer, the group of senior orators presented to the council their conclusions reached the previous night in the secret meeting.

The presence in this meeting of chiefs and orators from the normally independent subvillage of Si'utu, important chiefs such as Fa'atoafe and Mulipola, marked the seriousness of the occasion and its general significance to the village. It was, however, Tuiatua Onosa'i, speaking as the senior orator of the Sālemuliaga, who took the floor. The speech was markedly different from most initial orations in its lack of elaborate oratorical flourish. It was a spare and affecting speech, delivered with sober dignity, and without the usual elaborate emphasis on courtly honorifics and the use of arcane language heavy with proverbial allusion.

Tuiatua's purpose was to present to the assembled chiefs and orators the decision of the Sālemuliaga as to the proper punishment for the immediate family of Tolova'a Aleki. "Tuatō and Tolova'a," he began, "are the captains of our village." In the somberest of tones, Tuiatua asked the assembled chiefs where the ship had ended up. "It has sprung a leak, and we are totally defeated, our name denigrated and bandied about in the ears of the nation. Your sacredness, *ali'i*, has been trampled, your dignity ruined by the stories that have gone out across Samoa."

It was, he reminded the chiefs, Tuatō and Tolova'a who had glorified the name of Sala'ilua. They carried the village's dignity to all the important sections of Western Samoa—to *pule, tūmua, ituau, ma alataua, 'āiga i le tai ma le va'a-o-Fonotī*.[4]

Since the founding of Sala'ilua village, however, nothing of such seriousness has shown its head in this village. This is something new to our generation. The eyes of our ancestors who rest now in their graves never beheld such a thing in their time as what we have seen here. Certainly, they knew their own problems, but these were all light ones. There were deaths, and fights, and all sorts of things that happened in the course of our life and in our culture. But in this last week, poison has been injected into our village. In the wisdom and judgment of our *ali'i* and *tulāfale*, it is indeed a poison in our village.

Tuiatua's words were compelling and the other *matai* sat and listened, clearly moved by the seriousness of the words. The next part of the speech appeared to be an accusation of irresponsibility on the part of the rest of the chiefs for allowing such a thing to happen in the village. "Where," he asked, "was the wisdom of the *ali'i*? Where were the honorable Leala'itafea and Savai'inaea? Where were the 'Āiga Sā Amituana'ī and the Children of Sina? Where were the Leulua'iali'i and the Ali'i o Paepae [chiefs of the foundation; i.e., the titles Va'a, Tia, Noa]? Where were Sala'ulu ma Suafa

[the Ali'i titles of Si'utu]?" Then, not failing to include himself by implication, he asked, "Where all this time have been the Sālemuliaga, the chosen
orators of the village?" The accusation thus appeared to be directed to all
the political titles of the village except for Tuatō and Tolova'a. But in fact
the implication was something quite different. The weakness of the political
powers of the village, Tuiatua continued, is not their own failing alone,
but follows from the arrogant pretentiousness of Tuatō and Tolova'a, which
has led to this "poisoned state of affairs."

"Never again," the speech continued, "must we see a thing like this
occur here. We must all turn to consider the care of our village, and the
proper running and internal ordering of Sala'ilua. If we can take care of our
own affairs and put this business in order ourselves, this will be our crown-
ing achievement in the eyes of God."

The term *teu* (to put in order) generally suggests internal or self-control
as distinct from *pule,* which implies an external source of order. The emphasis is thus on keeping the matter local insofar as it is possible to keep
outsiders out of it, and to demonstrate to the rest of Samoa that Sala'ilua
is capable of ordering its own affairs and reconciling even the most serious
internal problem. *Teu* is commonly used in relation to housekeeping, and
the suggestion of "keeping one's own house in order" is appropriate to
Tuiatua's message. What the orator was doing was to prepare the assembly
for the imminent announcement of the punishment, and to appeal for a
ready ratification of the judgment of the senior orators.

In this spirit, Tuiatua was admitting that all the chiefs were like youngs-
ters, and that not enough white heads were evident in the Sala'ilua council.
Nevertheless, he said, if the chiefs of the *fono,* youthful as they are, can still
order the crisis themselves, the country at large will know that Sala'ilua is
a village possessing great wisdom and its good name will be preserved.

In the next part of his speech, Tuiatua returned to the theme of the
arrogance of Tuatō and Tolova'a, suggesting that perhaps this event would
cause them to consider their power which had, until now, gone unchecked.

It was time, he implied, to assert some control. Gradually and with
caution, he moved toward the announcement of the punishment for Tolova'a Aleki and his family. For the first time his speech became formal
and marked by circumlocution.

He was preparing his audience for a difficult announcement and softening
the impact of his words. At last he announced, "I will not move on to some
other subject, or a different matter. We shall now speak from the wisdom
and profound judgment of the followers of Muliaga (founder of Sālemuliaga),
and speak from one voice."

Just before pronouncing judgment on the 'Āiga Sā Tolova'a, Tuiatua
consulted briefly with Fa'atoafe, who was at his side, probably to assure
himself that they were in agreement on what he was about to say. I shall
reproduce in translation most of what followed next in Tuiatua's speech.

Here then we have the decision of our body of orators for our gathering on this morning. Without any further hedging, I present our decision. For Tolova'a and his children who inspired this trouble, the plan we have made is as follows. Tolova'a and all those who spring from him, that is his children, and their descendants, are cast eternally out from this village. This does not apply to the (other) branches of the house of Tolova'a, that is to the other two Tolova'as. But Tolova'a Aleki, our decision goes, is banished forever from Sala'ilua. This means that his family will be swept away from here, and the decision passes on to his descendants who shall spring from him.

As we all know, he (Aleki) has just recently blossomed forth, not having served any village. No. He has never prepared the oven in any village. And the thing which has happened has come from what? Has it come from Sala'ilua? There is a voice of wisdom from the *ali'i* of the village and there is the profound judgment from us of the Sālemuliaga. But no, this thing has not come from us. We know how to show respect to Tuatō and Tolova'a. We know how to exalt them. But we also know how to protect our village. But the event that has occurred is really something special, and this is why we have here the decision of the Sālemuliaga, which I present humbly to you, the *ali'i* of the village.

Tolova'a Aleki and his descendants, all whom he produced, are cast out forever and ever from Sala'ilua. That goes for Tolova'a Aleki, with all due respect to the assembled dignity. There is also Tolova'a Etuali and his descendants. They have done no harm in our village. And there is Tolova'a Musumusu and that branch of the Sā Tolova'a, because of the covenant among the senior chiefs. He also does not enter into our decision. But for Tolova'a Aleki, I have just announced the decision.

In addition, we have decided on a fine of ten sows as the punishment for this day. This is relatively light in view of the other punishment, the banishment from the village. But we have decided on ten pigs together with the banishment from the village. Aleki will no longer be called a person of Sala'ilua. We shall all sign a petition [to this effect] and send it to the [government] authorities at Tuasivi. The speech of the Sālemuliaga is thus concluded. That is our complete decision. Good day.

Considering the rank of Tolova'a Aleki, the proposed sanctions were extremely severe. The speech also contained some rather harsh language expressing irritation—perhaps long-standing—with both Tuatō and Tolova'a. The reference to Aleki having served no village was particularly cutting. Aleki's parents, like Fatu's, had been away from the village because his father served as a Methodist pastor, and thus Aleki had not grown up in Sala'ilua. And like Fatu, he had gained his ultimate position in the village through a combination of personal talent, political cunning, and genealogical right, but had not earned his office through *tautua* (service) rendered in the village. The implication of the remark was thus that Aleki and, perhaps by innuendo, Fatu as well, had not earned the right to high rank in Sala'ilua and were not fully members of the village.

The sending of a written announcement about the banishment to government authorities is important because of the right of a village council to banish a chief from his own land has never consistently been affirmed by the government courts in Western Samoa. The second part of the fine, the payment of the ten mature sows, was never again brought up as far as

I know. It would seem that this part of the fine was announced to add weight and dignity to the decision, rather than with the hope of actually collecting the pigs.

Instead of prompting a chorus of assent or praise, Tuiatua's opening speech actually inspired a storm of angry protest from other members of the assembly, particularly from among the *ali'i*. Mulipola Se'evae from Si'utu was the first to respond. Stating that his heart was saddened by Tuiatua's words, he reminded the body of orators that the previous evening the village *ali'i* had expressed their opposition to the convening of a secret *fono māitu* among senior orators, and had suggested that an open meeting would be a more appropriate forum for discussion of the matter at hand. The body of orators, Mulipola went on to suggest, was perhaps unaware of proper procedure in these matters. While the judgment of the orators was certainly important, so also was that of the body of *ali'i*. Where in their deliberations had the orators sought the opinion of the noblemen of Sala'ilua?

Fa'atoafe, also from Si'utu subvillage, interrupted the speech at this point and attempted to mollify the assembled *ali'i* with a formal apology and invitation to take the floor and express to the assembly their dignified judgments. Sālemuliaga and the other orators of the village, he went on, have had their say and will now sit in silence.

Savai'inaea Alova'a, the ranking holder of the senior *ali'i* title Savai'inaea, was the next to take the floor. "The reason," he began, "that our meeting lies in error is that our procedures are all awry." Alova's was clearly angry and offended at having been overlooked in the decision-making process.

Is it you [i.e., the orators] who are the foundation of our village? You have already presented our meeting with a decision. What is left for us to do? What is there for us to say? You did not consider us at all in your judgment, but have made all the decisions alone. Thus is would appear that there is really nothing more to be said.

Once again, Mulipola Se'evae took the floor. He suggested that it was now too late to ask for the opinions of the *ali'i* families in the village. "The procedures are all awry," he said, repeating Alova'a's complaint. "The opinions of the *ali'i* families should have been solicited on the very day that the murder took place." Despite this objection to the decision-making process, Mulipola pleaded for unity in carrying out the decision of the orators. "Do not, in your anger, cast out Tuiatua and Fa'atoafe. We must all carry our burden together and this should thus be known as a joint decision."

Leulua'iali'i Faiva, holder of a leading *ali'i* title, was next to speak.

The judgment of Sālemuliaga has not always been correct or profound, and neither has that of the families of *ali'i*. Thus we have always met together. . . . Our practice has been that if the *ali'i* are wrong we count on Sālemuliaga, Tuatō, and Tolova'a. Should Tuatō and Tolova'a be in error, along with Sālemuliaga, then our hopes are on the *ali'i*. This is the way we have divided things.

In apparent contradiction of this plea for unity, Leulua'iali'i then turned to consider Tuatō and Tolova'a, raising again the theme of the arrogant abuse of power by the senior title-holders in the village. "Do you think that Tuatō and Tolova'a ever thought about the Sālemuliaga and the families of *ali'i*? No. The only consideration they have ever had was for Tuatō and Tolova'a, for God and for Sala'ilua."

Matapula Fa'ipula, a senior orator from Sala'ilua subvillage, then asked the assembly to put to one side these procedural questions for the time being, reminding the chiefs that they had an urgent matter pending resolution. "We have not, as yet, had any explanation of the crisis, and yet it is a major crisis for us. This is not a regular meeting." He advised the assembly to consider the crime in relation to the fine announced. "Banishment is, after all, a very serious penalty, and yet the crime too is of a most serious nature." For this reason, he suggested, it was crucial that the publicly announced punishment have behind it the weight of a unanimous decision.

Not content with these apparent moves to smooth over the procedural question, Savai'inaea Alova'a spoke again, reiterating in even stronger language his dissatisfaction with the procedures that had been used in arriving at the punishments to be meted out in the case: "We trusted you, the elders [orators], and then you go and make all the decisions yourselves, judging for yourselves, what is correct. Why did you not ask us to meet with you? Why? And then you tell us that you have brought with you a decision which you alone have arrived at!"

Both Tuiatua and Fa'atoafe tried to interrupt this speech throughout its delivery, but Alova'a was determined to have his say and prevent the matter from being smoothed over. Urging the senior orators to have patience and reminding them that they had indeed had their say, he suggested that it was now time to leave the floor to the assembled *ali'i*. He reminded the assembly of the *fa'alupega,* the formal village greeting: it includes, he said, not only the orators, but the *ali'i* titles as well.

Why have you forgotten the *ali'i* families of the village? . . . You have paid lip service to the term *'āiga* [i.e., the *ali'i* families] but then you go ahead and make decisions for us while we just sit and look idly on. Good heavens! I find this all rather amazing! . . . Our village has thrived on the *ali'i* and their collective wisdom. How many times have we been called in to settle problems in our village? We have always met together with the Sālemuliaga. But now, you don't pay any heed to us. . . . Where is the dignity [*mamalu*] and the sanctity [*pa'ia*] of this village?

Tuiatua finally managed to get the attention of the assembly. He was profusely apologetic and clearly embarrassed. The body of orators, he said, had met among themselves, had merely suggested one possible punishment. It had no intention of ignoring the wisdow of the *ali'i* or slighting any other sections on the matter at hand. They should voice their opinions so that a unanimous decision might be reached. Savai'inaea Alova'a replied that the original decision of the orators was good enough, and that it should be the one announced publicly. His only complaint, he emphasized, was not with the content of the decision itself, but rather with the means by which it was achieved.

This concluded the first part of the convocation; the *ali'i* and orators of the council were ready to present their decision to the village at large. Tuiatua stepped from the house onto the *malae,* where he stood with his orator's staff and flywhisk, symbols of his status as orator. His speech was short and solemn, repeating in almost identical words the pronouncement on the punishment which he had made earlier to the chiefly council.

After this speech, kava was again served in all four meeting houses. The next speaker was Tolova'a Musumusu, representing the 'Āiga Sā Tolova'ā. Tolova'a Etuali had left the village, presumably on some important family business, and Musumusu, another cousin and co-title holder, had come from his residence in Apia specifically for the occasion. A gentle, soft-spoken man, much younger than Aleki and Etuali, Musumusu was distant enough from the murder itself and from those involved to remain safely in the village with little possibility of violence. His speech, delivered in the polite t-pronunciation, was carefully formulated. Acquiescing to the will of the village, and by way of apology, Musumusu admitted that Tuatō and Tolova'a had indeed sinned and thus had to be punished. The emphasis was on the joint guilt of both senior orator families, thus softening the humiliation of his own family. The conventional linking of the two titles in formal oratory made this implication relatively easy to sustain.

After Musumusu's speech, kava was once again served around the *malae.* Then Sapati, a junior holder of the Tuatō title, made his way onto the *malae* to speak on behalf of the murdered man's families. His speech was brief. Sapati thanked Tolova'a Musumusu for having accepted the decision of the council and expressed the hope that the two families would once again be able to live together in peace and mutual love. Tuatō Sapati forgave Tolova'a and his family on behalf of his own family, telling them that the matter was now behind them and must no longer be remembered.

Once again kava was served in each of the four houses. Then one of the pastors spoke. Since the local Congregational pastor had been called away on family business of his own, the Congregational pastor from Si'utu offered the concluding speech of the meeting. Frequently it is expected that a pastor will ask formally for the announced punishment to be lightened, a convention that is generally acceded to by the chiefs. In this case, however, so serious was the crime that no reduction in the punishment was requested. The pastor simply offered a prayer of thanksgiving, and reiterated the hope that the villagers would once again live together in harmony and mutual love.

The formal part of the meeting was now finished. All that remained was for the chiefs to draft a letter to the Western Samoan Justice Department, informing them of the village council's decision. The following is a translation of the letter that was finally sent to the government officials.

The decision of the *fono tauati* by the two senior chiefs, Tuatō and Tolova'a, the dignity of the families of *ali'i,* the Children of Sina, and Leala'itafea. Also, the decision of the honorable Savai'inaea, Amituana'i, Mulipola, and the Ali'i-o-paepae. Due to the following causes: (1) Agafili Ioane, son of Tolova'a Aleki, shot Tuatō Fatu; (2) he [Tolova'a Aleki] has three times been banished from the village because of violations of village law; (3) we wish to protect the welfare of our village and protect the village from undesirable events. Therefore it is the unanimous opinion of the chiefs and orators of this village of Sala'ilua to cast him and his descendants from the lands belonging to this village. This goes for him, his descendants, and also for their descendants. It goes as well for his parliamentary vote.

Aftermath: Political Ramifications of the Murder

As far as the village was concerned, the conflict was officially reconciled by the *fono tauati*. Marshalling almost every traditional institution available for the reconciliation of intravillage conflict, the chiefs and orators of Sala'ilua had, in their terms, succeeded in ordering the crisis. For the families directly involved in the murder, however, and for the political life of the village as a whole, the matter was not so easily put to rest. To understand the political implications of the murder we must first examine the organization and the more recent histories of the descent groups involved most centrally in this conflict.

The descent group defined by the Tolova'a title, the 'Āiga Sā Tolova'a, has three title branches (*itū paepae*). Each branch is traced to a common holder of the title who had three daughters but no sons. Each of these three daughters founded a separate descent line of the descent group Sā Tolova'a and, in the absence of any brother, each of these lines is considered as *tamatane* (descending through brothers), despite its uterine origin. At the time of my stay in the village there were three holders of the Tolova'a title, two of whom, Etuali and Aleki, resided permanently in Sala'ilua. The youngest, Musumusu, was residing in Apia. Etuali, apparently not wishing for the burden of responsibility that goes with active power within the family, left the senior status open to his cousin Aleki, a more ambitious and energetic leader.

The situation within the 'Āiga Sā Tuatō is somewhat more complex. According to Fatu, there are six distinct divisions in the descent group. All present holders of the Tuatō title trace their common ancestry to the generation of Fatu's paternal grandfather, a man who reputedly had nine daughters and one son. Four of the daughters died childless, leaving five daughters and a son. Five of the title divisions of the Tuatō title thus trace their origin through uterine links and are *tamafafine* (sisters' children) in relation to the single division descended from a brother. This branch, Fatu's own, is considered *tamatane*.

There are at present seven holders of the Tuatō title, including two holders within a single branch. Fatu's seniority among the Tuatō was based, he claimed, on the unique *tamatane* status of his branch, descended as it was through an unbroken male line. According to Samoan custom, the *tamatane* branch has direct authority (*pule*) over the descent group, its members normally reserving the right to choose titleholders from among their ranks. *Tamafafine* members, tracing their descent through a sister to a titleholder, maintain advisorial rights.

In addition to his *tamatane* status among titleholders, Fatu was noted for his intelligence and political acumen as well as for a respectable command of genealogy and oratorial skills. Although called "old man" because of his senior rank, Fatu at fifty was relatively young for a man of his position. Not only was he clever and knowledgeable, but he prided himself on his courage and aggressiveness which, he said, made others fear and respect him. His senior rank within the village and among the Tuatō title holders did not, however, go unchallenged. Fatu's father, Finagalo, had been a pastor in the London Missionary Society Church, a missionary, and a well-known teacher at Mālua Theological Seminary. Fatu and his siblings had spent most of their childhood living in the seminary compound rather than in their father's village. As a pastor, Finagalo had been forbidden to hold a chiefly title. The title thus remained vacant until Fatu, the eldest son, assumed it in the early 1950s, at which time he moved to Sala'ilua with his young family to occupy the site on which his father had grown up. Fatu immediately began to construct a two-story house there, a house in which he and his family were to live for the next two decades.

Fatu's arrival in the village created several serious problems for others of the 'Āiga Sā Tuatō living there. For one thing, Fatu immediately took over the control of his paternal homestead, marking his claim with the construction of the large house. In so doing, he came into direct conflict with those who had been living on the land and who remained there under the authority of the young, newly arrived Fatu. The conflict between Fatu's own household and the distantly related group sharing their immediate village site was evident at the time of my stay in the village.

Within the larger Tuatō descent group, Fatu's arrival in the village created something of a crisis. Until his arrival, Tuatō Savai'inaea Filipo, an intelligent and respected Somoan associate judge of the Magistrate's Court, had enjoyed unchallenged seniority within the larger descent group. Gradually, however, Fatu's genealogical claim as *tamatane* to Filipo as well as his political ability and charismatic manner posed a clear threat to Filipo's seniority. The matter of intra-*'āiga* authority was taken to the Land and Titles Court three times, most recently the week before I arrived in Sala'ilua. Each time the court had upheld Fatu's right to his senior rank on the basis of his *tamatane* status. The tension between the families of Fatu and Filipo was evident throughout my stay.

The political, social, and legal repercussions of the murder diffused throughout the families and the village. Both senior holders of the two ranking titles of Sala'ilua were now dead, one physically, and the other socially and politically. Within both the 'Āiga Sā Tuatō and the 'Āiga Sā

Tolova'a a new, and perhaps long-term, struggle for dominance could be expected. Within the Tolova'a family the matter probably would not be complex, with only one titleholder remaining resident in Sala'ilua. But within the Sā Tuatō the succession issue might well be problematical and lead to future court cases. The title branch headed by Tuatō Savai'inaea Filipo would no doubt take the opportunity to reassert its former strength in family matters. But Filipo himself was now old and infirm. Furthermore, there would now be the problem of dealing with whoever was chosen as Fatu's successor, for this successor would certainly attempt to invoke the seniority of his title branch in asserting his preeminence within the whole Sā Tuatō. That seniority, it will be remembered, stemmed from the status of Tuatō and his descent line as the sole *tamatane* branch of the whole descent group.

Within the *'āiga potopoto,* a descent category composed of all those claiming a voice in the selection of a successor to Fatu—a group including Fatu's own children, his siblings, and their own children—signs of impending conflict were already emerging. There is in Samoa no clear rule or norm for political succession. There are only culturally sanctioned alternatives for making a claim to a title, each or any of which may be applied in any combination by interested parties in developing their strongest "path" or claim to a title (see Marsack 1958, Weston 1972, and Shore 1976a).

Within hours of the murder, after the initial shock and confusion had abated somewhat, Fatu's eldest son Galu searched through his father's clothes chest and found the book of family genealogies that had been begun by Fatu's grandfather. Such histories constitute invaluable evidence for title succession claims. Fatu's son, with the tacit approval of Fatu's wife, appeared determined to keep the book from the other factions of the family. When he was taken into custody by the police for his attack on his father's murderer, Galu had this book in his possession.

Within hours of the arrival of Fatu's five sisters and one brother in Sala'ilua for the funeral, informal discussions relating to the title succession had already begun. The elder sisters took the initiative in the matter, and were anxious to see that the title pass to Enele, their younger brother, a New Zealand-educated headmaster of a government junior high school on the northern coast of Savai'i. As the sole *toe 'o le uso* (remaining brother), Enele was in a very strong position to make a claim for the title. The only serious rivals to this claim could be Fatu's own sons. They, however, were relatively young, and none had reached a level of achievement in economic or educational terms to make an attractive candidate for the title.

In relation to the encompassing Sā Tuatō, the descent group including all title branches, the matter was still more complex. Fatu's own branch, it will be remembered, held an anomalous position within this larger family unit. Having reached his preeminent position in the village and the family mainly through a combination of personal ability, charisma, and genealogical right, Tuatō Fatu had also been in an unstable position because his family had not in fact resided in Sala'ilua for many years, and thus had not activated their status in the village through direct service. Thus, if Enelē were to take the vacated title but continue to reside on the opposite side of Savai'i, the power and prestige of the title and the family associated with this branch would certainly diminish considerably, being quickly eclipsed by one of the other branches. For Enelē to accept the title, therefore, obligated him to take up permanent residence in the village and give up his job. One possible solution to the problem would be for Enelē to apply to the Education Department for a transfer and to assume the headmaster post at the local intermediate school, near Sala'ilua.

Fatu's sisters began to discuss the possibility of constructing a large new house on the family compound, estimating the monetary contribution required of each of the siblings for such a project. A new official orator's residence, known formally as a *laoa,* would solidify the position and rights of Fatu's siblings in relation to the house site and associated land. Since Tuatō had already been sharing the immediate house site with another related family, primary authority over the rights to the land was also at stake here. A new house would serve as a symbol of the continuing presence and power of Fatu's branch of the descent group within the village. Finally, a new *pālagi*-style house would serve as an attractive residence for Enelē and his family, long accustomed to living in European-style houses. Perhaps such a house would induce Fatu's younger brother to make the necessary move to Sala'ilua, and protect the family's interests there. The succession issue remained complex and uncertain.

Plate 1. Village *taupou* prepares kava for a village meeting. The youth at her side helps with the preparation and will serve the drink to the assembled chiefs.

Plate 2. Tuatō Fatu is served kava at a meeting of village chiefs.

Plate 3. Surrounded by his family and neighbors, Tuatō's body is displayed just prior to his burial.

Plate 4. Village chiefs bearing clusters of leaves make their way in an *'auala* (mourning party) to Tuatō's house to pay their last respects.

Plate 5. Chiefs representing Tolova'a's descent group (seated) present fine mats to Tuatō's family on the day of his funeral. Woman on the right is making a formal display of a mat to the village.

Plate 6. *Fono tauati*. Tuiatua announces the formal order of banishment for the family of Tuato's murderer. Village chiefs and orators can be seen in the meeting house in the upper left-hand corner, while members of the *'aumaga* listen attentively to the speech just to the right of the speaker.

PART II

STRUCTURES

CHAPTER THREE

Sala'ilua Village

Long after Tuatō was buried and the events surrounding his death had receded in favor of more immediate concerns, I continued to puzzle over what I had seen. I had come to Sala'ilua to study patterns of conflict and social control. Yet surely there was a large element of coincidence in the tragic occurrences that I had witnessed, and much of the affair could be accounted for in terms of unique circumstances and specific personalites. And certainly deaths—even deaths of such tragic proportions—do occur now and then. It could have happened anywhere, I supposed. . . . But it didn't happen anywhere, and I was keen to understand what part, if any, the village of Sala'ilua had to play in the tragedy.

The question itself was not alien to Samoan musings on conflict. The casual Samoan explanation for disorder in a village is the weakness of the chiefs, and the consequent lack of regard by villagers for their laws. Yet such an explanation, while it might account for social disorder in the Apia urban area, was simplistic in the case of Sala'ilua. The village was indeed a particularly exuberant place in many ways, but it was far from lax in authority. The chiefs of the village prided themselves on the strength of their authority, and the respect with which their laws were viewed. The authority of God was given splendid representation as well, in the persons of two talented and energetic pastors and a resident Catholic priest. Church attendance was mandatory, as in most traditional villages, and delinquents were subject to fines. In addition, Sala'ilua supported a set of thriving traditional organizations whose activities occupied the greater part of the lives of the villagers. Thus on the surface, at least, there was no evidence that social disorder sprang from a simple weakness of traditional authority in the village.

Either my initial suspicions were correct, that the murder of Fatu was a matter of a very particular set of circumstances, or else I had to look deeper into the social and political life of Sala'ilua for the sort of structural explanation with which anthropologists are more at home.

In this chapter, I will refocus my attention on the village of Sala'ilua, and the complex set of institutions that give it structure and provide for its residents a framework for ordering much of their daily lives. In many ways, of course, Sala'ilua may be taken to represent a "typical" Samoan village, retaining many of the more traditional institutions no longer found nearer the urban area. Yet, each village in Samoa is also distinctive, and Sala'ilua possesses a number of unusual structural features. It is in these unique aspects of Sala'ilua that I was especially interested, since they might provide significant insights into some of the less obvious forces underlying Fatu's death.

Approaching the Village

The village of Sala'ilua, on the western coast of Savai'i, is today only a ten-minute flight by single-engine plane from Faleolo Airport on Upolu (see map, Figure 3.1). Psychological distance is rapidly changing for Samoans. When I lived in the village in mid-1973, the airstrip at Si'utu had barely been cleared and, while the residents awaited government aid in the form of leveling machinery, was being used as a cricket field. Savai'i was then far in the rural "back" of Samoa as Apia residents often said, clucking in surprise at the remoteness of "my" village. And certainly, climbing aboard a rickety bus at 3:00 A.M. to begin the six- to eight-hour journey by bus and launch to the "back" of Samoa, Sala'ilua seemed far off to me.

A twenty-five-mile trip along the northwest coast of Upolu leads through the most densely populated rural part of Samoa, past Faleolo Airport and on to the main wharf at Mulifanua, at the western tip of the island. The motor-launch trip across the often turbulent thirteen miles of Apolima Strait takes another one and a half to two hours, depending on the weather and the particular boat that is in service. Three buses make the thirty-one-mile journey from Salelologa Wharf, where the launch docks at Savai'i, to Sala'ilua. If one is fortunate enough to find a bus waiting at the wharf, and the bus has collected enough passengers to make an early departure worthwhile, the total time of the trip may be shortened by an hour or two.

The final bus ride to Sala'ilua normally takes about two hours. Recently, the government road has been paved for a mile west of the commercial center at Salelogoa, at which point it cuts inland across the densely forested and sparsely populated southeastern tip of Savai'i, and remains unpaved

Figure 3.1. Western Samoa.

and only partially graded for the next five miles. At the village of Fa'ala, at the beginning of the Palauli district, the road emerges from the forest and, for the next several miles, is paved as it hugs the coastline through a string of three contiguous villages. The road then turns again inland and is unpaved for the remainder of the trip. After a mile through land dense with coconut trees and cattle from the Nelson Plantation at Letolo, the road forks south to Satupa'itea. But the bus continues northwest on the main branch of the road and once again loses sight of the coast as it bumps through sparsely populated plantation lands.

Most of the south coast of Savai'i comprises volcanic rock cliffs of recent origin, and is thus inhospitable to coastal settlements. Six miles through the forest, the road suddenly meets the coast again, and the lava rock fringing the shore gradually becomes level and gives way to sandy beaches along which lie the four villages of Papa, Puleia, Gātaivai, and Gautavai. From this point the bus will remain mainly inland from one-half to one mile as it heads west along what the Samoans call "the road of poverty." This ten- to twelve-mile stretch of poorly graded road is so named because, lacking a source of fresh water or inhabited settlement, it was considered a particularly trying part of the journey around the island, which was made on foot before the advent of motor-vehicle service on Savai'i.

At the village of Taga, the road emerges briefly near the coast, then turns sharply north and inland for the remaining ten miles to Sala'ilua. This part of the journey is through a region of mixed vegetation. Rain forest gives way near the coast to cultivated patches of taro, ta'amū (Alocasia, a large edible root crop related to taro), coconut palms, bananas, and cocoa trees. About three miles before Sala'ilua the plantation lands belonging to village families begin to appear along the side of the road, and house sites of families who have moved onto their plantation lands for more or less extended stays become increasingly prevalent. At this point it is a common sight in the morning and early evening to see village youths making their way on foot to and from their family plantations, baskets of taro or clusters of coconuts slung on the ends of carrying sticks, which are balanced over their shoulders.

The road suddenly meets the coast again at Si'utu, a settlement associated politically with Sala'ilua village. Several hundred yards later, the plantation zone gives way to the 'a'ai or central village area of Sala'ilua proper (see figure 2.1).

Sala'ilua is a commercial and unofficial administrative center of its district, much like the villages of 'Auala to the north in the Asau district, Fagamalo in the Itū-O-Tane district on the northeast of Savai'i, Tuasivi, the government administrative center in the Fa'asaleleaga district on the southeast coast, and Vailoa in the Palauli district. No sleepy backwater, Sala'ilua contained until recently the District Intermediate School, several trading shops including the district's largest store, a "club" used for dances and weekly movies, three major churches, including the district's sole Catholic church, and the residence of the district's only priest. Nearby are the district agriculture station, the district hospital, and the post office and telegraph station. Until 1966, when it was virtually destroyed by a hurricane, Sala'ilua possessed a large concrete wharf which provided a landing for cargo and passenger launches. Sala'ilua is the usual setting for the monthly circuit court sessions, while nearby Si'utu contains the district constabulary.

Sala'ilua village is thus unusually active in its district, and was considered a district capital in German times. Reminders of this focal status of the village appear in the form of a large number of older European-style houses still standing from the days of German colonization of Western Samoa. The village prides itself on its reputation as an active place, pointing out that Sala'ilua is often called Apia Lua (Second Apia). Sala'ilua people, visitors are advised, "know how to get things done." Typical is the following statement by a senior *tulāfale* of the village.

There is one thing commonly said of Sala'ilua: the people here are very smart. That's the reputation of our orators. In the German times, Sala'ilua was called Laumua [capital], for if there was a flag-raising ceremony in Apia, we had one here in Sala'ilua. Haven't you heard the saying that Upolu has Apia Number One, but Sala'ilua is Apia the Second? We're very good in doing things concerned with Samoan custom. That's because we are very smart. I don't like to say this myself, for you may not believe it, but nowadays in Samoa, other villages are very scared of me. If something is going on in a village, and orators from all over come, I go and do battle with my words.

Sala'ilua's reputation is earned, at least in part. Traveling throughout the archipelago, one gets the impression of more or less subtle differences in ambience from village to village, despite the general homogeneity in culture and social organization throughout. My impression of Sala'ilua, one that has been supported by the observations of other visitors, is of an unusually active, energetic, proud, and assertive settlement.

Historically, Sala'ilua appears to have been something of an economic center in its district. Relatively isolated from the more or less endemic warfare that plagued the Tuamasaga and A'ana districts on Upolu, and the Fa'asaleleaga district in Savai'i in the early nineteenth century, Sala'ilua was an attractive commercial prospect for European traders seeking local business in Samoa. Possessing the best reef passage on the southwest coast of Savai'i, Sala'ilua afforded relatively easy access by sea, despite its remoteness from Apia. Gilson (1970:213–216), who indicates that Sala'ilua had by the middle of the nineteenth century attracted a large number of European traders, cites a case that reveals Sala'ilua's longstanding reputation as a strong and vital village.

In 1856 William Fox, A European trader based in Sala'ilua, was murdered by a young man of rank from Sagone village in the northern part of the district. Fox, it seems, had accused the young man of stealing, an accusation that had been answered with a bullet. Gilson's account of what followed is suggestive:

In turn, the murder provoked the Sala'ilua people, for through it they suffered the indignity of having a man whom they protected cut down within their village, while losing their trader into the bargain. Sagone therefore offered its *ifoga* but was turned away and, had it not been for the timely intervention of the nearest London Missionary teacher, might have been attacked forthwith. Subsequently, however, the *'aumaga* Sala'ilua evened the score by ambushing and killing a Sagone chief who had had nothing to do with Fox's murder. (Gilson 1970:213)

The incident, Gilson goes on to explain, created a political crisis for the British and American consuls resident in Apia, who were faced with arbitrating a dispute involving both Samoans and Europeans.

Today Sala'ilua remains a center of economic and political activity. The signs of activity are everywhere. Alone in its district, Sala'ilua possesses a generator for its own use and a set of power lines connecting the various houses in the village. As of 1974, however, the system was in a state of disrepair and chiefs insisted that they were awaiting the arrival of new lines.

Sala'ilua has something of a reputation for large-scale projects. To raise money for village projects several years ago, villagers organized a traveling concert party complete with original comedy skits and songs. This concert tour was recorded by the government radio station and occasionally may be heard in public broadcast.

In 1954, the village also contracted an infamous arranged marriage (*fale tautū*) between one of its *ali'i* and a young, beautiful titled girl (*taupou*) from the village of Lefaga on Upolu. The affair has something of a fabulous reputation, and is commemorated in story and song. The celebration of this marriage appears to have been on a particularly grand scale, involving an alleged exchange of twenty thousand United States dollars *'oloa* (bride price) for about 4,000 fine mats as *tōga*, or dowry. These figures may have been exaggerated over the years but this was clearly an ambitious undertaking for a village.

By way of a final and more recent example of the effervescence of the village, church activity, which is a good indication in Samoa of the level of village energy, is unusually vigorous in Sala'ilua. Three large congregations (Congregational, Methodist, and Catholic) are active in the village, with a fourth, also Congregational, in Si'utu. The Methodist and Congregational congregations have constructed enormous and impressive multi-storied pastors' houses. The Methodist pastor is housed in a three-story structure, the only such house I have ever seen in Samoa.

While I was in New Zealand following my fieldwork period in Samoa, the Methodist community of Sala'ilua sponsored a trip of about thirty chiefs and young, untitled men to Auckland, New Zealand, to work for several months in order to raise money for a new and larger church building. The airfare for each man was borrowed from a bank and repaid as he worked. In addition, each worker had the obligation of contributing a total of six hundred New Zealand dollars for the church through weekly voluntary payments to the treasurer of the group, and could keep the rest of his earnings for personal and family use. The entire project was conceived by a group of brothers who were originally from Sala'ilua but have been long-time residents of New Zealand. Such village projects, while not unique to

Sala'ilua, are relatively uncommon elsewhere, and reflect the strong sense of community activity associated with this village.

Sala'ilua is thus, in some ways, not a "typical" Samoan village.[1] It is a product of both its particular history and general Samoan village structure. It has a long history of commercial and political contacts within the district and beyond, within the archipelago as a whole. As a minor port and a Catholic mission center, it has had continual, though superficial, contacts with the outside world, both *pālagi* and Samoan. Yet Sala'ilua, in its institutional structure, is highly conservative, maintaining a full and active set of more or less "traditional" organizations and activities, many of which are no longer found in the urbanized or urbanizing centers of Upolu. It is considered a rural, "back" village where traditions are strong and ancient institutions flourish.

The Village: Orientations

From the sketch-map of Sala'ilua (figure 3.2) it is apparent that the village is a linear, nucleated settlement characteristic of Samoan coastal villages lying along the main government road. The residential core (*'a'ai*) of the village lies along a stretch of government road just over half a mile long, although plantation lands exploited by the villagers extend several miles southeast, and from three quarters of a mile to over two miles inland of the road. Si'utu, an associated (sub)village of Sala'ilua, is geographically separated from the other two subvillages, Sala'ilua and Sataputu, which are contiguous. Si'utu lies off the main road, just south of the rest of the village, on a coastal section of sand and lava rock where the coastline bends sharply south. The shore bordering the village alternates patches of lava rock with short stretches of sandy beach. A fringing coral reef lies about five hundred yards from the shore along the length of the village, creating a wide lagoon

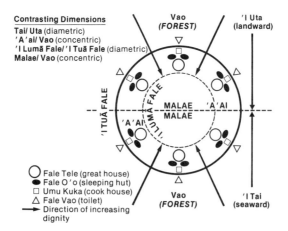

Figure 3.2. Spatial Orientations in a Samoan Village.

exploited by fishing parties. Moving inland, the land slopes upward at a gradual but steady incline of approximately fifty feet for every two hundred fifty yards, creating a broad, sloping coastal plain conducive to intensive horticulture.

Samoan spatial and social orientation in a village is based on two kinds of distinction. The first is the familiar Polynesian directional orientation *tai/ uta* (seaward/landward). *Tai* and *uta* may be interpreted both as places (the shore and the forest or bush, respectively), or as relative directions. The directional use is the more common.

From a position within the village in a coastal linear settlement like Sala'ilua, *'i tai* generally means "toward the sea" or lagoon or beach, while *'i uta* means either "toward the rear part of the village" (*'i tuā fale*) or "toward the plantation or bush." From a position in the lagoon, *'i uta* usually refers to the village, while *'i tai* means farther out to sea, perhaps the *vasa* or deep sea beyond the reef. Finally, from the perspective of the plantation, *'i tai* generally signifies the village, while *uta* indicates the forest (*vao matua*) of the highlands.

Symbolically, however, *i tai* suggests primarily the more populated and ordered arenas of Samoan life. Women's work, generally lighter and cleaner than that of men, is associated with the coast rather than the bush. The *fale tele* (guest house) of each household group is positioned seaward of the compound's other houses, and it is here that important guests are housed, important meetings are held, and ideally where the girls of the family are supposed to sleep under the watchful eye of the chief and his wife. *I tai* is associated with light and clean work, with bathing, and most suggestively with the maintenance of decorous and controlled behavior under the gaze of a dense population and watchful chiefs. *Uta*, on the other hand, suggests the bush, populated by ghosts (*āitu*) rather than people. To go *i uta* commonly suggests leaving a center of order and population, and thus leaving the control of the chiefs and village regulations. Positioned *'i uta* in the household compound are the *fale o'o* (small sleeping huts) in which the young men normally sleep. Still further *i uta* is the cookhouse, the scene of the dirtiest and heaviest work in the compound. Finally, at the very back of the compound, just where the bush meets the cleared land, lie the *fale vao* (bush house)—the outhouses. Guests are entertained on the seaward side of the compound, and are discouraged from wandering to the back of the compound, particularly near the cookhouse.

I uta is the direction in which men and boys go for their work, the site of gardens, the bush, and most of the dirty and heavy work of Samoan life. It is the bush that provides the "heavy" (starchy foods), the staples of the Samoan diet, while *mea lelei* (good food), lighter protein foods such as fish and imported canned foods, are caught or purchased *'i tai*, from the sea or from the village shops. Finally, the *uta* is dangerous, uncontrolled by chiefs and their regulations, out of range of human sight and thus of civilization. The bush (*vao* suggests both physical and moral darkness. To live in the bush is to live alone, out of reach and control of society. Ghosts are one's neighbors, as is trouble, which is seen to occur more frequently in the bush than in the center of the village.

The second dimension of spatial orientation within a village divides the village into concentric zones of center and periphery. The focus is on the *'a'ai* or residential core of the village. The ideal village is thus conceived of as circular rather than linear, with the *malae* or sacred political ground as a center of dignified activity, a secondary ring of *fale* with the large guest or meeting houses closer to the center, and the smaller huts and cookhouses radiating outward. Finally, at the periphery of this ideal village, there are the boundaries with other villages or the bush and the sea. These are the areas outside the control of village chiefs.

While most villages in modern Samoa are now linear, the circular village model is still a powerful conceptual pattern in Samoan thought. Lepea village in the Faleata district near Apia, which was the official residence of Fiamē Mata'afa Faumuinā Mulinu'u, the late prime minister of Western Samoa, is organized in this circular pattern, clearly a deliberate effort to realize the ideal village pattern. This circular pattern is also evident in a number of other villages, such as Matāvai Sāfune in the Itu-O-Tane district of Savai'i. This pattern of concentric circles is not clearly evident in most linear villages. However, if we view the government road as a kind of central focus and the household compounds on either side of it as an inner core, with the bush, sea, and village boundaries as the outer periphery, then the circular pattern is suggested, with all of its major symbolic associations. The *'a'ai*, and especially the *malae*, are centers of village political life, and are thus more dignified than the periphery. As we shall see, village regulations tend to be more rigidly enforced in the core, and traditional etiquette is frequently specified as applying only to the core and more especially to the *malae*.

Notably, in recent years the village road has become a major focus of control, and a place where a person must be particularly careful to order his behavior properly. As with the *malae*, certain village regulations (especially curfew regulations) and many government laws apply mainly or exclusively to behavior on the road. In this way the main road has a significance in relation to behavioral control parallel to that of the *malae*. There is, therefore, in the Samoan village, a general symbolic association between the two dimensions of spatial orientation, such that *tai* : *uta* :: *'a'ai* : periphery :: greater control : lesser control. The relationship is graphically represented in figure 3.2.

These distinctions between seaward and inland on the one hand, and center and periphery on the other, are associated in turn with a set of distinctions between front (*luma*) and back (*tua*). Guests arriving at the main house are asked to sit *'i luma*, in the front of the house, which is to say the part of the house closest to the sea. Low rank or subordination in general is linguistically associated with the "back." To serve one's chief is to *tautua*, while the wife of the *ali'i* is called his *faletua* (literally, "back house"). The rear of the household compound, or the village in general, is called *'i tuāfale* (the rear of the house(s)), while rural (and thus "backward") Samoa is often referred to as the "back" of Samoa by urban dwellers. Finally, to do something 'i luma o le tulāfono, is to act "in front of the law" or "because" of the law. To be up front is to be in a public, dignified context, the focus of control, and is thus to be cautious and on one's best behavior. We shall explore in later chapters this dichotomy in considerably more detail.

The center/periphery distinction also operates in relation to periodic centers of power and prestige that occur in a village. These include chiefly council meetings, the appearance of important guests, and the occurrence of various sorts of celebration. These occasional events establish temporary centers of dignity and formal activity within the village. Those who are excluded from direct participation, such as children or the untitled, form a deferential periphery in relation to these highly charged centers of ritual activity. Those on the periphery may serve those in these focal centers, but are constrained to keep a respectful and low profile. But to anyone who has witnessed such events in a Samoan village, the attitudes of those on the periphery, particularly the young children and the youth, are not simple deference and passivity. Rather, a marked ambivalence is evident toward those at the centers of power and dignity, a passive–aggressive stance in which the boundaries separating those in the center from those on the periphery are constantly challenged, tested, and reaffirmed. This "boundary testing" is characteristic of Samoan social interaction.[2]

Village and Subvillage

In examining the structure and constitution of a Samoan village we are faced with two definitional problems. The first is to delineate the territorial units which we label as district, village, and subvillage. The second is to define the nature of the household unit to be used as a basic demographic unit in a census of the village.

Nu'u is a generic Samoan (and western Polynesian) term for settlement. To translate this term, however, as a segment of some inherent size or population such as are suggested by the terms "village" or "district" is to misconstrue the significance of the term and the logic that underlies its usage. When the morpheme pito (part) is prefixed to nu'u, the resulting term pitonu'u signifies a segment or subsection of a nu'u. Pitonu'u is frequently translated as "subvillage."[3] This translation is often misleading, appearing to define an absolute rather than a relational unit. Any encompassed unit of settlement may be called a pitonu'u if it includes more than one household group, is conceived to have a distinct identity, and is embedded within an even larger territorial organization, which is a nu'u in relation to it.

The nu'u Sala'ilua comprises two pitonu'u (what we shall call subvillages), called Sataputu and Sala'ilua (see figure 3.2). There is, in addition, another subvillage, Si'utu, which has an ambiguous association with Sala'ilua village. Si'utu is represented at times in Sala'ilua's *fa'alupega*, a village courtesy address including all important political units comprising the village. But when it does not desire recognition or inclusion as a subvillage of Sala'ilua, references to it may be deleted. Si'utu also has its own chiefly council. On occasion, however, the subvillages of Sataputu and Sala'ilua can also have their own councils. When matters properly concern all three subvillages, then they meet as a single village. But when matters are internal to Sataputu and Sala'ilua subvillages, and do not concern Si'utu, then only the former two subvillages meet as a single village.

Historically, Si'utu appears to have been associated with the village of Gātaivai, but broke away under circumstances unclear to me. Over time, and largely because of its proximity to Sala'ilua, Si'utu became progressively involved in the affairs of that village and, for some purposes, a "part" of it. Aside from its own council, however, Si'utu maintains an independent Women's Committee, Congregational Church, weaving house, *aualuma* (girls' organization) and *'aumaga* (untitled mens' organization), as well as some curfew laws that differ from those of Sala'ilua village. At times Sala'ilua chiefs are heard to grumble that Si'utu no longer wished to *fai nu'u* (literally, to "make-village") with Sala'ilua. Characteristically, it is the making or doing that is stressed in the identity of a settlement rather than simple "status" or "being." To the extent and on those occasions that Si'utu does not *act* as a part of Sala'ilua, it *is* not a subvillage. Because of its marginal status in relation to Sala'ilua as a whole and because, even without the inclusion of Si'utu I was already working with what is, for Samoa, a large resident population, I have omitted Si'utu from the demographic profile of Sala'ilua, and include it in the study only when that inclusion is situationally warranted.

The second problem in describing the structure of a Samoan village is the definition of a household unit for the census. Because of the ambiguous and shifting character of group boundaries in Samoa, including those defining residence groups, I asked several informants what they considered to be the best unit in terms of which to frame the census of Sala'ilua. The answers were identical: the *matai* and his *'au'āiga*.[4] *Matai* in this usage refers to the titled head of a household, and the *'au'āiga* (literally, "family cluster") comprises all the people who are directly under his authority who serve him, reside on a single household compound in which he has his main house, and all of whom cook and eat from the same ground oven.

Insofar as all titled household heads are chiefs, it becomes readily apparent that formal political power is widely dispersed within a Samoan village, with almost all men over the age of twenty-six holding some sort of *matai* title. This egalitarian aspect of Samoan chiefhood is offset by the clearly hierarchical distribution of power characteristic of political units beyond the household level. Thus, as household heads, Tuatō and Tolova'a are simply *matai*, two of many Sala'ilua-based titles; within the Sala'ilua village council, however, they are ranking titles of considerable power. Finally, as we shall see, they are orator titles, with a distinctive sort of power and meaning for Samoans, understood in complementary opposition to the power of *ali'i* titles. In this context, however, we are to understand the chief in his most local role as head of a household unit called an *'au'āiga*.

In the definition of *'au'āiga*, no mention is made of shared blood or other idioms of biological kinship. Although it is assumed that most of the *'au'āiga* members will be cognatic kin or affines and usually closely related, household compounds include not only nuclear or extended families, but also kin who are classed as *'āiga fāimai* (literally, "increasing kin" or "outside kin") who are more distant relatives, temporarily resident in the *'au'āiga*, exercising their rights as kinsmen to hospitality and potential residence with any of their families. Because of the frequency of such visitors in a household and the absence of those normally resident who have gone temporarily to live in other households, household composition and thus census figures are very unstable.

In June 1973, the Sataputu and Sala'ilua subsections of Sala'ilua village contained 828 reported residents, distributed over 55 *'au'āiga* (figure 2.1).[5] The largest of these *'au'āiga*, number 16 in figure 2.1, contained 52 residents, while the smallest (number 17) contained but two, a married couple.[6] This smallest *'au'āiga* was thus a one-generation unit, the only such unit in the village. Sixteen other *'au'āiga* comprised only two generations, parents and their young children. Many of these newer and smaller households are located at the extreme southeastern end of the village, somewhat remote from the village center. These constitute, for the most part, the households of young *matai* who have chosen to establish households on or near family gardens or on previously uncleared family lands. In thus establishing their own households, these young *matai* create new *'au'āiga*, although retaining frequent and intimate contacts with their parental households.

In general, then, the larger three-generation households headed by older, more established chiefs appear to cluster in the *'a'ai* or center of the village, with younger chiefs establishing new households on the periphery. Approximately 70 percent of the Sala'ilua households comprise three generations. The average number of residents in an *'au'aiga* in Sala'ilua is 14.8, and slightly lower (14.3) when the largest and smallest *'au'āiga* are excluded.

Well over half the population of Sala'ilua is under the age of 16 (see table 3.1). According to the last several census enumerations this is true for the Western Samoan population at large. The fact that there are almost three times the number of children 15 years and under for each year of the time span than there are young adults of 16–25 is probably a function of (a) increasing birth rates and (b) migration of young adults to Apia and overseas for schooling and employment.

Thus Sala'ilua is demographically a youthful village, with a significant drop in representation by the group of adolescents and young adults who normally constitute the bulk of the work force in a village. Assuming that many of these young adults have left the village, we should turn to see where the expatriate villagers are now residing.

In the census, 291 people who had grown up in the village and had lived

Table 3.1
Age Composition of Sala'ilua

Age Category	Number	Percent of Total Population	Number for Each of Age Spread
0–15	457	55.2	30.5
16–25	107[a]	12.9	10.7
26–60	219	26.4	6.4
60+	45[b]	5.4	–

[a] 20 *'au'āiga* with none.
[b] 28 *'au'āiga* with none.

there for significant periods of time were reported to be residing outside the village.[7] This group includes both villagers who have established marital residence outside of the village and those who have emigrated to urban centers in Apia, American Samoa, or elsewhere overseas for educational and economic reasons. Table 3.2 gives a breakdown of residence of these expatriated villagers at the time of the census. Of these expatriate members, 112 (38 percent) make some financial contribution to Sala'ilua families. Of the 52 households in Sala'ilua, 42 (81.1 percent) reported receiving some significant and regular monetary contributions from expatriate members.

District Level Organization

While, for many day-to-day matters, Sala'ilua residents are concerned with village and subvillage affairs, remaining relatively self-sufficient, the village is also articulated in a number of ways into three types of organization: localized political units, dispersed political alliances, and administrative units for government services.

Localized Political Units

In the nineteenth century, the island of Savai'i was a power base for powerful groups of orators with six centers of *pule*, or orator power. With the exception of the Malietoa family, which had an important branch in Sapapāli'i in the Fa'asaleleaga district as well as in Upolu, the lineages comprising the traditional power bases of Savai'i tended to be widely dispersed rather than localized within single districts.[8]

During the nineteenth century, however, a loose organization of military alliances within Savai'i divided the island into three districts: Fa'asaleleaga to the east, with the western part of the island divided into an upper half called Itū-O-Tane (Side of the Men) and a southern district Itū-O-Fafine (Side of the Women) (see map, figure 3.3). Of the latter two districts, the

Table 3.2
Sala'ilua: Residence of Expatriate Villagers

Location	Number	Percent of Total Expatriates
Rural Samoa	59	20.3
Apia area	111	38.2
New Zealand	53	18.2
American Samoa	56	19.3
United States	7	2.4
Elsewhere[a]	5	1.7

[a] Tonga and Japan.

former had the status of *Mālō* (Conqueror) and was thus called the "Side of the Men," the latter gaining its humiliating name in defeat. Sala'ilua lies within the boundaries of Itū-O-Fafine and, more specifically, within a political district (or subdistrict) known as Palauli-i-Sisifo (Palauli West). Palauli West, known in former times as the Fa'atoafe district, was actually a part of a larger Palauli district which was split in half by the Satupaitea district. Within the greater Itū-O-Fafine district, there were four politically significant descent groups dispersed throughout the area and, through marital alliances, beyond it, linking Itū-O-Fafine with other districts in Upolu and Savai'i. These great political "families" are the 'Āiga Sā Lilomaiava, 'Āiga Sā Tonumaipe'a, the 'Āiga Sā Moeleoi, and the 'Āiga Sā Muliaga. An important branch of this last family, as we shall see, is a major political component of Sala'ilua.

The modern political map of Savai'i is based generally on this more traditional arrangement, but includes further subdivisions. There are today in Western Samoa thirteen parliamentary districts, each electing through

Figure 3.3. Savai'i: Nineteenth-Century District Organization.

the vote of district *matai* a *Faipule*, or representative to the legislative assembly of the central government. Sala'ilua is part of Palauli-i-Sisifo political
district which comprises the western half of the old Fa'atoafe subdistrict.
The concept of territorial district, translated as *itū mālō* (literally, "side of
the government"), suggests for Sala'ilua several distinct associations: the
older Itū-O-Fafine; Palauli; Palauli-i-Sisifo (parliamentary district); and
Fa'atoafe.

Dispersed Political Alliances

The major political alliance which is still important within Sala'ilua is the
Sālemuliaga. Sālemuliaga (also known as Sā Muliaga) is one of the great
Fale'upolu, or orator "families" of Savai'i, and is dispersed throughout the
island in nine different villages. These are: Sala'ilua, Gātaivai, Taga, Faga,
Saipipi, Sa'asa'ai, Pu'apu'a, Asaga, and Lealatele (see map, figure 3.4).
Actually this last village, on the northeast coast of Savai'i, was destroyed
by the volcanic eruptions of 1910, and its members re-established their
village in northwest Upolu, calling it Le'auva'a (boat crew) to commem-
orate their flight to sea from the lava flow. Thus today the larger Sālemuliaga
descent group is represented in one Upolu village, although in traditional
terms it remains an exclusively Savai'i-based family.[9]
    Aside from genealogical, political, and ritual ties among the nine villages
associated with the Sālemuliaga, ties that give orators from any of these
villages rights to be present at ceremonial occasions of any Sālemuliaga
base, Sala'ilua is also connected by a web of less direct and more diffuse
links to many of the other villages in the Samoa group. For the most part,
these ties originated as links of kinship through the subdivision and proliferation of titles throughout the archipelago by multiple marriages of title
holders, which thereby created different *faletama* (descent group branches
created by the serial unions of an important chief).[10] In Sala'ilua, for in-

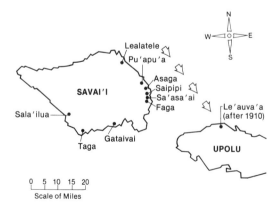

Figure 3.4. Centers of Sālemuliaga Power.

stance, the descent group defined by the *ali'i* title Leala'itafea is referred to collectively as Alo-O-Sina (Children of Sina). The Sina referred to in the address was the sister of Taufau Tui A'ana, a king of the A'ana district in northwestern Upolu. The founder of the Leala'itafea title was the son of the *ali'i* Seumanatafa of Falealupo (and originally from Apia village). Seumanatafa, in turn, was descended from Sina through a daughter of the original Leatualevao, a Sala'ilua man, brother of Tuatō and founder of the 'Āiga Sā Tualevao. Wherever the Seumanatafa title spread through the marriages of titleholders, the name Alo-O-Sina spread with it. Thus today, one finds Alo-O-Sina in Falealupo, in Apia village (through Seumanatafa), and in Sala'ilua (through Leala'itafea).

Such ceremonial connections through common title, or honorific name, do not necessarily suggest close genealogical links. Although such ties are frequently remembered by orators, it is the title, rather than a descent principle, that carries the weight in structuring the links. As in the process of bestowing personal names and political titles, the descent relationship is transformed into a name and remembered through it, a linguistic medium replacing a biological medium as the carrier of descent connections. Any "Child of Sina" will be welcomed into Sala'ilua village and, in all likelihood, his right to be present at a Sala'ilua ceremonial occasion will be accepted by local orators. In practice, however, names are weaker links than blood, and such formal ties do tend to diminish over time as different branches develop distinct identities. Gradually local ties of village and district eclipse in importance these dispersed alliances. While the connections among the Sālemuliaga villages have remained viable politically, others, such as among the Alo-O-Sina, are rarely exploited with distant villages. They are remembered, however, and remain potential connections which may be exploited should an occasion warrant it.

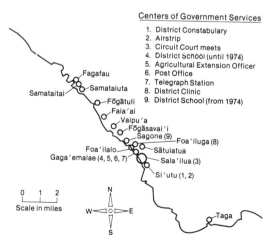

Figure 3.5. Itū-Sālega: Government Administrative District.

Government Administrative Districts

Aside from the more traditional political divisions among districts, Savai'i has been divided into sets of administrative districts for government departments. These districts administer the services of the Departments of Health, Education, Justice, Agriculture, and Post Office and tend to be based more on territorial contiguity and convenience than on traditional political alliances. Thus Sala'ilua is an unofficial district center for the administrative services of government. Si'utu houses the office of the district constable and, until recently, a neighboring village was the location of the district intermediate school. The district post office and telegraph station, together with the house of the district agricultural extension officer, are also located on a compound just outside Sala'ilua. A district clinic lies several miles to the north of Sala'ilua in Foa'iluga village. Although the precise boundaries for these various administrative districts vary from department to department, they tend to extend from Taga in the south to Fagafau, a distance of about fourteen miles, including fifteen villages. Geographically, Sala'ilua is almost exactly in the center of this district (see map, figure 3.5).

CHAPTER FOUR

The Matai System

If asked to suggest the single most important pillar upon which their culture rested, most Samoans would probably respond without hesitation that it was their system of chiefs. In an important sense, the existence of their culture for Samoans is predicated on those institutions and practices associated with chiefs in which Samoan culture—the *fa'a-Samoa*—finds its most elegant distillation. To understand the political organization of Sala'ilua, therefore, requires an examination of the *matai* system which is at its heart.

I have already suggested something of the complexity of the *matai* system, the fact that a chief is simultaneously part of a village system and the leader of a dispersed descent group with a complex network of diffuse alliances. To clarify the complex structure of the chiefly system, it is useful to think of a title as involved in a number of distinct relationships. A *matai* in Samoan is a chief, a person empowered through possession of a chiefly name or title, with authority (*pule*) over lands and people. The power of the chief lies not so much in the personal qualities of the holder (though these can significantly affect the title's power and dignity), but rather in the title itself; a name confers power on its holder. All chiefs share a number of characteristics including possession of a title, *pule* within both kinship groups and villages, and a general honor and dignity that attaches to his title. *Matai* are also importantly different from each other in terms of rank, general prestige, and power, and in the *kind* of power they possess. Some are *ali'i*, noblemen with formal powers to command. Other *matai* are *tulāfale*, orators for the *ali'i*, who speak on their behalf and wield other more active, executive power that we recognize as explicitly "political."

Relation of Title to Land and Property

Each chiefly title gives to its elected holder control over the disposition of certain house sites and garden lands already under cultivation. Such properties are controlled by the titleholder in trust for his descent group, which he leads, and to which he is responsible for the management of their joint properties. In theory, there is often overlapping stewardship over lands and houses in cases where there are closely related, ranked titles. A subordinate but resident chief may have immediate control over his lands and house sites, but in theory at least a superordinate title holder within the same descent group has overriding authority. In fact residence, direct use of, and control over title lands and properties appear to carry great weight in stewardship, and such overriding authority is rarely tested. This ambiguity in the boundaries of authority is characteristic of all ranked relationships in Samoa. In relation to house sites, chiefly dwellings, and lands, local authority is normally respected.

Samoan land tenure is a particularly problematical subject, particularly if one seeks general principles or rules. Investigating land tenure and the specific nature of the land title relationship is made particularly difficult in Samoa where informants are especially reluctant to discuss matters pertaining to land with outsiders. With some senior titles, rights to parcels of land already under cultivation or to houses already occupied or built come automatically on assumption of the title. Other lesser titles or newly created divisions of older titles do not have specific lands attached to them, but are often associated with land, the authority over which lies with another superordinate title. Finally, land that is exploited and developed by a title-holder in the village where he holds his title, or by members of his household, come under the control of his title, and by extension of those who succeed him to power.

While Samoans generally claim that land is controlled by a *matai* and belongs to a title rather than to the person who actually clears or works the land, practice governing succession to control seems to vary considerably. Some informants insist that, should an untitled man clear and develop plantation lands on his own within his village, primary authority over the land would be passed to his own children, independent of the succession to the title of his chief. Others insist that all such land would be under the control of a title, and should the title pass to a distant branch of his family, the original cultivator would lose primary rights to his land and its fruits. When title succession remains within a primary household unit, passing from father to son, or to a brother, such issues may well not arise. However, conflicts over interpretation of land tenure norms may well arise where title succession does not follow the more normal paths, and where land is scarce. Such cases today are settled not by norms of inheritance or title succession, but rather by rules of negotiation in the Land and Titles Court.

One final way of gaining control over a parcel of land is through a bequest or gift of land from another, perhaps unrelated, descent group. Sometimes such bequests of land are accompanied by a gift of a title associated with that descent group, while at other times only land is given. Such a bequest of land is called a *matū palapala*, and is generally an expression of gratitude for generous hospitality, service, or aid rendered to the donor or his descent group. Land may be given without a title, just as a title may be given without any associated lands. Any land worked by the new title holder in his own village may come under the control of the new title, and the new title may thus become included in the council of its new village. This is one way in which titles become regionally dispersed and individuals not related through consanguinity or marriage may be said to be "connected through a common title."

Most informants agree that an *'āiga* member who had rendered proper service to his chief and contributed a share of his harvest to the chief as part of his *monotaga* (contribution to collective village projects) could not summarily be chased from his own lands and houses without extreme cause. The basic rights of a cultivator to remain on his lands apply normally even in the case when title succession is in another branch of the family. Conflicts in such cases do occur, however.

The one clear exception to this right of residential continuity for *'āiga* members in good standing relates to the main or title house of the senior chief. For many high-ranking *ali'i*, there is a special house site and chiefly residence (*māota*) attached to the title. These houses are often located on the *malae* associated historically with the title group of which the house occupant is the senior chief. On the village map of Sala'ilua (figure 3.2), the *malae* of the senior *ali'i* of Sataputu and that of the senior *ali'i* of Sala'ilua subvillage are clearly marked. Sataputu is the home of the descent group of Savai'inaea ('Āiga Sā Savai'inaea), as well as those of Leala'itafea and Leulua'iali'i. The house of the 'Āiga Sā Leala'itafea is the largest Samoan house on compound 9 (figure 3.2). The large grassy area surrounding their house is their *malae*, called Vā-i-Paepae (Between the Foundations). The large house on compound 8 represents the house of the 'Āiga Sā Savai'inaea and its *malae*, known as Mutiatele (Great Lawn) is beside it.[1] It is clear, then, that the *malae*, the Samoan political center analogous to the religious *marae* of eastern Polynesia, is primarily associated with constituent descent groups of village *ali'i*, rather than with the village as a whole.

All senior chiefs have their main title houses. Those belonging to ranking orators are called *laoa* and are associated neither with traditional names nor with *malae*. For senior *ali'i* and *tulāfale*, title succession does imply a residence shift for these main houses, the new title bearer and his household gaining the right to occupy the main title house. The family of the former titleholder become *tautua* or servants of the new holder. Such transitions, particularly when the title passes between only distantly connected individuals, are inevitably charged with tension, sometimes leading to serious friction between the two parties. Due to the vagaries of title succession in Samoa, there is an inherent instability in control of title lands and residence rights in chiefly dwellings over time.

Relation of Title to Household

Within the *'au'āiga*, which is the domestic unit of primary cooperation, distinctions in chiefly status between *ali'i* and *tulāfale* have little or no importance. A household chief is simply the *matai* or titled headman of the *'au'āiga*, whatever his status and rank in the larger political context. Though a chief may be of little account in village or district political affairs, holding a rank of *vā-i-matai* (between the chiefs) or *vā-i-pou* (between the house posts)—indicating the lack of important voice of the title in political affairs—he wields primary authority over the members of his own household, allocating tasks and receiving food and monetary contributions from its members, as well as controlling access to local lands under the control of his title. Lines of authority among chiefs who may share a common household (often brothers or father–son pairs), or between closely related household groups sharing common lands or trees, can be problematical and are often negotiated in terms of relative age, rank, or length of residence. A chief has the clearest autonomy in authority over his immediate family (wife, children, and attached relatives), but less clear-cut authority over trees or lands that are shared with another household. While each *'au'āiga* is normally headed by a chief who is resident in the household, there are cases in which no one has been given a title, and domestic authority is in the hands of a senior, untitled member of the *'au'āiga*. In such cases, however, overriding authority is possessed by the chief in whose name the lands are in trust. This chief may issue orders and allocate work roles for larger-scale undertakings, while the untitled household head carries on the normal business of daily life within the *'au'āiga*.

Related households, such as those headed by siblings each of whom possesses a distinct title, which are located close enough to each other to provide for continual exchange of services and goods, are known as each other's *pui'āiga*.[2] This term is used somewhat loosely and ambiguously in modern Samoa and is sometimes asserted to be synonymous with *'au'āiga*. Careful questioning of informants, however, reveals that the *pui'āiga* always refers to a closely related household, other than one's own household. Ties of consanguinity are a necessary but not sufficient condition for calling a household one's *pui'āiga*. It is, characteristically for Samoa, factors of residence and cooperation that along with the genealogical criteria, classify a household as a *pui'āiga*.

The Sala'ilua *Matai* Organization

There are a total of 29 distinct chiefly names or titles associated directly with the Sala'ilua subvillages of Sataputu and Sala'ilua. Of these, 14 are of *ali'i* status, while the remaining 15 are *tulāfale* titles. Taking into account title subdivisions, there are 106 titles in Sala'ilua (excluding Si'utu), 60 of which are *ali'i* titles, and 46 of which are orator titles. Thus, while the number of distinct orator titles exceeds the number of *ali'i* titles, the *ali'i* titles are broken into far more title divisions than is true for the orator titles, and the number of *ali'i*-status chiefs in Sala'ilua actually exceeds the number of orators.

Eleven men hold two Sala'ilua titles each, bringing the total number of individuals holding village titles to 95.[3] Thus just over 11 percent of the Sala'ilua titleholders possess two village titles, frequently in different local descent groups. Nineteen (20 percent) of these titleholders reside permanently outside Sala'ilua, either overseas in the Apia urban area or in another rural village with their wives' families or other of their several activated family connections. Of the 95 individuals holding Salai'ilua titles, 13 (13.5 percent) also hold at least one additional title in another village. There are thus 22 chiefs in Sala'ilua holding multiple titles, constituting 29 percent of all Sala'ilua chiefs. This figure includes one chief holding three titles. Of the 106 Sala'ilua titles held, 22 (20.5 percent) are held by affines to the title's descent group. That is, just over one-fifth of all Sala'ilua titleholders hold their titles as *faiavā* (affines).

In table 4.1 I have listed each of the Sala'ilua titles, dividing them into columns according to their status as *ali'i* or *tulāfale*. Each title is followed by a number indicating the number of title divisions into which the title has been subdivided. Each column is in three sections, suggesting the general rank distinctions among the different titles. The first section in each column lists the titles that have undisputed senior rank within a village. The second section lists titles of somewhat lesser rank in the village, while the third section contains the lowest-ranking titles, some of *pito vao* or *vā-i-matai* rank.[4] It should be stressed that this is no more than an impressionistic ranking, and is more accurate at either end of the scale than in the middle. No attempt at any more elaborate or fine-grained ranking has been made, since such an attempt would be misleading and ultimately indeterminate.

Relationships of Subordination Among Titles

I only became aware of the *pito vao* rank late in my fieldwork and was able to elicit only an incomplete list of these subordinate relationships. This list is shown in table 4.2.

Table 4.1
Sala'ilua *Matai* Titles: Rank, Status, and
Title Divisions

Ali'i Status		Tulfāle Status	
Savai'inaea	(11)	Tolova'a	(3)
Leala'itafea	(5)	Tuatō	(6)
Amituana'i	(7)	Matapula	(7)
Leulua'iali'i	(5)	Fotu'a'ava	(7)
Seigafo	(14)	Agafili	(13)
Leatualevao	(8)	Tuiatua	(1)
Tia	(1)	Leusoga	(1)
Taito	(1)	La'ifai	(1)
Faumuinā	(2)	Selegaiatoto	(1)
Va'ā	(1)	Tauleo'o	(1)
Su'a	(3)	Va'asili	(1)
Olo'apu	(0)	Saufatu	(1)
Noa	(1)	Tupa'i	(1)
Mua'imalae	(1)	Pale'ita'au	(1)
		Fa'aolofaiva	(1)

Table 4.2
***Pito Vao* Relationships Among**
Sala'ilua Titles

Superordinate Title	Subordinate Title(s)
Savai'inaea	Seigafo
	Matapula
Leulua'iali'i	Noa
Tolova'a	Agafili
	Su'a
Tuatō	Fotu'a'ava (?)

I have inferred the junior rank of the Fotu'a'ava title in relation to the Tuatō from the close relationship between several holders of the Fotu'a'ava title and Tuatō Fatu, a relationship that appeared to parallel that of the Agafili title to the Tolova'a. Since I discovered this *pito vao* classification of titles in Sala'ilua only after the death of Tuatō Fatu, I was unable to confirm whether this relationship was so recognized by Tuatō. This list is incomplete and intended as merely suggestive of the kinds of subordinate relationships that exist among sets of titles. Not surprisingly, such relationships are generally not discussed openly among villagers, rank relations being among the more sensitive issues of Samoan political life. These relations may be at the heart of disputes among villagers. For instance, one of the holders of the Tuatō title suggested to me that the Agafili title served both the Tuatō and Tolova's titles; but this contention was seriously disputed by some other villagers, particularly those affiliated with the Tolova'a title.

Becoming a *Matai*

"The path to power," a common Samoan saying goes, "is through service" ('o le ala i le pule 'o le tautua). Power itself is most clearly signified in Samoa through the assumption of a chiefly title. From puberty until he is selected by his family to hold a chiefly title, a boy is called a *taule'ale'a*, a term suggesting both youth and untitled status.[5] Should he remain untitled, he will always be known as a *taule'ale'a*, socially a youth, despite advancing age. Conversely, a youth on whom *matai* status has been conferred is no longer a *taule'ale'a*. He immediately gains in prestige and is regarded with greater respect and seriousness by his family and by other villagers. On assuming his title, even a relatively insignificant one, a youth will no longer attend the meetings of the *'aumaga*, the village association of untitled males. His proper place is now in the chiefly council among those of similar status. Instead of passively receiving instructions and decisions from the chiefs, as he had when a *taule'ale'a*, the new chief will be expected to lend his voice to the formulation of village regulations. He has been empowered with *pule*, secular authority to govern in village and family matters.

While Polynesian chieftaincies have been generally characterized as hereditary offices and contrasted with the more clearly achieved status of "big man" in Melanesia (Sahlins 1963), succession to Samoan *matai* status is neither clearly through achievement nor through ascribed status. Rather, a chief is selected by consensus of the assembled members of the descent group following what are often protracted discussion and debate. Instead of employing a single "rule" for succession, Samoans characteristically maintain a number of different, often conflicting, norms for selecting a chief, and employ them as alternatives or in combination. The actual choice of a chief, then, becomes a result of complex negotiations and a successor can rarely be predicted on the basis of abstract norms alone.

Such a flexible system of determining political succession permits the selection of a chief to be finely attuned to a particular situation, and allows a descent group the widest scope in choosing a new chief. Not limited to conferring *matai* status on an eldest child of the former title holder, or even on a direct blood descendant, the descent group can place power and responsibility in the hands of the ablest members of the group and bring into the fold those talented or wealthy members who may threaten to become alienated from the *matai* system and its authority. Further, in cases wherein a descent group is unable to agree on a single candidate or each faction within the descent group presses the case of its own representative, there is always the option of subdividing the descent group into title branches. Such subdivision of titles has enabled the *matai* system to keep pace with demographic changes, and has assured almost any talented person access to formal political power.

The Samoan emphasis on "service" to the chiefs and to the family as a basis for selecting new title holders has been mentioned. Traditionally such service has consisted of providing one's own chief with labor and food, as well as contributing work to family and village projects. In recent times, the concept of "service" has been expanded considerably to allow for the contributions of money and other material goods from those descent group members who may reside far from the village, perhaps overseas. At times, more abstract qualities such as fame and prestige of family members who have gained distinction academically or in professional careers also may be considered as service to the family.

So great is the Samoan emphasis on service as a criterion for political succession that adopted children, sometimes with no blood ties to the descent group, may be chosen as successors. Such adopted children are frequently referred to as *tautua*, suggesting that their path to the title has been through their service to the descent group rather than through genealogical links. In the nineteenth century, it was sometimes the practice of a descent group to adopt a child from a distinguished or high-ranking descent group, and to confer an important chiefly title on that child, giving official validation to the link or *faiā* that had been created between the two descent groups. Such adopted children were known as *tama si'i* (transferred children) and played a significant role at the highest levels of Samoan politics.[6]

Apart from his service the new *matai* should, Samoans claim, demonstrate that he is *agava'a*, clever and knowledgeable in the intricacies of Samoan lore, genealogy, and oratory. Nowadays, business skills and managerial abilities may be implicitly included in the concept of *agava'a*, adapting traditional concepts to altered circumstances. In addition to skills gained in formal schooling, chiefs should have gained some competence in more traditional kinds of knowledge dealing with ceremonial life, genealogical traditions, and the complex historical links that exist between villages and titles. Such knowledge should ideally be combined with discretion and wisdom in its employment, qualities that are alluded to in formal oratory as *tōfā mamao* and *utaga*, profound wisdom and cautiousness.

In addition to these more achieved skills, Samoans do indeed stress genealogical connection to former title holders as an important—but not absolute—criterion for succession. Heirs (*suli*) to the title through direct descent have an important claim to the title, and are certainly the most likely successors if they also possess the necessary skills and have demonstrated service to the descent group. The "true heir" (*suli moni*) is often held to be the son of the last titleholder. Such direct succession is known in Samoan as *nofo soso'o*, and is the most common form of political succession for the very high-ranking titles. Interestingly, Samoans have a term for eldest child, *ulu matua*, suggesting primogeniture. There is, however, no special term for an eldest son, even though males are far more likely to inherit titles than are females. Despite the term *ulu matua*, direct succession implies only that a title has passed from father to child, rather than father to eldest child. Primogeniture, although given some recognition in Samoa, does not constitute an important norm for political succession.

Samoans often insist that, in addition to the norm of direct lineal succession, there is a prior genealogical right of a remaining brother of the former title holder to succeed to his title. This right of the "remaining brothers" (*toe 'o le uso*) emphasizes collateral claims over lineal, and is justified by Samoans in terms of the rights of members of a senior generation over those of junior generations. It was this sort of claim, as younger brother to the former titleholder, that Enelē made to the Tuatō title after Fatu's death.

Formal Conferral of a Title

When using English, Samoans often refer to the "taking" of a title by a newly appointed chief. While in the past important titles may well have been forcibly "taken" by warfare, and even in present-day Samoa disgruntled unsuccessful claimants at the Land and Titles Court may feel that a title has been snatched from their rightful possession, a chiefly title is not taken by a holder so much as it is laid upon him by a descent group. A title, in Samoan thought, is simultaneously a name, a position or place in a council, a collection of rights and powers summarized by the term *pule*, and finally a "side" of the person who assumes it. Conceptually separable from the individual who happens to bear it, the possession of a title also transforms the holder from untitled status to that of chief—from secular or "common" status to one imbued with *mamalu* (dignity), *pa'ia* (sacredness), *pule* (authority), and *afio*, a formal term indicating stately or majesterial presence.

The process of becoming a chief has several distinct stages. Following discussion among various branches or factions of a descent group, and the arrival at a consensus on the proper holder (or holders) for a title, the descent group will announce its decision publicly (nowadays through the newspaper). It will also announce the date of the *saofa'i* (entitlement ceremony). *Saofa'i* is a polite term for *nofo* (sit) and its use in relation to entitlement suggests that to assume a title means to be accorded a place or seat in a council. A *saofa'i* is really an elaborate kava ceremony, enhanced by much oratory, in which the new titleholder is served kava for the first time under his new name.

Following the installation, which may be attended by members of the chief's descent group, members of the village in which the title is located, and those bearing political relations to the title and its holder, the new chief may assume his rightful place in the council of the village. Should the title be an important one, it may confer on the holder the additional right to occupy the official house and house site of the title, sometimes requiring the removal of the former occupants. While the installation validates the status of the new chief in relations to his descent group, the titleholder is under a tacit obligation to validate his status in his village by providing a feast for its members. Feeding the village publicly demonstrates the chief's commitment to his village and his obligation to support and protect even those members who are not his own kin.

Authority and Obligations of Chieftaincy

Primary authority over a title is, as I have stated earlier, in the hands of a descent group. Not only does the descent group have the right to bestow a title or to subdivide it, but it also reserves the right to revoke a title from any holder who is judged unfit or unworthy to continue in office. While to an outsider a Samoan chief may appear to wield unlimited authority over both his family and untitled villagers, he is in fact considered to hold his title in trust for those under its authority. In a sense, the chief as well as those he controls is under the authority of the title. Such authority not only confers power on the titleholder, but also considerable economic and social obligations of aid and support for those over whom he rules. This responsibility is commonly held to be a heavy—often onerous—burden for the chief, who is usually the object of a continual stream of requests from family members who look to him as a source of material, moral, and political support, especially in times of crisis. Further, the norms of *matai* status make it especially difficult for a chief to deny aid to his dependents, making skillful and tactful management of resources—both human and economic—an important asset for a chief.

Of all the responsibilities that a chief owes to his descent group, as well as to the community at large, none is more serious or consequential than the obligation to take formal responsibility for the behavior of those under his authority. As we shall see, moral responsibility in Samoan though focuses on the maintenance of proper relationships. Among these important relationships none is more significant than that of the chief to his descent group. The chief "stands for" (or, more precisely, "sits for") his family in the local council. An honorable, clever, or otherwise outstanding chief casts a favorable light on his entire *'āiga*, just as a disgrace for a chief is necessarily a disgrace for those under him. More generally, the actions of any family member are held to reflect primarily and directly on the good name of the family as a whole and, as its official representative, on its chief most immediately.

In Samoa, it would seem, the sins of the sons may be laid rather weightily upon their fathers, and bearing the consequences of those sins is one of the less glamorous aspects of the *matai* position. We have seen, for example, how Tolova'a Aleki, the father of Tuatō Fatu's murderer, was held formally responsible for his son's act in the traditional judicial proceedings, even though Ioane was himself a chief.[7] Indeed, Aleki, recognizing a kind of contradiction in this attribution of responsibility, attempted to deny responsibility for Ioane's acts by focusing on the fact of his son's own title. Ioane's acts, he claimed, were the acts of an Agafili, rather than of a Tolova'a, and Ioane's direct political links to the Sā Agafili should be stressed, not his genealogical ties to his father and his father's title. Aleki indeed had a valid point to make within Samoan custom, but for a number of reasons, which will be discussed in a later chapter, the Sala'ilua chiefs felt it appropriate to hold Tolova'a, and by extension his direct descendants, responsible for the murder. Since guilt by association is tantamount to a formal legal principle in Samoan custom, the orators of Sala'ilua were quick to make precisely clear the limits on responsibility for the murder. We recall here Tuiatua's powerful denunciation and the banishment of Aleki, his immediate family, and "all who shall spring from him." At the same time, Tuiatua made it clear that the guilt stopped there, and that the other branches of the Sā Tolova'a were not to be held responsible for the act.

Another quite different aspect of the Samoan stress on representative responsibility was the attitude of villagers toward Fatu's son's attempt on the life of his father's murderer. On the one hand, revenge is strongly discouraged by the church. Forgiveness, we recall, was the principal theme of the pastor's numerous speeches in the hours and days immediately following the murder. Within Samoan custom as well, revenge, particularly within a descent group or a village, is recognized as a powerful cause of prolonged feuding and thus as disruptive of the ideal of mutual love that should characterize village life. On the other hand, a man's sons are held to represent him, indeed to replace him in his death and, by virtue of their filial tie, a son is understood to be the proper person to avenge his father's murder. "If Galu does not try to avenge Fatu's death," a local pastor had confided to me privately, "he is no son of his father." That a pastor should admit the logic of such an act suggests the strong ambivalence most villagers feel toward a violent act of revenge.

This ambivalence was further reflected in the treatment that Galu received at the hands of the police. Obliged by law to arrest him and charge him with assault with intent to kill, Galu was in fact treated as something of a hero and a model son. The police were generally sympathetic, as was the Court, which gave him a relatively light prison term for an offense that could have earned him a far more serious punishment.

The Title and the Man

Margaret Mead (1930) relates a revealing story from Manu'a, the site of her famous early fieldwork. The story recounts a legendary rivalry between two half-brothers, Alia-Tama, the younger, and Alia-Matua, the elder, for political power in Manu'a. The two men, the legend goes, were walking along a path on a particularly hot afternoon. Suddenly seized by a thirst—for power, it turns out—the younger Alia begs his older brother to climb a coconut tree to pluck a green drinking coconut. The elder brother demurs, complaining that the dignity and *mana* of his chiefly status prevents him from performing menial services. Alia-Tama then suggests that his brother simply remove his tapa crown, which was the symbol and repository of his chiefly power. The suggestion appearing logical enough to Alia-Matua, he takes off his headpiece, places it on the ground, and climbs the tree. Wasting no time, the younger brother snatches the tapa crown, places it on his own head, and runs off to Fitiuta in Manu'a, where he is proclaimed Tui Manu'a.

Personal qualities may certainly enhance political power in Samoa, but power per se is clearly separable from any particular person who may wield it. Political power lies primarily in a title and is conceived of as external to the person who might happen to bear it. Without a title, as many talented and otherwise distinguished Samoans have discovered, one is—in an important sense—nobody. With it, even the most unprepossessing person is imbued with the dignity and distinction of his office.

Just as a titleholder is selected for a combination of qualities, both structural and personal, so also the chief remains at once a person and a position, holding both aspects of his status as distinct sides of his identity. Much of Samoan history, and of the complexities of Samoan political lie, are involved with the dynamic relations between these more stable structural aspects of power and the personal, more idiosyncratic character of those who use that power. This distinction is of great significance in Samoan culture, and much of the third part of the book will be taken up with an exploration of its implications.

In tracing the network of important ramifications and implications of the murder of Tuatō Fatu, it is important to remember that the death constitutes both a political and a personal tragedy. On the one hand, there are the characters involved in the sad drama, particular people at a particular time, with a unique rivalry between them. Fatu's death brought grief to many who knew him. On the other hand, it was also an event of political history with significant and far-reaching consequences for the balance of power in Sala'ilua. To understand something about that power, one must understand the more formal aspects of the structure of authority in Sala'ilua and, in more abstract and general terms, the important political institutions that together constitue the *matai* system in modern Samoa.

CHAPTER FIVE

Fa'alupega and Fono: The Framework of a Local Political Order

A Samoan proverb insists, "Samoa is the land where all positions have been allocated" ('O Samoa 'o le atunu'u 'ua uma ona tofi). It is possible to define for Samoa two types of social order: a political order stressing ties through territory, and a kinship order emphasizing links through blood, marriage, and adoption as the basis for affiliation. While as providing ideal types for analytical purposes, such a distinction is useful, it becomes difficult to maintain at the level of village and subvillage.[1] If the individual household ('au'āiga) is clearly based on ties of kinship, common residence is also a defining feature of the unit, and distinguishes the 'au'āiga from other 'āiga categories. At a slightly higher level of organization is the village or subvillage. It is at this level that the defining criteria for membership most clearly merge criteria for ties through kinship and those through territorial and political links.

The political identity of a Samoan settlement is associated with its chiefly fono by a fa'alupega or honorific address recognizing directly or by implication all the important constituent families and titles of the village, and by the chiefly titles that have a place in the village council but are primarily associated with the descent groups located there. The council is both a plan or formal arrangement for a gathering of chiefs, comprising a seating plan and a general order for kava service, and also a particular meeting at a particular time and place (see Larkin 1972). This same distinction between formal plan and particular realization applies to the village address as well. The fa'alupega suggests a timeless ordering of village segments as well as particular rankings of the constituent parts of the village at any time in history. Thus, both fono and fa'alupega are simultaneously general patterns for social organization and particular political configurations at any particular time.

The political order of a village is phrased largely in terms of the kinship idiom, and at this level it becomes difficult to conceive of the two orders separately. The fono in any realization of a general plan is a gathering of chiefs who are seated in a generally determinate order within a house, an order reflecting distinctions of both rank and status. Chiefs and chiefly titles are linked to kinship units. Titles are the primary property of named descent groups and confer upon their bearers descent group and household authority. As constituent units of the village council, titles are also fundamental to local political organization. A chiefly title belongs to the village by virtue of its inclusion in the village political structure and of its holder's place in the village *fono*. Rights of succession (or, more properly, election) to a vacant title belong to the members of a dispersed title-based descent group called the *'āiga potopoto* (assembling kindred). A *matai* is thus a village head man, household leader, representative, and authority. While a chief is selected by and from a descent group whose members do not necessarily live in the village or district where the title is based, his political status must be confirmed by his accepting kava in council as recognition of his village authority, and by his sponsoring a large feast for the village in whose council he will have a voice. Full chiefship in Samoa is thus validated both in terms of kinship and territorial organization.[2]

While the chiefly title is primarily a feature of the *'āiga* system and secondarily (though importantly) a village institution, the converse is the case for the *fa'alupega*. Primarily a charter for the integrity of a territorial unit that may well comprise distinct descent groups, the village greeting is nonetheless phrased in the idiom of kinship. The greeting defines the unity of a settlement. Common territory, important marriages, and political alliances with other groups are the bases of political cohesion. The *fa'alupega* also defines the internal differentiation of a settlement in terms of its constituent descent groups.

Every important encounter between members of different villages in Samoa begins with a formal exchange of *fa'alupega*, each party reciting in the most elevated of tones the greeting of the other. Such recitations constitute the public acknowledgment by each group of the political integrity of the other. The honor and name of a village or district are at stake in these recitations, so orators are careful to include in their greetings all important titles and descent groups, particularly those of the other village whose members are actually present. Mistakes—particularly omissions— are serious matters for Samoans, which is why *ali'i* traveling about Samoa make sure they are accompanied by a knowledgeable orator. In discussing the *fa'alupega* in this way, I am implying its essential flexibility and sensitivity to local context.

The Sala'ilua *Fa'alupega*

It is easy for a student of Samoan social organization to assume that the greeting of a village is a determinate "thing," and one, moreover, that has a form and structure standardized for each district. It was such a set of assumptions, for instance, that led Kraemer (1902) to collect the greeting of each village and publish them along with descriptions of house building, cooking techniques, and genealogies of political families. It was because of such assumptions that the London Missionary Society saw fit to "correct" many of Kraemer's published village greetings by publishing their own *Tusi Fa'alupega*, or book of greetings, in 1958. This view of the greeting recognizes the existence of a single greeting for each district and village, having an unambiguous and stable form and content. Variations in that structure or order are generally assumed to reflect historical shifts from one structure of power to another (see, for example, Pitt 1969:79).

While obviously such shifts in local power configuration do occur, it is misleading to account for variations in a single *fa'alupega* solely in terms of historical shifts in power. There is as much variation in the greeting due to contextually motivated stressing of certain elements of village organization at the expense of others, as there is variation due to historical political changes. In table 5.1, I have juxtaposed three versions of the Sala'ilua greeting. In each greeting I have included references to Si'utu subvillage as well as to the other two divisions of Sala'ilua, but have distinguished Si'utu from the others. Si'utu might or might not be included in the Sala'ilua greeting, depending on whether the speaker wanted to stress the inclusion or exclusion of Si'utu from the rest of the settlement. If Si'utu chiefs were meeting alone to discuss some matter relevant only to their settlement, then only the Si'utu references would be included, and the same would be true of the other two constituent subvillages of Sala'ilua.

To facilitate comparisons among the three versions, I have provided interlinear translations of each. Version A is from Kraemer (1902); version B is from the London Missionary Society's *Tusi Fa'alupega* (1958); version C was collected by me from Tuatō Fatu in 1973.

In these three variants of the greeting eight elements appear to be structurally stable, four somewhat less stable, and three of the elements appear only in the most recent version. Of the three versions, the most recent one, collected from an orator of the village, has by far the most differences. As represented in table 5.1, each of the versions has eleven elements, though there are places where the division between elements seems to be more arbitrary than significant. In fact, the number eleven appears to be a coincidence, rather than a necessary feature of the *fa'alupega*. The absence of reference to the important Sālemuliaga orator group in version C is difficult to account for, since the importance of the group is commonly recognized in modern Sala'ilua. It is conceivable that Tuatō Fatu omitted the main orator group from the greeting in order to emphasize the place of the two orators in the village not included in the Sālemuliaga: Tuatō and Tolova'a. Instead, the informant placed reference of Tuatō and Tolova'a in the first position, that reserved for the Sālemuliaga in the other two versions of the greeting. Fatu's only reference to the Sālemuliaga was indirect. The reference in 8C to Matapula, an orator title within the Sālemuliaga, is unique among the three variants. The only explanation that I can see for this inclusion is the fact that Matapula is the title of Tuatō's eldest daughter's husband.

Order of Inclusion of Elements

As suggested in the preceding section, the particular order of elements in a greeting and the difference in ordering between different versions may

Table 5.1
Three Versions of the Sala'ilua *Fa'alupega*

Version A 1903	*Version B* 1958	*Version C* 1973
1. *Tulouga a 'oe Sālemuliana* Greetings to you, Sālemuliaga	*Tulouna a 'oe Sālemuliaga* (see 1A)	*'Oulua matua mai Sala'ilua* You two senior ones from Sala'ilua
2. *Tulouga 'oulua matua* Greetings to you, two senior ones	*Tulouna 'oulua matua o Tuatō ma Tolova'a* Greetings to you two senior ones, Tuatō and Tolova'a	*Susū mai le Savai'inaea* Welcome to Savia'inaea
3. *Alāla mai 'oulua āitutagata* Welcome to you two demon-men (see 1C, 2A, 2B)	*Tulouna Lau Afioga a Leulua'iali'i* Greetings to the honorable Leulua'iali'i (s. of Malietoa Taulapapa)	*Le 'Āiga Sā Amituana'i* The family of Amituana'i
4. *Tuatō ma Tolova'a*	*Susū mai ali'i o paepae* Welcome, chiefs of the foundation (group of *ali'i* titles)	*Afio mai Leala'itafea* Welcome to Leala'itafea
5. *Afio mai Alo-O-Sina* Welcome to the children of Sina (*ali'i* family of Leala'itafea)	*Tulouna a lo 'outou 'āiga o Alo-O-Sina* Greetings to your family, Children of Sina	*Ma-Alo-O-Sina* (see 5A, 5B)
6. *Ma lau afioga Leala'itafea* and your honor, Leala'itafea (S. of Seumanatafa of Falealupo descended from Sina, through d. of Leatualevao of Sala'ilua)	*Afio mai lau Afioga a Leala'itafea* (see 6A)	*Le matua o Seigafo* the elder Seigafo (*ali'i* of Si'utu)

7.	*Tulouga (Afio mai) le 'āiga Sā Amituana'i ma lau susuga a Savai'inaea* Greetings (be welcomed) the family of Amituana'i and your honor Savai'inaea (both senior *ali'i.* s. of Amituana'i married d. of Leala'itafea and bore Savai'inaea Oloitefu)	*Tulouna le 'āiga Sā Amituana'i* (see 7A)	*Ma le tamatane o Popupu* and the fraternal descent group of Popupu (?)
8.	*Tulouga Sāla'ulu ma le nu'u faigatā* Greetings Sala'ulu (La'ulu family) and the difficult village (Si'utu). La'ulu is from Gātaivai village, but Si'utu broke from this village, earning perhaps their name "difficult village"	*Susū mai lau susuga a Savai'inaea* (see 7A, 2C)	*Maliu mai Matapula* Welcome to Matapula (important orator of Sālemuliaga
9.	*Susū mai 'oulua suafa 'o Mulipola ma Mulipola* Greetings to you two titles, Mulipola and Mulipola (M. originally son of Tolufale of Maneno Island, *ali'i* title of Si'utu	*Tulouna a 'oulua suafa 'o Mulipola ma Mulipola* (see 9A)	*Afio mai Sala'ulu ma suafa* Welcome family of La'ulu and titles (of Mulipola and Mulipola; see 8A, 9A)
10.	*Tulouna na ali'i o Paepae* (see 4B)	*Susū mai lo 'outou 'āiga Sāla'ulu* (see 8A, 9C)	*Alāla mai le nu'u faigatā* Be greeted, the difficult village (Si'utu; see 8A)
11.	*Susū mai 'oe Leulua'iali'i* Welcome to you Leulua'iali'i (s. of Malietoa Taulapaᴐa; see 3B)	*Alāla mai 'oe le nu'u faigatā ma lau fetalaiga a Fa'atoafe* Be greeted to you the difficult village, and the honored orator Fa'atoafe (Fa'atoafe is the senior orator of Si'utu)	*Ma lau fetalaiga Fa'atoafe* and your honor the speaker Fa'atoafe; see 11B)

be significant. We may compare the order of inclusion for the constituent elements (families, titles) of the three versions, by giving the relative order in which each of the elements appears in each version. This ranking is set out in table 5.2.

Following the name of each element is an indication of whether the elements refer to an *ali'i* title [A] or a *tulāfale* title [T]. The elements are listed in overall rank order, based on both frequency and order of inclusion for each element.

The preeminence given to orator groups and titles in the greeting is obvious in terms of positioning, if not in terms of number of units included. The emphasis on the two major orator elements in the village, the Sālemuliaga group and the senior orators Tuatō and Tolova'a, is clear in that they occupy the two first positions in each variant of the greeting. The shifting of the reference to Tuatō and Tolova'a to first place, and the omission of any direct reference to the Sālemuliaga, in version C has been discussed above.

Reference to the two senior men of the village, Tuatō and Tolova'a, appears in second position in the two earlier versions of the greeting, and in first position in the most recent. Along with the reference to the Sālemuliaga, orators rather than the expected *ali'i* occupy the important opening positions of all three versions of the Sala'ilua greeting, while the village *ali'i* titles all come toward the middle of the greeting.

Significantly there is not, among the three versions of the greeting, a single case of matching rank-ordering of the included titles. While the positioning of the first one or two, and the last elements of the greeting does seem to be significant, it does not appear that the precise ordering of

Table 5.2
Order of Inclusion of Elements in Sala'ilua *Fa'alupega*

Version			Element
A	B	C	
1	1	—	Sālemuliaga [T]
2	2	1	Tuatō and Tolova'a (*'oulua matua*) [T]
7	7	3	Sā Amituana'i [A]
7	8	2	Savai'inaea [A]
6	6	4	Leala'itafea [A]
5	5	5	Alo o Sina [A]
8	10	9	Sāla'ulu [A] (Si'utu)
9	9	9	Mulipola/Suafa [A] (Si'utu)
8	11	10	Nu'u Faigatā ("Difficult Village" Si'utu)
10	4	—	Ali'i o Paepae [A]
—	11	11	Fa'atoafe [T] (Si'utu)
—	—	6	Seigafo [A] (Si'utu)
—	—	7	Tamatane o Popupu [?]
—	—	8	Matapula [T]
11	3	—	Leulua'iali'i [A]

elements in the middle of the greeting is structurally predictable, or that it denotes exact ranking.

The Structure of a Fa'alupega

The question of what constitutes the structure of a Samoan greeting is important for a more general understanding of social structure in Samoa. Many of what have been assumed to be invariable features of a village greeting, including features of specific content inclusion, content ordering, and segment grouping are actually open to a good deal of free play. To interpret each variation as a basic structural modification of the *fa'alupega* itself is to overstate the case for structure and to misunderstand the nature of the *fa'alupega*.

A greeting, just like the political unit it symbolizes, is an ordering of constituent elements in a series of ambiguously hierarchical relationships. Some of these elements seem to be relatively stable over time, and from use to use, and might be taken to be mandatory. Others are less stable, open to manipulation by users, and thus appear less structurally basic than the others.

Instead of examining what a greeting of a district or village is in general, it would be more revealing and appropriate to investigate the structural features in the *use* of the greeting as reflected by contextual variations in its realization. Such varying use of a greeting stresses some links at the expense of others, and suggests situationally relevant degrees of inclusion or exclusion. In addition, of course, broader and more stable shifts in relative power and prestige of groups in the village are also reflected. Some of the variations in the different versions may well suggest such general historical vicissitudes in power and rank. It is important, however, to recognize the degree to which variation may be accounted for in terms of a synchronic structuring of contexts, and the susceptibility of elements in the greeting to collapsing, elaboration, and reordering in order to shift focus from use to use.

Organization of the Sala'ilua *Fono*

It was Mead (1930:11) who first suggested that the chiefly council in Manu'a was more of an ideal conceptual arrangement comprising "names and their ranks" rather than any particular title holders. As an ideal plan, the *fono* is repeated at three levels of village organization. The basic plan, from which the others are derived, is the ranking of chiefly titles in the council of a particular village. The *aualuma* (village girls' association) and the *'aumaga* (association of village untitled men) derive their organization of rank and status from this chiefly council arrangement. When the wives of chiefs meet, or the wives of untitled village men, their meetings are also organized according to the status and rank of the associated *matai*. Thus whatever the particular village organization, it is always the relevant links to village *matai* titles, through fathers, husbands, or other family connections, that determine the seating and speaking order of the council.

Three general types of council in Samoa must be distinguished. The *fono fale* (house meeting) is most common, and deals with everyday matters. It generally includes only one segment of the village, whether chiefs, their wives, sons, or daughters, or the women's committee. The meeting is held in a single meeting house.

To deal with more serious matters, there are two other types of *fono*. Both, it will be remembered, figured prominently in Tuatō Fatu's murder case. A secret meeting, or *fono māitu*, is a closed and secret gathering of senior orators, meeting at night behind lowered blinds, discussing is whispers a particularly serious matter. The purpose of such a meeting is for a body of orators, usually in consultation with *ali'i*, to reach a consensus on an important issue before the public meeting. When this consensus has been reached, a *fono tauati* or public meeting of the entire village on the *malae* is called for the following morning. Chapter 2 provides a rather detailed account of one such meeting.

During the time I spent in Sala'ilua, I had the opportunity to attend a number of different *fono*, including both *fono tauati* and *fono fale*. No two meetings were exactly the same in particular structuring, and yet one could easily identify a general structuring to these meetings and, in the case of meetings of the *'aumaga* or Women's Committee, one could see the derived organization from the more basic council of village chiefs.

It is possible, for Sala'ilua, to distinguish three levels at which the *fono* is structured. There is the common and most general structuring of the council that links it with other Samoan gatherings throughout the archipelago. This general pattern enables any Samoan to participate in a *fono* anywhere throughout Samoa, and to fit his particular status and rank into the local organization. There is also a particular version or realization of the general pattern in a local setting. This local plan may include some deviations from the general *fono* scheme. In this local version, particular positions and functions are allocated to specific titles, groups, and individuals within a subvillage, village, or district. This local version of the *fono* is also a kind of ideal plan. Finally, there is the particular council meeting at a specific time and place, with specific individuals occupying the formal positions. While any particular *fono* conforms generally to the formal *fono* pattern and is consistent with the local version, it may also involve specific elaborations and modifications to suit the needs of the circumstances. One person may, for instance, occupy the seat of an absent chief, sitting in under his name. One title may replace another in precedence in the kava service, and in the subsequent weighting of voices for the discussion. Such variations are functions of specific context, but operate within the general structural framework of the kava service and the *fono* more generally.

The General Scheme of a *Fono*

Of all the arts, it is those associated with political relations that receive the most attention in Samoa. Samoans nowhere express more elegantly their love of courtliness than in their chiefly council. The great round meeting houses of Samoa are among the finest architectural achievements in all of Oceania. It is a prerogative of an *ali'i*, a titled nobleman, to have an official meeting house built on his land. Every village will have at least one of these grand *māota*, as they are called, usually located at the edge of a *malae*. For the most important titles, the house site itself is remembered with reverence, long after the building itself has been dismantled. As with titles, or places in the council, a *māota* retains an existence even when not in use. Important orators have their houses too, called *laoa*, but on the most important occasions, a *fono* will be convened in one of the larger and grander of the *māota* in the village.

The structure of the *fono* includes distinctions of both status and rank. Status differences refer to distinctions in role, while rank distinctions refer to a gradient of power, prestige, and so forth within any particular role. Status distinctions in the *fono* include those between *ali'i, tulāfale,* and untitled servants. There is also a place for the *taupou*, a titled daughter or close relative of an *ali'i*, who presides over the preparation of kava. A further status distinction may be made between hosts and guests in the case of a kava ceremony welcoming guests. The meeting house is conceived as comprising two rounded ends or *tala* with the *atualuma* (sides) connecting them. The extreme ends of the house are called *matuatala* and are the appropriate positions for the highest-ranking *ali'i*. The *atualuma* or sides are generally reserved for the orators and for those making the kava. The "corners" between the ends and sides of the house are called *pepe*, and are set aside for chiefs of lesser rank. Kava makers and attendants sit on the landward side of the house, along with the overflow of lower-ranking orators.

In the case of an intervillage meeting, two senior *ali'i*, one from each village, will face each other from opposite ends of the house while senior members of each village's body of orators (*fale'upolu*) will face each other on opposing sides of the house. An alternate plan is for opposed orator groups to share the seaward side of the house, positioned on adjacent sides of the center post on the *atualuma*. If the meeting includes only members of a single village or other unit, then two senior *ali'i* from within the village take opposing ends of the house and the orators sit on the seaward side, with the kava makers and attendants on the landward side of the house. Thus a general scheme is maintained, but variations are possible to suit local circumstances.

In the *fono* floor plan represented in figure 5.1, *ali'i* face each other, as do the orators. The *ali'i* and *tulāfale* are adjacent and at right angles to each other. The symbolism of *ali'i* and *tulāfale* in the more general scheme of power relations in Samoan thought will be explored in chapter 12. When

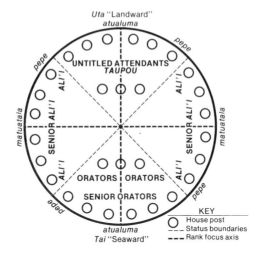

Figure 5.1. General Seating Plan for a Kava Ceremony.

outsiders are present at a *fono*, hosts usually sit facing guests, again with chiefs of parallel status facing each other and chiefs of complementary status at right angles. In terms of status, the *fale* may be thought of as comprising four quadrants formed by two intersecting lines, the first formed by the two *matuatala*, seating places for the highest-ranking *ali'i*, and the second by the *atualuma* or side positions. These intersecting axes of status and rank are represented in figure 5.1 by the dotted lines. While status distinctions are clearly symbolized by adjoining sides of the house, rank distinctions are indicated by a center/periphery distinction in which senior rank is focused at the central posts at both the ends of the house and the sides, with lesser titles radiating outward in diminishing rank. Whereas status distinctions suggest a clear binary opposition, those of rank are appropriately graduated, allowing for the expression of subtle and gradual rank distinctions. While such a scheme theoretically permits a precise indication of rank, the tendency is for ranking distinctions to be left relatively ambiguous, with the extremes of center posts and no post as the only clear indices of rank. This tendency suggests the reluctance of Samoans to be explicit or rigid about ranking in any but a very general way.

Local Instances and Local Version of the Sala'ilua Fono Structure

During a period of three and one-half years, I had the opportunity to attend and witness many *fono*, and my observations support the power of the general plan outlined above to structure the actual process of a council gathering. In fact, this general plan seems not only to structure local council meetings in Samoa, but was also evident in the gatherings of Sala'ilua chiefs temporarily resident in Auckland, New Zealand. In all variations of the

Sala'ilua *fono* that I witnessed, there was a clear attempt to maintain the *tai/ uta* distinctions in seating, the opposition of chiefs of equivalent status, and the focal seating positions at the center of the side and the end of a house or room. There was some tendency in local variations to place all the orators at the seaward side of the house, leaving the landward side for the kava makers. The positions for the senior *ali'i* were invariable.

In Sala'ilua there was a fair degree of variability in the seating position of any specific title, due largely to changing composition of each particular meeting as well as to the type of meeting. No title can be said to have an absolute position in a meeting house, since its rank is dependent on the scale of the meeting and the particular composition of *matai* present. It is therefore the combination of specific circumstances and general principles for status and rank allocation that determine the seating at any particular *fono*. For instance, while the Mulipola title of Si'utu would enjoy a focal rank position at any Si'utu gathering, he would share that position, or even defer to another chief at a more general meeting of all Sala'ilua, or at a district gathering. In a general *fono* which I attended of all three segments of Sala'ilua, Mulipola Fiatau shared focal position with Savai'inaea Alova'a.

On the orators' side, Tuatō and Tolova'a, when present, share focal position. At the general village meeting convened to deal with the murder of Tuatō Fatu, the 'Āiga Sā Tuatō and the 'Āiga Sā Tolova'ā each took a separate meeting house around the *malae*, while the other chiefs and orators of the village, occupying their own house, rearranged the rank positions among the orators to reflect the new circumstances. Fa'atoafe, Tuiatua, and Matapula occupied senior rank positions on the orators' side of the house for this occasion.

This general scheme for the *fono* is flexible enough to allow for a collapsing of distinctions, with one unit representing a general group. This sort of collapsing was evident in a district *fono* in which Tolova'a Aleki and Savai'inaea Alova'a represented all of the chiefs of Sala'ilua. Conversely, the scheme also allows for elaboration of fine distinctions, as when a sub-village meets in a separate *fono* and previously submerged elements take on a new significance.

While it is possible to describe the general structure of a *fa'alupega* or *fono*, it is only in relation to a specific configuration of titles and their holders that these institutions have any life. The following chapter will focus on these chiefly titles and examine what they are in terms of a number of important connections in Samoan thought which they suggest.

CHAPTER SIX

Titles: The Articulation of an Aristocracy

In one sense, Samoans characterize the *matai* system as the foundation of their society because the chiefs provide Samoans with a sense of their own immortality as a people. People die in Samoa, of course, and sometimes they die suddenly and tragically, as Fatu did in Sala'ilua. But Tuatō did not die with Fatu, for it is a name already borne by others and a title sure to be carried again by a successor to Fatu. Titles thus represent the institutionalization of persons as enduring offices and positions that have a life of their own.

It is difficult to enter into the life and thought of Samoans as we have without very quickly encountering the striking double life that Samoans accord people as titleholders. In his private moments with intimates, Fatu, like all chiefs, was just a man among men. He was Fatu. But in his public moments Fatu was more than this: he was Tuatō and Tualevao and carried with him the dignities and powers of these names. In death too he was double, for, as we have seen, the conflict was understood at one level as a fight between persons (Fatu and Ioane) and at another level as a political battle engaging titles and their associated families. It was thus through the titles associated with Fatu and Ioane that the fight took on genuine political implications.

Because of the centrality of titles and of the chiefs they define to the way in which Samoans understood the murder of Tuatō Fatu, it is useful to inquire into the system of chiefs in Sala'ilua and examine more closely the meanings of a chiefly name.

Aspects of a Title

Title and Titleholder

In Samoan thought, the *matai* is an association of a name and a person. The crucial distinction between the title and the person who holds the title (i.e., the office and the officeholder) is important in Samoan thought and will be taken up again in a different context in chapter 12. Titles and their holders are conceptually independent, but structurally interdependent entities in Samoan thought. In the Samoan conception both person and names are divisible into many potential parts or sides. A single name or title may have different parts or divisions, known as *fasi igoa* (pieces of the name).

Each division has a distinct holder. With the agreement of the dispersed descent group, a title may be split into several divisions, each given to a different holder. Such splits are made as a reaction to population pressures or political conflict within the descent group.

Just as each title may have a number of holders, each person has potentially a number of distinct "sides," each associated with a different name or title. Thus, Tuatō Fatu was also Tualevao Fatu. A *gafa* is a descent line or pedigree tracing the descent from person to person either to find a linkage between two contemporaries, or to define a relationship between a person and a particular ancestor. An *'augānofo,* sometimes confused with the *gafa* by observers, is a title succession line in which the title provides the organizing focus rather than either an ancestor or a person tracing a pedigree. Were political succession strictly on the basis of a descent principle, the two lines might be conceptually identical. In Samoa, where lineal descent is only one of a number of criteria for political succession, an *'augānofo* parallels a descent line or *gafa* only rarely, and significantly, it does so usually only in the case of a very high-ranking title.[1]

In formal Samoan, this distinction between the title and the person is reflected in the polite address in which an individual is addressed by the dual pronoun *'oulua* (you two), reflecting the conceptual separability of the person (*tagata*) from the dignity of his office (*āfio*). For a chief, the primary dignity attaches to the title.[2]

Itū Paepae: Title Divisions

We have already seen how, through successive marriages, adoptions, and gifts, a title can become alienated from its original village or even from its original descent group, and come to have several distinct local bases. Often, the original ties of common descent or origin of these title branches become weak and are all but forgotten. Within a single descent group and village, however, there are frequently multiple title divisions called *itū paepae* (sides of the foundation) or, more simply, *itū* (sides). The nature of the relationships among these title branches and among their holders varies considerably, depending on the history of the particular title division, how many generations back the division took place, and the genealogical propinquity of the various holders. A title division may have been agreed upon by all parties concerned within the original descent group, leaving relations among the coholders amicable and close. In cases in which the split came through dissension or was imposed by the Land and Titles Court, a title division may attempt to deny that the title had ever been split or, more commonly, stress the autonomy of each of the title branches.

Most splits occur originally between brothers or between their children. The splitting of a title is one way of avoiding open conflict among contending branches. This division of a title between competing branches of a descent group creates two or more *itū paepae*. A common alternative to splitting a title has been for the Land and Titles Court to impose an alternating succession of a title among two or more branches.

There are no norms regulating the relations among these different title branches. Particularly interesting is the lack of clear norms relating to title succession. In some cases where the split is relatively recent, or occurred amicably, members of the one branch may retain a voice in selecting a successor to the second. In other instances, and more commonly, there is considerable autonomy of different title branches. In fact, where such autonomy is absent in the relations between different title branches, the term *itū paepae* is often held to be inappropriate.

The term "'Āiga Sā" prefixed to the name of the title indicates the descent group whose identity is defined by the title . This group is also known as the *'āiga potopoto*, literally the "assembling kin" and sometimes as the *'āiga 'ātoa* (the entire body of kin). This descent group comprises a cognatic stock traced through bilateral descent ties or through links of adoption from the original titleholder, any subsequent titleholder, or the most recent titleholder. It is thus the title, rather than a descendant per se, that provides the focus for structuring this descent category, and in terms of which this category is realized on specific occasions as a concrete group. The term *'āiga potopoto* may be used abstractly to suggest the broadest possible extensions of this stock, embracing many title branches. Alternately, it may have a more restricted use, and refer implicitly to a single autonous branch only.[3]

Titleholder and Coholders of Same Title

The degree of cooperation and solidarity among coholders of a single title varies considerably and depends on factors of genealogy, residence, history, or particular circumstances. The rank relation among such coholders is particularly sensitive, and is the frequent focus of conflict and stress. There is always an official parity in rank among coholders of a title, but in fact there is frequently an implicit and sometimes an explicit internal ranking among them. It is significant that such rank differences are poorly reflected in the Samoan vocabulary, and are represented ambiguously by terms such as *matua* (senior, elder) or *sa'o* (correct, straight). Such terms, however, are historically associated only with certain titles, rather than with the general concept of rank within a chiefly status. For example, *matua* refers to a title that has given active control to a junior title descended from it, and has taken a passive but respected role in political life. *Sa'o*, by contrast, is an honorific term associated with certain senior titles within a village, and indicating senior village rank. Again it is commonly the title, rather than any particular holders of the title, that is referred to and is overtly ranked. Among orators there are distinctions between *tulāfale,* an ordinary orator, and a *fai lāuga*, a senior orator. The latter suggests the rank of important spokesman for the village and descent group. Finally, the *tu'ua* is a rank-related term for orators, suggesting a kind of elder statesman who is supposed to be (by lucky coincidence) both the oldest and the wisest orator in a village. In fact, the term is frequently applied to a younger, but particularly active and capable orator. Once again, none of these terms focuses on rank distinctions within a body of coholders of a single title, although undoubtedly they may support such rank discriminations.

This linguistic masking of rank differences among coholders is a significant and characteristic feature of Samoan relationships to which I shall return in chapter 11. While Samoans are quick to insist publicly that all holders of a title are the same and equal, it is also evident from observing political life in a village that there is often a member of a body of coholders who is accorded greater deference than the others. Sometimes this seniority of rank is explicit, but more often it must be inferred from elite interactions. Formally, any holder of a title may become a *sui* (replacement) for any other and represent the entire title-based descent group.

There are many criteria involved in this internal ranking of coholders of a title, criteria that comprise alternative paths to prestige, and thereby to rank. These alternatives are not formalized as norms of rank definition by Samoans, but may be inferred from case histories. Thus seniority appears to be determined by a combination of ascribed and achieved statuses. Age, wisdom, length of village residence, prowess in war, genealogical knowledge, *tamatane* status, patrilineal links to the title's founder, Land and Titles Court decisions, and general political cunning all enter into the determination of particular rankings. The relevant genealogical criteria, for example, might include descent from senior sibling, or descent status as *tamatane* to the title. The multilateral and thus ambiguous nature of these criteria make any particular incumbency or claim to seniority indeterminate and unstable over a long period of time. One informant, himself a senior-ranking holder of a title, commented that a senior chief must always be wary.

Associated Political Titles

Generally a title-based descent group (*'āiga potopoto*) is associated primarily with senior-ranking titles, although the concept potentially includes any title as the basis for a distinct *'āiga potopoto*. Senior titles commonly frame the village greeting and are seen as the basis of the political structure of a village. Associated with these senior titles in a village or district settlement, however, are subordinate or junior titles, sometimes called *pito vao* (literally, "bush section") titles. Such subordinate titles are sometimes the creation of senior titleholders, and their holders act as retainers of the senior chief.[4] They are thus subordinate in rank, both within the village and within the larger descent group, although such minor titles still confer upon the holder the right to be present at council meetings and to act as spokesman and leader of a household unit. A title may be created for a son or other junior relative as a reward for service, or to confer an official status on a relative to support his *de facto* status as head of household.

Holders of such subordinate titles often have relatively little say in village affairs, their power being restricted to formal recognition of their chiefly status and to the power that every chief exerts within his own household. As we have seen, such chiefs are sometimes known as *vā-i-matai* (between the chiefs) or *vā-i-pou* (between the house posts), referring to the title's lack of real power within the village council. *Pito vao* status, not surprisingly, is generally a status ascribed to titles other than one's own, and rarely will a chief admit to having such a low status within the village, although the seniority of other titles may be admitted. Clear determination of subordinate status for titles is thus difficult, and is a matter of one's own assessment of deference accorded to, and power exerted by, a title.

One of the greatest difficulties in the determination of rank is that title autonomy is more relative than absolute. Thus, in terms of a particular household, any title may be said to wield undisputed authority, whatever its village-wide rank. Similarly, a title that is seen as subordinate to another in certain contexts may be recognized as defining an autonomous descent group in others. For instance, the Agafili title was described to me on the one hand as a servant title to Tuatō and, especially, Tolova'a. On the other, it is also the focal title in the descent group called the 'Āiga Sā Agafili and members of the descent group, whatever other affiliations they held in the village, would attend succession discussions for this title as members of the 'Āiga Sā Agafili, rather than as members of the 'Āiga Sā Tolova'a.

Finally, a particularly distinguished titleholder of a junior title may increase the prestige and eventually raise the relative rank of his title to the point where it is no longer clearly a subordinate title. Such instability in rank boundaries, whereby an encompassed unit may assert its autonomy and rank equivalence to a formerly encompassing and superordinate title, is in this sense analogous to the instabilities between the *nu'u* (village) and *pitonu'u* (subvillage).

The Dispersed Descent Group

Not all relations between linked titles are ranked. Thus, two titles within a village, each relatively autonomous in most village affairs, and each defining a distinct descent group (with overlapping membership) for purposes of succession, may bear a fraternal relation to the other. Such a relationship, casting the titles as each other's brother, suggests the status of the two titles' founders as brothers. Gradually, the names of the brothers, passed down to their heirs, become political titles, and the genealogical connections between the brothers and their descendants structure the relations between their names. In Sala'ilua, for example, Tuatō and Leatualevao are held to be related as brothers, and this close relationship between titles is reflected in the fact that the titles are held jointly by a single person in two cases in the village. While Leatualevao is an *ali'i* title, in contrast to the orator title Tuatō, it is the Tuatō title which is seen as senior in the village. However, when paired together, informants generally refused to say that Leatualevao was inferior in rank to the Tuatō title. Certainly, Tuatō never considered Leatualevao to be a subsidiary title to the Tuatō.

Titles may also be linked through filiation. Frequently titles, villages, and even districts in Samoa are held to originate from a common ancestor. The common pattern is for a powerful chief to marry his sons off to daughters of important chiefs in other villages, and send the sons to reside with their wives' families, thereby creating and solidifying links between the villages and founding local descent lines with supralocal links.[5] These sons are sometimes the originators of local titles, which trace their connections to important titles in other villages.

There is a common relation between paternal and filial-based titles. This relationship is modeled after the common practice in Samoa that an old man will "retire," giving to his son the *pule* or secular authority over household and village affairs, but retaining the *fa'aaloalo* or formal honor. This relation between father and son is paralleled frequently by relations between titles deriving from this relationship. In such a relationship, the elder title becomes a *matua* (elder title) which may be given ceremonial respect and deference, but retains little of its actual power.[6] This elder status of a title, distinguishing a kind of sacred honor from secular power, has resulted in the most powerful titles in some districts of Samoa actually being junior in genealogical status.[7]

Such a situation exists, for example, in the 'Āiga Sā Tunumafono in the Sāfata district on the southwestern coast of Upolu. This great political family derives its name from Tunumafono, its founder. Whenever the district meets as a unit, the holder of the Tunumafono title is given the highest honor in the kava ceremony. In fact, however, it is not the "father" but his "sons" who actually have supreme authority within the district, power that is realized in the senior titles of the villages of Sātaoa, Sa'anapu, Nu'usuatia, and Lotofagā.

As far as I know, there is no analogous relationship in Sala'ilua to this *matua* status in Sāfata. There are, however, several significant filial links between Sala'ilua titles of approximately equal rank. There is, for instance, a direct lineal relationship among the founders of the *ali'i* titles Leatualevao (and through him, Tuatō), Leala'itafea, and Savai'inaea. Savai'inaea is the specific link between Leala'itafea and Amituana'i. Their interrelations are evident in figure 6.1.

The original Leulua'iali'i (a Sala'ilua *ali'i* title), was the son of Malietoa Taulapapa, a link that connects him and his descendants to the powerful Sā Malietoā, with power bases in the Tuamasaga district of Upolu, in Sapapāli'i village of the Fa'asaleleaga district in southeastern Savai'i, and on Manono Island.

We have already discussed how titles proliferate through alliances of marriage and adoption, forming an overarching supralocal network of ra-

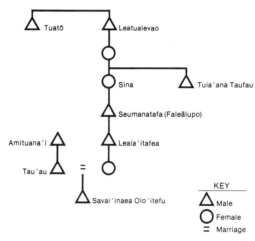

Figure 6.1. Relations Among Original Holders of Important Sala'ilua Titles.

mifying descent group links. The Sālemuliaga descent group is an example of one such network of localized descent group branches which are found throughout the island of Savai'i. Panoff (1964) has argued that such a widely dispersed ramage-like descent-group structure is more characteristic of Upolu social organization than that of Savai'i which, being somewhat more localized and less dependent on supralocal connections, conforms more to what Sahlins (1957) has called a truncated descent line, and Ember (1959, 1962) has termed a sept. Clearly, whatever the different tendencies, the existence of a ramage-like (though unranked) political structure relating sets of both individuals and titles is certain for both Savai'i and Upolu.

Links of Kinship Among Sala'ilua Matai

Detailed genealogical information bearing on the composition of a village, and particularly information about ties among chiefs, can be extremely sensitive, since it is this sort of information that is the basis for title claim disputes in the Land and Titles Court. Thus, like information on land tenure and boundaries, it is always difficult to collect from Samoans. I was able, however, to collect from my main informant in Sala'ilua detailed information on the affinal and consanguineal links among all the village chiefs. I then attempted to have this information checked by one other member of the village, who belonged to a different descent group from that of the first informant. Several corrections and additions were suggested dealing mainly with relations among the chiefs associated with the descent groups related to this second informant.[8]

There are almost sixty cases of chiefs who are related to other village chiefs as affines, indicating a recent marital alliance between village households. The matrix also indicates a far greater number of agnatic links among village chiefs than uterine links through sisters or mothers. This agnatic bias in *matai* relations is not unexpected considering the predominance of virilocal marriages, in which case a man's sisters and daughters are more likely to reside outside their natal villages upon reaching adulthood. Thus one's mother is more likely to be related to one's residential village as an affine than to be residing in her natal village. Further, this agnatic bias is comprehensible in terms of the agnatic stress in title succession, whereby titles commonly remain in the possession of those related through *tamatane* links through or from males. There is however considerable deviation from these patterns, both in marriage residence and in political succession. Uterine links to titles, or affinal connections, whereby a chief holds his title in the descent group of his wife, his mother, or as *tamafafine* to the title, are sometimes masked by the male stress in the ideology of secular power in Samoa. Thus, I suspect that if more careful genealogical tracing had been done for Sala'ilua, a greater number of uterine links would be discovered than was reported to me by my informant. For instance, *tamafafine* links to title by a holder are sometimes translated by informants into *tamatane* links. Such a situation holds in the 'Āiga Sā Tuatō, where five of the six title branches are actually *tamafafine* branches since these five titles are descended from a sibling set in which there was a single brother and five sisters. However, informants tended to translate these connections into *tamatane* links, related as the titles are through a common male ancestor. More interesting yet is the situation in the 'Āiga Sā Tolova'a, where the three branches are descended from a sibling set in which there were three sisters and no brothers. In such a case, where there is the lack of male ancestors in the founding generation, all lines are interpreted as *tamatane* links to the title.

Thus Sala'ilua is more than a cluster of distinct localized descent groups. Through generations of intermarriage among the constituent descent groups in the village, the village has virtually become a solidary kinship unit as well as a territorially based political unit. Kinship boundaries are inevitably fuzzy, but become clarified in relation to specific occasions. Today Samoans often claim that it is unwise to marry within one's own village, since the likelihood that husband and wife will be related is extremely high.

There are twenty-two sets of brothers who possess chiefly titles in Sala'ilua, including two sets of half-brothers. Of these, three fraternal sets hold the same title (Agafili in two cases and Savai'inaea in a single instance). There are also thirteen father–son pairs holding village *matai* titles. Of these pairs, only two fathers hold the same title as their sons (Agafili and Matapula). Three fathers have two sons each who are title holders. Within the closest range of genealogical proximity, kin-group boundaries tend to overlap boundaries between title groups.

While there is a widely ramifying network of kinship ties among all major village descent groups as well as within each of the title groups, a few patterns deserve special attention. Most notable is the number of kinship links (fifteen) between holders of the Agafili title and two of the three holders of the Tolova'a title. These links suggest the *pito vao* connection that had been reported between the Agafili and Tolova'a titles. Similarly, the Su'a title, another title subordinate to the Tolova'a, is linked to both this title and the Agafili title through each of its three holders. A weaker link holds between the Agafili title and Leulua'iali'i, and between the Tuatō and the Leatualevao titles. Some titleholders have far more diffused and greater numbers of links of kinship and marriage throughout the village than do others. Significant among these are Tolova'a Aleki, Tuatō Fatu, and Savai'inaea Alova'a. These three men are among the highest-ranking chiefs in the village, suggesting at least a correlation between the extent of one's network of supporting kin ties throughout a settlement and political power there. This observation is supported by Samoan beliefs, which view political power as a function of the elaboration of one's network of kinship ties and other alliances.[9]

Male Lines and Female Lines

Just as a village is conceived of as comprising two distinct sets of organizations, the village of men, and that of women, so also descent groups are understood to comprise female and male divisions. The character of these divisions is complex, however, and has been frequently misunderstood in the literature about Samoa. The problem seems to be that the male/female distinction in relation to descent-group segments has two quite distinct structures, which have often been confused. The one, stressing the husband/wife or mother/father relationship divides any assembly of cognatic kin into *toto mālosi* (strong blood) and *toto vaivai* (weak blood).[10] Those with "strong" blood ties to a group claim a "path" to the descent group through unbroken agnatic links, a chain of "fathers." "Weak blood," by contrast, implies that the connection to the descent group is through an individual's mother, or some other uterine link. In its simplest form then, the distinction between strong and weak blood suggests that descent through fathers is preferable to descent through mothers in making claims on a political title. Thus, although Samoans may be said to reckon descent bilaterally, there is clearly what Goldman (1970) has referred to as a propatrilineal bias in descent reckoning in terms of political succession. The higher the title in question is ranked, the more likely it is that this patrilateral bias in succession will become an important factor in selecting a successor.

A man may hold a title in his father's family or in his mother's family. In either case he claims the title through one of his descent lines (*gafa*). Alternatively, a man may be given a title in his own wife's family, in which case his title is claimed through a link of *pāolo* or affinal connection. In such cases, a man may be referred to as *fai āvā*, a term indicating either residence in his wife's village or possession of a title through her. As we have seen, just over 20 percent of the chiefs in Sala'ilua hold titles in their wives' families. It is important to note that children of such *fai āvā* maintain their claim to their father's titles through their mothers rather than through their fathers. They are thus "weak blood" in relation to their own father's title.

While the status of agnatic or uterine connection to a title implies a clear-cut distinction, in fact we are dealing with a difference in degree, rather than with a distinction of kind. In the limiting cases, there is indeed an unambiguous distinction between someone who descends from a pure pa-trilineal line of title holders and someone descending from an unbroken line of "mothers," which is to say "wives," to the title holders. In many cases, however, descent is through a mixed line of agnatic and uterine connections. In these cases, the distinction between "strong" and "weak" blood is really one of degree. The greater the number of agnatic links, the stronger the connection. Further, the concept of connections is itself ambiguous, since one may claim a title based on direct descent from the original founder of a title, from any subsequent holder of the title, or from the most recent title holder. Since many of the older and more distinguished title holders may be traced back twenty-five or more generations, there is clearly much room to maneuver in finding a strong basis for a claim.

Tamatane/Tamafafine

Of greater importance to a Samoan descent group than the distinction between agnatic and uterine descent is the distinction between *tamatane* and *tamafafine* status. In its simplest formulation, *tamatane* refers to descendants of a brother (i.e., a title holder or his brother) and *tamafafine* to descendants from a sister of a titleholder. This distinction is most commonly invoked in relation to title succession, and distinguishes those members of a descent group with direct claims to select a titleholder (*tamatane*) from those with indirect power over a title, who can advise and can veto a selection but cannot hold a title themselves (*tamafafine*). These roles are derived by ex-tension from the relation of brother to sister. The *tamafafine* traditionally fulfill a role of restraining and controlling the *tamatane*, much as a sister restrains her brothers.[11]

While the formal definitions of *tamatane* and *tamafafine* are simple enough, in practice they are far less straightforward. A number of factors have made it particularly difficult for observers to understand how these categories of fraternal and sororal lines operate. To clarify some of the subtler and more complex aspects of the *tamatane/tamafafine* distinction, let us turn to Sala'ilua and the *'āiga* of Tuatō Fatu for an example of how these descent categories operate.

Fatu's claim to the Tuatō title, it will be remembered, was as a repre-sentative of the sole *tamatane* branch of the title. The *tamatane* status of his particular branch gave Tuatō Fatu an advantage over the other holders of the Tuatō title who were considered *tamafafine* to the title. Moreover, within his own title division, Fatu had a second *tamatane* status, being a direct lineal descendant through an unbroken series of agnatic links to the sole male heir to the title at the time it was subdivided.

After Fatu's funeral, the question of the precise meaning of the *tamatane/ tamafafine* distinction arose in relation to the various succession claims within Fatu's own title branch. For instance, I was curious about the status of any of Fatu's own sisters' children in pursuing a claim to succession of the Tuatō title. The most likely of these claimants was Lōia, the eldest son of Fatu's eldest sister. Lōia possessed both a good education and a secure job, both of which added to his attractiveness as a candidate. Although he was in line for the now-vacant title of his own father, long deceased, I was curious what his claim to the Tuatō title would be.

When I suggested this possibility, his mother responded that he had indeed a legitimate claim to the Tuatō title, but probably would not pursue it. Most significantly, she claimed that her son's status was as *tamatane* to the title, since his point of linkage to the Tuatō title was his great-grand-father, himself the sole male child at the time the title was first subdivided. However, when I put the question of the status of Lōia's claim to the Tuatō title to Fatu's own son Galu, this young man admitted that his cousin did indeed have a claim to the title, but insisted that it was a weak claim of *tamafafine* rather than a *tamatane* claim. The logic used in this case was that the immediate link of Fatu's nephew to the title was through a woman, sister of the most recent titleholder. Thus his status would have to be considered that of a *tamafafine*. To clarify the bases of these conflicting claims, the genealogical situation is outlined in figure 6.2.

The recently deceased incumbent, Fatu, is represented by position D in figure 6.2. His claim to *tamatane* status is based on his descent through an unbroken line of agnates (C–B–A), including the sole male sibling in gen-eration II, the generation at which the title subdivided. Fatu's younger brother, E, has an identical claim to the title through an unbroken succession of agnates. Lōia (H), the eldest son of Fatu's eldest sister (F) has, however,

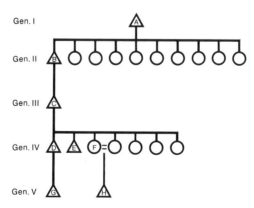

Figure 6.2. Succession to the Tuatō Title: *Tamatane* **and** *Tamafafine* **Claims.**

an ambiguous status. *F* claims that her own *tamatane* status is transferred to her son. Thus *H* is *tamatane* to the title when the significant point of emphasis is taken to be descent from *B* in generation II. When status is reckoned in relation to generation IV, however, *H* is classified as *tamafafine* to the title rather than *tamatane*.

The nature of *tamatane* and *tamafafine* status has never been fully clarified in the literature on Samoa. Mead, for instance, characterized *tamatane* and *tamafafine* as "a curious bilateral grouping in which all the descendants of a male line are balanced against the descendants of the women of the family" (Mead 1930:18). Several important ambiguities are apparent in this statement. Left unclear is the nature of these male and female "lines." The composition of the "family" involved in the groupings is also not clear. Mead's characterization also suggests that a family is divided into clear, concrete groups or segments but, again, we are not told how such a distinction is unambiguously drawn. Samoans, by this account, would seem to possess some kind of double-descent system recognizing both matrilines and patrilines.

If we are to understand these Samoan descent categories, then a number of questions remain to be answered: 1) What is the relation of the *tamatane/ tamafafine* distinction to patrilineal and matrilineal descent? 2) Do *tamatane* and *tamafafine* represent actual groups of people, descent lines, or abstract categories? 3) To what extent do these descent "groups" unambiguously classify members of any particular family?

At first glance it would seem that the *tamatane/tamafafine* distinction is simply an alternate cultural idiom for patrilineal and matrilineal descent reckoning. Were this the case, then *tamatane* would identify the "strong side" of a descent group while *tamafafine* would identify the "weak side." As we have seen, Mead seems to take this view. The example drawn from Fatu's family suggests that the actual relation between *tamatane* and *tamafafine* on the one hand, and paternal and maternal descent on the other, is more complex. To illustrate the relation, let us take a hypothetical case drawn out over three generations (see fig. 6.3).

B is a titleholder in generation I. *A* is his sister and *C* his wife. *G* and *H* are the offspring of *B* and *C*. Their father, *B*, and his sister are their links to their patrilineal kin. In Samoan terms this would be their "strong side."

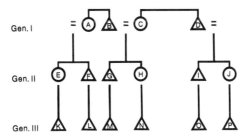

Figure 6.3. Hypothetical Case of *Tamatane/Tamafafine* Distinction.

G is a clear heir of his father, with a strong claim on title *B*. Any of *B*'s brothers also share a claim to this title. All of their heirs would be known as *tamatane* in relation to the title *B* and in relation to any of *A*'s descendants (*E*, *F*, *K*, and *L*), who would be *tamafafine*. The mother of *G* and H (*C*) and her brother (Chief *D*) are maternal links, the "weak side" of *G* and *H*. Thus linked to title *D* through a mother, *G* and *H* have no strong claim ever to hold this title. They are *tamafafine* in relation to title *D* and in relation to *D*'s offspring (*I, J, O,* and *P*). In the second descending generation (II), therefore, there is indeed an overlap between *tamatane* and patrilaterality and between *tamafafine* and matrilaterality. The only difference between these usages is that *tamafafine* views the woman in her capacity as a sister, while 'weak side" views her from the point of view of her maternal role.

The complications come in generation III and beyond. *M*, descending from *B* through an unbroken set of male links, is unambiguously *tamatane* in relation to the title. In this case *tamatane* and patrilineal descent continue to overlap. The status of *N* is less clear-cut. His immediate link to title *B* is through his "weak side"—his maternal kin. It could be claimed that *N* was *tamafafine* to title *B*, especially if his mother's brother succeeded to the title. However, by comparison with his second cross-cousins *K* and *L*, *N* could lodge a claim as *tamatane* in relation to title *B*. This claim is possible since *N* does descend from a title-holder (*B*) rather than from his sister (*A*). In this interpretation of the situation, *N* would be *tamafafine* only in relation to *O* and *P* and the title *D* once held by their "mother's brother" two generations earlier. *N*'s mother represents a "weak" (i.e., matrilateral) link to title *B* and thus a diminished claim to that title. Nonetheless, this weak claim is still arguably a *tamatane* claim to title *B*. Thus there is no longer a direct correspondence between *tamafafine* status and maternal descent.

That *tamatane/tamafafine* does not represent a simple rephrasing of patrilineal and matrilineal descent is clear from figure 6.4.

Figure 6.4 is set out to emphasize the patrilineal tendencies in title succession, rather than any strictly lineal descent scheme. Insofar as both *tamatane* and *tamafafine* status are commonly structured by titles, this is an appropriate way of illustrating this system of descent-category reckoning. *W*, *X*, *Y*, and *Z* represent different political titles in relation to which *tamatane* and *tama-*

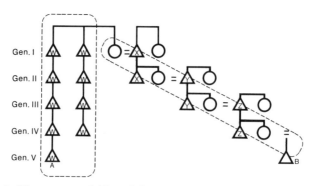

Figure 6.4. *Tamatane* **and** *Tamafafine* **Reckoning in Relation to Lineality.**

fafine status are reckoned. *A* and *B* are both males in generation V. I have delineated with dash lines *A*'s patrilineal descent links and *B*'s matrilineal descent links.[12] I have also indicated with dash-dotted lines the most probable direction of title succession (in this case for title *W*). This direction is through agnates, with remaining brothers in the senior generation having some priority over claims from sons. *A* is *tamatane* together with all previous title holders of title *W*, and the *tamatane* links coincide with both the normal path of title succession and an agnatic descent line. In the case of *B*, however, the diagram stresses *tamafafine* links that accrue to him by virtue of his uterine ancestors, but in their relation as sisters rather than as mothers. It is evident that the matrilateral connections determine *B*'s *tamafafine* status in generations I, II, III, and IV, but in each generation this status is in relation to a different title. It is, furthermore, the titles that structure the *tamafafine/tamatane* descent categories. Thus in generation I, *B*'s matrilineal ancestor is his *tamafafine* link to title *W*; in generation II, the matrilineal ancestor provides him with *tamafafine* claims on title *X*; in generation III, it is in relation to title *Y* that *B* is *tamafafine*; and finally he is *tamafafine* in relation to title *Z* in generation IV. It is thus clear that while a single *tamatane* status may be traced through a single agnatic descent line, *tamafafine* status in relation to a single descent group does not follow a maternal descent line.

A person's link to a title through a woman can be phrased in two ways. When that woman is understood to be one's mother, then one has a weak claim to direct control of that title. When that same woman is viewed instead as a sister to a titleholder, then the relationship is expressed as *tamafafine* in relation to *tamatane*. In this view of the relationship the descendants of the sister are not regarded as "weak" but rather as possessing a sacred but indirect power over the title, and the right to veto a decision by the *tamatane*.

Clearly, these distinctions can become quite subtle and involve inherent ambiguity and indeterminacy about one's precise status. As we have seen, a person linked through a woman to a title can be classified as either *tamatane* or *tamafafine* depending on which generation is used in calculating the descent link.[13] Sometimes a generation is agreed upon by a descent group for calculating claims. More often, however, the issue is left ambiguous and is argued in family meetings or in the Land and Titles Court.

It should be clear by now that *tamatane* and *tamafafine* represent categories for the classification of individuals rather than concrete groups or coherent descent lines. The terms are inherently relational and contextual. Particular titles and specific holders of those titles structure *tamatane* and *tamafafine* status: in themselves, the terms are meaningless. *Tamatane* and *tamafafine* are relationships rather than concrete persons or groups.

Other Considerations in the Bestowal of Titles

In addition to the criteria for selecting titleholders discussed previously, several others should be mentioned. It is possible for a dying chief to name his own successor. Such a bequest of one's own title is called a *māvaega*, and is made when a chief wishes to pass up an expected heir in favor of someone who has gained the incumbent's favor through devoted service. It is through such specific title bequests that important titles in Samoa have gone to adopted sons over direct heirs. In such cases, the bequest is usually recognized by the descent group, though a provision is often made in the bestowal of such titles that the title will revert to the true heirs of the title on the death of the adopted heir, rather than continue in his line. In other cases, such as that of the paramount title Tamasese, the title has stayed in the line of the adopted child (Shore 1976a).

While in most cases the final decision about title succession rests with the descent group, the situation is different in the case of paramount titles. Until the nineteenth century, there were four paramount titles for Upolu, titles referred to as *pāpā*.[14] Two of these paramount titles, the Tui A'ana (of the A'ana district) and Tui Atua (of the Atua district) were the property of a very large descent group called Sā Tupuā, embracing a number of dispersed lineages focused in the Atua and A'ana districts of Upolu. The other two *pāpā* titles, Gato'aitele and Tamasoāli'i, were the property of another maximal descent group, the Sā Malietoā, with political centers in the Fa'asaleleaga district of Savai'i, in Manono Island, and in the Tuamasaga district of Upolu. These two *pāpā* titles of the Sā Malietoā orginated with women of the Malietoa line, and were frequently conferred as honorific titles on the paramount chief Malietoa.

Actual succession to all of these paramount titles was, ideally at least, in the hands of certain groups of orators rather than the general membership of the descent group. Thus, when the Tui A'ana title became vacant, certain orators from the A'ana district met to decide on a new title holder. Similarly, orators from the Atua district were responsible for the conferring of the Tui Atua title. The Malietoa title was in the hands of orators from the villages of Afega and Malie, two of the Tuamasaga centers of Sā Malietoā power. These orators were empowered to bestow the title on a successor of their choice after conferring with ranking members of the descent group in the Safata district of Upolu, Fa'asaleleaga district of Savai'i, and Manono. The honorific title Gato'aitele was conferred by orators from Afega village, while that of Tamasoāli'i was under the control of orators from Safata.[15]

The present political system of Western Samoa no longer officially recognizes these four *pāpā* titles. Instead, there has evolved from this older system another set of paramount titles, referred to generally as *tama 'āiga* (children of many families). This name suggests something about the basis of the power of these important titles, their wide political support through complex alliances. These four titles are Malietoa, Tamasese, Mata'afa, and Tuimaleali'ifano. The traditional power of certain orator groups in the bestowal of paramount titles has been retained for these titles, connecting them with the older paramount titles of Samoa.

No consideration of factors in the bestowal of titles would be complete without a mention of the importance of the Land and Titles Court. Growing from the Land and Titles Commission established by German colonial authorities in 1903, the Court has come to have an ever-increasing importance in the disposition of land rights and political titles. Originally established as a forum for adjudicating disputed title and land claims that descent groups could not resolve peacefully, the Land and Titles Court has grown in importance as the population has expanded and the number of titles and title division has increased. Along with growing population pressure on land, the importance of agriculture in the subsistence and cash economies of Western Samoa has meant that the number of disputes over land rights and title claims has grown steadily. Increasingly, the Land and Titles Court has come to replace the descent group as the final arbiter of conflicting claims.

Although the Court is officially headed by the Chief Justice of Western Samoa, until now always a non-Samoan, the Court's decisions are largely based on the judgements of a panel of Samoan judges and assessors, men who have high standing in the traditional Samoan polity, and who are respected for their wide knowledge of traditional Samoan lore and abilities to cross-examine claimants on details of genealogy and history. Significantly, the Western Samoan Land and Titles Court has remained faithful to customary practice in matters of titles and lands, and has avoided rigidly codifying the flexible and pragmatically oriented criteria used by descent groups in deciding title and land inheritance.[16]

The principles used by the Court for deciding cases have been the ones that we have discussed in relation to title succession, principles of ability, service, genealogical status, and the wishes of the former titleholder.[17] The principles are applied pragmatically, however, and the Court has never allowed simple precedent to determine the outcome of any case. As the Registrar of the Court once told me, each case is decided on its own merits. Further enhancing this flexibility is the practice of not publicly revealing the basis of any decision by the Court.

While we may rightly identify the *matai* system as the heart of village authority, it is by no means the only major social or political institution. While the term *social organization* is commonly applied by anthropologists to units that have little formal or self-conscious structure, a Samoan village is organized explicitly on a number of different levels. It is to the structure of these local organizations in Sala'ilua to which we turn in following chapter.

CHAPTER SEVEN

Village Organization: Structures of Social Control

The South Pacific has been a palette for the Western imagination, from which a portrait of life free from the sexual, economic, and social restrictions of European society has been painted in story, song, and image. Food, the vision usually goes, abounds naturally for the plucking, hunger being as easily and delightfully satisfied as other appetites. The model for social life assumed in this myth was the beachcomber, free from severe social constraints and from the arbitrary tyrannies of political or economic necessity.

Such an image, in one form or another, prepares the sensibilities of even a sophisticated newcomer to Samoa, and sets the stage for a series of shocks. For village life in Samoa is far from liberating, and engages the lives and attentions of the villagers to a degree quite extraordinary to an unaccustomed observer. Far from a carefree existence geared only to the requirements of the moment, a well-run village defines for its residents an intricate system of long-term social and economic obligations, strictly enforced by the chiefs and their power to levy fines for noncompliance. These obligations are, in turn, linked to membership in corporate groups whose activities constitute much of the active lives of the villagers.

When someone in Samoa suggests that a certain village is strong in Samoan custom, the implication is usually that there is a vigorous *matai* system at work there, and also that the village contains a full complement of traditional organizations through which important public works projects are carried out. As Samoans understand it, such a traditional village is made up of two large conceptual entities, *'o le nu'u o ali'i* (the village of men) and *'o le nu'u o tama'ita'i* (the village of women). In fact, these names do not actually refer to two distinct groups or institutions, but rather to the fact that almost all of the traditional village institutions in Samoa are based on a sexual division of labor. As we will see, the only institutions that normally include both male and female members are those that have been introduced relatively recently through European contact. All traditional village institutions base their membership on a few key criteria. In addition to sex, a combination of age, marital status, political status, and a distinction between those "born" into the village and those married into it is the basis for allocating individuals to village groups. Such a system leaves no one unaccounted for and imposes a number of different obligations on all members of the village.

In this chapter we move further into the system of social control in Sala'ilua by turning to examine the functional organization of Sala'ilua and the system of regulations and activities through which village groups exert their influence over the lives of the villagers.

While our first glimpse of Sala'ilua in the heat of the afternoon confirmed the initial expectation of a sleepy, quiescent place, the lives of the villagers are actually framed by a ceaseless round of regular activities. Many of these, of course, are domestic chores: cooking, gathering firewood, sweeping out the house, cutting the grass and, for women, the seemingly endless washing of laundry. Men focus on subsistence activities which keep all but the youngest and oldest at a distance from the village center during much of the day, usually in the gardens and occasionally at sea fishing.

But in addition to these subsistence chores, it is common to see, in the morning or late afternoon, when there is some relief from the most intense heat, small groups of men or women making rounds through the village, engaged in any one of the normal village inspection tours or other forms of regular communal work. These rounds are usually carried out with little formality, and the more serious moments of the work are often punctuated by rounds of laughter as someone relates a particularly amusing incident. Such work provides a good occasion to catch up on village gossip or to share news with someone just returned from Apia. It is also a break from the tedium of domestic chores. Communal inspection and work parties form a relatively gentle system of continual vigilance in the maintenance of social order.

To understand a Samoan village is to recognize its dual character. On the other hand, a village is a loose confederation of distinct descent groups. On the other hand, the village constitutes a set of village-based organizations that cross-cut families and demand allegiances to the village as a corporation in its own right. It is to these village-wide organizations and their claims on the lives of villagers that we turn.

The Village of Men

Control over men's work in Samoa is maintained through a number of male organizations. Most important is the council of chiefs and its associated committees, through which specific tasks are allocated to village men. The other men's group is the *'aumaga,* the untitled men's organization.

Council of Chiefs

The chiefs' council has already been examined at some length. It is at once a legislative, executive, and judicial body, the ultimate authority in village affairs, and the chief representative in intervillage or district matters.

The council includes in its membership all holders of village titles, whether the holders derive the titles from their own families or from their wives' descent group. No formal distinction is made in the council between true members of the village by birth and those with affinal ties. Indeed, several of the ranking title holders in Sala'ilua have no direct connection to the village except by marriage. The council may also admit to its membership villagers holding titles in other villages, but such membership is a matter of courtesy to these chiefs and is always at the discretion of the village chiefs.

The chiefs' council enacts, promulgates, and enforces village regulations of the most general sort. It is also responsible for establishing committees or appointing individuals to enforce the regulations and acts as a judicial body in handling transgressions of village law. If a conflict coming under the primary jurisdiction of another village body cannot be satisfactorily or amicably resolved by that body, it is frequently referred to the council as a court of last resort. In some extreme cases, the council may be bypassed and the matter taken directly to the government, either to the constable in the district or to the Land and Titles Court. The chiefs' council meets regularly, usually on Monday mornings, the usual day in Samoa for council meetings. Additional meetings may be convened on an ad hoc basis when the situation requires.

Committees of the Chiefs' Council

The work of the council is done through an elaborate committee system. In Sala'ilua, most of the *komiti* are ad hoc, constituted to deal with particular problems or projects. A few, however, are more or less permanent institutions of the *fono*, since they are responsible for general and enduring village functions.

Perhaps the most important of these committees in Sala'ilua is the Judicial Committee of the council, called simply *Komiti*. The Judicial Committee enforces villages regulations through numerous inspections and patrols. It is also empowered to levy fines in both money and foodstuffs for breaches of regulations. Most of the actual work of Sala'ilua committee falls to an appointed group of younger chiefs called the junior chiefs (*matai lāiti*), who report to a group of senior and older chiefs, the *'aupuletua,* (those who rule from behind). The Judicial Committee of Sala'ilua is led by a committee leader selected from among the *'aupuletua,* while a younger chief serves as secretary to the committee, overseeing the actual collection and recording of fines. Each of the three subvillages of Sala'ilua is represented by at least one chief who represents the interests of his subvillage in the committee. Finally, *ex officio* membership on this committee is accorded to the village "mayor" (*pulenu'u*) who is a paid representative of the national government in the village, elected by the village to act as a link between the Apia government and the village *fono.* (This office seems to have become something of a sinecure in Sala'ilua.)[1] The junior chiefs meet on Sunday evenings to discuss infractions of village regulations during the week and to levy fines. Their decisions are then carried on to the body of senior chiefs for approval. Most of the fines are levied for failure to abide by village curfews. A subcommittee of chiefs is charged with patrolling the village road at night to enforce the curfews and to warn or apprehend violators.

In addition to the Judicial Committee, Sala'ilua's *fono* includes a number of smaller committees. The Hospital Committee represents Sala'ilua in the district-wide Hospital Committee, which helps to oversee the district hospital and deal with the National Department of Health. The local School Committee looks after the local primary school, and sends members to represent Sala'ilua on the District School Committee, which is responsible for the district junior high school. There are also a Water Pipe Committee, an Electric Generator Committee, and a "Committee of the Village," which is responsible for inspecting land boundaries for village and plantation lands, and for adjudicating boundary disputes. This latter committee is especially important, since land boundary disputes are the most common source of intravillage squabbling.

'Aumaga (Untitled Men's Organization)

Like the chiefs' council, the *'aumaga* predates European contact with Samoa. The name *'aumaga* means literally "kava chewers," suggesting a now obsolete function of chewing kava roots in the preparation of kava liquid for ceremonial drinking. Today, the *'aumaga* includes in its membership all village *taulele'a* (untitled males) from the time of adolescence until they take titles or move out of the village. While in school, children are automatically excluded from *'aumaga* membership, but begin their *'aumaga* responsibilities on completing their education.

Traditionally, leadership in this group lay in the office of the *mānaia,* a position normally held by the son of a ranking village *ali'i* who possessed a political title attached to his father's own title. Nowadays, however, the *'aumaga* is led by sons of Tuatō and Tolova'a, senior orators and senior village chiefs. (The association of leadership in the *'aumaga* with the sons of orators rather than with those of *ali'i* is important and will be discussed further in chapter 13.) At the time of my stay in the village, *'aumaga* leadership was in the hands of a son of one of the older Tuatō, who shared his post with a sister's son of a Tolova'a title holder. *'Aumaga* leaders have the power to fine other members of the group for violations of group regulations, missed work parties, or failure to meet planting quotas set by the *'aumaga.* As with the chiefs' council and the *aualuma,* the *'aumaga* is potentially divisible into a number of segments, each being realized in a number of discrete contexts. Thus there are church, subvillage, and village level *'aumaga.*

Called *'o le mālosi o le nu'u* (the strength of the village), the *'aumaga* functions as servants of the chiefs' council as well as an institution for socializing young men in political and oratorical skills useful when they become *matai*. It is through membership in the *'aumaga* that a *taule'ale'a* can *tautua* (serve) the chiefs, and thus earn himself a title one day.

In addition to its general role in doing the bidding of the village chiefs, the *'aumaga* of Sala'ilua has a number of specific obligations to the village. The *'aumaga* encourages in its members the development of skills and attitudes appropriate for young men. Thus one day a month the Sala'ilua *'aumaga* makes the rounds of members' taro gardens to check that quotas for new plantings have been met. These quotas are set each month at a meeting of the *'aumaga*, and failure of any *taule'ale'a* to meet his planting quota results in a monetary fine. The fine is said to be the same for any failure to meet the quota, whether by one taro or by hundreds. Positive incentives are also provided for planting in the form of monthly prizes—an axe and a machete for first and second place, respectively—for the *taule'ale'a* who has planted the most taro shoots.

The *'aumaga* is also responsible for maintaining the grounds of the village and district school compounds. The grounds are cleared of any unwanted growth or trash, and the grass is cut. This work is usually carried out one day during the first week of each month.

The Village of Women

The women's associations in the village are more complex and numerous than those for men. This difference between men's and women's organizations is highly significant.

The Women's Committee

The Women's Committee is the most inclusive and active of the village organizations for women. It is a distinctly modern organization, originating during the German colonization of Samoa, although its functions are traditionally "feminine." Sometimes known as the *fono aofia* (collective council) for village women, the Women's Committee includes in its membership all village women, both those who are "true girls" of the village and those who are village affines, and comprises all village girls who are no longer in school. The Women's Committee is led by a wife of a senior chief, often but not always a senior *ali'i*. She is called the committee *pelestene* (president), one of a number of terms of English origin reflecting the exogenous origins of the organization.

In Sala'ilua, the committee president is the wife of Savai'inaea Alova'a; she enjoys a place in the village roughly equivalent in power and prestige to that of her husband. Like so many of the village organizations, Women's

Committee structure is segmentary and may include, contextually, women of one subvillage, two of the three subvillages, or the entire village of Sala'ilua.

The Women's Committee is charged primarily with the responsibilities related to the public presentability of the village. Village sanitation and the provisioning of individual households for guests are the major concerns of the Women's Committee. Much of the work of the committee, like that of the chiefs' council, is carried on through subcommittees. The three sub-committees of the Sala'ilua Women's Committee are all concerned with aspects of village cleanliness and public presentability. The Sanitation Com-mittee carries out regular inspections of village households and latrines to make sure that they conform to village codes of cleanliness. Households are also expected to be well provisioned for guests, and failure to have on hand such items as extra mosquito netting, fancy dishes, and adequate bedding for village guests may lead to monetary fines by the committee. Treatment of guests in the village is understood to reflect on the name of the village as a whole. The Sanitation Committee also cooperates with the district nurse in the national government program of care for infants and young children. Distribution of medicine or inoculations is done through this committee. The Latrine Committee, a recent addition to the Women's Committee, has been charged with overseeing the work of installing new water-seal toilets in Sala'ilua. Women in this committee work closely with representatives of the government Department of Health. The Bathing Pool Committee makes and enforces regulations associated with use of the village bathing pool. This natural spring is used for both bathing and laundry and is divided into men's and women's sections. Infractions of committee reg-ulations open the offender to small monetary fines. Finally, other subcom-mittees of the Women's Committee deal with cemetery maintenance and inspection of mulberry tree groves used in tapa cloth making and pandanus groves used in the weaving of mats. A Hospital Committee oversees the village's contribution in the monthly round of chores for maintaining the district hospital.

Faletua ma Tausi (Chiefs' Wives)

The chiefs' wives have their own organization, headed by the wives of Tuatō and Tolova'a title holders. Like their husbands, these women are expected to provide village-wide leadership; except that, in the case of this group, control extends only over the activities of village women. The actual position of this group in the village appears to be largely ceremonial and symbolic. The chiefs' wives are a corporate group in relation to the weaving house where they have their own sessions, distinct from those of the other village women, and in relation to a Sunday to'ona'i, a kind of brunch, which these women sometimes share.

Fafine Lāiti (Wives of Untitled Men)

This organization, comprising the wives of the untitled men belonging to the village, recruits its membership through the untitled men who are true members of the village. In this sense, the *fafine lāiti* does not parallel the organization of chiefs' wives, which is structured by village titles. The wife of a chief who holds his title in his wife's family is thus not considered a member of this organization.

Both of these wives' groups are more clearly categories than fully corporate groups. The latter, in particular, has very few corporate functions. I did see one day the group of *fafine lāiti* sitting together weaving fine mats. I was also told that they held a common Sunday meal like the wives of the chiefs, but never witnessed one. It is striking that the organization of *fafine lāiti* persists despite the absence of distinctive functions for the group.

The *Aualuma*

The *aualuma* (organization of village girls) parallels the men's *'aumaga* in many ways. Both are the traditional gender-based youth groups. There is a sense in which the parallel breaks down, however. The primary criterion for inclusion as a village "girl" is the fact of having been born or raised in a village, and having a claim to being "the true flesh and body" of the village in terms of descent links. On marrying, a girl becomes a "woman" (*fafine*) in relation to her husband and household. In terms of the political organization of the village as a whole, however, she remains a "girl" (*teine*) of her own village, and always has the right to participate in *aualuma* activities there.

For men, a "boy" (*tama*) becomes a man (*tamāloa*) when he marries. Age does play a part in his designation, however, such that an older man, though unmarried, may be referred to as a *tamāloa*. The same is decidedly not true in the case of an older unmarried lady. As with females, a man is always a "boy" in reference to the larger context of his natal village, although addressed as a "man" in relation to domestic activities. Whereas a girl becomes a member of the *aualuma* merely by virtue of her birth in the village, a status which she can never lose, the man has a right to membership in the *'aumaga* only as long as he remains untitled. On assuming a village title, he is no longer a *taule'ale'a*, and thus loses his rights to *'aumaga* membership.

An *aualuma* may operate in relation to any subvillage or combination of subvillages, or in relation to an entire village unit. The *aualuma* functions mainly as a ceremonial unit. Its traditional responsibility is for entertaining guests, a function relative to the public presentability of the village, similar to the functions of the Women's Committee. Led by a *taupou* who is also known as *sa'otama'ita'i* (chiefly lady) or the *sa'oaualuma*, the *aualuma* takes charge of any large traveling parties to visit the village. In most cases, festivities for the guests as well as all provisions for their welfare fall traditionally under the control of the *aualuma*. The *taupou*, an institution whose decline in modern Samoa parallels that of the *mānaia*, is ideally a daughter or sister's daughter of an important *ali'i* who bestowed a special *taupou* name upon a suitably attractive and dignified girl in his household. Virginity and general chastity are traditionally formal requirements of the position holder, since the status of *taupou* is a kind of summary symbol for Samoan maidenhood.

Nowadays, many of the functions of the *aualuma* seem to have been assumed by the Women's Committee. I did, however, witness a kava ceremony in Si'utu to welcome a party of visitors from American Samoa, related by marriage to the village. Typical of such ceremonial affairs involving sons, daughters, or wives of chiefs, the girls took ceremonial positions in the kava service derived from the positions of their fathers' titles. Aside from such occasional hospitality to visitors (the large traveling party having become something of a rarity), the *aualuma* today remains more of a conceptual part of a village structure than an active institution. In fact, sometimes one hears members of a Women's Committee referring to themselves as an *aualuma*, though as we have seen the two are conceptually distinct.

The Weaving House

Each subvillage has its own *fale lalaga* (weaving house), though frequently those from Sataputu and Sala'ilua subvillages meet jointly. The weaving house appears to be a precontact institution for the instruction of young girls in the art of weaving fine mats (*'ie tōga*). Older women participate as well in these houses, to make the tedious job of weaving more enjoyable by communal enterprise. At times, the chiefs' wives may meet separately in their own weaving house, in which case the fundamental purpose of the house is social intercourse and mutual encouragement of work rather than actual instruction.

The weaving house possesses its own rules, authority structure, and a power to impose fines upon offenders. Authority within the house lies with two offices: *matua u'u* and the *lātū o faiva*. The *matua u'u*, ideally the wife of a ranking *ali'i*, is the resident weaving expert and the teacher of the younger women. Clearly here criteria of skill and experience outweigh those of specific political status in the selection of an incumbent to the office. The *lātū o faiva*, ideally the wife of an important orator, is a ceremonial position with responsibilities for the distribution of food during common meals. The *lātū o faiva* also organizes the ceremonies marking the completion of a set of mats by the weaving house. Both senior weavers sit in the *atualuma* or side of the house, the position reserved for orators during a kava ceremony. The body of weavers under their direction is called the *'ausese'e*. The weaving house has regulations regarding unwarranted absence or tardiness and disrespectful behavior while in the house. The *fale lalaga* generally meets twice weekly, on Tuesdays and Thursdays.

'Autalavou

Crosscutting the *'aumaga* and the *aualuma* is the *'autalavou*, the body of village youth. This group, composed of both young men and women, makes regular visits to the district hospital to visit with patients, and this was the only corporate activity of the youth group that I could elicit from informants.

Church-Based Organizations

The Congregation

Each church congregation (*'aulotu*) is a distinct village group. In addition to church attendance and participation in common church-related activities of many sorts, congregation members cooperate in a scheduled monthly cleaning of the church building and grounds, with men doing the grass cutting, and women the weeding and cleaning.

Youth Groups

Each of the three village congregations has its own *'autalavou* (youth group). This group is active in sports events, traveling parties, hosting visiting groups from other churches, and in organizing dances and other fund-raising activities. Each youth group has its responsibilities for the maintenance of the church building and grounds and for working in the plantation of the pastor to help provide for his upkeep.

The Pastor's School

The missionaries established Samoa's first schools, and in the Protestant churches of Samoa this tradition of educating the children persists. Until late adolescence, all Protestant children in Samoa, with few exceptions, attend Sunday School. The younger children attend the daily Pastor's School where the pastor and his wife teach basic literacy and Bible lessons. Much of the early socialization of young children, in terms of basic manners, speech styles, proper sitting posture, and reading and writing skills, is in the hands of the pastors.

It is evident from this brief survey of village organizations in Sala'ilua that the village is, in a sense, highly structured and that lines of authority are clearly drawn for the many kinds of joint activity of villagers. There are within the village two fundamental and irreducible sources of authority. One is the *matai* council; the other is the church and pastor. Normally, the pastors work closely with village chiefs to run the village, and cooperate in supporting each other's authority in various village activities. Pastors and chiefs are careful not to trespass on each other's authority. In handling serious conflicts in the village, the chiefs and pastors play largely complementary roles. However, the authority of the pastors and that of the chiefs are potentially in conflict, since there are areas of overlapping or at least ambiguous jurisdiction. Sometimes chiefs and pastors may conflict directly, when a pastor seeks to exert his considerable influence in a political dispute or intervene where a chief would normally have jurisdiction. Catholic priests, often non-Samoans, and even the lay preachers who represent the Catholic church in the village, tend to have somewhat less direct impact on village politics, remaining for the most part on the periphery of secular affairs, than do the pastors.

Another area of potential conflict is between the authority of the leading women of the village over the "village of women" and the overriding authority of village chiefs over the village as a whole. Although the chiefs exert an indirect control over the Women's Committee, that authority is far from clear-cut, and would only be exerted at the specific request of the senior women, in a case where the women could not resolve an internal conflict amicably in their own councils, or where a conflict between women also involved others in the village or from outside the village. In the same way that paramount chiefs with ultimate *pule* over a distinct village and its lands would intervene in local affairs only in exceptional circumstances, chiefs are careful to respect the fragile boundaries between their own power and that of the leaders of other village organizations.

Local Restrictions

Curfews

The village chiefs have a broad range of specific responsibilities in Sala'ilua, many of which are carried out through committees, the members of which are appointed in the general council. Most visible of these committees is undoubtedly the Judicial Committee in Sala'ilua, which oversees the enforcement of general village regulations. Members of this committee may be seen every evening patrolling the main road of the village during either of the two daily curfews. At about 6:00 P.M., one of the chiefs blows a conch shell as a signal that villagers should leave the public areas of the village for their homes. At 6:15 or so, another blast of the conch signals the start of evening family prayers. Quickly the village fills with a sacred cacophony of a dozen different hymns emanating from each compound of the village. Following the singing are Bible reading and prayers, all of which take about half an hour. A final blast from the conch sounds the end of the service, freeing the road and other public areas of the village for an evening stroll or perhaps an impromptu round of song in praise of the virtues of Samoa, or the beauties of a lover. It is in the evenings, particularly when the village is lit with the cool white light of a full moon, that Sala'ilua comes closest to satisfying the romantic vision that is popularly associated with Polynesia. At 9:00, however, the festivities officially come to an end for school children, as the conch sounds once again to start the evening curfew for the young. An hour later it will sound again, and villagers will slowly make their way home. By 10:30 or so, the road will be virtually deserted except for a few stragglers, and the inevitable patrol of one or two chiefs who gently urge anyone still left on the road that the time has come for sleep.

The curfew, however, cannot enforce sleep, and is intended only to clear the public areas of the village. Many will stay awake for another hour or two, playing cards by the dim light of a kerosene lantern, listening to the latest popular Samoan songs on the radio, perhaps sharing a good tale with friends or family, or just reclining on a sleeping mat, thinking over the events of the day, or making plans for the morning.

Mosquito nets are eventually hung into place as the evening grows late, sleeping mats are unrolled and married couples retire with the smaller children behind a hastily erected wall of cloth which has been draped from a wire. The lights are gradually extinguished around the village, except for the muted glow of a single lantern, preserving the house from total darkness.

Chiefs have the authority to fine offenders, usually less than a dollar, for breaking the curfew. In fact, however, it appeared to me that fines were rarely levied; chiefs seldom needed to give more than a gentle reminder to any stragglers. Further, while the main road was usually empty by eleven at night, it is always possible to move about the village through the trees to the rear of the household compounds, or to get from one place to another after the *matai* patrol has gone off to sleep. In these late night and early morning hours, Samoans say, ghosts and dogs take over the road, sharing it with an occasional youth quietly making his way to or from a tryst with a lover. Such surreptitious wandering through the village is one of the reasons for the institution of the evening curfew, but no curfew has ever prevented such late night meetings, and they are tacitly understood to be a normal, if officially discouraged, part of the life of youth.

In addition to the nightly curfew, there are special restrictions on movement on Sundays, when the sabbath is strictly enforced by the chiefs. Preparations for the large brunch, called *to'ona'i*, begin in the plantations all day Saturday, when taro, bananas, yams, and breadfruit will be gathered. On Sunday the food preparation begins early, well before dawn, and by sunrise the strong smell of smoke from the ground oven in each compound envelops the village. By about 7:45, at the first sounding of the church bell, the villagers have already put in several hours of hard work, and the bell signals a curfew on further work. All oven preparations must be completed, the food to be baked or steamed, well covered with layers of green banana leaves. Any work after this first bell is punishable by a nominal monetary fine.

At eight, the sounding of the church bell means that all members of the Congregational or Methodist congregations must be in church. Latecomers are fined ten cents at the door by a chief. Also, any villagers who fail to attend church are fined by a committee of chiefs, except for the infirm or a single person who stays behind to tend the cooking fire.

Deportment and Dress

In addition to these restrictions on movement within the public areas of the village, the chiefs of Sala'ilua enforce restrictions on the personal appearance of villagers and guests in the village. Traditionally, chiefs had the right to set a standard for personal comportment in the village. Acts such as raising one's arms over the head, carrying a load on a stick slung over the back, or (for a male) wearing a *lavalava* draped from the shoulders around the body rather than properly tied around the waist were forbidden in the residential core of the village. Even more serious was the practice of yelling a kind of war cry (*ususū*) anywhere in central village. This central part of the village is seen as the center of social life, and behavior must be carefully controlled. Raising one's arms or making war cries were once taken to be challenges to the chiefs of the village, and are still thought to show serious disrespect to the village and its chiefs.

Today these restrictions are not always enforced, but others have taken their place as foci of the public control over private appearance. In recent years chiefs from Sala'ilua have joined those of other villages in publishing regulations forbidding men to wear beards or long hair, and women from dressing in miniskirts, shorts, or slacks. In general, the chiefs of the village take these regulations seriously, since they view the adoption of these *pālagi* customs as a direct assertion of personal rights over the authority of custom and its guardians, the chiefs. Offenders are ususally given ample warning to adopt a more conservative appearance, but fines up to a *tālā* ($1.40) or more may be levied for continued failure to observe the dress regulations.

Numerous other inspections and work projects, many of them ad hoc, add to the constant round of public activities that keep villagers active and require attention to be turned almost continually to public and communal affairs. Clearly, little in Sala'ilua is left to purely personal initiative or chance. Villagers pride themselves on the elaborate texture of their lives, in which the affairs of their dispersed descent groups compete with the equally complex and demanding regime of village life continually coopting their attentions and fixing their priorities on affairs of a decidedly public nature.

Law and Goverment

Village Law

In terms of the degree of formalization, a village-based legal system in Samoa falls somewhere between the looseness and informality that characterizes conflict resolution in many New Guinea societies, and the extreme elaboration of explicitly judicial norms, bodies, and processes in Euro-American and some West African civil societies. Samoans did not institute a distinct and independent set of judicial institutions, such as courts and legal specialists, but they did build into their political institutions a fairly sophisticated set of processes to deal with conflict of many sorts.

Samoans recognize the concept of "law" as an explicit set of statements prescribing and proscribing certain behaviors which are backed by legitimate public authority. Such a conception of law appears to predate European contacts with Samoa. In 1884, Turner, writing on ancient Samoan society, made the following comment.

Having no written language, of course, they had no written laws; still as far back as we can trace, they had well understood laws for the prevention of theft, adultery, assault and murder, together with many other minor things such as disrespectful language to a chief, calling him a pig, for instance, rude behavior to strangers, pulling down a fence, or maliciously cutting down a fruit tree. (Turner 1884:178)

There was a fair amount of disagreement among different informants as to what all the village laws are, since they are generally neither codified nor written down. Villagers in Sala'ilua frequently were unaware of which laws were purely local and which were part of central government's legal code.

Samoans use the word *tulāfono* for the "law." The word means, literally, "position of the council," and can suggest either a single regulation or the entire body of prescriptive statements that constitute the "law." This latter usage of the term *tulāfono* tends to be limited to central government laws and legal institutions, and is almost never used in its collective sense to refer to a body of village-based regulations. When Samoans speak about taking a matter to "the law," it is inevitably the government in Apia or its representative that is referred to, not the local council. Samoans appear before contact not to have had a conception of "the law" as a unified institutional complex, distinct structurally and functionally from other social and political institutions.

Tulāfono suggests at once "rule," "regulation," and "law." *Solitulāfono* means a trampling on or desecration of the law. A punishment meted out for such a breach is a *fa'asalaga*, from the word *sala* which means at once "to err" and "to be punished for erring." The heavier term *agasala* (literally, "action which places one in punishable error") is the most common translation of the English word "sin."

The legal "system" in Sala'ilua operates in four distinct institutional complexes: the *'āiga*, the village/district, the church, and the central government. Although the word *tulāfono* is never applied to parental or *matai*-based household regulations, and these are not properly part of a Samoan legal system, there are traditional judicial processes that operate within and between extended families—such as the *ifoga* (humbling) that the senior chief of family must undergo toward the chief of another group against which an offense has been committed. This humiliation involves, for the chief, publicly kneeling or sitting before the house of the offended group with a mat placed over his head. The mat is then offered, often along with a payment in money, in the hope of reconciling the descent groups involved and avoiding serious reprisals by the offended group. Primary legal authority at the local level is vested in the council of chiefs. As we have seen, numerous other corporations exist at village and district levels that make and enforce their own regulations.

The churches have regulations governing the conduct of their members. These regulations cover all members, and most especially those within the Protestant churches who wish to have the special status of members of the *Ekalesia*—an inner church or body of full Christians. Church regulations forbid such things as theft, drunkenness, adultery, murder, and for those wishing to become deacons or members of the Ekalesia, such traditional practices as tattooing. The only sanction the church has in controlling its members is the threat of barring someone from the Ekalesia or deaconship, and the ever-present fear of the curse that a pastor is held to be able to inflict on anyone who incurs his wrath.

Central Government

Western Samoans are all subject to the laws and statutes of the central government's legal code, which is largely a modification of a New Zealand legal code. The district constable is the most direct link between the villager and the government's legal apparatus. Minor cases brought to the attention of government authorities are tried in a circuit court that meets monthly in Sala'ilua. More serious cases are taken for trial to the High Court in the government compound at Tausivi, Fa'asaleleaga district in southeastern Savai'i or, alternately, to the High Court in Apia.

In many cases, an act may be at once contrary to village law, government law, and church regulations, as well as repugnant to the extended family of the offender. Multiple jeopardy is thus an inherent part of the total legal system of Samoa, a fact which, although it is expressly denied by the Western Samoan Constitution, is recognized commonly by Samoans who complain of being placed in the position of "dying twice" for the same delict. Generally, this double jeopardy refers to the fact that villagers are liable for punishment by both local, traditional authorities and government judicial authorities.

In my interviews I asked informants to state what they considered to be important village "laws," using the term *tulāfono*. From the responses I compiled a list of important explicit and implicit laws and regulations recognized by villagers in Sala'ilua. It is possible to distinguish four categories of implicit and explicit norms: moral law, explicit legislation, customary principles of propriety, and public etiquette.

Moral Law

Informants frequently neglected to include in their listing of village laws the proscription of murder, readily agreeing that there was indeed a prohibition of murder in the village, but that it was "a law of God" or the church as well as a village regulation. Some laws, then, appear to be fundamental moral proscriptions and are assumed to exist despite the absence of specific local legislation. Such proscriptions cover both *solitulāfono* (offenses against the law) and *agasala* (sins). Theft is often included in this category by informants. *Matai* appear to see no need to translate these implicit moral beliefs into explicit laws. Many villagers felt that in addition to specific fines and other punishments meted out to those who broke such moral laws, automatic supernatural sanctions such as illness, death, or other misfortunes might well befall an offender.

Legislation

Other laws are seen as products of specific legislation and are promulgated by chiefs. They include such regulations as those dealing with disrespectful behavior to chiefs, adultery, land boundaries, and fights within the village. Transgressions of these regulations are classified primarily as crimes and only secondarily or marginally as sins.

Important Principles of Propriety

While murder or violent rape are considered as *leaga* (bad/evil) in the sight of God as well as man, other acts are disapproved of because they are *matagā* (repugnant) in the eyes of man. Drunkeness, cursing or causing a disturbance in the village center, and incest are *'inosia* (disgusting) to the sensibilities of others, suggesting disorder and pollution. There is some suggestion that the most offensive aspect of these acts is getting caught, so that private drunkenness undetected or illicit sexual behavior is not the object of serious disapproval, in the same way that murder is. A characteristic of these proscriptions is that they are generally recognized by villagers as part of traditional Samoan custom rather than as a body of formal legislation.

Public Etiquette

These aspects of Samoan custom are similar to those in the preceding category, differing only in relative degree of seriousness. Acts such as *'ai sāvali* (eating while walking) or sitting in a formal gathering with one's legs stretched out are neither sins nor crimes and rarely incur any punishment aside from scolding or mockery from others. These acts are *matagā* (unsightly) but almost never called *leaga* (bad/evil). The attitude is one of mild reproach, the offender being described as *lē a'oa'oina* (ill-taught) or *lē māfaufau* (thoughtless or lacking judgment).

These four categories of social prescriptions and proscriptions on behavior clearly do not unambiguously classify every Samoan law, rule, or regulation, but do suggest some of the distinctions Samoans make when they discuss and evaluate behavior.

Sanctions

While the concept of formal punishment for offenses against custom and chiefly authority appears to be traditional, predating European contacts with the archipelago, the particular sanctions employed have undergone considerable change in modern Samoa. According to Turner (1884:178), aboriginal Samoans had punishments for a wide range of delicts and punishments were inflicted on both individual offenders and the descent group, depending on the circumstances. Stair (1897:91) records a Samoan distinction between *sala*, which were general punishments to entire households such as banishment or destruction of crops and houses, and *tua* which were personal punishments inflicted upon the offender himself and were considered less serious than *sala*. *Sala* had behind them the force of an entire district or settlement, and Stair records how such punishments were put into effect.

the leading men of the settlement rising from the place of the meeting, proceeded towards the residence of the obnoxious family, attended by their followers, where they quickly seated themselves on the ground in full view of the family they had decided to banish. The latter had often heard of the sentence in sufficient time to enable them to remove their mats and other household property to a place of safety; but the livestock generally fell into the hands of the expelling party, who reserved them to feast upon after the work of the day. (1897:91–92)

A formal speech was made by one of the orators of the party, announcing the punishment arrived at by the council, after which the family's breadfruit trees were ringed above the stump, rendering the trees barren for two or three growing seasons. The outcast family then either had to resist, or give in to the will of the village or district and abandon their compound, which was set afire.

According to Stair, the exact terms of banishment were never specified, but were left open to later negotiations. In some cases, in fact, the banishment was never actually carried out.

Should the expelling party be influential, it sometimes happened that having ac-knowledged the power of their settlement by submitting quietly to his punishment, some friend would suggest to his companions that, their authority having been assented to and acknowledged, it would be desirable to recall the banished party, so as not to lose strength. (1897:94)

The party would then be recalled after a series of conciliatory speeches on both sides had been delivered. Occasionally, feeling on the part of the banished party would be such that they would voluntarily absent themselves from the settlement for years, or even permanently.

Murder and adultery, particularly in cases involving a chief, were pun-ishable by death. Banishment of the culprit, along with his entire family, was usual, although the acceptance of vengeance by the kin of the victim against those of the culprit as a legitimate form of retribution frequently obviated the need for formal banishment. A murderer or adulterer and his *'āiga* were often quick to absent themselves from the village, seeking refuge among distant kin in another part of the island or archipelago.

While food fines were often levied by chiefs on an offender's household, some offenses invited personal punishments against the guilty party. Turner mentions certain forms of physical disfigurement such as the loss of an eye, ear, or nose for an adulterer. Offenders were also liable to be trussed up naked like pigs intended for the oven and carried on a pole as an offering to the offended family. An individual might also be publicly humiliated by being hung by his feet from a tree or forced to kneel for hours in the sun, punishments that could prove lethal in the tropics. Turner also alludes to some horrifying and imaginative tortures inflicted on culprits, practices such as forcing a person to chew on roots pungent enough to kill a man in some cases, or at least leave him in terrible pain. Or a guilty party might be forced to beat his own head with stones, inflicting severe gashes on himself, or to play catch with a sharp, prickly sea urchin (Turner 1884:179ff.).

Under the influence of the missions, however, most of these practices, including the distinction between *tua* and *sala*, disappeared. All traditional forms of capital punishment and physical abuse and torture quickly withered under the missionary eye. The village was left with the power to fine culprits and the *'āiga* in both money and crops, power to inflict certain kinds of public humiliation upon a guilty party, and finally power of ban-ishment. In addition, Occidental political and religious forms introduced in the archipelago added new dimensions to legal and moral culpability by providing new judicial and ethical codes and institutions to deal with of-fenses against them. The remaining negative sanctions against kin groups for breaches of customary and *fono*-based regulations are various forms of fining and destruction of personal crops; for individuals, as well as their kin groups, banishment is the sole potent sanction left to the village.

Traditionally all fines are in food, which is distributed among the village households and groups according to rank and status. Heavy fines include mature sows and might in serious cases, such as rape or murder, range from fifteen to fifty sows, a devastating economic blow to any kin group. Such a number of pigs could be raised only by solicitation from dispersed kin and the consequent placing of the fined family in heavy debt to their relatives. Another particularly serious food fine is *'ati ma le lau*—the uprooting of a group's entire garden and the distribution of the mature crops among the sections of the village.

Lighter fines range from one to five sows, or one hundred mature taro roots. Since contact with the West, imported foodstuffs have added a number of new items to the list of fineables. Most common are forty-pound tins of *masi* (hardtack biscuits) and cans of pilchard or herring. Heavy fines, particularly in the urban area where quantities of pigs and taro may be much harder to secure, are frequently levied in forty-pound cases of biscuits or cartons containing forty cans of fish. The cartons of fish are particulary suitable as media of fining since they may be subdivided easily for redistribution within a village. There is a rough conversion schedule used by chiefs in assessing relative severity of fines and equivalences among different fining media. While the schedule may well vary as prices fluctuate, the approximate equivalences in fining are: one carton of forty cans of herring or pilchard = one mature sow = one forty-pound tin of hardtack biscuits.

While heavier fines are generally levied in foodstuffs, less serious delicts may be fined in money. Monetary fines tend to be levied for breaches of relatively minor regulations such as curfew transgressions or breaches of the dress code. Many of the transgressions that result in monetary fines involve institutions in the archipelago, although this is not a rigid rule. Monetary fines are always relatively light and range from 10 Samoan cents (14¢) to one Samoan dollar ($1.40) for transgressions involving an entire household.

In addition to fines, larger sums of money and fine mats may be paid as death or adultery payments between descent groups when an *ifoga* is performed. These payments are distinct from the aforementioned fines, since they are voluntary offerings made by the family of an offender rather than obligations imposed upon them by political authorities.

Justice and Social Harmony

Margaret Mead justly noted the "Samoan flair for schematization, for theoretical arrangements which disregard individuals and override geography" (Mead 1930/1969:10). Yet it would be wrong on several counts to conclude from the impressive array of regulatory institutions and legal procedures described above that Samoans possess a jurist's passion for fine legal distinctions and the pursuit of justice in the abstract. While a great deal of attention was paid to matters of protocol, rank, and procedure in all of the judicial proceedings I witnessed in Samoa, there was not a comparable stress on the subtleties of motivation, intention, or circumstances surrounding the conflict. One might say, more generally, that there was an absence of publicly expressed interest in causality.

In a survey of local and district government commissions by the New Zealand colonial government of Samoa in 1949, one of the questions put to the chiefs of each village in Western Samoa concerned the rights of an accused person to testify and to provide for his own defense. This question was based on an assumed priority in a legal system of the personal rights of the accused. Without exception, each village indicated to the commission that its members were indeed accorded such rights as defendants in local judicial proceedings. My own experience with such judicial proceedings, however, does not support this reported emphasis on the rights of defendants.

In each of the cases of conflict I studied, including Tuatō's murder, the primary concern of the judicial tribunal, whether it be the assembled Women's Committee, the 'aumaga trying one of its members, or the assembled chiefs, was clearly with the restoration of harmonious social relations within the village or district. It appears that this concern frequently precludes confronting in too great detail the precise circumstances surrounding the genesis of the conflict. These details were often the subject of local gossip but, in my experience, did not play any significant part in official judicial proceedings in a village or district. The emphasis was rather on social effects than on the particular causes of conflict. Maintaining peace in a small, stable community can understandably outweigh the more absolute dictates of what we normally think of as "justice."

To be sure, there was in all of the cases I observed an underlying concern to get to the root of the conflict. But interestingly this concern for bringing to light the origins of a conflict was never in fact translated into a thorough investigation of the conflict itself. Whereas there is in Samoa a great emphasis on and elaboration of institutions for restoring harmony among disputants, negotiating sanctions, and achieving consensus among village segments, there seems to be a corresponding lack of focus on investigation of the origins of the conflict itself. While Samoan has a term for witness (molimau), no witnesses were ever called to testify in any judicial tribunal I witnessed. In fact, of the six disputes I witnessed in council there was only one in which the disputants themselves were actually present. In no case studied did those directly involved actually testify.

This lack of emphasis on the causes or surrounding circumstances of conflict does not result, I think, from a lack of interest in such questions. Rather, those in authority appear deliberately to avoid confronting any subjects that would exacerbate the conflict and widen the breach in social relations.

In the account of the general village meeting convened to pass judgment on the family of Tuatō Fatu's murderer (chapter 2), I reproduced at length a series of speeches within the main meeting house, speeches that might be expected to involve themselves with questions of justice, guilt, and causes, but which in fact avoided these issues almost completely. The subject at this meeting appears to have had little to do with the conflict itself. Instead, the stress was on the subtleties of negotiation and protocol for decision-making. The meeting was more obviously focused on these subjects and on the relationships among village leaders than on discovering the complex facts surrounding the murder.

In this context, it is not surprising that social reconciliation is often given greater emphasis than punishment. There is among Samoans a stress on the maintenance of interpersonal harmony, at least in its external manifestations, and on *fealofani* (mutual love). It is, for example, a common practice to hold a public reconciliation between the disputants to demonstrate openly that the relationship has been ordered and harmony restored. At times, reconciliation includes discussion of the origins or causes of a conflict. Yet, where feelings run particularly high and guilt is unclear, the attempt to discover the causes of a conflict may well be bypassed in the interests of the maintenance of harmony. In these cases, whatever private feelings lie behind the overt conflict are left to be sorted out in other ways and at other times. In a number of cases I witnessed, a conflict was "buried" after an emotional confrontation at a council meeting, or was referred to the local constable for attention, rather than to village authorities.

In attempting to find clues to understand better the social and cultural implications of Tuatō Fatu's murder, I seem to have arrived at something of a paradox. In moving from event to structure, I have sought some insights into an act suggesting profound social disorder. Sala'ilua, I hinted, might have been more than simply the passive scene of the crime, and in the last few chapters the social and political structures of the village have been studied for evidence of complicity. And yet, what seems to be found here is not a paradigm for conflict so much as a model of social order, a village whose people's lives would seem to be choreographed from birth until death by an articulated set of institutions, laws, and behavioral customs whose explicit function is to prevent the sort of conflict that took Fatu's life.

Thus far, there are two noticeable features of Sala'ilua that distinguish it from most other Samoan villages. The first is historical. Sala'ilua's importance in its district is not due to its political status, but to a long-standing economic preeminence. Possessing a fairly good deep-water passage through the reef, Sala'ilua has been a center of commerce in its district since the mid-nineteenth century. The Germans recognized this, and Sala'ilua was a local center for the colonial administration of Western Savai'i in the first quarter of the century. The reputation that the village has earned for ambitiousness and vitality may well be due in part to a long history of intercourse with European traders.

The second feature of Sala'ilua is structural, and distinguishes it from all but a handful of villages. This is the inversion of power relations between *ali'i* and *tulāfale* in the political structure of the village. This inversion of the normal *ali'i–tulāfale* relation appears to have had noticeable and far-reaching effects on political relations within Sala'ilua. During the general village meeting convened to pass judgment on Fatu's murderer, Savai'inaea Alova'a again and again asked the assembled *matai* of the village where the dignity and sanctity of the village *ali'i* were, and why the orators of the village paid the *ali'i* so little heed. The arrogance of the two ranking holders of the Tuatō and Tolova'a titles appears to have been an important underlying theme of the meeting. The occasion of a judicial council to settle a serious dispute between these two ranking families seems to have been interpreted as an appropriate occasion to vent some strong resentment on the part of the village *ali'i* against the power of Tuatō and Tolova'a specifically and the body of orators more generally. The message underlying these complaints dealt with a sense of loss of balance in the village, a failure of political equilibrium.

It might be suggested here that the aggressive character of Sala'ilua village is, in part at least, structurally comprehensible in terms of this inversion in *ali'i* and *tulāfale* relations. To understand the nature of this structural inversion in power relations and its consequences for Sala'ilua, we must first turn to a more general investigation of the symbolic relations between *ali'i* and *tulāfale* in the context of a more general ideology of power and social control. This investigation will be the subject of the third part of this study.

Law and Behavior

In a well-run village, life is *māopoopo* (well ordered), and the lives of its residents are *puipuia* (protected or, literally, "walled in") by customary institutions. As Samoans understand it, this protection is not simply from malevolent outsiders, or even from others in the village. Perhaps most significantly, village law and authority are understood to protect people from themselves—from passions and desires that, uncontained by culture and customary authority, would lead to moral and social chaos.

With such assumptions, it is not surprising that the extent of public authority in Sala'ilua over private behavior is impressive by any standard. From morning until night, the villager is subjected to explicit constraints on his behavior in the form of village regulations, government laws, public inspections, and curfews. Authority to make and enforce these regulations lies in the various organizations discussed in this chapter. Above all the others, the chiefs' council has the responsibility for establishing and maintaining social order.

It is all too easy to infer an ordered life from a highly ordered social system, to assume that behavior emerges directly from the formal institutions that have evolved to shape it. Obviously, such an assumption is inevitably simplistic in any culture. In Samoa, it is particularly misleading, because it does not take into account the Samoans' own understanding of the relationship between the formal dignity of explicit social institutions and the dynamics of real behavior.

As one listens to Samoans talking among themselves about their own or others' delicts, and as one observes the behavior of villagers, even those who make and enforce many of these regulations, it becomes clear that despite the Samoan passion for public order there is not an unqualified respect for authority or for law-abiding behavior. *Usita'i* (obedience) is, to be sure, a central and explicit Samoan value, especially for children. But consistent or blind obedience is not really admired by most Samoans. Conformity with laws and regulations is, like so many aspects of Samoan behavior, a function of particular contexts, as are verbal demonstrations of respect for those regulations. There are times when blind submissiveness to authority is appropriate; there are times when it is not. Laws and legislative authorities form one part of a more general system of social controls, a system that includes, among other things, classifications of social contexts and norms for violating official rules. Laws and regulations function in Samoan belief as the dignified outer limits or constraints on behavior, giving a moral shape to a world that is otherwise *sa'oloto* (free or unbounded).

No boundary is, however, intended to provide an absolute limit on behavior. All boundaries are assumed to include opportunities for testing and occasional trespassing. "Getting away" from time to time with officially proscribed behavior is a matter of personal pride for many Samoans, and they admit this in intimate conversation. Such pride in overstepping official and social limits on personal behavior provides social life with a vitality that Samoans cherish, and is in no significant sense inconsistent with a professed reverence for the very laws and regulations that are being tested. Only a respected law is one worth making a great effort to test.

Simultaneous respect for the boundaries of social behavior and willingness to challenge them may appear illogical to a Western observer, since internal consistency and an ideal "integrity" between professed belief and demonstrated act are often the implicit basis of judgment of behavior as "logical." For Samoans, respecting laws means finding them worthy of testing and, when they assert themselves in their full authority, when one has pushed too far, it means demonstrating public deference to them. It is common for young Samoans who have energetically applied themselves to pursuing illicit sexual gratification or to taking chickens of another family without permission or, perhaps, to gambling illegally, to submit themselves with equal enthusiasm to the punishments that are meted out to them when they have been caught. There is, as we shall see, some evidence that reverence for authority and law among Samoans is associated with private desires to trespass precisely those laws and the authorities behind them. For boundaries to be dignified, they must be asserted strongly from time to time. For the world to be vital, however, and charged with possibilities of manipulation and sociopolitical mobility, they must not be imposed too rigidly or consistently.

This relationship between formal law and behavior, built into the Samoan system of social control, is paralleled by the relationship between the official fine as announced and the actual fine as paid in cases of fining by village authorities. An announced penalty is not always expected to be realized exactly. Like a law, a fine is dignified and worthy of serious regard if it is heavy and, further, if it is enforced from time to time. Yet because it is understood as the upper limit of punishment, announced often to underscore the dignity of the regulation it is enforcing, and of the authorities who have passed the regulation, a fine is also a boundary open to manipulation and testing. As with laws, announced fines are translated into behavior through a process of negotiation. This process is partly formalized in Samoa in the form of a chief or pastor who functions in judicial tribunals to request officially that an announced fine be lightened. This request is part of the structure of such tribunals, and is thus commonly expected and usually acceded to.

Frequently fine reductions are carried out through a less formal procedure. The level of fine paid is negotiated by a testing process for ascertaining what level of fine payment will be accepted by authorities. In each case study I collected of conflict resolution that included fines, the fine paid was never that which had been officially announced. Even in cases involving banishment, the banished party may test the viability of the sentence several times before finally submitting to it. Further, what is announced as "eternal banishment" is, in fact, interpreted as a five- to ten-year period of enforced absence from a village. The fact that, in the case of Tuatō's murder, the culprit's family insisted upon appealing what seemed to be a hopeless case twice in government courts represents not simply an appreciation of European legal procedures, but also an attempt to apply Samoan norms of sanction-testing to a non-Samoan legal arena.

The disobedience that seems to characterize fine payment in Samoa is culturally expected behavior, regulated by cultural norms of boundary negotiation that are as fully a part of Samoan culture as the official rules that were violated. Laws and official fines are both important to Samoans because they provide a moral skin or framework within which a great deal of manipulation and testing take place. Without such outer limits there would be, for the Samoan actor, no shape to his moral life.

Plate 7. *Fono tauati.* Facing the house of the village chiefs and orators, Tolova'a Musumusu formally accepts the banishment order for his cousin and his cousin's family. See figure 2.2 for a schematic plan of this meeting.

Plate 8. Village orators engage in a formal debate (*fa'atau*) for the right to make the formal presentation of kava roots to visiting chiefs.

Plate 9. Two orators face each other in a formal exchange of speeches.

Plate 10. The village pastor and his wife provide nightly Bible lessons for village children.

Plate 11. View of a village on Savai'i. Note the house foundation in the foreground. In traditional fashion, the village houses encircle a central *malae*.

PART III

MEANINGS

Introduction

It is a common mistake to assume that the web of mysteries, minor and major, that constitutes an alien culture may be resolved by careful observation alone. Even the most painstaking and perceptive observer eventually discovers that the key to many of the most intriguing and significant aspects of a culture lies within the minds of those he observes. Simple observation may be deceived by the lack of clear "fit" between the apparent patterns of behavior and the framework of beliefs and concepts that lies behind them. Another way of putting the problem is that human action is in large part symbolic action, and human acts have not merely effects and mechanical causes, but also intentions and meanings. To uncover the structure of those meanings that are shared, and rescue some of the intentions that inform human acts, is one of the most challenging and engaging aspects of fieldwork.

In these final chapters, I shift perspective to explore some of the symbols and meanings that link apparently disparate aspects of Samoan social life into meaningful patterns. While appearing to move away from Sala'ilua specifically and the murder on which our attentions have focused, such an exploration will actually take us much closer to the heart of the conflict and help to clarify some of the significant cultural factors that underlie it.

The formal structures of political, kinship, and local organizations that may be observed directly are obviously not identical with the patterns of symbols and meanings that can be elicited in intensive interviews. Yet I believe it is important to recognize that the two perspectives are, in many ways, complementary and refer to a common set of experiences. To assume that social structure and cultural patterns are simply two distinct and irreducible aspects of social life must be at least partially wrong. I believe it is possible to show, for instance, that sociological constructs like "bilateral descent," "propatrilineal succession," "optative descent," or "ambilocal residence" are sociological clues to distinct cultural conceptions of what a person is, and how he understands the social world in which he acts. These conceptions have, in turn, important implications for his moral evaluations, constituting assumptions in terms of which acts are understood and judged.

Properly described, every social system tells us something important about how a person is defined. From there we may move on to explore the social arena in which that person lives the public moments of his life. We may also look behind this field to a more private stage (or rather, offstage) with which these public moments are contrasted. The social arena is really a complex network of social relations. These are not simply the concrete, observable relationships by which Radcliffe Brown defined social structure. They are also conceptual relations defining abstract types of human linkage, with distinct valences and implications for evaluating behavior. Finally we turn to behavior itself, distinguishing from observable behavior "in the raw" sets of patterned acts linked to social contexts. These culturally stand-ardized patterns of behavior, are distinguished (following Parsons 1937) as social action.

In using such analytical concepts as cultural categories, shared beliefs, common symbols and meanings, and norms or rules for interaction, there is always the danger of misrepresenting the nature of the relationship be-tween a culture and its members. In arguing for the sharedness of cultural norms and values (Parsons 1951), the effectiveness of rules (Douglas 1966, 1973), the power of cultural templates (Schneider 1968) to guide action and shape experience (Geertz 1973), cultural anthropologists frequently imply the essential passivity of an actor in relation to a cultural system, although such a relationship would not be entertained as appropriate to our own lives. Further, the quest for pattern or configuration, the cultural gestalts that have dominated the working assumptions of anthropologists since Benedict's early work (1946), sometimes leads anthropologists to assume a degree to coherence and sharedness of "culture" that may be misleading.

Our problem is, then, to account in a significant way for the intuitive sense one gets in Samoa that Samoans do indeed share an important set of beliefs, symbols, and presuppositions about behavior that makes their per-ceptions of experience in some sense distinctive. Samoans themselves are quick to underscore their common cultural identity. At the same time, however, we must try to define a common "intersubjective" framework in such a way as to account for important local and individual variations in practice and understanding. Moreover, it should be possible to show that Samoans maintain an active relationship with their cultural environment, in such a way that they shape it at the same time as it is shaping them.

Writers on Samoa have frequently commented on the Samoan passion for diversity and the graceful manipulation of social forms (Mead 1930). Milner, in the introduction to his *Samoan Dictionary*, notes the difficulty that the fieldworker in Samoa encounters in eliciting consistent explanations of even noncontroversial matters. He refers to what he calls the "dialectical nature" of Samoan culture where "it is rare for information to be given, even from a reputedly sound and authentic source, without its being soon contradicted from another equally reputable and reliable source" (Milner 1966:xii–xiii). The character of this variation is a major subject of this study and will underlie most of the analysis in the last section.

Samoans, as well as outsiders, have recognized the paradoxical character of their *fa'a-Samoa,* a cultural tradition defined in terms of both its coherence and its malleability. To understand in what sense both characterizations are accurate without being simply paradoxical or contradictory we turn to the problem of meaning in Samoa.

CHAPTER EIGHT

Persons

In one of the versions of the Samoan story of creation,[1] the universe is created through an act of will by the god Tagaloa Fa'atutupunu'u (Tagaloa the Creator of Places).[2]

Tagaloa is the god who dwells in the illimitable void. He made all things. He alone (at first) existed. When there was no heaven, no people, no sea, no earth, he traversed the illimitable void; but, at a point at which he took his stand, up sprang a rock. His name is Tagaloa-faatutupunuu (i.e., Tagaloa-Creator; literally, the People-producing Tagaloa), because he made all things when nothing had been made. (Mead 1930:149)

The "creation" of lands begins when Tagaloa Fa'atutupunu'u commands the rock to divide and it splits several times:

and thereupon were born, in immediate succession, the reclining rock, the lava rock, the branching rock, and the cellular rock. Tagaloa then, looking towards the west, said (again) to the rock, "Divide!" He then smote it with his right hand: the rock divided on the right, and immediately the earth and the sea were born. That (the earth) is the parent of all the men (mankind) in the world. (Ibid.)

In subsequent sequences, all similar to the first, various parts (sky, clouds, watery abyss, hollow abyss) and characteristics (immensity and space, human heart, human will, and suspicion) of the universe and certain forms of flora come into existence.

In the next part of the myth, Tagaloa assigns these progeny of the initial rock to various stations: heart, spirit, and will are given to man, immensity and space to the heavens, abyss and voids are appointed to inhabit the watery regions of the earth and zoophyte and coral the sea, and the rock and the earth are given to the land (Mead 1930:51).[3] The genetic or evolutionary processes then continue, and the heavens and the sea and the earth become inhabited by their own offspring. Thus it is that the universe with its manifold qualities and aspects grows into existence.

Tagaloa the Creator then sat down, and produced Tagaloa the Unchangeable, and Tagaloa the Visitor of the Peoples, and Tagaloa the Prohibitor of the Peoples, and Tagaloa the Messenger, and Tuli and Logonoa.

Then Tagaloa the Creator said to Tagaloa the Unchangeable, "Be thou King of heaven!" (1930:150)

With the creation of the constituent elements and qualities of the universe completed, the Tagaloas turn to the task of conjuring into being the islands composing the world:

Then Tagaloa the Messenger, having assumed the form of the Turi [sic], went about to visit the lands; but no land could be seen. . . . Commencing at the group or range where the Eastern group now stands, he caused that group to emerge from the waters. Then he proceeded to where Fiti (Fiji) stands, and caused it to emerge. Then, wearied with traversing so wide an expanse of ocean, he stood and looked towards Tagaloa the Creator, in the heavens. Tagaloa the Creator looked down and the Tongan lands emerged. Again he looked towards Samoa (Manu'a is meant); but, unable to continue his course, he looked again to the heavens. Tagaloa the Creator and Tagaloa the Unchangeable looked down, and the land called Savai'i emerged. (1930:151)

After creating all the lands in the universe, the Tagaloas turn their attention to human creation. Tagaloa the Creator commands: "Take the man-producing vine, and go and plant it exposed to the sun. Leave it to bring forth spontaneously, and when it has done so inform me." This being done at a place on the eastern end of Upolu, it is discovered that what the vine produces is not of human form, but rather a shapeless mass of *ilo* (maggots). Tagaloa the Creator, seeing that his people-producing vine has brought forth only maggots, "straightened them out so as to develop their heads, faces, hands, and arms, moulding them into perfect human forms, and he gave them heart and soul."[4] Then, characteristically, these first (four) humans are given their assignments (*tofi*)—their proper places and functions. Upolu and Tele are, together, given over to the smaller of the two main western islands, which became known henceforth as Upolu Tele (Great Upolu). The other pair, Tutu and Ila, are assigned to a smaller island to the east, henceforth known as Tutuila.[5]

In addition to the prose creation story, Mead reproduces in its entirety a verse *solo* (chant) dealing with the same events. It is said that the chant belongs to Tuli, the *ata* or manifestation (Mead uses the translation "emblem") of Tagaloa the Messenger, and is addressed to Tagaloa the Creator. Although the events of this version of the myth broadly parallel the prose story, the chant places somewhat greater stress of the evolutionary or genetic origins of the world at the expense of an emphasis on mechanical creation.

The words used in the chant to express the process of origin are *tupu* (grow or become), *foa* (hatch, be born, grow) and *fānau* (to give birth). Proper creation by Tagaloa the Creator (Fa'atutupunu'u) occurs only after the people-producing vine bears the maggots. The vine is said to *fa'atagataina* Tutuila (to populate Tutuila) by an internal dynamic of its own. Then Tagaloa the Creator descends to *totosi fa'asinosino* (fashion into membered form) human beings from the formless mass of maggots. To the maggots are thus imparted will, face, and body; they are given shape and order.

The chant concludes with section that the translators render as Tagaloa's Counsel, although there is no such heading in the original Samoan version.

This section appears to the Western reader as a non sequitur. Tagaloa distinguishes between two *malae*: *Malae a Vevesi* (the Ground of Confusion) and *Malae a Toto'a* (the Ground of Tranquility). According to the chant, the gods may hold council at either of these meeting grounds, or alternatively at the Meeting Ground of the Rock (*Malae Papa*), or at any of several others. But when a ship or house is to be built, the gods are bidden to assemble only at the Ground of Tranquility, to drink kava with the builders. Tagaloa and his court will then remain in the heavens, at the Ground of Tranquility, while the builders descend to do their work.

Steubel has recorded still other versions of the same legend, each differing from the others in several significant aspects. In one (Steubel 1896: Samoan edition 1972), the story begins with a genealogical account of the successive "births" of various types of stones, flora, and fauna. Finally, following the birth of Fe'e (octopus), we have a cosmic flood when the sac of the Fe'e ruptures, inundating the dry land.

At this point Tagaloa Lagi looks down and, seeing the *puga* (a kind of coral) floating unanchored, lifeless, and unordered in the sea, he dispatches his helper Gaio to obtain from Tagaloa Nimonimo (Tagaloa the Illimitable) *agāga* (spirit) and *mauli* (life force/guts) with which to invest the coral with life. The coral is then wedded to a woman, created by Tagaloa Lagi, who gives birth to Tuli, the messenger of Tagaloa (a kind of Samoan Hermes). Tagaloa then sends Tuli to find himself a home below on earth, but Tuli complains of the heat of the sun. Tagaloa provides Tuli with a shade-producing vine, which is the people-producing vine of the main story.[6] The maggots, however, do not spring of their own accord from the vine, as in the other versions, but rather are sent by an angry Tagaloa (the reason for the anger is unclear to me) to devour the shade vine of Tuli.

When Tuli complains that his vine has been eaten away, Tagaloa requests that the remains of the vine be brought to him. Tuli uproots the vine and discovers maggots at its roots, and he brings them with the vine to Tagaloa. Tagaloa then orders Gaio to draw out the various human parts from the maggots, and this is done by an act of punning. Gaio forms the head (*ulu*) first of all and Tuli says, "Wait until I speak my name," at which point the *tuliulu* (back of the neck) comes into being. Similar acts of punning create the *tulilima* (elbow), *tulivae* (knee) and the *tulimanava* (loins). Gaio is sent again to fetch the spirit and the life force, but instead, brings back the snake (*gata*). Tagaloa commands Gaio to *tā ane* (beat upon) the snake, at which point was created—verbally and ontologically—*taane* or *tāne* (man), and *tāgata* (person).

In each of these myth variants, the world is created in parts. Islands are created one by one and then endowed with characteristics. Characteristics (heart, will, suspicion, life force, spirit) have an independent existence from the bodies that will incorporate them. People are created as parts, pieces, components to be assembled. And the act of creation itself is a process of composing, or articulating, the parts. Tuli, the messenger, is the go-between, the filler of the *vā*, or space. The *tuli* is also the physical articulation or relation between parts of the body, so that as a prefix it means "joint" or "joiner."

Two particularly interesting themes run through the various versions of the Samoan story of creation. One is the focus on discrete parts or aspects of the universe having an existence independent of the wholes they may comprise. Thus, for instance, it is difficult to know whether the Samoans' central deity Tagaloa is one or many gods, since each of the particular characteristics is accorded a separate personification. We have in these stories Tagaloa the Creator of Places, Tagaloa the Illimitable, and Tagaloa Lagi (Tagaloa of the Heavens). They are, like the Christian trinity, simultaneously the many and the one. Tagaloa Lagi, moreover, has his *ata* (shadow), Tuli, which is again an active manifestation of himself, and yet is also endowed with an independent will.

Creation also describes the origin of qualities and parts of existence rather than totalities, such that will, spirit, hands, head, or feet are grasped as primary elements of the created world. Creation constitutes both the generation of these parts and also a linking together of the parts into proper relations with each other.

The second, related theme evident throughout the different versions of the creation legend is a pervasive and interesting union of two perspectives on creation, distinguished by Mead (following Handy) as important variants within Polynesian mythology—an older evolutionary model for creation, and a more recent type of myth in which the world is made through a deliberate act of creation. Of the Samoan creation myth, Mead has commented:

There are two versions of genealogical creation, one, the characteristic series of different kinds of rock; the other, the characteristic Maori series of voids and a series of qualities; and later in the myth the progeny of immensity and space. . . . Coupled with the genealogical elements which Samoa shares with the Maori are found other elements which Handy has distinguished as the creation type. . . . Here Tagaloa is seen as the creator and orderer of the universe. (Mead 1930:155)

While it is possible to identify these tendencies within different versions of the myth, a closer reading of the myths indicates that what Mead calls the evolutionary and creation themes are complementary threads woven together within any one of the versions. I have already suggested that the term "creator" is a misleading translation of Tagaloa Fa'atutupunu'u, and that "conjurer" or "inspirer" would be more appropriate approximations of the Samoan sense. The myth suggests that creation involves, rather than the imposition of life on totally inanimate or passive matter or the creation of that matter *ex nihilo,* the activation of potential life forces which are given in the world. In this sense, creation is the infusion into matter of reproductive power and a capacity for growth. Such a vision of creation is clearly neither simple fabrication nor simple evolution, but something of both at once, a harnessing of potential energy through a creative act of will.

This complementary intermingling of forces is suggested at several places in the myths. Tagaloa the Creator of Places, the instrument of change and activity, generates his own antithesis: Tagaloa the Illimitible. To create Savai'i, the largest of the islands, the complementary forces of changer and unchangeable were required. Among the most important *malae* for the gods is another complementary pair: the Ground of Tranquility and the Ground of Confusion. The gods, we are told, meet at both, and the existence of the one presupposes the existence of the other. As Samoans say, "'ua tua'oi āfā ma maninoa" (the storm and the calm are neighbors).

The same kind of duality evident in the creation myths was noted by Goldman as implicit in the criteria for status that Samoans use as the basis of political power:

Samoa represents more clearly than any other Polynesian society the special combination of organic and "made" features that give to a status system a dual character. The Samoan status systems were . . . bipolar. That is to say, whether one considers the authenticity of a single status or the table of the organization of statuses, some combination of organic (genealogical) or "made" (political or military) will be involved. (Goldman 1970:251)

Goldman distinguishes between "dual" systems that separate the organic and achieved aspects of status, and "bipolar" systems such as Samoa's, wherein the two poles are combined "almost in the way an electric circuit is formed" (ibid.). In opposing systems that separate aspects of power to those that combine them, Goldman has bypassed the possibility of complementarity, in which separation and combination are reconciled in the notion of interdependence between linked opposites.

The Person as a Cultural Artifact

While intuition may lead to valuable hunches in approaching most mysteries, cultural puzzles are less likely to be solved by following intuitive leads. Here, our unquestioned assumptions frequently lead us astray, and it is precisely at this rarely conscious level of our understanding that we find the most stubborn barrier to accurate interpretation. This is why good cultural interpretation often begins with a clarification of the implicit biases brought by an outsider to the perception of another culture.

There is, perhaps, no more powerful barrier to our accurate perception of Samoan culture than a complex set of assumptions that most Westerners (and perhaps especially contemporary Americans) hold about the nature of the person. Underlying many of our everyday assessments of ourselves and others, as well as implicit in a number of scientific paradigms of social relations, is a set of beliefs, priorities, and attitudes that cannot help but frame our vision of others, even when those others may not share the assumptions. Clues to these assumptions are found in certain key terms that dominate both scholarly and popular discourse on the person—terms such as "personality," "self," "integration," "the individual," and "social role." Clifford Geertz remarked on this problem.

The Western conception of the person as a bounded, unique, more or less integrated motivational and cognitive universe, a dynamic center of awareness, emotion, judgment, and action organized into a distinctive whole and set contrastively against other such wholes and against other social and natural background is, however incorrigible it might seem to us, a rather peculiar idea within the context of the world's cultures. (Geertz 1975:48)

Dumont (1965, 1970) has examined the implications of a dominant atomistic and individualistic ideological bias on Western perceptions of such hierarchical societies as India. Clearly, this bias constitutes an important obstacle to the illumination of a culture that does not share it.

Erikson (1964a) recounts the story of an old Jew who visited his doctor burdened with complaints. "My feet ache, my back hurts, and my breathing is a bit sluggish too. And you know, doctor, I'm not feeling so well myself either." The sense of self, that profound certainty we all entertain about the unique and coherent quality of our personal essence both within and beyond our corporeal shell, is among the most telling of our fundamental social concepts. It is also a concept whose historical development in the West can be traced. Trilling, in his study *Sincerity and Authenticity* (1971), illuminates moments in the intellectual and moral history of the past four centuries when a progressively conscious sense of a person as a personality and a self became apparent in literature and social philosophy. The psychological evolution involved a parallel reification and externalization of a complementary concept: "society."

Sincerity, authenticity and, eventually, personality become tantamount to moral values, according to Trilling. He points to the English Renaissance and particularly to the works of Shakespeare for the earliest expressions of this new self-consciousness. In what Trilling calls a moment of "self-transcendence" in *Hamlet,* Polonius rises above his own moral dimness and pomposity in advising his son Laertes: "This above all: to thine own self be true / And it doth follow, as the night the day, / Thou canst not be false to any man" (1. 3. 18–20). Laertes is counseled to know himself first in order to know other men. He is advised, moreover, to know himself truly, suggesting the possibility of a false knowledge of oneself. The theme of turning inward for truth, looking beyond the phenomenal world of appearance, is a recurring Shakespearean theme. Nature, for Shakespeare, is a book to be properly read—or misread, at one's peril. Yet true knowledge lies, for him beyond this phenomenal realm, in an interior vision or "insight." Trilling suggests that the emergence of this self-concept brought with it an entirely new vocabulary for assessing action. Shakespearean figures like those who inhabit the novels of Jane Austen possess "character" and may be judged in terms of criteria of sincerity and personal authenticity in a way that Homeric heroes cannot. The use of terms such as "sincere," "honest," or "hypocritical" as moral attributes is predicated on a set of implicit questions and assumptions about actors that are more a historical product of a particular time and place than of human experience in general. They are, that is, to be understood largely as aspects of culture rather than of human nature.

As with "substance" or "essence," the self is at best glimpsed with difficulty. Both within the skin and beyond it, self is intuited rather than perceived. The search in the physical sciences for an ultimate particle of matter and that in metaphysics for essence or substance are paralleled in theology by the search for soul and in psychology by that for self, identity, and personality.

While Trilling seeks to demonstrate the origins of this notion of personal authenticity and selfhood in the sixteenth century, it appears that the concept goes back considerably earlier in Western history. Linking the development of the concept of "self" to that of "mind," Bruno Snell (1960) has argued that Mind was a discovery of the Greeks after Homer. The psychological universe of Homeric Greece, Snell tells us, was pluralistic, grounded in perception and sensory experience in a way that is not true in Greece of the fifth century B.C. Snell reminds us that Homer had no words corresponding to our concepts of "mind" and "soul." In early Hellenic writing, human actions appear as externally "caused" rather than internally "motivated" or "intended." Snell explains: "Aristotle's 'first mover' is absent from Homer's ken, as is the concept of any vital centre which controls the organic system. Mental and spiritual acts are due to the impact of external factors, and man is the open target of a great many forces which impinge on him" (1960:20).

Further, the Homeric world did not recognize a distinction between internal and external aspects of reality. Merit and appearance were distinguished from each other, but neither was clearly distinguished from internal or essential qualities of phenomena. Snell asserts that early Greek drawings did not represent the human body as an integrated, organic entity, but rather as an aggregate of limbs and parts. Only in what has come to be known as the Classical period of Greek art, the fifth century B.C., do we find attempts to depict the human body as an entity with an essential unity, whose various parts are subordinate to and interrelated by a larger sense of wholeness. Says Snell (1960:6–7): "The early Greek drawings seem to demonstrate the agility of the human figure (while) . . . the drawing of the modern child (demonstrates) its compactness and unity."

Thus it is only in the fifth century B.C. that we see, in Greece, the beginning of a recognition of the person as a distinct whole, an integrated unit both physiologically and psychologically. From this notion of person emerges that of personality in the same way that the notion of mind arises from the concepts of thought and intention. Once a person has been accorded an interiority, complete with intention and will, he becomes a "character" or "personality," mindful of his actions and of an external world about him.[7] Homeric actors, Snell says, do not reveal "character," that self-awareness and coherent identity which becomes evident in later Greek writings. By the time of Sappho or Anacreon ". . . they are evidently concerned to place a genuine reality, to find Being instead of Appearance" (1960:50). They have, in Snell's terms, discovered mind and self.

The Samoan Concept of Person

Not only are there in Samoan no terms corresponding to the English "personality," "self" or "character," but there is also an absence of the corresponding assumptions about the relation of person to social action. A clue to the Samoan notion of person is found in the popular Samoan saying *teu le vā* (take care of the relationship).[8] Contrasted with the Greek dicta "Know thyself" or "To thine own self be true," this saying suggests something of the difference between Occidental and Samoan orientations.

Lacking any epistemological bias that would lead them to focus on "things in themselves" or the essential qualities of experience, Samoans instead focus on things in their relationships, and the contextual grounding of experience.[9] This difference between European and Samoan perceptions of experience has not been lost on Samoans themselves. One young Samoan, a youth of about eighteen, gave me the following account of the differences between the Samoan and the *pālagi*.

In their cultures, the Samoans look after their culture, while the *pālagi* look after themselves. Cultures are all different. So if you grew up in the one place that had customs and law, then they are the proper things to look after you. But if you grew up in a place where there were no customs or laws [i.e., in *pālagi* societies] then it would be good for you to look after your own behavior. The Samoan looks after relationships; the *pālagi* looks after himself.

It is striking that in this statement, the informant frames the relationship between Samoan society and the actor as a passive one, while the *pālagi* is understood to have an active one. In other words, in this informant's conception, Samoan behavior is (externally) "caused" while that of the *pālagi* is (internally) "motivated."

Another informant, a middle-aged woman who has worked for many years in an institution also employing Europeans, explained the cultural differences in the following terms.

The Samoans look after the relationship first and foremost. For example, in my own work, the *pālagi* orders the workers about directly. He has no concern with the social relations involved. Do this, and this, and this! But we Samoans must be careful what we say or do. We must care first for the relationship as our custom dictates. If I feel that something is wrong, I hesitate to say it, for in our culture we must be very cautious with relationships.

This Samoan emphasis on correct perception of social relations and their requirements goes far beyond a concern for etiquette or tact. It is a moral and epistemological axiom.

When speaking of themselves or others, Samoans often characterize people in terms of specific "sides" (*itū*) or "parts" (*pito*) or particular "characteristics" (*'uiga*). No attempt is made to provide a summary characterization of a whole integrated person. By parts or sides, Samoans usually mean specific connections that people bear to villages, descent groups, or titles. While at any given time one particular linkage will be stressed and the person's identity will appear to lie in a single descent group or village affiliation, no such assumption is made by Samoans.

Thus while no unitary social identity is suggested by any particular reference, Samoans frequently go to great lengths to isolate, at any particular occasion, one of the many possible sides or relations a person has. This contextual specification of social identity from the various possibilities is evident in the following excerpt from an interview that I had with an elderly *ali'i* from Savai'i. The informant had been talking about another man, Eti, a close relative of his. A distinguished man, Eti holds five different chiefly titles. In this conversation, two of these titles (and the relations they imply) were relevant.

Tofilau Eti is a cousin of mine. One of his sides is the Tofilau [title], but another of his sides (the Va'aelua title) is me. After the meeting in the village, the other chiefs said to Tofilau—for he is, in one of his parts, my true body—that someone had to report to me what the council had decided.

In this case, the specification of the relevant genealogical connection of Eti to the speaker (the Va'aelua title) is embedded in a report of an event in which the Tofilau title was the relevant "side" of Eti. The speaker here was very careful to distinguish the different sides and to specify clearly the relevant context for each. Note also how my informant referred to Eti (or "part of Eti") as one of the parts of his "own true body."

On another occasion, a middle-aged Samoan man was recounting to me the story of a woman who had been possessed by a ghost. The woman was living in a village where the informant had grown up, and where the informant's father had been for many years the resident pastor of the Congregational church. The possessing spirit was held to be that of Sauma'eafe, a well-known and feared spirit in Samoa, believed to be that of a young girl from Sale'imoa village, the home of my informant's paternal grandfather. The story, which was told to me in fluent English, contains the following statements.

My father, the pastor, came in, sat down, and made the proper greetings. Then the ghost (within the possessed woman) said: "I'll go now." She was very quiet during the time that the pastor was in the house. He asked about the patient: what was happening, what her condition was, et cetera. Her father explained that she was taken up to the hospital, and had come back, and that they had decided to get this old lady (a spirit medium) from Sale'imoa village who was famed for exorcising this particular spirit. Another thing is that my father is a member of one of the families of Sale'imoa. He is a member of that village, so then in that situation the lady (medium) knows him as a member of her own village.

The constant modulations in social identity made within this brief passage are remarkable. A man is known as "father," "pastor," or "man of Sale'imoa" and the speaker is careful at each reference to specify which aspect of the man is being highlighted. What may appear as the diffracted quality of such a personal identification in which the essential person appears to be lost within a prism of shifting social relations is a perfectly normal way in which Samoans conceive personal identity.

This sort of isolation of relevant "sides" of people to particular contexts is an important part of any large political or social gathering of importance. Many people will attend such gatherings from distant villages, both to pay respects to the person or family at the center of the celebration, and also to gain some social or political advantage through the activation of relations that have been dormant or to acquire fine mats in the gift exchanges that are a highlight of all such gatherings. Sometimes someone will come who is not personally known to the orators presiding over the formal greetings, or else a person might be known but might have a number of different kinds of connection with the village or family, any of which might be relevant.

When such a person arrives, he will normally be greeted respectfully and then asked to make public the *'auala* or path by which he comes. This defines what the visitor hopes will be recognized as an important connection through descent, marriage, political alliance, or village association with the host for whom the celebration is being held. Sometimes, when the visitor is not generally known, this specification simply tells all present who the visitor is in sociological terms. At other times, however, the person is too well known, linked through several different kinds of connection; so the requested path reduces the ambiguity by singling out one particular connection by which the visitor wishes to be known at the gathering.

Thus, for instance, at a funeral a visitor may be related to the deceased both by common descent and through the deceased's spouse. In such a situation, by no means farfetched, a person's "path" may be either as *gafa* (a descent link) or as *pāolo* (an affinal link), but it cannot be both for any single occasion. Other possible specifications might be a uterine connection (*'āiga o le tinā*), an agnatic link (*'āiga o le tamā*), a direct agnatic link to a title (*tamatane*), or a connection to the title through a sister (*tamafafine*). Adoption too provides a legitimate claim for recognition at a celebration.[10] The path may also be less clearly kin-based, focusing instead on connections through linked titles. We have already seen how such formal associations between titles are an important part of any *fa'alupega* in a village or district, and these connections are potential paths to any important affair involving the titles.

Once such a path is asserted by a visitor, the group of orators hosting the celebration has the right to either accept or reject the claims made. If the path is recognized as legitimate (the usual result) the visitor is welcomed into the gathering, and any gifts brought are accepted publicly. "'O le ala 'ua mutia, 'ae le'o se ala fati" (It is a grassy path, and not a newly beaten track) would be an appropriate formal welcome, recognizing the connection as an old and viable one.

Even in everyday discourse, where these more formal levels of status are not important, statements or evaluations are made with an implicit "part" of one's identity in mind. On one occasion, for instance, a young man in the course of a fifteen-minute conversation asserted that he both supported and opposed a prominent politician. Baffled by the apparent contradiction, I pressed him for clarification. It turned out that for each opinion a different "side" of the man was being invoked. His father's family was related to the politician in question, and this relationship was the basis of the loyalty expressed. On his mother's side, however, the man was linked to a branch of a descent group that had a long-standing claim on the title that the politician held. From this perspective the politician was a rival, to be opposed rather than supported. Whereas our perceptions of the situation recognize a thorny conflict of loyalties in these relations, the young man simply localized his judgments to different kinship contexts.

Samoan (and all Polynesian) pronouns are particularly well suited for this kind of contextual specification of identity. "We" is realized in either a dual or a plural (more than two) form. Even more significant is the required specification of whether the person addressed is included in the "we" or excluded. Thus *tatou 'āiga* refers to "our family" in which the person being addressed is considered part of the group. *Matou 'āiga,* however, refers to "our family" in a sense excluding the person addressed from membership. What is most striking about these forms is the way in which they are frequently used to expand or contract the flexible boundaries of a group, according to context.

Thus, for instance, when requesting a cigarette a Samoan may well ask someone "Pe iai se ta sikaleti?" (Do you have our [*ta*: dual inclusive] cigarette?). The cigarette is linguistically appropriated by the requester, making a refusal all but impossible. The subtle modulations in relationship that can be suggested by a skillful shift in pronouns was demonstrated to me one day when I ran into an elderly lady in Apia with whose family I had lived for about a year. "Did you not hear," she asked "about the death in our (*tatou*) family?" I had not, and was being implicitly rebuked for not having contributed to the funeral of a distant relative whom I had known, and who was considered to be within the circle of relatives to whom I bore social responsibility. After we chatted briefly and exchanged recent news, I asked the woman where she was headed. "To a wedding in our (*matou*) family." The change to the exclusive form of "we" suggested that this particular kin connection lay beyond my social responsibilities to "my family," either because the genealogical link was too distant to include a mere anthropologist-turned-son, or because I had never met these relations and had not thereby maintained a well-trodden path to what remained only potential kin.[11]

Personal Traits

The various dimensions that make up a total person in Samoan thought are not limited to political or kinship status. In addition to the socially articulated "parts" or "sides" through which a person is known, people also possess 'uiga or particular personal qualities. 'Uiga, which also refers to "meaning," suggests something close to what psychologists mean by "trait." Fa'ali'i (ill-tempered), tausua (good-humored), fa'afāfine (effeminate, for males), loto alofa (thoughtful/generous), fia sili (pretentious), or 'augatā (lazy, dilatory) are all possible traits by which people may be characterized. In fact, Samoans are quick to pin such labels on people, in the form of either compliments or accusations.

While such characterizations seem to suggest a Samoan personality concept similar to that used by Europeans and Americans, there is a crucial difference. For Samoans, these traits are never used as summary terms to characterize or distinguish a person "in general." They are understood to be merely aspects of people, possessed in different degrees and combinations by different people. While different 'uiga may differentiate people from one another, they are used in a way that suggests they are understood primarily as aspects of particular contexts rather than of particular types of people. Samoans on the whole do not focus on a temperamental or behavioral consistency within a person, although they may recognize one or more traits as strong within that person. The emphasis for evaluating people is not the consistency of behavior with behavior, or of trait with trait, but rather the appropriateness of a trait to a given situation. There is no term in Samoan that clearly expresses the English concept of (self-)consistency.

When a Samoan says of someone's behavior e lē fetaui (it does not fit), the reference is to the lack of fit between action and setting rather than to any lack of fit between a particular behavior and an individual personality type. The judgment is about appropriateness to context, and not about consistency to personality.[12]

Samoans commonly characterize themselves as inconsistent, especially when they compare themselves to the pālagi. "E fiafia pu'upu'u 'o tagata Samoa" (Samoans are easily bored) is the most common way in which this difference is expressed, while the European "e alu so'o 'i le mea e tasi" (always sticks to one thing), as one informant expressed it. Further, it is inconceivable to Samoans that a person could be summarized by a single characteristic. For example, in response to my question of whether he knew anyone who was totally good, one young Samoan male responded as follows.

There is no one I can think of who is completely good. [In other places] there may
be, but certainly not many. Among the *pālagi* there is consistency [one thing stays
put]. He [the *pālagi*] has his talents and sticks to what he does. He is content for
long periods of time with what he does. But in Samoa, people are happy for only
brief periods [with any one thing]. People look and see that others are up to other
things and they become discontent. That's where you get your ill-will [*loto leaga*]
rising up.

While the European concept of the integrated, coherent, and "rounded"
personality suggests the metaphor of a sphere, that most perfectly "integrated" of objects, the contrasting Samoan metaphor implicit in the Samoan
conception of person is a many-faceted gem. A sphere maintains its shape,
its integrity, by a denial of sides, or what is called in contemporary American
slang by "getting it all together." By contrast, a faceted gem maintains its
own form through differentiation, a maintenance of distinct sides, and a
denial of that integration which would render it without sides. Further, as
with a gem, the greater the number of facets, the more brilliant the form.
Richness comes from multiplying sides, but such multiplication carried on
past a certain point confuses the sides, merges one into the other, and the
object loses its shape. Such a potential blurring of sides is the constant
danger of too ambitious an attempt to enrich one's identity in Samoa by
activating too many sides. Such manipulation of potential relationships is
a craft that only the most skillful may ply without courting social chaos.
Indeed, the status of the present paramount chiefs, the *tama'āiga* (children
of many families), suggests the ultimate elaboration of sides, while the
fragility of these titles over time also suggests the problems inherent in
maintaining an enormous number of active sides simultaneously.

In describing what I understand to be a Samoan conception of person,
it should be evident that I have simply provided a Samoan account of what
anthropologists have been struggling with under the terms of ambilineality,
bilateral systems, cognatic descent, and ambilocal postmarital residence.
Firth pointed to the cognitive implications of these social systems (1957)
when he termed them examples of "optative descent systems," and Silverman (1978) underscored Firth's observation by suggesting that Oceanic
social systems of this sort might be characterized by their stress on the
maximization of options for social affiliations.

In sum, then, the Samoan concept of an identity consists of an identification of particular parts of an individual, and a relative weighting of those
parts. Fundamental in any assessment of a person's makeup is an evaluation
of the particular behavioral and social context in which the assessment is
being made.

That this notion of personal identity should appear to Western observers
as illogical, and suggest the kind of failure of "ego-integration" that Erikson
(1950) suggested would result from role diffusion, is no more strange than
that the logic of cognatic descent should have eluded anthropologists for

so long. As Schneider (1965) has aptly pointed out, anthropologists have
simply assumed that any social system required the unambiguous commitment of a whole person to a social group. This assumption presupposes
a particular psychology that, as we have seen, is in no sense universal.

Of the many scientific observers of Samoan society, Mead and Maxwell
appear most clearly aware of these differences between the Samoan and
Western accounts of personal identity. For instance, Mead (1928:161) noted
that "Samoans have a low level of appreciation of personal differences and
a poverty of conception of personal relations." Insofar as Samoan relations
are more "social" than "personal," defined as they are by social contexts
rather than in terms of personality constructs, Mead's formulation is similar
to my own. Samoans are, however, extremely keen observers of certain
types of distinctions among different actors. Yet these differences are interpreted by Samoans as distinctions of particular characteristics and behaviors, and of their relative prominence in different actors, rather than in
terms of discrete personality types.

In accounting for individual behavior, especially unusual or disapproved-
of behavior, Samoans frequently assert that " 'ua 'ese'ese tagata" (people
are different), "e lē tutusa tagata" (people are not equal), or " 'ua salasala
tagata" (people are "cut up" differently). These statements appear to express
clear-cut notions of personality differences. Yet closer examination of such
statements reveals quite a different stress. While Samoan statements of the
type "X acts in one way while Y acts in another way" may be heard now
and then, it is almost always differences in the number or power of particular
sides of actors that are being discussed. The implications of this depersonalization of action or feeling in the Samoan conception of the person will
be taken up in chapter 10.[13]

Sides or facets of people act up, arise, are strange, or become strong. This
is not equivalent to explanation in terms of personalities. There is an interesting ambiguity in the Samoan phrases mentioned above, " 'ua salasala
tagata" (people are all "cut up" in different ways) and " 'ua 'ese'ese tagata"
(people are all different). Both salasala and 'ese'ese are ambiguous in that
they suggest both that people are different from each other and that people
are all differentiated internally. Samoan conceptions of behavioral variation
link a notion of individual differences within a population with a notion
of the internal differentiation of each actor, such that personal differences
seem to be a function of situation type and not of discrete person type.
Sometimes, such conceptions of the relationship between actor and act
produce Samoan statements with a strangely "illogical" quality to Western
sensibilities. Consider, for instance, the following statements.

Here in Samoa there are no bad characteristics or actions as there are in overseas
countries.

(Is this village different from other villages in which you have lived?) They are
pretty much the same, although the behaviors are different.

(Different in what way?) The behavior of some youth is good. They don't go and throw stones at [the movie theater]. For youth are very bad. They go, for instance, if there is a meeting in the back of that house over there—some youth will go and bombard the house with stones. They will gather together and decide to bombard the movie theater. That's what we call being uneducated. For the lives of the youth are all different. They are not the same.

People are not all the same. There are some people who are good and then there comes a time when they do bad things. That's just the way that people are.

Samoans appear to speak of behavioral differences as if they emerged from differences among actors, while simultaneously placing a great stress on the situational determination of behavior. The formulations are more clearly understood, however, when we look to persons not as discrete and self-consistent units but as bundles of different behavioral potentials that are activated in relation to particular social contexts. Observed variability in individual behavior may, in such a formulation, be related either to different contexts in which a single actor has behaved, or to distinct sides of an actor which have been activated in similar contexts. The phrase "people are all different" is thus ambiguous in a critical sense, suggesting both individual differentiation and internal differentiation of a single actor.

Mead stressed the lack of a Samoan conception of "fixed role," remarking that "most individuals play a series of parts of differing importance in a series of differently organized activities" (1965:257). Clearly, however, the phrase "fixed role" suggests something of a contradiction in terms, since a role is normally defined as part of a set of roles, and thus no single role can be "fixed." Perhaps the term "self" or "personality" might have been more apt. Further, Mead appears to recognize that a behaviorist theory of action would better account for Samoan social action than a personality-trait theory. For instance, Mead asserted that "Whereas in a different kind of society [from Samoa], it would be possible to predict what a given individual, A, will do as compared with a given individual, B, in Samoa it is much more possible to predict what a series of men, A, B, and C will do in a given situation" (ibid.).

Maxwell, picking up on these insights of Mead's, noted that Samoans seem to conceptualize behaviors as independent from the people who act them.

In Samoa, terms describing motor and verbal behavior are used only in certain *situations*. A child being boisterous in the presence of an adult is said to be "not acting in the way a person of his age should act," he is *tautala la'ititi*. But the same sort of behavior towards one of his peers would receive no notice. That is, most of the adjectival forms describe *behaviors*, not people. (Maxwell 1969:148)

Although Maxwell's study is called *Samoan Temperament*, really a misnomer for what would be more properly called aspects of personality, Maxwell himself notes ironically that he "could not elicit any Samoan classification of people in terms of temperament, and in fact there is a characteristic unconcern about the analysis or classification of personalities" (ibid.).

Names and Persons

One of the most revealing ways to illuminate the Samoan concept of person is to examine the structure of the naming system by which persons are identified in social interactions. An examination of a naming system necessarily highlights the crucial understandings a society has about personal identity, while important cultural differences emerge in the comparison of different naming systems.

There is in the Samoan language no close approximation to the English "self." To do something "by oneself" is to do it *to'atasi* (alone). There is also the self-reflexive form *e a'u lava* indicating an act done by a person and referred to by the actor. By contrast, to do something "to oneself" may be rendered in Samoan in several ways. The same self-reflexive form mentioned above may be employed here: "'iate a'u lava" (literally, "to me indeed"). However, a more colloquial form employs the word for "body" as a kind of metonym for the "whole self": "sa 'ou fai ifo i lo'u tino" (I spoke down to my body). While these forms do express a notion of self-reflexive action, none suggest the Western notion of wholeness implicit in the word "self," an identity of a person wholly within the skin and yet transcending the body.

In referring to a third person, Samoan provides a number of forms. One may, for example, ask "Po'o ai le tagata lenā?" (Who is that person?), which is the most common way of referring to an unknown third person. Alternatively, one may ask "Po'o ai le igoa lenā?" (Who is that name?) in which a person is metonymically defined by his name, much as he may be by his body, a part taken for the whole. If it is possible, then, to identify person with name, it should be particularly revealing of the conception of person to examine Samoan personal names and the modes by which a person is attached to his names.

At birth a Samoan child is given a personal name, referred to in Samoan as his *igoa taule'ale'a* (untitled person's name). There is no formal ceremony to mark the bestowal of a name, although the missionaries have introduced baptism. Most Samoan *igoa* (names) are not marked for gender. Sina, the generic Polynesian name for moon goddess, is a partial exception, however, and there are several other exceptions as well. Samoanized borrowings of personal names from the English Bible, or from English or German names, are all marked for gender as they are in their original languages. Samoans are frequently named after close relatives, both living and dead. There is no cultural preference for which relative a child should be named after, or any pattern of alternation between father or mother in the choice of names for children as in Rarotonga (Mackenzie, personal communication). Normally, however, babies are named after relatives of the same sex.

Another naming pattern concerns the naming of children after events or places prominent at the time of the child's birth. These events may have no particular direct connection with the child's birth except that they link the birth with a co-occurrence and anchor it to some event in the wider social sphere. One child, for instance, was named Tusilomifefiloi (dictionary), commemorating the fact that George Milner was residing in his village at the time of his birth while researching his *Samoan Dictionary*. Another child, a girl, was named *Taulago* (battle of the flies) since, I was told, the family members were battling "like flies" at the time that the baby was born.

A common structural feature of Samoan naming is that it stresses the relation of the person named to something significant in his social environment. In this sense, names establish relationships more clearly than they suggest personal identity. It is significant, for example, that the event a child is named after need not have any "personal" connection to the child named, but may rather merely link the new child with his social environment at the time of birth.

In addition to these personal names, there are also *suafa matai* (chiefly titles), *suafa* being simply the equivalent term in the chiefly respect vocabulary to the common form *igoa* (name). There are several thousand such chiefly titles registered in the Land and Titles Court in Western Samoa, and each is the property of a title-based descent group. These title-based descent groups are distinguished by the fact that they are referred to with the prefix Sā (cf. Tongan *ha'a*) to which is attached the title name. Thus, the descent group claiming rights through the title Malietoa is addressed as the Sā Malietoā, with the final vowel commonly lengthened. Such a descent group is dispersed and its boundaries are ill defined. In fact, because the group or category is defined primarily in relation to the name or title by which it is named rather than in relation to a descent principle per se, this particular descent group is more properly a title group. Each title bears relations to other titles, usually through the genealogical connections of the title founders, and thus there is an inevitable overlapping of membership in title-based groups. As we have seen in the ethnography of Sala'ilua village, senior titles may also have associated dependent and minor titles attached to them, and the larger *'āiga* thus encompasses in membership this smaller and subordinate group.

Over time, and in response to population and resource pressures, titles may be "split" into more or less autonomous segments, and the associated descent group undergoes a parallel splitting into *itū paepae* (title branches). *Itū 'āiga* (literally, "side of the *'āiga*") is a more general term for descent group branch, while *itū paepae* refers exclusively to segmentation through the splitting of a single title. Titles may split several times, and some titles have as many as twenty "parts" or branches. The nature of the relations between different branches depends largely on the time-depth of the split and the circumstances surrounding it. In some cases, members in one branch have a voice in the election of a title holder in another, but commonly such rights are eroded with time. It is commonly believed in Samoa that the title's dignity is diluted by splitting it, and this belief is reflected in the fact that none of the four paramount titles has ever been split.

The potentially infinite divisibility of titles in Samoa provides the political system with an adaptive flexibility in the face of population changes. It is a traditional alternative to the creation of new titles and, more significantly, a powerful force for generalizing and diffusing political power, and for preventing the creation of a large class of untitled commoners under the sway of a small class of chiefs.

Just as *matai* titles are in theory infinitely divisible and conceptually in-dependent of their holders, so also is a person infinitely divisible into dif-ferent titles. One man (or, rarely, woman) may hold as many different chiefly titles as he can secure through election by the title's associated descent group. The only constraints on the number of titles an individual may hold are the number of distinct genealogical links he can trace to title-based groups, the ability to devote time, energy, and wealth to fulfilling obli-gations of service to the members of the title group, and the possession of sufficient prestige to make one a desirable holder to the bestowing group. Because of these constraints, most title holders hold a single title, while those holding multiple titles tend to hold no more than two. It is rare that someone would hold more than four titles. Multiple titles may be from related title groups (as in the case of Tuatō Tualevao Fatu in Sala'ilua), or they may come from unrelated groups, as when a man holds one title in his father's family, another in his wife's family, and another in his mother's family.[14]

Just as there is a conceptual distinction between personal name and chiefly title (the former focusing on an individual, the latter on a political group), so Samoans differentiate a personal descent line or *gafa* from a title sucession line or *'augānofo*. The title line is structured by the title, and traces the line of holders. The descent line is traced through the double focus on an ancestor or title, and a person in a subsequent generation whose descent (or as Sahlins, in a personal communication, put it, "ascent") is being traced. Person and name, bearer and title are conceptually separable, but interde-pendent. Each is divisible into a number of different parts or sides, each side having a life and history of its own.

In addition to their personal names, Samoans may use a surname or *fa'ai'u* as an individuating marker. Generally, a child uses a patronymic form as his surname, either his father's personal name, or one or more of his father's titles if he is a chief. The use of one name in one context does not preclude the use of an alternate appellation in another context, and indeed, such contextualization of naming is at the very heart of the Samoan naming system.

If, for example, my personal name is Alo and my father, whose own personal name is Vili, holds two *matai* titles, Tuataga and Māmea, then my own name may be realized as: Alo Vili, Alo Māmea, or Alo Tuataga. I might choose, however, a three- or four-place name, using any combination of my father's names in any order, as long as title precedes personal name for any single individual. Depending on which connection I wished to stress, the following variations are all possible: Alo Māmea Vili, Alo Māmea Tuataga, Alo Tuataga Māmea, Alo Tuataga Vili, or Alo Māmea Tuataga Vili. Should I receive a title of my own, my personal name would then follow my title name, and would serve as a distinguishing marker of my particular branch of the title if it had been subdivided. For example, should I receive the title Tuatō, the most common form of address for me would be Tuatō Alo. In intimate situations, however, I might still be referred to as Alo, or even as Alo + patronym. Even with my own title, any of my patronymic names might be postpended as further distinguishing markers. Again, the particular name chosen would depend on the relationship to be stressed.

Should I receive a second title, Te'o for example, then either of my titles could be the initial segment of my name. Both titles might be used together, with the stressed name going first, but it is not necessary to use all of a person's titles. Commonly, only a contextually stressed title is used at any one time. Finally, my name would conclude with my personal name and, rarely, with the addition of a patronymic form. Thus, given my two titles, my name might be realized with any of the following forms: Tuatō Alo, Tuatō Tc'o, Tc'o Alo, Tc'o Tuatō, Tc'o Tuatō Alo, Tuatō Tc'o Alo, Tuatō Alo Vili, Te'o Alo Vili, Te'o Tuatō Alo Vili, Tuatō Te'o Alo Vili, and so on. My father's titles instead of or in addition to his personal name offer many possibilities.

In general, the proper ordering of elements is: own title(s) + own personal name + father's title(s) + father's personal name. The last two segments are both optional and rare forms, and neither requires the inclusion of the other. Women may and do become chiefs, though chiefship is normally a male prerogative. A woman would use her title and personal name exactly as does a male title holder. An unmarried girl normally uses her father's title or personal name as her surname. Upon marriage, however, she adopts her husband's personal name and/or title(s) as her surname, while her patronymic would be used whenever she returned to her natal village, or in any other context where her status before marriage was stressed.

We can get some idea of the myriad of possible names that a single individual has in his repertory. The addition of a single title (either own title, or that of a father or husband) makes for an increment of a whole new set of appellations. Many of the more elaborate sequences of name segments would be used only rarely, when extreme deference or honor was indicated. Generally, the stressed name or title precedes an unstressed element. Further, the greater the number of segments comprising a name, the greater the honor accruing to the holder.

The Samoan naming system is an excellent paradigm for the Samoan conception of person, reflecting as it does the multiplicity and contextualization of personal identity. A particular name form in Samoan suggests a certain relationship between the named and another social unit. Names thus mark relationships far more clearly than they mark distinct individuals. Relations are to persons, localities, parcels of land, and, even in the case of personal names, to events. Throughout his life a Samoan adds to his repertory new potential name segments, thereby enriching and multiplying his identity. Significantly, while names are easily added, they are, like all parts of a person, rarely lost. They remain as potential sides of a person.

Relationships and contexts—what we would normally consider extrinsic aspects of identity—are the important factors in name selection. The use of title rather than personal name, or in addition to personal name, indicates deference in a formal situation. Personal naming and particularly nicknaming convey intimacy of relationship and lack of significant rank difference. A particular local or kinship link is emphasized by pre-positioning the associated title, while a reference to one's own father's village or family is suggested by the inclusion of a patronym. The stress is on the flexibility in contextualization of identity. Names are the primary markers of complex relationships, and only secondarily define discrete individuals.

Personal Experience

Probably the most striking aspect of Samoan personal identity, as I have described it, is its strongly social and public nature. Notably absent from our discussion thus far have been the more private dimensions of identity, dimensions that are a baseline for the Western sense of a person. To assert as I have that Samoans do not clearly formulate a conception of personality or focus on "the self" is not to say that no personal feelings and inner demands exist for Samoans. On the contrary, we shall see in the following chapter that Samoans have a very lively conception of private experience, but it is a conception of forces that are understood as an ineradicable residue of destructive energy, or will, against which social life is set.

Samoans live most of their lives in a very public arena. The more private aspects of experience are strongly discouraged by the absence of walls in a Samoan house, and by powerful norms of social life, which keep people in almost constant social interaction. Samoans do not seem, on the whole, to like being alone. If they do, they rarely admit to it publicly, since sociability is a strongly approved value. To be alone appears to be equated with being lonely, and Samoan speakers of English frequently cannot understand the distinction between the two terms. Moreover, as we shall see in the following chapters, social isolation not only brings unhappiness, but is also seen to encourage antisocial urges and acts.

Levy (1973) has described in Tahitians a kind of uncanny panic, an existential fear called *me'ame'a* that describes the feelings Tahitians claim to have when they are alone. While I know of no parallel term used by Samoans other than *fefe* (afraid), there is among Samoans nonetheless a similar resistance to any sort of social isolation.

This reluctance to discuss or pursue purely private experience is understandable in light of the largely relational identities that Samoans develop. If a person is understood in terms of particular dimensions of social identity that are selected from a large number of possibilities, then in a significant sense there is for Samoans no absolute reference point for personal identity once they are outside any social context. Alone one remains a bundle of potential relations, with no key for focusing on one rather than another. Lacking any stress on the ultimate resolution or integration of these relations, Samoans will normally avoid any situation that will leave them in social isolation.

Whatever the "scientific" status of such units as persons or personalities, they are important kinds of cultural constructs that may or may not be part of the intersubjective premises of a particular culture. We assume that the presence or absence of such cultural constructs in a particular culture does not provide evidence for the objective existence or nonexistence of these constructs. The lack of a Samoan term for "personality" is certainly not sufficient evidence for the lack of usefulness of the concept in relation to Samoans. On the other hand, it is assumed that such cultural premises do have an important impact on social action within the setting that posits them. For example, comprehending social action in a society that posits a concept of self or of individual is quite different from understanding such action in a society where individual and self are not part of the community's cultural assumptions.

Attributing to cultural beliefs or constructs such moderating influence on social action obliges us to examine our own analytical constructs to determine if they are appropriately neutral or general to apply to the culture under examination. In this chapter, Samoan and Occidental conceptions of the person and of structure have been examined. While both cultures stress a concept of person, it is clear that "personality" and "self" are not appropriate analytical concepts for Samoa.

Understanding the actor's orientation in Samoan social action leads to a consideration of the structuring of that action's social contexts. Differentiation rather than integration of perceptions and of persons is the suggested Samoan mode of orientation in social action. A behaviorist or situationist social theory, stressing perception, social learning, classification of interaction situations, and appropriateness of responses appears more applicable to Samoan social action than does personality disposition or trait theory.

CHAPTER NINE

Action

Although I had lived in Samoa for a number of years in close contact with family and village life, for a long time I remained puzzled by what seemed a paradox. Reserved, dignified, even courtly in bearing, Samoans were also notably aggressive at times. Cautious and meticulous in their skillful negotiation of social relations, they have nonetheless gained something of a reputation in the Pacific for toughness and personal assertiveness in relations with others.

These apparent contradictions have long been noted in one form or another by observers of Samoa. Lemert, a social psychologist with an interest in cross-cultural comparisons of deviance, compared three Polynesian societies in terms of alcohol consumption. He noted what he characterized as disruptive and unintegrated effects of alcoholic consumption on Samoan personality, particularly as compared with Tahiti and Rarotonga.[1] Lemert characterized Samoan personality as suggesting "a deep sub-stratum of aggression . . . which readily comes to the surface with intoxication" (1972:230). This aggression, he asserts, "is in part culturally inculcated . . . [and] encouraged in certain kinds of structural situations." More specifically, for Lemert,

Samoan aggression differs from that in Tahitians and Cook Islanders in being cumulative, slow-burning and explosive. In some forms it comes very close to the psychiatric concept of "free-floating" aggression, subject to hair-trigger release. A Samoan may brood for weeks over what he regards as an injustice and then with an apparently trivial provocation burst into a murderous rage. (ibid.)

The aggression is explained by Lemert in terms of the frustration–aggression hypothesis. Samoan aggressiveness, says Lemert, rather than being normally distributed throughout the Samoan population, appears to characterize untitled men. It is this group, the explanation goes, that is most directly under the authority of the chiefs, most commonly called on to do their bidding, and thus, in some sense, the most "oppressed" segment of Samoan society. Lemert stresses Samoa's generally "conservative emphasis" that places a high value on "conformity, acceptance of group decisions, ceremonial compliance and politeness in interpersonal interaction" (ibid.). Samoan drinking, Lemert asserts, "while it indirectly expresses some of the values of Samoan culture . . . is much more conspicuously a mechanism or device through which individuals in group settings find release for a variety of unintegrated feelings and impulses" (1972:225). Oppressed most severely, their personal expression most restricted by their subservient relationship to the chiefs, the youth find a natural outlet for their frustrations in alcohol.

In Lemert's account of Samoan drinking behavior, disruptive and aggressive behavior appear simultaneously to express and also deny basic Samoan values. Thus implicitly at least, Samoan values seem to assert contradictory messages, a primary set of values denying aggression and stressing obedience, authority, and passivity, and a secondary set encouraging egocentric and aggressive behavior.

Aggression, in this account, appears to be largely a phenomenon of "individual" needs and drives frustrated by the "social." Some variant of this assumption is characteristic of most aggression-as-frustration theories (LeVine 1973:63–64). There are significant parallels here, as we shall see, with Mead's handling of Samoan aggression.

A third point is that Lemert assumes that "normally" feelings and impulses must be integrated in some way within the individual, and when they are not, as in the apparent case of the Samoan youth, they become destructively expressed in aggression. What these impulses are to be integrated with, however, is not so clear in this account. Aggression seems to be, for Lemert, a negative or residual phenomenon, the product óf poorly integrated personality or social institutions. Aggression is thus a release, or outlet, for frustration, for badly integrated parts of personality; that is, for unsocialized drives. Harmony, integration, and a "fit" among all parts of a "personality system" are presumed to be normal.

At the other end of the spectrum are such observations as the following, made by an early German resident of Samoa in the first quarter of the century.

The Samoans are the most polite people in the South Seas; they alone have a word for please: *fa'a-molemole.* . . . You promise him anything, or even refuse to comply with his greatest wish most politely he will say *"fa'afetai"* and never be angry with you. But inwardly he will curse you, but that does not matter   His politeness is often the cause of what one calls lies. . . . Why does he so? For his respect to you. . . . Nor he [sic] will ever a Samoan ever contest you. (Neffgen n.d.)

A naive observation by an untrained eye, clouded with the romantic mystique of the South Seas, we might conclude, and thus dismiss the case. And yet, this characterization is echoed in Margaret Mead's characterization of Samoan personality.

In the field of personal relationships the freedom of choice allowed the individuals is prevented from having more important results by the low level of appreciation of personality differences. . . . So that the freedom in personal choices operates mainly in reducing the poignancy of personal relations, the element of conflict, the need for making painful choices. The emotional tone of the society is consequently more moderate, less charged with strain and violence. It never exerts sufficient repression to call forth a significant rebellion from the individual. . . . The individual need commit no murder, need not even muster up a fine rage to escape from a disagreeable situation—he simply slips out of it into the house next door. Such a setting does not provoke violent, strikingly marked personalities; it is kind to all and does not make sufficient demands upon any. (Mead 1928:494)

Mead's characterization of Samoan personality as low key, passive, and gentle appears also in *Coming of Age in Samoa,* where it is seen as a product of a gradual and benign socialization "which makes growing up so easy, so simple a matter" (1929:198). The society that produces such a personality type is, to Mead, casual in tone, "a place where no one plays for very high stakes, no one pays very high prices" (*ibid.*). Despite the contradictory evidence that has been published since her own research, Mead has held firmly to this characterization of Samoan personality. In her recent autobiography, for instance, she remembers Samoans as "the happiest people I have ever known. . . . From childhood they moved slowly and easily into an adult world that was wholly familiar and enjoyable. Year after year from childhood on they could sing the same songs and dance the same dances . . . with pleasure" (Mead 1970:29).

While some observers appear to have viewed Samoan personality with one eye shut, observing half truths, whether polite passivity without aggression or an aggressiveness lacking reserve and control, other observers have noted the strongly contradictory tendencies of Samoan personality. The Keesings, for instance, have summarized the contradictions that have characterized descriptions of Samoan personality, noting that there has been a paradoxical stress on " 'security,' 'conformity,' and 'group responsibility' and the symmetrical balancing of social structures on the one hand . . . [and] 'devisiveness,' 'deviousness,' 'turbulence,' and the potential of 'violence' on the other" (Keesing and Keesing 1956:8). A similar observation is made of the Samoan male personality by Maxwell. The male, says Maxwell, "must strike a balance between his inclination to dominate others . . . and the necessity for sometimes maintaining a respectful or dignified silence" (Maxwell 1969:156). Although strikingly similar to the Keesings' account of the paradoxical nature of Samoan personality, Maxwell's formulation differs from it in a subtle, yet significant sense. The aggressive dimension of Samoan behavior is attributed by Maxwell to the Samoan's "inclination to dominate others." Aggression is thus an expression of inner drives. Passivity and politeness, however, are social "necessity" and, by implication, external to the individual and located in the social order itself.

This pervasive tendency to translate the opposition between passivity and aggressiveness into one between social controls and individual drives is clearly evident in the writing of Mead on Samoan personality. Just as her account of Samoan personality stresses the passivity and balance over aggression and poor integration, so also her account of cultural patterns in Samoa stresses the social as dominating the individual. "The dominant note in Samoan society," she writes,

is its prevailingly social emphasis. All of a Samoan's interests, all of his emotion, is centered upon his relationship to his fellows within an elaborate and cherished social pattern . . . individual work and play, individual religious activity, art and personal relationships have never been admitted, and receive scant attention from the society. . . . All attempts at a development of personality along other than social lines . . . wither in the chilly atmosphere of negligent disapproval. (Mead 1930:10)

Similarly, Mead asserts that in Samoa social activities are judged "important and deserving of endless ritual respect," while there is a "complementary feeling that those things done alone are at least suspect, if not downright wrong." (1930:81)

For Mead, then, maturation and socialization suggest the imposition of the social pattern on "individual tendencies," thereby creating a child who can *māfaufau* (judge). In this respect Mead's vision of what it means to come of age in Samoa suggests the attainment of harmony "between the individual tendencies and the pattern requirements" (*ibid.*).

Individual and social tendencies differ, in this account, not simply in their origin but also in their character. The two are polar opposites that Mead, in a later paper, describes as follows.

. . . two tendencies of Samoan social organization, the tendency to place each individual, each household, each village, even (in Western Samoa) each district in a hierarchy, wherein each is dignified only by its relationship to the whole, each performs tasks which contribute to the honor and well-being of the whole, and competition is completely impossible. The opposite tendency, the rebellion of units against this subordination to a plan and their use of a place within a component unit to foment trouble and rivalry with other units, while not so strong, is always present. (1965:263)

Mead has left unanalyzed and thus unclarified the issue of whether we are to understand this dualism as (a) an opposition between the social pattern and the individual (i.e., unsocialized) drives, (b) an opposition between two aspects of social organization, or (c) a dichotomy between two dimensions of the socialized personality. Despite her assertion that we can understand these tendencies as inherent in social organization, Mead appears far more committed to the nature:culture :: individual:society paradigm that sees culture as a "field" upon which each individual attempts to "exercise . . . his particular talents." (1929:481)

Āmio and *Aga*: Fundamental Samoan Categories of Action

Turning from outsiders' perceptions of Samoan behavior to Samoans' own understandings of action, we are in a much better position to understand the "logic" of the apparent contradictions we have noted. Samoans themselves have a fairly elaborate ideology of human behavior in relation to human nature and society. An exploration of this ideology is, in light of what is shown in the characterizations of Samoan behavior presented above, particularly enlightening.

Several years after I had become acquainted with Samoa, I gradually became aware that Samoans sorted human behavior into two fundamental categories. Moreover, each of the categories could be distinguished by name: *aga* on the one hand, and *āmio* on the other. Over the years, I have become aware of just how significant this distinction is in understanding Samoans' own assessments of human behavior.

Āmio describes a category of behavior that might be called "personal," focusing on the individual will or drives as the source of behavior. *Āmio* is a largely descriptive category of behavior, characterizing the actions of particular people. *Aga,* on the other hand, is more clearly prescriptive, suggesting categories of abstract behavioral styles appropriate to certain socially defined statuses. "Social conduct" or (in the Parsonian sense) "social action" might better describe *aga* than the term "behavior."

Āmio represents the socially unconditioned aspects of behavior that point away from social norms, toward personal drives or desires as the conditioning factors.[2] One's *āmio* may be virtuous (*āmio lelei*) (good *āmio*) or (more likely) it will be described as bad behavior (*āmio leaga*). In either case, a judgment about *āmio* focuses on a particular person rather than on social types of behavior. On the other hand, *aga lelei* (good social conduct) and its specific forms such as *agāli'i* (chiefly action) or *agavaivai* (humble conduct) or *aga leaga* (improper social conduct) and its specific forms such as *agamālosi* (crude conduct) or *agasala* (sinful conduct) are judgments that observers make about one's conduct in terms of socially prescribed styles of conduct. They are thus implicit statements about socialization—the degree of "fit" between actual behavior and social norms.

One very perceptive informant, a male of twenty-six, was able to describe the differences between these terms clearly.

The word *āmio* means the things you do that originate from yourself. It's your own choice; your *āmio* is your option. But the word *aga,* that's the view of the other people as they observe you (*faitauina 'oe*). That's the considered judgment (*maitau mai*) of others about you. . . . Whereas you can say to yourself "my *āmio*," you can never say "my *aga*" referring to yourself. That's an expression used by others when they judge you.

In that *aga* is a social category of behavior it can never be known to the actor himself except through his relations with others, a point that suggests the dependence of Samoans on other's knowledge of their actions for social control.

While virtuous *āmio* or evil *aga* are both conceivable to Samoans, it is significant that most of the compound terms made from *āmio* refer to acts that are socially disruptive, while *aga* is found principally in compound terms denoting forms of virtue. Thus *āmio pua'a* (piggish behavior), *āmio 'inosia* (disgusting behavior), and *āmio valea* (stupid/idiotic behavior) are all common ways of commenting negatively on someone's behavior. *Āmio tonu* (righteous behavior) is also possible, suggesting that personal impulse may lead to socially desirable consequences. Conversely, *agatonu* (righteous conduct), *agāli'i* and *agavaivai* are the dominant kinds of compound terms using *aga*. The fact that less virtuous behaviors such as *aga leaga* or *agamālosi* may also be expressed by *aga* suggests that social norms may include certain forms of behavior from particular classes of people (like children, untitled youth, or even from *tulāfale*) that are both socially disapproved and yet normally expected.[3]

Used alone, *āmio* frequently implies aggressive acts motivated by self-serving impulses and appetites. Erotic desires or hunger are most commonly suggested by the term. *Fai le āmio* (literally, "do" the *āmio*) implies following such drives, usually at the expense of others. It is sometimes used to refer to young men prowling about at night in search of amorous adventure or to the stealing of chickens or pigs to gratify a sudden protein hunger. It is interesting to note that while human beings are understood to possess the potential for both *āmio* and *aga*, animals may be described only in terms of *āmio*. *Āmio pua'a* (the behavior of pigs) or *āmio maile* (the behavior of dogs) are possible forms, but *aga pua'a* or *aga maile* would sound ludicrous to Samoan ears.

The term *aganu'u* (the *aga* of human settlements) is the Samoan word for human culture. The form *āmionu'u*, however, would sound as silly as would the association of *aga* with animals. Thus it would seem that the capacity for *aga* separates humans from animals, while the capacity for *āmio* suggests the animal in man.[4]

Both *āmio* and *aga* have derivitive forms made by appending the nominalizing suffix *-ga* to the base terms. The effect is to generalize the terms from specific kinds of acts and characteristics to more general classes of such characteristics. Thus, while *āmio* describes the actual acts of a particular person, the nominalized form *āmioga* refers to acts typical of a group or type of person. More specifically, the term *āmioga* would be used in reference to characteristic acts of children (*tamaiti*), young people (*tagata talavou*), or most characteristically the acts of the younger generation (*tupulaga fou*), but never to the acts of those of mature age or noble rank. One informant insisted that *āmioga* was nearly like *aga*, but was a less dignified term. Certainly, in generalizing acts to characterize whole groups, *āmioga* suggests behavior one step more socialized than simple *āmio*.

The parallel modification of *aga* with the nominalizing suffix results in the form *agaga*, which is often translated as "soul" or "spirit."[5] In fact, the term *agaga* is more complex than this, and its original meaning seems to have become at least partially obscured through the use of *agaga* in the Samoan Bible for "soul" or "spirit." On the one hand, the term refers to an intention to perform an act, or to the essential core of an act or saying.

This ambiguity implicit in locating the intention in action both in the actor and in the act itself is characteristic of Samoan thought about the relation of actor to act. On the other hand, the term does appear to suggest something like an inner essence of a person, a kind of source of human action. Notably, however, this core or "inner" soul appears to be derived from the term for social (role-based) conduct, and (linguistically at least) identifies the "innermost" aspect of the personality with public norms rather than with private experience.

In the parallel sets *āmio/āmioga* and *aga/agaga* there is an implicit paradigm for socialization in Samoan conception. In *āmioga* we have the externalization of a personal impulse in its application to a general category of people. In *agaga,* by contrast, we have the internalization of a set of social forms as an aggregate of role-based norms for conduct. The model for socialization implied by these sets is the gradual replacement of purely personal and asocial impulses by a set of socially derived conventional norms approaching the point where one's inner life is in some sort of harmony with the demands of social life.[6] Such a harmony is understood to be evanescent at best, and generally unattainable, *āmio* always reserving a voice in an endless dialogue with society.

In the rest of this chapter, I shall explore in greater detail some of the important assumptions that underlie this fundamental Samoan distinction between *āmio* and *aga.*[7]

The Anatomy of Āmio: Samoan Conceptions of Human Nature

The distinction between *āmio* and *aga*, two important "sides" of each person, is really a kind of Samoan ideology distinguishing human nature from culture. This nature/culture distinction, which Levi-Strauss has made famous in anthropology as a basic intellectual problem underlying many social institutions, is an important Samoan assumption. Possessing both a natural component of aggressive drives and a social aspect of cultural norms for proper conduct, *tagata* or man has two general natures, each a facet of his total makeup. Samoan legends are replete with references to creatures in which this dual nature is clearly manifest, creatures that are said to be *itū lua*, made of two sides, one human and the other demonic or animal-like. The first humans, as described in Chapter 8, had a kind of double origin. Initially, they were merely parts—heads and limbs, which emerged from *ilo* or maggots. In their final form, however, they were the product of the proper juxtaposition of these parts, an act of Tuli the Connector or Messenger, himself a manifestation of the god Tagaloa.

Most of the remainder of this study will explore Samoan conceptions of human culture. First, however, I will examine a Samoan vision of natural man: an anatomy of *āmio*.

One of the first questions that I put to the approximately fifty informants interviewed concerned their characterization of an unsocialized human nature. I asked informants to characterize life in Samoa were all laws and regulations suddenly rescinded, and also to describe a society that had no laws and regulations or authorities. Informants' answers to both of these questions were virtually unanimous. The vision of human nature emerging from these responses suggests a Hobbesian state of nature marked by passions, self-interests, and ubiquitous conflict. The following comments were typical.

If there were no such things as laws in Samoa, this land would be the wildest, most uncontrollable place, with evil behavior [*āmio leaga*] on the part of the youth [*tupulaga*]. . . . If there were no laws at all everyone would behave badly. (Male, eighteen years old, rural Upolu)

There would be universal ill will/envy [*loto leaga*]. If people had the run of their own personal feelings, were allowed to express their own wills, they would soon come to have ill will against each other. One person would see that another family had something nice, and he'd go and destroy it. (Male, fourteen years old, rural Savai'i)

If there were no laws this village would be no good because each person would live according to his own thoughts. If I wanted to be a big shot [*fia sili*] I'd go ahead and do it; if I wanted to take charge of everything [*fia pule*] then I'd do that. In this life we have here, we are cautious and respectful because of our laws. If we had no laws, then we'd have an unsightly [*matagā*] village, in terms of the behavior of the residents. [This is] because there are differences in the lives of the people; there are people who have controlled behavior [*āmio pulea*] and also those whose actions are uncontrolled [*āmio lē pulea*]; those who are properly educated [*a'oa'oina*] and those who are not properly educated. (Female, twenty-eight, rural Savai'i)

Everyone would go about raping, murdering, and stealing at will. Mainly because this village just can't seem to make honest laws and stick to them. They make them, put them aside, make them again, and then ignore them once again. (Female, elderly, rural Savai'i)

They would be all heathens [*fa'apaupau*]. That means that they would all live in disrespectful ways [*tū fa'alēmigao*], doing things they should/must not do. (Male, twenty-three, Manono)

If there were no laws, people would go about happily killing each other, for they would have no fear of jail to stop them. They wouldn't worry since there was no law. They'd do whatever they wanted. (Male, twenty, rural Savai'i, employed in Apia)

Behavior would be very evil [*leaga*]. If someone wanted to eat he would just walk into a house, and if the man and woman [i.e., the residents] were there, he'd take over the house. The whole village would be broken apart. (Male, sixteen years old, Apia)

If you live free, then you'll have some people killing others, fighting and doing all sorts of bad things [*mea leaga*]. For there would be no laws to advise people [*faufautuaina*] of the proper way to act. If the law perishes [*oti*] so will the judgment [*māfaufau*] of the people. They will no longer think about doing any good thing. People will just go about indiscriminately doing that which is good [*lelei*] and that which is bad [*leaga*] with nothing to advise their thoughts. (Female, seventeen years old, Apia)

In the Samoan conception, human nature appears to be selfish, impulsive, and destructive. The last of the above statements, moreover, suggests that the function of laws (and perhaps, by extension, society in general) is to provide a moral template or "adviser" enabling people to discriminate good from evil. There is some indication in the interviews that Samoans associate this state of nature in certain aspects with pre-Christian Samoa, a time when Samoans were heathens (*fa'apaupau*) and lived in darkness (*fa'apouliuli*). Take for instance the following statement, which is representative of many of the views expressed by informants.

In ancient times people were wild. People killed each other. People were delivered up as gifts to other people. People lived like wild animals. But nowadays, since the arrival of the Church [*lotu*] we have all been enlightened and people have changed. . . . In the days before the Church arrived here, people lived uncontrolled lives. Now we have the Church as well as the authority of the *matai* and their laws. But in those ancient days, as our tales tell us, people lived like animals. People ate each other. . . . The Bible was brought here before there were any chiefs to rule Samoa. . . . There was no real authority over people. Each person was his own master. Now, however, we have the Church.

Laws and other external impositions of control and authority not only prevent destructive and selfish acts, but they constrain people to stay put rather than to roam about as is their natural impulse. Social laws channel energy to socially useful tasks. One informant felt that without laws: "There would be no thought given to planting and to doing useful chores, but only to living it up, having a good time. People would move about [*alu solo*] and continually eat here and there ['*ai'ai solo*]."

Freedom and Constraint

Given these Samoan assumptions about human nature and the state of social life in a society lacking strong external authority over individual impulses, we would expect Samoans to possess a negative ethics of constraint, as opposed to a directed ethics whose prescriptions are based on positively articulated and directed goals such as happiness, health, or pleasure. A negative ethics of constraint is based on a goal of achieving the good through the avoidance of evil. In fact, Samoans do appear to articulate positive ends or goals for social life such as mutual love, health, or peace, but these are often described in terms of the containment of their opposite states.

The Samoan language places a far greater emphasis on concepts of constraint than on freedom. I know of but a single word for "free," *sa'oloto*, which means literally feelings that are correct or straight. Samoan concepts of constraints on behavior are expressed with a more elaborate vocabulary. *Pule* is the most general word for authority, and its derivative *taupulega* refers to general or extensive authority. *Teu* means "to put in order" or "to clean up" and may refer to ordering one's feelings or behavior which, like a lawn or a house, may have grown disorderly. One may *teu* a conflict or one's own behavior, and while such an ordering of behavior may occur in the face of strong external authority, the stress is on the internal ordering of one's own actions in the face of a shame-producing or punishing threat. Whereas *pule* generally suggests externalized control over another, *teu lau āmio* (putting one's feelings in order) stresses a kind of self-control.

Most emphatically external is the control suggested by the term *puipui,* which means literally "to wall in" or "to protect." The adjective *māopopo* means "well organized" or "properly run" and would describe a village that had an effective chiefs' system. The word derives from the root *opo* "to grasp" or "to hold firm" and does not suggest, as *teu* does, that there has been disorder that has been set straight.

Pulea, the perfect form of the verb *pule,* means "controlled" or "under control" and is frequently used in the form *āmio pulea* suggesting behavior that is under control. *Loto pulea* means "controlled feelings," *loto* being a quasi-bodily organ or part of the anatomy located in the abdomen, which may become filled with various emotions.

Several terms connote more negative aspects of control. *Saesaetia,* meaning "tied up" or "bound," is often used with *loto* when one's feelings are all bottled up, and free expression is prohibited. The word expressing sadness of feelings, *fa'anoanoa,* has a similar semantic association, deriving from the word *noa* (to tie up). While these words suggesting the binding of one's feelings are frequently used to express undesirable and unpleasant aspects of social control, they are not unambiguous in this context, and have clear positive associations as well. I shall return to this ambiguity below.

Loss of control is generally expressed through the negation of the words for control. Thus *lē pulea* and *lē maopōpo* refer to various kinds of social disorganization. *Mo'i'ini* is a positive expression for being "out of control."

Despite the clear linguistic stress on concepts of constraint as opposed to those suggesting freedom, Samoans express a marked ambivalence in their attitudes toward both constraint and freedom. This ambivalence suggests a strong internal conflict or contradiction in Samoan attitudes toward authority. For instance, the desirable and undesirable aspects of freedom that Samoans express are often essentially identical. One informant, for instance, an Apia youth of seventeen, described why he felt ambivalent about what he called the "free life," and why it was good on the one hand but bad on the other.

Freedom is good in the sense that I wouldn't have to touch any work. I'd be free to sit around the house and go to the pictures when I wanted to. It would be up to me when I went and played around. That's good. But on the other hand it's bad in the same sense that you would just go on your own way and do whatever you wanted, and you wouldn't do any chores like plantation work, which you should do. You wouldn't do any other useful work.

Here good and bad could be interchanged, and the meaning would be the same.

Constraint and freedom have, for Samoans, certain temporal and spatial associations. I asked informants, for instance, where they felt most free, and received three distinct responses, each suggesting a distinct implicit semantic opposition.

Freedom: Home and Family

Some informants said that they felt most free (*sa'oloto*) in their own households, with their own family. The implicit contrast here is that between kinsman and stranger, in which context "stranger" (*tagata 'ese*) can mean unknown person, as well as a known individual from an unrelated kin group. This equation of freedom and family life constitutes something of a convention in popular songs and verse. The following song, for example, belongs to a class of hortatory popular songs encouraging virtue and discouraging vice.

> Greetings to those who have lived enslaved,
> Brothers who have misused their lives,
> Who have no freedom,
> Like He who died, the Savior.
> Only in the family, with your true parents
> Will true joy be found.
>
> Only in the family, with your true parents
> Will true joy be found.
>
> If you live among strangers,
> You will work with great caution.
> You will not joke loudly,
> And if reprimanded, you will be afraid.
> In your own family, you may rest,
> Act however you wish.
> Go back to your own people,
> Just like the penitent son.
>
> This is just a word of advice
> For the youth of Samoa.
> Lead cautious lives, lest you be enslaved.
> Honest service will be a crowning achievement.
> Samoans, this is my advice
> So that you may lead useful lives.

This popular attitude toward living with strangers was echoed by a Savai'i woman in a statement about the life of a married woman residing with her husband's household.

The life of a woman who lives with her husband's *'āiga* is all bound up [*saesaetia*]. She cannot simply decide to go somewhere without the approval of her husband. But if I have no husband and want to go to Apia, then I simply pack my bags and go. There is no one to hold me back.

Freedom: The Urban Area

For Samoans, the urban area (Apia or, in American Samoa, Pagopago) and all overseas countries are associated with personal freedom. With no chiefs on the spot to observe one's actions, and without the omnipresent intimate social ties that lead to gossip and enjoin cautious social relations, Apia is for many Samoans an attractive escape from the obligations of village and domestic life. Life is Apia, for rural villagers, is seen as free from the drudgery of Samoan chores to which one is committed in the village. A woman of twenty-eight residing in rural Savai'i but educated in the urban area, expressed the following common attitude towards the town.

Here in Samoa, I am not really free [*sa'oloto*] anywhere I go. There are so many different chores to be done. In my understanding of the word, the only place you can be "free" [uses English word] is in the "town" [English word]. Just eating, bathing, going to have some fun, and sleeping. There's nothing to enslave their thoughts and feelings as there is here.

Later in the interview, this informant expressed ambivalence about Apia life, contrasting the control and orderliness of village life with the freedom and disorder of Apia life. However, life in Apia was also more enlightened than that in the rural villages.

In Apia, people live in an enlightened way. They live a good, clean life. Here in the rural area, life is very different. In the urban area, you wake up in the morning, drink your tea, while here you wake up and immediately begin to do your chores, since your chores to get done are always heavy on your mind. You can only eat at noon, when the morning chores are finished. . . . People are far better controlled here in the rural areas than in the urban area. In Apia there's not just one kind of person, but many sorts of people mixed up together. And there's no one to look after all the people except for the police department, which can look after the bad behavior of people. . . . In Apia we find badly behaved people. But here in Savai'i we find them too. It's just that [here] the authority is heavier, and so people live more cautiously.

Freedom: The Bush and the Plantation

The bush or plantation was the third area associated with freedom. If life in Apia provides freedom from obligations and malicious gossip and freedom to roam about at will, and the household provides freedom from dangerous or uncertain encounters with strangers, the bush or plantation lands suggest freedom from the distractions of all social intercourse, and the opportunity to pursue domestic chores in relative tranquillity. One Savai'i woman admitted her longing for this freedom in an interview.

I would love to live in a house far away from here [the village], in the plantation, because I would no longer have to listen to tales or hear about the fights that were going on. I wouldn't go about doing mischief. I would go and do the chores I had to get done, and when I had finished, I'd go to sleep. But here in the center of the village ['a'ai] I go about here and there listening to gossip from the various parts of the village, and I return home filled with anger. Then maybe the kids will come home and start to make noise, and cry, and ears will ache and so I'll beat them and throw them out of the house. My head hurts because of all of the noise the kids make. Then we'd hear about the fight that the family over there was having, and I'd run to watch it. The Samoan, he loves to watch such things because then he can gossip about it. But living alone in the bush, he gets into no trouble. He is happy and has his evening worship to God every night, then rests and goes to sleep. No trouble.

This view was echoed by a youth of twenty who came from rural Savai'i but employed in Apia. "It's best if I go and live by myself. Just me. And if I have a wife and kids, then that's fine too. But then we should live by ourselves so that my feelings don't get troubled by other people, and we can live peacefully."

For many Samoans, it appears that intense social life provides control on behavior, and yet presents precisely the temptations and incitements to passions that lead to conflict. Life in the village means the control from *matai* and fellow villagers over private passions, but it also provides the very conditions in which those passions thrive. In the urban area there is freedom *to* move about, and this is one sort of freedom for Samoans. In the bush there is freedom *from* such excitement. One lives in the plantation a still, tranquil existence.

The bush is a morally ambiguous setting, however, since it is associated not only with freedom from the complex personal entanglements of village life, but also with the darker passions of unsocialized or uncivilized existence. This ambiguous status associated with the periphery of the village is the converse of the status of life in the village center. Samoans interviewed showed a marked ambivalence toward intense social relations, seeing in them at once the seeds of social conflict and the controls on that potential conflict.

If the geographic areas peripheral to traditional social life—Apia on the one hand, and the bush and plantation on the other—are associated with a certain freedom from constraint, this leaves the village proper, specifically the residential core, the *'a'ai* and the *malae,* as the center of control and authority. One must be particularly cautious when on the main road or the *malae,* and many of the village regulations, as has been noted, apply specifically to these focal points of dignified and cautious behavior.

Freedom for Samoans is not simply a desired state; nor is constraint solely to be avoided. Given Samoan assumptions about human nature, it is understandable that freedom is largely valued negatively and associated with uncontrolled passions, selfish and therefore antisocial desires, and disorder. I have considered the state of anarchy that Samoans associate with freedom from laws. "A free life," suggested one informant, "is like a life of animals. One has no responsibilities." To another, freedom suggested the absence of *mamalu* (dignity): "if we lived," he said, "according to our own desires, there would be no dignity in our culture. Things are kept well ordered in order to keep the culture dignified."

In the Samoan conception, dignity and social order are negative qualities in the sense that they are defined as the constraint or containment of natural urges and tendencies. Commitment to law and village authority proceeds in this understanding from the desire to contain or "bind up" destructive passions. An elderly lady from Savai'i was asked a question about whether she approved of all village laws and regulations.

Yes. For all laws of the village are very good. Everyone in the village is very happy about them. They protect [*puipui*] us from evil acts of all sorts. . . . Another thing: if a boy wants to go [sexually] to a girl, then he goes creeping to her at night [*moetolo*] while she sleeps. You know what [*moetolo*] is? Well, it's things like that which are bound up [*saesae*] by the chiefs. So that boys will not drink beer or gamble, and so that everyone will be bound up.

The practice in some villages of banning communal sleeping houses both for boys and for girls is justified on the ground that intense social life encourages antisocial urges or temptations. One youth from Savai'i explained in the following terms why he felt that sleeping houses had been banned in his village.

This has been banned, because it is from such houses that willful and destructive behavior springs. If we boys have our sleeping houses here, and we have cemented a good relationship, then surely notions will rise up [*tauosooso*] in us, if not to go creeping to sleeping girls, then to go and steal pigs or chickens to eat, or some other sort of theft.

Of the sleeping house, a woman in the same village as this informant made the following remarks.

[The sleeping houses are now prohibited] to protect the girls from things that might happen if they all slept together. Especially things by other boys. Some girl might go and take one of the other girls with her to her boyfriend. . . . The girls would go *fa'asoa* [mediate in love affairs] as we call it. The women protect them from this, so that nothing evil occurs.

Although I have here translated *puipui* as "protect," it is important to recognize that it has here a sense quite foreign to Western concepts of protection. The Samoan use of the term *puipui* suggests not an external threat to the individual, but rather forces at once within the individual and external to him, which the actor must be protected against. Temptations, desires, and even actions provoked by situations are within the actors but not equated with them. I shall return to this interesting Samoan conception of the separation of the actor from his feelings or thoughts in chapter 10, in the context of Samoan notions of responsibility for action.

In addition to spatial dimensions, control and freedom also have temporal dimensions. In one sense, freedom is associated with daylight, where there is *mālamalama* (light/understanding). The constraints of law and chiefly authority are not so important in the daylight, when everyone and their actions are in full public view, but operate mainly at night (*pō*) when the world is, both literally and figuratively, bathed in darkness (*pōuliuli*). One youth from the island of Manono said that he felt that people were free in the daytime but not at night.

I've heard that some of our ancestors had set things down so that in the day if evil erupts [*osofia*, "springs up"] like spirit possession, it's up to you yourself to deal with it. But when night falls, then it is the chiefs' business. Then if you think you can handle these things yourself in the nighttime, well, bad things happen. For at night it's very dark and no living person can see what's going on, and even if they can see, they can't see very far. This [constraint on night activities] is correct, too, in my opinion.

The freedom associated with the daylight hours is the relative freedom from formal control institutions, such as curfews or *matai* patrols. This freedom is made possible by the general effectiveness of informal controls in the daytime, when eye and tongue provide effective instruments of social constraint. As one informant put it, "in the daylight people can see each other; while in the night, when people are preparing to sleep, we can each do our will." Formal and informal controls in this sense occupy complementary arenas both spatially and temporally. In the daytime, one is relatively (though hardly totally) free from law and chiefly authority, because social life is most intensely public at this time. It is, in Samoan thought, such intense sociality that is both the greatest spur to private passion and the most effective control on it.

These ambivalent attitudes toward freedom and control characterize the attitudes of a great many Samoans with whom I am familiar. The two attitudes are, in fact, two "sides" of the same issue, and each attitude finds its normal expression in a distinctive set of contexts. Sometimes, however, this ambivalence emerges sharply in a single exchange with an informant.

I have two examples of such an interview. The first is an excerpt from an interview with a fifteen-year-old youth from the Apia area who, at the time of the talk, was a high school student. The entire exchange is reproduced below, with the interviewer's questions enclosed in parentheses.

(Where do you feel you are most free in your life?) I'm free if I'm bad and I don't help my mother, and only my small siblings do all the work. [I'm free if] I come home from school and only play around.

(Is this freedom good or bad?) It's good in Samoan custom. Samoans all like to be free like this, because then they can just sit around and not do any work or anything.

(How can you call it a good thing in Samoan culture if Samoans are rarely free in a village setting, and you are not free under the traditional authority of a *matai*?) People are all different. Some want the rule of the chiefs because they like it, but others think that they are enslaved by the chiefs.

(What do you think?) I don't like to live a free life. I'd prefer to live under the rule of the chiefs. I wouldn't want freedom because then I'd just go and roam about [*ta'a*] or go to the movies. I'd really prefer going to watch the chiefs in their meetings.

(Is it better to live under the authority of the chiefs, or is it better to control your own life?) It's better for me to live under the authority of the chiefs, for they can decide things for me until I'm older and can judge better.

The ambivalence and apparent contradictions in these responses were partly induced by my questioning style, through subtle shifts that were injected into my intonation and physical proximity to the informant to elicit what I had come to recognize as context-bound concealed beliefs. This tendency of Samoans to respond according to social interactional context rather than to express what we would call personal "conviction" is a characteristic feature of Samoan social action. In the following excerpt, again with an Apia youth, I was able gradually to shift the context of the interview through kinesic and linguistic cue changes (see chapter 13) from a formal, constrained situation to a relatively intimate and free situation. The effect of these shifts on the attitudes of the informant toward social constraint and freedom was marked. I had been discussing with the informant the system of village laws, and had asked him whether he felt that all of the various regulations and constraints on individual behavior were necessary and just. The conclusion of the interview is reproduced here.

(Do you think that the law prohibiting girls from wearing miniskirts is a good law?)
Yes, it is a very good law.

(Why do you think it is good?)
Well, the girls have not grown up wearing this type of clothes.

(Yes, but the boys in Samoa haven't grown up wearing pants, have they?)
Yes, but as you know, it's all right for *pālagi* girls to wear pants and miniskirts, but as for Samoan girls, it's not right. I don't know what the elders think, but as

for me, it is not really a good thing to forbid them to wear these clothes, and I think that minis and shorts should not be prohibited.

(In your opinion, which of the laws is the most important for the welfare and the protection of the villagers?)
For the good of the village?

(Yes.)
Well, the most important law of the village is that which says that you must all go to church. Oh, wait a minute! The most important law is the evening curfew; you know, the one at night.

(Why do you think that you should be controlled by others, and not by yourself?)
No! Each man is his own boss!

(But didn't you just say that the curfew is the most important law?)
Look, the real truth is that if all laws were suspended [literally, *tatala* "opened"], that would be the best thing.

(Why?)
There should no longer be any laws at all. It's a bad thing that the village is doing.

(Why do you think it's a bad thing?)
Just because! That's my understanding of the matter. People should not be prevented from doing things that they want, and punished for it.

(In your understanding, if people lived according to their own wants, and all laws were suspended, would they behave well or badly?)
Badly.

(Why?)
That's just what people are like.

(If everyone lived outside the authority of other people, how would everyone act?)
Badly! I mean well behaved—for some people. The laws, they are useful for people who act badly.

The logic of this exchange appears diffracted and inconsistent to the Western reader. Both strong respect for and hostility toward strong external control on individual behavior is clear in the attitude of the informant. The boundary between the expression of one or the other attitude is that between formal and intimate contexts. Both opinions, however, must be considered equally as the informant's true "convictions" and are contradictory only because here the context-defining cues have been purposely confused, and thus the context is rendered illogical. The problem is thus more with the ambiguity of the context than with the inconsistency of the informant.

In human affairs, Samoans recognize an essential duality to experience, two opposed human capacities. In identifying the one that Samoans call *āmio* with natural impulses linking man with animals, and the other—*aga*— with the distinctly human capacities for cultural life, we have identified a Samoan version of a dualism popular with anthropologists. It is important to recognize, though, that the opposition between *āmio* and *aga* is not quite the same as a simple dualism of nature and culture. For while *aga* does suggest the culturally derived aspects of behavior, *āmio* represents a *conception* of natural impulse, not nature itself.

In succeeding chapters I shall trace some of the ways in which Samoan culture reifies and thus coopts this conception of human nature, in the form of symbolic representations of what are understood as natural human capacities. While *āmio* "in the raw" may be glimpsed when violence erupts and passions spill over, no longer bound by the normal restraints of social life, one can also see in many Samoan institutions—political, linguistic, aesthetic—a Samoan attempt to control *āmio* by according it a carefully modulated cultural representation.

CHAPTER TEN

Knowledge and Judgment

In the West, the relation between sensing and knowing the world is problematical and complex. At best, accessible knowledge may be a diminished version of the deeper truth that is inaccessible to human understanding. This is the basic Kantian distinction between the accessible phenomena and the inaccessible noumena. Seeing may be believing, but it is not quite knowing. Samoan categories of knowledge are, by contrast, firmly rooted in external perception. The Samoan word for "to know" (*iloa*) also means "to shed light on." To know is to see, and "to understand" (*mālamalama*) refers also to light, sunlight, daylight, and consciousness. Knowledge, by implication, lies within the phenomenal world and not beyond it.[1] Of the blind in Samoa it is said "latou te lē iloa se mea" (they do not know/see anything). To the extent that a person's sensory access to the world is diminished or to the extent that he is turned inward on himself, deprived of the power to *faitau* (read/judge) the world, to that extent is he in darkness, neither knowing nor seeing himself in relation to the external world.[2]

While the most common forms of knowledge in Samoan thought are associated with visual perception, these do not exhaust the Samoan epistemology. In addition to *iloa* and *mālamalama*, the Samoan lexicon includes *lāgona* (to feel/sense) and the closely related *lāloga*, a more intuitive kind of sensing. Of one's mistakes, one can say "'Ua 'ou iloa lo'u sese" (I know my error) or equally, "'Ua 'ou lāgona lo'u sese" (I feel/sense my error). To suspect something without certain knowledge is *māsalosalo* (*masalo* = perhaps); merely to guess at something is *taumate* or *mate*. To have precise knowledge is *masino*, from which derives the verb *fa'amasino* (to adjudicate). Certainty of knowledge is suggested by *mautinoa*, and uncertainty by its negation, *lē mautinoa*. A pan-Polynesian term for general knowledge, *kite*, has its Samoan cognate *'i'ite*, oracular knowledge or a foretelling through mystical intuition, from the word *'ite* (to be in view).

Particularly striking about Samoan categories of knowing is the prominence accorded to vision as a basis for understanding.[3] As I have suggested, most of the basic Samoan terms for knowing are derived from words having to do with visual perception. In contrast, knowledge gained from aural perception seems to have a secondary status in Samoan thought. Despite the prominence of oral tradition in political life, the important place of the orator, and the importance of remembering spoken genealogy, oral report does not have the epistemological impact of the visual. Thus *tala* or oral report suggests not simply news, but the possibility of distortion. *Faitala* (to make tales) is gossip. *Fa'alogo* (to listen) and *logo* (to hear) are recognized as paths to understanding, but appear to be paths of secondary importance. The stress on visual coding of knowledge appears to be distinctly Polynesian in character (see, for instance, Levy 1973) and in strong contrast to the importance of hearing in general (Schieffelin 1976, especially chapter 5) and, more specifically, of verbal knowledge in the form of spells and other secrets throughout Melanesia (Barth 1975; Malinowski 1932, 1935). Secrecy in matters of genealogy or oratorical devices has its place in Samoa, primarily in permitting the manipulation of traditional knowledge for the advantage of an interested party. But in no sense does secrecy invest knowledge with greater "truth value."

Important features distinguishing visual from aural knowledge are the directness of visual knowledge, its capacity for immediate disconfirmation, and its grounding in a particular context. Spoken knowledge, by contrast, is far less likely to depend on a particular context, is far more easily stored, and is more readily transferred between contexts. I shall return to these differences. To suggest that Samoans focus on the directly perceptible basis of knowledge is not to say that Samoans rely on "common-sense under-standing." While Levy has suggested (1973) such a common-sense basis for Tahitian knowledge, Samoan perceptions, direct as they may seem, are nonetheless mediated by a complex set of cultural categories for distin-guishing contexts in terms of which perceptions are evaluated.

Fa'alavelave: A Passion for Complexity

To know the world by perceiving it is to embrace the complexity and variability of experience. Here we find no interest in reducing the world's complexities to general principles, but rather a passion for apprehending experience as complex and appropriating distinct facets of life to their proper contexts. The Samoan concern with the particulars of experience and their placement in the scheme of things is suggested by the Samoan love of the local and the idiosyncratic. New twists to old tales, local variants of ritual forms, and a proliferation of conflicting origin myths are all characteristic of the Samoan passion for elaboration of cultural forms. Such variation is not simply local dialect or even idiosyncratic, but frequently is context-bound, the same individual sometimes adhering to conflicting versions of a genealogy, myth, or village address on two different occasions.

This characteristic elaboration of simple basic forms into a pattern of great apparent complexity and surface density has been termed "cultural involution" (Goldenweiser 1937). Samoans have their own term for such cultural elaboration: *fa'alavalave*. Literally, the term means "to make com-plex" or "to tangle" and commonly refers to the life-crisis celebrations that punctuate the normal course of Samoan life.[4] The term is also used for any kind of trouble or disturbance that disrupts and complicates life.

If Samoans constantly complain about the burden that these various sorts of *fa'alavelave* impose on them in terms of money, time, goods, and energy expended, one cannot but notice at the same time a sense of exhilaration, of heightened possibilities for the reaffirmation of old relationships and the creation of new ones, that accompany these complaints. *Fa'alavelave* both deplete life and replenish it. Material resources are expended, social resources are revitalized. Sapping a household group of its mats, pigs, taro, and money, *fa'alavelave* also energize Samoan life, providing arenas for the maximization of social encounters and the elaboration and deepening of ties that were only potential or nascent. Ties of kinship or residence, political loyalties, or friendships may all be put to the test, denied, created, reaffirmed. Family honor and title prestige are put on the line to be raised gloriously or to suffer humiliating diminution when the fine mats and food are redistributed at the end of the ceremony.

What are at issue on these occasions are not simply specific social relationships, but also the very norms and traditional practices of Samoan society, which undergo a testing and renewal. The sense of the renegotiation of traditional understandings and norms of rank and of particular social configurations is apparent in the charged atmosphere of *fa'alavelave*. Much of what anthropologists often assign to the level of "shared" structural norms and rules is actually subject to this process of renegotiation and gradual modification.

To complicate and to elaborate are, in Samoa, to celebrate the *fa'a Samoa*, to enrich a world understood as multi-dimensional. Like a person, the social world is understood to possess many "sides" and "parts" and is to be understood in terms of its contexts. The whole is thus not reducible to any simply monad, for such a simplification of structure is a kind of death. Life is a process of elaboration; understanding life means both creating and grasping that complexity. Such elaboration is a challenge to find a proper place for each variant such that the new are an increment of the old rather than a displacement. Elements are added; rarely are they dropped. They are simply held in reserve.

Judgment: Cause and Effect

Causality is linguistically suggested in Samoan by the morpheme *fa'a-* which, appended to a verb, implies that the action is caused by an external agent. Appended to a noun, *fa'a-* suggests the creation of the object, such that *susu* means "milk" while *fa'asusu* means to produce milk from a breast or "to suckle." The particle *e* following the verb introduces the agent of an action. Thus, *igoa* (name) becomes, with the addition of *fa'a-*, *fa'aigoa* (to name) and "Sa fa'aigoa le tama e lona tinā" (The boy was named by his mother). Similarly, "Sa fa'aoso le solofanua e le tama" (The boy jumped the horse) employs the causative verb *fa'aoso* (to cause to jump) from the addition of *fa'a-* to the verb base *oso* (jump).

The concept of causation itself is expressed in its closest Samoan approximation by the verb *māfua* (to originate/cause) from which derives the noun *māfuaga* (origin). *Māfua* itself derives from the verb *fua* (to blossom/ bear fruit), stressing both the organic and the genetic rather than the mechanical notion of causation implied by the Samoan terms. Also implicit in these origins of the term *māfua* is that it stresses the effects or results of causation rather than the means.

Another meaning of *fua* is "gratuitously" or "without effect." While I am not sure that this form is related genetically to the homophone meaning "blossom" or "fruit" (both nouns and verbs), the links between the two sets of meanings are suggestive. To do something *fua* means that it was done both with no cause, and to no effect. *Fua* in this sense is the common Samoan translation for the English term "gratuitous" (free/without payment). This linguistic collapsing of cause and effect in the term *fua* suggests the Samoan emphasis on evaluation of cause in terms of its perceptual effects. This is a genetic or genealogical notion of succession, rather than a mechanistic concept of causation.[5] Final rather than efficient causation is stressed, along with organic results rather than mechanical causes. For instance, the Samoan sentence "Sa tagi fua le pepe" (The baby cried *fua*) implies both that the baby cried for no cause, and that it cried to no effect, or to no avail.

In relation to human behavior, Samoans assume that evil is "caused" in a sense quite different from virtue. Evil dispositions of actors are recognized in Samoan thought as inherent while, in accordance with a negative ethics of constraint, virtue is commonly seen as the result of the containment of these evil predispositions. Evil erupts or grows (*tupu* means "to grow" and "to happen"); it springs up (*oso*) and thus manifests itself in behavior. Virtue, by contrast, is "caused" only in a negative sense, as vice is contained. One would never say in Samoa that "goodness sprang up" or that "virtue was caused," but rather that "evil was kept at bay." Society, in this conception, is an arena for the encouragement of virtue through the containment of vice. We recall, in this context, that the term *aga*, suggesting the socially conditioned aspects of conduct (or, in other words, social action or style), is more commonly associated with virtuous actions than with evil. *Āmio*, on the other hand, being socially unconditioned, is more commonly associated with evil than with virtue. "Fai le āmio" (do the behavior), it will be remembered, is a common euphemism for acting freely on a private impulse, especially sexual impulse, and is charged with negative connotations.

Fealofani (mutual love) or *filemū* (peace) are not, in Samoan conception, "caused" states in the positive sense. It would not be a natural Samoan question to inquire what "caused" the peace or love, since they are generally interpreted as the carefully managed residua of the containment of their opposite states of discord. Causation, however, might indeed be questioned, if the topics were forms of vice and discord. "Who caused the fight?" or "Who caused the war?" are more logical Samoan questions—although characteristically, as we have seen, the stress is more often on the social effects of discord than on their causes.

Samoan notions of causation require neither spatial nor temporal proximity of an agent to the object or effects. Thus a sickness may spring from
one or more evil deeds committed in the distant past, or from a curse that
had been pronounced a great distance from its intended victim. Similarly,
causation need not be unilateral, and causes are often interpreted as multiple
both in the sense of different causes at the same level, and in the sense of
different layers or links of causes in a chain. Emphasis in assessing the causes
of conflict is placed on immediate as opposed to deeper causes, and on the
social effects of conflict more than on efficient causes. In fact, as we saw
in Sala'ilua, there appears to be a reluctance on the part of Samoans to
investigate causes of conflict, perhaps not so much from a lack of interest
as from a desire to avoid exacerbating the conflict.

Motivation and Personal Responsibility

The Samoan language is relatively poor in descriptive terms for types of
people, while relatively rich in terms describing behaviors. The focus is on
discrete actions rather than on discrete persons. Samoan does distinguish,
however, between discrete behaviors (*āmio*) and general styles of behavior
(*aga*).

While this section has "motivation" in its title, the use of the term in a
Samoan theory of action is somewhat misleading and requires explication.
To the Western mind, motivation is frequently associated with unilateral
or at least self-consistent causation of behavior. The term itself suggests the
mechanical models of behavior common in Western social theory and popular conception alike, and implies an energy or force acting to move an
object. Impulse is another such term. The causes that Samoans attribute to
acts do not assume either a simple force–movement paradigm, or that
causation is self-consistent and thus unitary. Further, the term "motivation," as used commonly in English, focuses the impulse for behavior
within the actor rather than on external features of social interaction.

Samoans, however, seem to conceive of motivation as uncentralized and
as only partially identified with an actor, never centrally located within
him. Chapter 8 explored the concept of the person in Samoan thought and
its implicit metaphor of a faceted gem, with the emphasis on discrete "sides"
and the maintenance of boundaries within them. This metaphor was contrasted with the sphere metaphor, the integration or unity of which I suggested characterized the Western conception of person. The *itū* (sides) or
pito (parts) that comprise people in Samoan thought define their various
'uiga (traits/characteristics), their *āmio* (behaviors), and their various affiliations and links. Mead (1928, 1930/69) and Maxwell (1969) both recognized
the Samoan tendency to speak about actions, behaviors, or situations rather
than about whole actors in discussing behavior.

In relation to motivation, Samoans do not appear to conceive of the
person as an integrated unit with a central will, but instead as an arena

within and upon which different behaviors, traits, and urges manifest themselves. The control function is *māfaufau* or discriminative judgment.

Samoans commonly talk about actions and feelings as if the body were
a decentralized agglomeration of discrete parts, each imbued with its own
will. Thus, such constructions as "my thoughts are angry," "my feelings
are happy," "my eyes cried," "his feelings are pained," "the desire to sleep/
eat/go has come," "his hand touched (i.e., stole) the money," and "the
sadness has sprung up" are all common ways of relating an actor to actions
or feelings. This list could be considerably expanded, so common is this
method of expression. To be sure, an alternate structure permits many of
these statements to be cast in a form stressing the actor rather than the
feeling or the act. For example, "my feelings are happy" could be expressed
as "'ua 'ou fiafia" (I am happy), yet the decentralized forms stressing the
actions or feelings as discrete entities represent the most common form of
expression in Samoan.

The term *oso* (jump) is frequently used to describe the cause of an action
or an emotion. Young men may sit around the sleeping house, and suddenly
the desire to steal a pig or to find a sexual partner may spring up. Temptations, *fa'aosoosoga* (literally, "the causing of springing up") are associated
with certain kinds of social intercourse.

A gifted Samoan artist recently painted a picture of four abstract dancing
figures. I have reproduced these forms in figure 10.1 because they vividly
illustrate this conception of the actor that I have been describing. These
figures show a lack of what we would call central motivation or unity of
action. The centers of the figures are empty, and do not appear to focus
the actors' movements or energies. Each limb appears to fly off on its own
impulse. This drawing suggests precisely the qualities of agility combined
with lack of organic unity that Snell (1960) used to describe pre-Homeric
art, and that suggest to him the lack of a conception of "character" in pre-

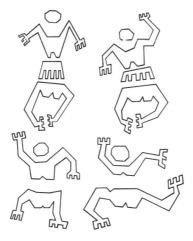

Figure 10.1 Four Stylized Human Figures by a Samoan Artist.

Homeric Greek literature. One need only compare these drawings to the classical figure and anatomical drawings by Leonardo da Vinci and other artists of the European Renaissance, in which the limbs are represented as radiating symmetrically from a central core, about the navel, a core that is commonly circled to emphasize its centrality. The European renderings of the human figure provide a vivid illustration, when compared with the Samoan figure drawings in figure 10.1, of some important differences between contemporary Western and Samoan conceptions of the relation of movement to actor.

The Attribution of Responsibility

In Samoan thought, responsibility for misbehavior is generally attributed to evil impulses that arise within actors, to a careless hand which "touches" something it should not, to "bad feelings" (*loto leaga*), or to a lack of proper judgment (*māfaufau*) associated with lack of proper guidance and training (*a'o'aoina*) by parents and other caretakers. The tendency to externalize responsibility for actions in relation to the actor as a whole is also suggested by the figure of the *āitu* (ghost) or of *Sātani*, or the *tiapolo* (Satan, or the devil), or more generally the *fili* (enemy). All of these figures are frequently pointed to as the causes of discord and of ill will. The devil, for instance, was repeatedly invoked in speeches and prayers during the various meetings surrounding the murder of Tuatō Fatu. It was to the devil that the incident was traced, and the villagers were urged to cast the enemy from their hearts and minds.

Samoans generally attribute responsibility for evil to distortions of proper relationships and situations rather than to agents. The chiefs' authority (*pulega*) was weak; children had not been properly taught by their parents; a person was foolish enough to leave food around where others might take it; a youth had momentarily forgotten his sisters and committed a theft; an offender was entered by a ghost, and spoke harshly to his father. This emphasis on the quality of relationships is evident in the representative nature of punishments inflicted for offenses. Chiefs are punished for the offenses of those in their charge, parents for the sins of their children. Brothers are humiliated by sexual promiscuity in their sisters, and sisters are shamed when their brothers are lazy or get drunk. In chapter 12 I shall examine in detail how Samoans categorize human relationships and the place of these categories in the definition of social contexts.

The externalization of responsibility for behavior is reflected in the emphasis placed on obedience to those in authority. Most informants insisted that, despite this stress on obedience, they would not obey any "bad" order given to them by their chief, adding in most cases that it would be inconceivable for a chief to give such a bad order. Several informants (including, significantly, all three inmates of Tafa'igata Prison whom I interviewed) did in fact assert that they would obey any command given to them by their chiefs. One young *taule'ale'a* from Savai'i explained this claim.

I'd obey [an order from a *matai* even if it were bad]. If the chief told me that I should go and take the pig from that family and cook it so we could eat it, I'd do it. Because of obedience. If the village should punish the act, it would be the *matai* who would be punished and not me. I'd merely have been obeying orders. And if we got away with it, if no one caught us, then good enough! But whatever the result, be it a fine or getting away free, it would be the *matai* who would take the burden. We just obey orders. I certainly would not want to be accused of silly behavior or of wanting to take upon myself the authority that is not properly mine. In our culture we are told that we must obey our mother, father, and chief. If the chief is not our father but our brother, then we obey him. We obey his good orders. And if he should ask us to do anything bad, then we do that too, for that's what it means to obey.

In fact, chiefs' orders are rarely questioned, and such questioning is not encouraged in subordinates. Chiefs are expected to possess not only *pule* (authority), but also special moral competence because of their election to a title. The logic, however, tends to be circular, since the rightness of a chief's command is often seen to be a function of his *matai* status.

Knowledge and Responsibility

The relationship between knowledge and personal reponsibility for one's actions in Samoan thought may be summarized by two general principles. The first is that knowledge of one's own actions is a necessary condition for being held responsible for them. Conversely, an ignorant actor bears no responsibility for his actions. The second principle is that private or purely personal knowledge of one's own actions is not sufficient grounds for responsibility for them. Knowledge of one's actions must be public to some extent for one to be responsible.

For instance, the definition of *mata'ifale* (incest, but literally "looking into the house") includes knowledge on the part of the offender(s)—so that Oedipus would not have been seen as committing *mata'ifale*. Significantly, a couple who, when caught in an incestuous relationship, attempted to excuse or justify their liaison, would invoke the conventional excuse "E lē faia ni tamaiti ni 'āiga" (Children do not constitute families). By this is meant that, being young, children are not quite responsible for knowing their genealogical connections and can thus be excused for an incestuous relationship (Shore 1976b). On being caught in any wrong action, an offender will commonly hang his head and admit in shame, "I know my error," by which he indicates in fact that someone else has discovered his error, and now it is publicly known. In a sense, knowledge of one's action means the seeing of it, the equation being suggested by the term *iloa* (know/

be seen) and to see an act means that it is known to someone other than oneself. One informant, a twenty-three-year-old untitled man from Savai'i, made this point clearly.

These days it is as if people don't think about others in what they do. People don't want other people to control them. They want to control themselves.

(Are these people right in desiring to control themselves?) It is right for me to be my own boss. But others can advise me what to do: to put this thing aside, to do this, to avoid that. There is a Samoan saying: "E lē iloa se tagata lona sesē." [A person does not known his own error]. It means that if I go and do something wrong, I cannot know it is wrong unless another person tells me that such and such a thing is wrong; stop doing it.

(Do you mean that a person can know the errors of other people but never those he himself commits?) That's right. We can know/see each other's wrongdoings . . . because if I look at what another does, I am able to see that it is wrong. He does the wrong thing, but with the thought that it is the right thing to do.

A second informant made a similar statement in response to my question about whether an act could be judged as "bad" (*leaga*) if no person other than the actor knew of it.

Well, when you think about [your action] you'll think that it's a good thing [*lelei*]; only when other people think about it do they call it bad [*leaga*]. If you do something [bad] and keep on doing it, and no one else knows, then you'll continue with the act and you'll think it's good. Only when other people know of it, and they start speaking of it, then you know that it's a bad thing.

Moral knowledge—knowledge, that is, of the rightness or wrongness of actions—lies not with the observer himself (a person per se is not a moral unit in Samoan thought), but rather in the relationship between actors, or between actor and observer. Samoan conceptions of moral responsibility thus make actors dependent on relationships, rather than morally autonomous.

Emphasis on public knowledge of action as a precondition for responsibility and social control is paralleled by belief in the inevitability of public knowledge of private delicts. For instance, Schultz (1965) cites several proverbs whose interpretations underscore this assumption.

"'Ua pona i vao, 'ae liai'ina i ala." (The fault was committed in the bush, but is now talked about on the road.) (104)

"Fa'alia i le tolotolo usu." (Revealed on Usu Promonitory.) (205)

"E nanā fua le tetea, 'ae lē lilo." (The albino was hidden in vain; but did not remain concealed.) (453)

According to Schultz's commentary, the theme of each of these proberbs is identical: "hidden vices will come to light." A more modern version of this proverb in Samoa is "E leai se mea lilo i lalo o le lā" (There is nothing hidden under the sun).

Belief in the inevitable discovery and public knowledge of private offenses, which is fundamental to the Samoan moral system, is expressed in the following statement, excerpted from an interview with an Apia high school student, a male of sixteen. I had asked him if he would ever feel ashamed if he had done something wrong, but no one had discovered his action.

You feel ashamed only if you are caught, or if others know of what you did. If no one knew then you wouldn't feel ashamed. You'd be pleased, for you had stolen and had gotten away with the act. But then there's a Samoan saying, "E leai se mea lilo e lē fa'ailoina" (There's no secret that does not come to light). No matter what kind of secret thing you do or say, you just can't keep it secret. You may steal and steal and steal and keep on getting away in secret with what you are doing. And then one day, you walk along the road, unaware that you are being followed by someone else, and you say, perhaps, "I haven't yet been caught," or something like that. Then this other person will tell someone else "perhaps that fellow has been stealing from the plantation for years or more." You'll be found out sooner or later. There's also another Samoan saying, "E sola le āmio leaga, 'ae tuliloina" (Evil behavior escapes, but is pursued). This means that if you are a thief or something and think that you are escaping, you'll run and run, but eventually someone will catch up with you and you'll be taken to the police.

One knows about others' misdeeds through various "signs." Such signs may have no direct or apparent relation to the offense, but may simply mark a person as open to suspicion. In this sense, the concept of a pure accident is foreign to Samoan thought, since every mischance that may befall a person may in fact be a sign to reveal a hidden vice. A twenty-eight-year-old Savai'i woman vividly described the sort of misfortune that could befall a guilty person.

You've gone and committed some wrong—say stealing money, and that crime is heavy on your mind. Then one day you're struck down by an epidemic that is going around, like the flu. You just don't know why it is that you're sick, the money or something else. Or maybe, you're just sick. But you sit and think about what you did, and you grow afraid that you may die, so in the end you go and admit what you did. . . . I may also be possessed by ghosts . . . in that sort of sickness I'd start raving and telling what I had committed.

Cursing (*fetu'u, fa'amālaia, tautu'i*) of an unapprehended offender by a pastor, chief, or parent is also a powerful way of bringing an offender to light either through voluntary admission in the hope of avoiding a curse, or by implication, as the victim of the curse. Blindness, swelling, or the sudden onset of any disease or physical abnormality may be taken as an indication that the individual is hiding a delict, and has thus incurred a curse. Such beliefs are still common today.

Generally, a person is not responsible for acts until they are detected. When I asked a youth if he would feel constrained to give himself up to authorities for an undetected offense which he had committed, he replied as follows.

Only if I know my error. Some people will think about their children. Or else, if I steal or do something else bad, I'll suddenly think that God has been watching my behavior, and perhaps someone else—or God himself—will come and visit some horrible misfortune upon my wife or my children. So I give myself up, tell the police what I have done, and then my fine will be light. I will have clean feelings [*loto mamā*].

The emphasis in this statement is not on moral prescriptions in themselves, but on the effects of vice on social relations, relations with God, one's family, or other important ties. Ultimately, no act can go undetected, since God is an omniscient and omnipresent observer of all human actions. It is only in the face of such external discovery of actions and their effects that an individual can be said to "know his error" and thus feel constrained to surrender himself. The phrase "clean feelings" is the common expression for the relief one feels when sin and evil come to light; one thus "knows" one's wrongdoing, and sets it straight again. *Mamā* (clean) is associated with the word *mā* (shame), a connection that Levy (1973:336) suggests for the Tahitians as well.

Stair (1897), in an early European observation of the behavior of Samoan children, noted that "Children were accustomed to witness all kinds of evil, and encouraged to follow deception as a virtue, the only evil attaching to a crime being that of detection" (178). If detection is an "evil attaching to a crime," it is nonetheless recognized as morally necessary for attribution of responsibility. When I asked a seventeen-year-old Apia youth if it were forbidden in his village to go roaming about at night, he replied: "Well, it's permitted for you to go out late at night and roam about on the road, but it's forbidden for you to be seen by anybody, especially by a chief. You are permitted to go, but you can't be seen/known by anyone." Detection may, however, be welcomed even by the guilty parties, confirming the moral order to which they are all ultimately committed. Samoan prisoners whom I interviewed all expressed satisfaction with the fact that they had been apprehended, and a commitment to the authorities who were the agents of their punishments. These attitudes would not, I think, be shared by most of these prisoners' Western counterparts.

It is easier to understand Samoan associations of light and dark in the context of their notions about knowledge and responsibility. Disruptive behavior is most likely to occur at night, in the darkness, when people cannot be seen and thus cannot know their own actions. External authority is most strongly in force at these times to bring antisocial actions to light, and to prevent their occurrence. In the daytime, knowledge of others' actions is easier, and thus behavior is most likely to be controlled. A significant aspect of many Samoan laws is that they are seen to be dependent on the existence of an enforcing agency. Many regulations are enforced during the day through the effects of informal social controls, such as gossip and public exposure of behavior. At night, control is more difficult. When the *matai* patrol committee that enforces the nighttime curfew decides to disband, the law is automatically disbanded as well. The regulation itself is said to have become "opened" or to "have rotted" and is thus no longer in force. One informant, when discussing the status of the chiefs' regulations in her village in the urban area, stated that the village used to have its own laws "but at the moment the [*matai*] committee has disbanded and they no longer have these laws."

If public knowledge of one's actions is necessary for the attribution of responsibility for them it is not surprising that village life is organized in Samoa to keep behavior as public as possible. The public, the open, actions done in the light of day, are controlled. Those done at night, in private, alone, behind the walls of European-style houses, or in private rooms, are often assumed to be antisocial and destructive. Such bad behavior is sometimes referred to as *āmio fa'apōuliuli* (behavior in the dark/night) or *pogisā* (darkness). When Samoans say that the Church, the chiefs, or their laws have brought *mālamalama* (light/understanding) to Samoa, the implication is that life has been brought into the realm of daylight where things are seen and thus controlled.

A striking feature of the Samoan village is the Samoan *fale* or house which has no walls and, except for blinds which may be lowered in case of rain or wind or strong sunlight, is open to public view. Life in such a *fale* is, even by the communal standards of most Polynesian societies, strikingly public.

Most Samoans do not immediately associate their open houses with social control. A conventional explanation for the lack of walls in the Samoan house (when such an explanation is demanded of a Samoan by an outsider) is the climate: it is cool and one gets the breezes more easily. Another explanation I collected was that the open *fale* symbolizes Samoan hospitality, and the ease with which a stranger can enter any house for a rest or a meal. When I asked the respondents of my questionnaire why Samoans had open houses, 77 (54.6 percent) invoked the climatic explanation, 35 (24.8 percent) noted simply that this was the traditional Samoan house style, while only 6 (less than 5 percent) volunteered that the house offered protection and control by keeping people in constant public view.

The Samoan association of control with the open house seems to be a largely implicit understanding, which informants readily recognize when presented with relevant hypothetical situations. For example, a woman was presented with a situation that had in fact really occurred, in which the women of one village were angry at a local Peace Corps volunteer for living in a closed house. When asked to explain the probable reason for the women's fear, the respondent explained: "People want to know what happens inside of a house. Many Samoans feel that if your house is all closed up, then you'll do secret things inside that others cannot see. Peoples' thoughts on this vary, though." Another informant, this time from Savai'i, gave this answer.

In a *pālagi* house, which is walled up, you cannot see the kind of behaviors that go on inside. If people do bad things you cannot see them. But you can always see from one Samoan house the sort of behavior that is going on inside another. But from a Samoan house, you cannot see the kind of behavior that is going on inside a *pālagi* house.

This informant added, however, that she believed it was bad that people could see into each other's houses, since it was this sort of watching of other people that led to rumors and malicious gossip.

Yet another informant, an Apia high school student, vividly described to me the effects on a person's behavior of living in an open house.

You must be careful to control [*teuteu*, literally "decorate" or make presentable] your behavior inside an open house. If you want to change your clothes, you don't want to do it if other people can see you. Your thoughts are all different when you live in a Samoan house, and the same goes for your behavior. If you know that others are looking at you, you think differently. In a Samoan house when you do things, others see you. Your "feelings" [English word] are different.

A point raised by several informants about the open *fale* was that it simultaneously encouraged the sharing of food and discouraged hoarding. Sharing, especially the sharing of food, is a very important Samoan value of which Samoans are highly conscious. A woman from Sala'ilua explained: "The life of a Samoan is such that if we are eating a pig, we distribute it here and there to other families, because they can see into our house and they know that we are eating. If, however, we had our walled-up *pālagi*-style house, we would no longer give away food, because then no one would know what we were eating." This informant, while stressing the effects of the open house on food sharing, denied that it had any effect on other kinds of behavior. Another Sala'ilua informant, an elderly lady, related the open house explicitly to more general aspects of Samoan behavior.

Today in Samoan custom, everything is shared. If we have something good to eat, and if we have had a good feast, we divide it all up and distribute it around to all the nearby *'āiga*. That's the Samoan way . . . we Samoans have a loving and generous spirit and we share everything with everyone. . . . We help freely and never expect a thing in return. It's not because we want to get back a string of fish or anything else in return. No. We act out of a loving spirit. . . . If we had . . . houses with walls closed off, then if we got good food, we wouldn't share anything. We'd just eat and eat it all for ourselves. There wouldn't be any more sharing. . . . If our lives were all walled in [*puipuia*] and our houses all had walls to block us off from others, then we wouldn't ever know what they were doing. For then they would be all blocked off from our sight.

Pursuing this topic with the informant, I asked her what she would feel if she were sitting with her family inside a Samoan house and eating a great feast, but had shared none of it with her neighbors. "I'd feel ashamed [*mā*]," she replied, "for we wouldn't have sent anything for the other families."

When I described the identical situation, except for the fact of the setting of the feast being a walled *pālagi* house, and asked if she would still feel ashamed, the old lady responded, with an ironic laugh, "Yeah! Oh sure! How could I possibly feel ashamed then?" Then, suddenly becoming serious, she added, "I'd be ashamed. How could we possibly eat without others having gotten any?" I reminded her that the house was walled in, and that on one could see the feasting, but before she could respond, a younger woman, who had been listening to the interview, called out: "Of course they'd find out! They'd hear the noise, and then the next day they'd ask us, "What was that great feast you were having last night?" That's why we'd be ashamed if we hadn't sent any food over to them."

In a society such as Samoa, where social control is associated with constant and intense social contacts, it is not surprising to find at the center of formal control institutions one that functions forcefully in keeping people engaged in continual social interaction and public observation.

Moral Evaluation

For the Samoan case, a distinction could be made between judgments rendered about actions, and judgments about actors. We in the West tend to equate the two, with insanity or sleep-walking as legitimate exceptions. Samoans evaluate actions more frequently than they evaluate actors, and for an actor who doesn't "know" his actions, he himself may be only lightly implicated in the condemnation of his actions.

While some acts, like murder, are violations of fundamental moral proscriptions, the moral evaluation of most acts is for Samoans highly sensitive to the settings in which they are performed. *'Ai sāvali* (eating while walking) is condemned by most Samoans when it is done on the main road or on the *malae* and also when it is done in the daylight. It is, however, no longer a bad act when these conditions do not prevail. Implicit in the prescription or proscription is the social context in which the act is carried out. Theft is somewhat anomalous in this respect. To some informants, the prohibition of theft was a basic moral proscription, and was seen as inherently bad, independent of context. For other informants, however, theft (*gāoi*) was indeed context-bound in its moral aspect in the same way as was *'ai sāvali*. One informant, an Apia youth of nineteen, told me that he felt that it was bad (*leaga*) to steal in the daytime, but added: "It's good at night, because no one can see you. And for some people it's good to steal in the daytime from the plantation when no one else is about." Another informant, after asserting that theft was good at night because no one could see you, continued as follows.

It's not too bad in the daytime actually. It's good in the daytime if you can get away with it. . . . In the daytime, people can see your face, and everything you are doing, your movements and other things. So they can walk straight up to you if you are stealing. But at night it's very bad to steal on the land of another. Many people have rifles and you'll be shot then. It's bad [*leaga*] to steal in the day, but not so bad as at night, for in the night it seems to be something which you had planned, while in the day, you might have been sitting and saying to yourself, "I really wish I had something to eat," while at night you think that no one knows what you are doing and so you will go and steal.

The judgments in this statement are complex. They involve several kinds of considerations including those of efficacy, intention, possible consequences if caught, and the relation of the act to socially accepted notions of right and wrong. The terms *lelei* (good) and *leaga* (bad) are used both in a moral sense and in a utilitarian sense judging the appropriateness and potential efficacy of an act. At times, the several meanings of the terms reinforce each other, as in statements that "It's bad to steal at night," but frequently the moral and instrumental connotations of the terms "good" and "bad" are mutually exclusive, and the statement becomes ambiguous.

The evaluation of acts in terms of instrumental effectiveness in relation to intended or desired ends is an important aspect of Samoan judgments. For instance, when I questioned informants about the relative seriousness of different misdeeds, their tendency was to base their evaluations on the results for the actor of the actions rather than on any intrinsic quality of the act. The following are samples of this sort of *a posteriori* evaluation of action.

I think that stealing is the worst sin [*agasala*] because a person gets a bad reputation from it. It's very bad [*leaga*].

If we consider the seriousness of each crime according to the fine that is levied for it, then we see that it is theft that has the heaviest penalty, while the penalty for nonattendance of church services is light.

The greatest crime is getting a pastor's daughter pregnant. The fine is about twenty or thirty pigs and a hundred taros. I think that this must be the worst crime, because it is the crime that has the heaviest punishment attached to it. That's how I know that it is the most important of all laws.

All crimes called *soli tōfāga* [adultery with a chief's wife] are the same. I know that this is the worst crime, because a person found guilty of it will no longer be found in the village [i.e., will be banished].

The ill-mannered person is he who is fined today by the village, and then fined again tomorrow.

Rape is bad [*leaga*]. Well, it's called bad, and you get about ten years of prison for it. But if someone is a murderer he is given life imprisonment, and he will never again go to his family. That's why murder is heavier than rape.

Theft is a serious crime, for if you are caught doing that crime you are heavily fined.

The term for sin (*agasala*) itself suggests this is *a posteriori* evaluation of behavior, since it means literally, "punished behavior." This is ambiguous, however, suggesting both that all sins are punished, and that all punished actions are sins. Unpunished behavior, by this definition, is not sinful.

This same kind of *a posteriori* evaluation is employed frequently in positive judgments of actors and actions. A good person, in the words of one informant, is a person who has a good name. "It has not been bandied about by the village or brought in front of the chiefs. This person is what we call a well-behaved, a good person [*tagata lelei*]." The characteristics of a negative ethics of constraint, in which goodness is defined as the avoidance of evil, are clearly expressed here.

Several informants described *mamalu* (dignity/honor) as a quality not inhering in the person, but rather in his relations with others, or in his effects on others. To one informant, a person's *mamalu* is defined by the number of persons honoring him. To another, *mamalu* meant that a person had a title attached to him. It is not surprising that Samoan evaluations commonly attend to things in their relations rather than to intrinsic qualities. Things are thus commonly evaluated in relation to time, place, social context, and as we have just seen, the effects they have in social affairs.

Samoan evaluations of goodness and evil involve not only distinctions between instrumental and moral judgments, but also between acts that are bad, independent of their effects on others, and those that are bad only to the extent that they incur the disapproval of others. We have already distinguished between the former kind of prohibition as fundamental moral proscriptions, such as that enjoining murder, and the latter as forms of etiquette, or context-bound norms of behavior.

These two kinds of judgments are linguistically marked by the use of two different adjectives of disapproval. *Leaga* is the more general word for "bad" or "evil" and while it may include social unacceptability as part of its meaning, it may also be used in contradistinction to *matagā* (literally, "hard on the eyes") to suggest that an act is fundamentally evil, regardless of social context. *Matagā*, by contrast, is a judgment specifically about the social inappropriateness of actions. Eating while walking (*'ai sāvali*), because it is an offense against society and can occur only in a public context, is described as *matagā*, which could be translated as "unsightly" or "disgusting" but never as *leaga*. Murder, however, is always *leaga*, and could also be described as *matagā* when the judgment focuses on its social effects.

Rape is classed by some as *leaga*, while to others it is more properly described as *matagā*. In the sense that rape is classed as *āmio matagā* (unsightly behavior), it is part of a more general class of sexual offenses. One informant said: "They call sex something bad [*matagā*] if someone else knows. They think it's bad if the place is full of other people, but when they are alone they don't think it's *matagā*, unless others know, and then it becomes *matagā*." Rape is somewhat anomalous, however, because it is not simply sexual activity, but involves an unwilling partner and some degree of force. Thus some people insisted that it is *leaga* as well as *matagā*. One youth told me in an interview: "There are differences [between *matagā* and *leaga*].

Matagā means that [a bad act] looks bad, *leaga* means that 'it is condemned' [uses English]."

Of theft at night, another young man said: "I don't know if it is *matagā*, but it is *leaga*. Things you do which are *leaga*, these are things which [only] God sees you doing, like theft at night."

Illicit sexual activity is sometimes referred to euphemistically as *fai mea leaga* (doing bad things), reflecting perhaps a missionary influence.[6] I pressed several informants about why the term was used for such sexual activity, and one responded: "Others will call these acts *matagā* if people know about them. They are, however, *fai mea leaga* at the time when you are alone in the woods. *Leaga* is worse than *matagā*." Another informant explained: "To *fai mea leaga*, you do something to a girl. People will say that the boy has done something *leaga*, and it is called *fai mea leaga*. It is almost the same as *fai mea matagā* but there are occasions and times when it is different. If you do something and no one else can see it, then you can't describe it as *matagā*, for only you know about."

There is also a third term to express disapproval of behavior: *'inosia*, which is a stronger word than *matagā* and could be translated as repulsive. It suggests physical revulsion to an act, and is related to the term *'ino'ino*, which describes a feeling of revulsion at witnessing something extremely unpleasant. The term is frequently employed accompanied by a harsh gagging sound suggesting vomiting. Levy (1973) has made a similar observation about the Tahitian association of moral and gastric revulsion. *'Inosia* may be used to describe actions that are either *matagā* or *leaga*, or both. It suggests that an act is filthy. To several informants, a filthy sleeping hut was the perfect example of something that was *'inosia*. Incest and rape were both also described with this term. A part-European man from Apia, twenty-seven years old, gave the following description of acts which he would class as *'inosia*.

I think it is like what pigs do. Dirty animals. We use it for things that are not kept clean. If someone drinks beer and goes and beats people, we call his behavior *'inosia*. Other people don't want him. No one likes him. Well, you know that all people are really *leaga*, but if someone is *'inosia* in the eyes of others, he is worse than *leaga*.

A physical revulsion to acts of others and the social ostracism resulting from that revulsion was stressed by several informants in discussions about the term *'inosia*. For instance, one informant explained: " '*Inosia*? If I go and do something bad on the road, or force [i.e., rape] a girl, and people know, then our family will become *'inosia*. It is as if *'inosia* "comes inside of" [i.e., is implicit in] the word *leaga*."

Behavior judged to be *'inosia* is behavior that is *leaga* in that it is inherently wrong, and also *matagā* in that it is judged also by its social effect on people. Repulsive, unclean behavior causes, on the part of the actor, shame (*mā*), a term related, as we have seen, to the word *mamā*, and thus through *loto mamā* (clean feelings) to the restoration of order.

Self and Other: Two Voices in Moral Judgment

At the end of chapter 8, I discussed briefly the focus of Samoan conceptions of person on the public rather than the personal or private aspects of
self. We have seen in a number of ways the importance of social relations
as the basis of the moral assessment of acts and of behavior control. The
absence of an elaborate vocabulary for the discussion of personal motivations for behavior is associated with the stress on public culture, or *aga*, in
the ideology of social control. We have seen, however, that Samoans do
have a very vivid conception of a person outside the influence of public
culture, a conception bound up with the concept of *āmio*. It is not surprising
then that this dichotomy between *aga* and *āmio* should play an important
part in framing the judgments that Samoans make about behavior.

Private desires and feelings receive little formal recognition in Samoa,
in the same way that private actions are discouraged by the public nature
of Samoan social life. Society and official ethical prescriptions are thus not
the accommodation of private desire, but rather a containment and denial
of them. It is just such private feelings that were viewed as dangerous and
antisocial, and that Samoans felt one had to *teu* (put in order), that chiefs
and others in authority *puipui* (protect/wall in), and that laws and regulations
saesae (bind up). Public order is thus recognized as the result of the containment of private passion, and the two aspects of experience—public and
personal—are radically opposed. This opposition between public and personal evaluations was explored in the questionnaire, which was distributed
to 141 students. A detailed analysis of the results of that questionnaire is
found in appendix A.

The Ideology and Social Structure of Impulse
Expression

Despite the dependence on external controls suggested by the formal
systems of social controls, there is nonetheless a distinct stress in Samoan
thought on some forms of self-control. This stress is apparent, for example,
in the following statements elicited from a group of *taulele'a* on Savai'i. I
had asked them how they knew the best times to work and to rest.

Pālagi and Samoans are different in that respect. *Pālagi* work according to the clock,
while we Samoans have control over our own behavior.

In working, the *pālagi* must go at a certain time every day. Here, if we don't
want to go, we don't go. But we still get food. Samoans eat for free [*fua*] and sleep
for free too. We sit around and do as we please, because no one has any authority
over us.

The stress in these statements is on self-control and personal freedom to
do one's own will, they very things that these same informants had insisted

were controlled and constrained by formal social controls. Indeed, when I pursued these issues with this group of young men, asking them about the degrees of freedom and self-control exercized in particular situations, they immediately switched back to an expression of the value and need for strong external constraints.

As I have shown, social control is understood by Samoans as public constraint over private impulses or, in other words, as the imposition of *aga* over *āmio*. Laws and authorities that bind up and limit aggressive impulses are, in the statements of informants, positively valued, since they lead to order and dignity. Considering the positive value placed on such constraints, one might expect to hear expressed a complementary disapproval of those private impulses that are seen to be socially disruptive. Informants do indeed express such disapproval when discussing social control in general. However, when speaking about themselves they tend to assert the desirability of personal freedom for impulse expression as well as the ability of an individual to control his own behavior.

Because of the great emphasis that Samoans place on relationships and contexts external to the "individual," private feelings, drives, and desires find their expression in a very indirect and complex way. Samoans seem to make a radical separation between the moral assessment of others' actions, or of behavior "in general," and judgments about their own behavior and private desire. In other words, the perspectives of detached observer and of actor are clearly distinct in Samoan thought and suggest associations quite opposite from each other. There is some evidence that actors do not seem to recognize themselves as implicated in their own statements about "behavior in general" or about others' behavior.

There is, of course, nothing unique in this kind of ambivalence about public morality. That personal desire and public virtue frequently clash, and that people often find themselves of two minds about their own acts and those of others, are aspects of our humanness, not simply of a Samoan's Samoanness. What is distinctive and interesting here, however, is the degree to which this ambivalence is formalized in Samoan thinking. My informants quite readily and unself-consciously expressed this opposition between a strong commitment to public control over others' behavior and a desire to be free themselves of such constraints. There was no sense in their accounts of self-contradiction, since the two kinds of statements seem to have been radically dissociated from each other.

For example informants, particularly younger ones, commonly claimed that the appetites for food, sex, or sleep should be immediately gratified. This desire for immediate impulse gratification was most strongly expressed when the question was put in the personal form, and thus referred to the informants themselves. These impulses, conceived of as external to the individual will, as objects to the actor, are recognized as potentially destructive only when the question is put about their relation to society in general. Thus, speaking about the desires for sleep, food, and sexual gratification, a group of youths from Savai'i offered the following comments.

It's all one [i.e., the same] thing. It's up to us. We sleep at midnight, at ten P.M., or any time we are sleepy. It's up to the individual person when he eats. In European custom, hunger is controlled by the clock, but not here.

If hunger comes, you eat.

And if the desire for sex comes, then you leap and zap! it's done.

Not only did informants express the desirability of immediate gratification of urges, but many asserted that the frustration of such gratification was the saddest and most depressing thing that could happen to a person. One of the young men interviewed in Sala'ilua, when asked what the worst thing was that could happen to him, replied: "Well, if I really had a desire to do something, and I couldn't get it, it would be terrible. Then I would start to think sinful thoughts of how to get it, and that would be a terrible thing for me." Other youths gave similar accounts: "I think that the worst thing would be if I wanted something from someone and couldn't get what I wanted"; "The worst thing that could happen would be if there were something I wanted badly and couldn't have."

Loto leaga (bad feelings/ill will) is what results when such desires are frustrated. Such bad feelings are usually focused on the person who possesses what the frustrated individual wants, or else on a person who otherwise prevents the person from having his way. A middle-aged woman from Savai'i expressed in these words here impression of such ill will: "[Ill will] is the thing you'll find among all Samoans. Because, if I see someone else who has something nice, then my feelings are angered, since that person has something good and I don't."

This general attitude expressed by informants about frustrated desire is strongly supported by evidence from the questionnaire responses. Respondents overwhelmingly indicated that their response to anger was elaborate expression rather than repression. In filling in a sentence-completion item beginning: "When I am angry I usually. . . ," 69 (53.2 percent) of the respondents answered they would have a tantrum or go wild (*fa'ali'i*). The next most frequent responses were "run away" and "cry," both with only 23 (16.2 percent) of the responses.

Considering the emphasis Mead placed on avoidance of conflict and of open expression of strong emotion in her accounts of Samoan socialization and psychological structure, particularly in relation to certain social institutions such as freedom to move from household to household, this stress on violent expression of frustration and anger is striking.

Once again, we appear to have a series of contradictions in our account of Samoan attitudes toward impulse expression. Samoans seem to possess a strong emphasis on both external authority and self-control. These attitudes are paralleled by feelings that human impulse must be strongly expressed and gratified, and simultaneously that they must be contained and thus denied, or at least severely deferred. The significance of this set of paradoxical attitudes becomes clearer if we compare the ideological aspects of control, actors' attitudes about impulse expression, with the social structure of impulse control. The desirability of both self-control and the expression and gratification of irrational urges is emphasized by informants when they speak from the perspective of *actor*. Precisely the opposite emphases, those on the need for strong external constraints on individual behavior and on the irrational aspects of private experience, emanate from informants when they speak from the perspective of the *observer*, or the perspective of the society itself.

The institutional framework of formal controls actually gives little overt recognition to the personal freedom and self-control that individuals expressly value for themselves. Thus, when informants speak as detached observers, their statements tend to reflect the implications of the manifest structure of Samoan social controls. When speaking as actors, however, their statements reflect those very impulses that the formal control institutions constrain. What appear to be contradictory attitudes to an outsider are thus to be understood not as internal contradiction but as two distinct and complementary voices of the speaker. The one voice expresses the moral claims of society against private desire and impulse. The other voice is that of the actor himself expressing the private claims of impulse and appetite which the formal system of controls not only constrains but also, in a negative sense, suggests.

Considering now the formal organization of social controls in Samoa, we are struck by the extraordinary lack of structural recognition that the expressed desires for impulse gratification receive. Informants all assert the desirability of immediate gratification of hunger, sexual urges, or the desire for another's property, but in fact one of the harshest lessons a young child learns involves mastery over exactly these impulses. A small infant in Samoa normally meets with little resistance to its desires. Demand feeding and relaxed sphincter control are supported by elaborate attention which the infant receives from older siblings, its mother, and its father. A toddler will be spoiled frequently by a doting father, who allows it to eat with him. On learning to walk, and especially on the arrival of a new baby in the household, however, the growing child suddenly finds these immediate gratifications prohibited. Without much warning or preparation, a child finds itself relegated to the status of *tama'ititi* (small child), a status ranking only just above that of the family dogs. Children are normally among the first to see the food, since they help to prepare and serve it, but are almost always the last to eat. Sitting, legs properly folded under them, fanning away the flies from the plates of their elders and guests, young children normally receive only what is left over from the meals of the others. This food is normally adequate in quantity, though generally protein-poor. But the important point here is the enormous amount of control over their appetites and the delaying of gratification that children must exercise while quite young. Immediate gratification in eating is, during the greatest part of a Samoan's childhood and adolescence, impossible.[7]

The same delaying of gratification is required of young Samoans in relation to sexual impulses. Despite the expressed stress on immediate gratification of sex drives, such easy gratification is rendered difficult or im-possible by the physical openness of Samoan social life, by the strong official disapproval of premarital sex for women supported by (but not originating with) the Church, and by the role of a girl's brothers as the protectors of her chastity. Even married couples must learn to exercise restraint in the open ambiance of the Samoan *fale*. The existence of institutionalized forms of rape in Samoa, including *moe tolo* (sleep crawling) to a girl, who may or may not be aware of the intentions of the would-be lover, suggest the difficulties that the expressed desire for immediate sexual gratification en-counter in actual experience. Sex may be referred to as *ta'alo* (play), but it is necessarily a serious game and far from casual or easy in the Samoan social setting. The social system suggests the need for care and patience in achieving sexual gratification, much as personal accounts emphasize the desirability of immediate and easy satisfaction.

The acquisition of material goods is also problematical in Samoa. While informants stress frequently that Samoan values guarantee them free food and lodging wherever they go, in fact reciprocity plays an important part in Samoan life. Free food or lodging generally implies a tacit obligation of return hospitality or of the recipients helping out the host family with food gifts or labor. The food gifts, called *oso*, are normally provided when the rank or status of the guest precludes his working. Material or labor assistance may be requested by an individual of any relative with the expectation that they will comply. But in making such a request, particularly of more distant kin, the individual must consider the history of the relationship he is in-voking and the future obligations of reciprocal aid that his request incurs.

Finally, the acquisition of fine mats or other valuables is a very complex matter, especially when the desired object is valuable. The political art of extorting, manipulating, or otherwise peacefully wresting goods from those who have them is highly developed in Samoa. The manipulator *par excellence* is the orator, a skilled specialist in political arts. Like food or sex, the acquisition of goods is always a possibility, but one that is rarely immediate or easy. Such desires are gratified only through mastery over impulses and learning patience, as well as certain manipulative skills.

Personal attitudes expressed by so many informants-as-actors, attitudes stressing impulse gratification, freedom from constraint, and self-control, find little or no formal recognition in social organization. These attitudes do not appear to reflect the implications in any positive or direct way, but arise in contradistinction to the actual ordering of social relations. Samoans-as-actors thus think and talk about social action with a set of terms and concepts often the reverse of those used when they speak as observers, as the voice of society in general. The various conflicts that have been apparent in Samoan attitudes about self and society are not "reconciled" through any sort of integration. Instead, they are dissociated. In part the dissociation appears to be institutionalized, each "side" being appropriated to a distinct set of contexts, and provided with a distinct voice, the one appropriate for formal, public situations, the other for informal and intimate contexts.

No society is completely successful in dealing with its contradictions. In the Samoan case, the fact that certain values are strongly expressed in one set of contexts and then vigorously denied in another way makes a certain "sense" if understood properly. Nevertheless, one would suspect that there are certain residual problems created for individuals. The frequency of certain kinds of violence in Samoa, often associated with alcohol and the "floating aggression" referred to by Lemert certainly suggest some of these problems of dealing with unappropriated or misappropriated impulses. In general, however, and within the Samoan cultural and social setting, the complex system of Samoan behavioral regulators seems to work remarkably well.

Moral evaluations may be coded in two ways. On the one hand, judgments may be framed by simple binary oppositions such as good/bad, generous/selfish, thoughtful/thoughtless. An ethical system that included only such binary sets in its vocabulary might suggest an absolutistic moral system in which every act was given one of two possible values for any particular quality. The other way in which such evaluations could be coded is through a graded opposition defined by polar values that permitted or required acts to be evaluated by degrees of a quality. Thus one action might be judged as "better" than another, or getting better than it had been, or "fairly good," all suggesting a scale of virtue. While both forms of evaluation are probably employed universally in moral discourse, a difference in emphasis, stressing a binary or a graduated mode of judging, has some interesting implications for differences in moral thought.

Samoan is notably poor in its capacity to express differences of degree in discussing a quality. The comparative forms of adjectives (bigger, more beautiful, less generous) may be expressed in Samoan with the use of the adverbial form *atu* indicating relative position away from a reference object (much like the German *hin*) and by *ilō* (than). Thus "the boy is fatter than the girl" would be realized as "E puta atu le tama ilō le teine." A clumsy optional way of expressing comparisons is with the rarely used phrase *e sili ona*, in which *sili* means "higher" or "greater." Thus: "E sili ona puta le tama" (The boy is fatter).

Similarly, it is possible to express in Samoan the relative intensity of a quality. *Tele* means "great," "much," or "very" as in *e lelei tele* (very good). Diminished quality, comparable to the English "quite" for "fairly," is realized with the term *feoloolo* (fair/improved), as in "E feoloolo le tusi faitau" (The book is fair) or "E lelei feoloolo le tusi taitau" (The book is quite good). The concept of excess, as in "too much," is expressed in Samoan either by the use of the adverb *tele*, or *tele lava* (very . . . indeed), or else by the adverb *so'ona* used with a verb only. Thus "he ate too much" could be realized in Samoan as "Na so'ona 'ai le tama" (The boy overate).[8]

I have presented these linguistic forms in some detail to indicate that the Samoan language does possess some capacity for expressing differences of degree. It is thus all the more striking that such evaluations are so infrequently made in normal discourse. More commonly, evaluations are made using a simple binary coding, such as "Pe lelei le tama, pe leaga?" (Is the boy good or bad?); "Pe lāpo'a le fale, pe leai?" (Is the house large or not?). When I first arrived in Samoa, one of the most frequent questions put to me by Samoans was "Pe lelei Samoa, pe lelei Amelika?" (Is Samoa good, or is America good?) in which I was forced to make an absolute discrimination where my normal reaction was to make a relative one. Statements characterizing people in terms of moral qualities are most commonly phrased in the absolute. A resident of Upolu might well say, "People from Savai'i are bad, people from Upolu are good." Other common judgments are, "Samoans are generous/loving; *pālagi* are selfish," or "Young people are mischievous." Rarely will such judgments be framed by forms more expressive of subtle degrees of virtue or vice.

At first glance, there seems to be something of a contradiction in this account of Samoan moral evaluation. As I have described them, Samoan evaluations of behavior approach a situational and highly pragmatic ethics in which judgments are relative to contextual factors and to the perceived effects of behavior rather than to inferred motivations. We might expect such a relativistic ethical system to be expressed in similarly relativistic terms, which is to say in graded forms. Instead, we find judgments that are based on a shifting scale of evaluations couched in linguistic forms that are largely absolutistic.

This sense of contradiction is also felt by any European new to Samoa. Samoans appear, on the one hand, rigidly absolutistic in their loyalties and their judgments. On the other hand, an observer eventually gets the feeling that no judgment is absolute, and that no particular loyalty (as to a village or an *'āiga*) is exclusive.

This paradox disappears, however, once we recognize that any particular judgment is implicitly grounded in a context, and that consistency to context but not necessarily between contexts is the implicit logical basis of a Samoan moral system. Thus, for instance, if someone claimed when living in Savai'i that "Upolu people are bad, Savai'i people are good" and then shifted to another of his villages in Upolu, only to claim that "Savai'i people are bad; Upolu people are good" is not illogical in Samoan terms. The statements tell us little about Savai'i or Upolu people in themselves, but convey a lot of information about the implicit context from which the speaker is making the statements. It also tells us something about how relations between Upolu and Savai'i are viewed.

The apparently absolute judgments made are absolute only in relation to their contexts. What is lacking is a privileged moral viewpoint outside any social context.[9] There is no "objective" perspective in such moral discourse; the contexts themselves are never challenged. The use of simple binary terms of judgment focuses attention squarely on the situation in which the judgment is being made. The relations discussed within the context are the basis of the judgment, rather than an implicit external standard. By contrast a more modulated, relativistic set of judgments would actually draw attention to some outside and perhaps absolute perspective, against which the comparisons were being made. To judge one thing as "better" than something else implies an unrealized "Good" beyond the immediate situation, in relation to which the comparisons are being made.[10] Samoan judgments are thus to be understood as absolute in relation to their context, but relativistic from an "objective" perspective outside any particular context. The absence of this objective perspective in Samoan thought is a fundamental fact of moral discourse in that society.

CHAPTER ELEVEN

Conflict in the Context of Social Relations

A man is shot dead by another following a dispute during a poker game. An act of murder is committed in a public place in daylight. There is, it appears, little mystery here. Everyone knows the victim, a respected and powerful leader in the village. Equally apparent is the identity of the murderer, also a respected leader himself, a chief and son of a prominent village family. *Why* the murder occurred can be understood simultaneously from several perspectives. In part 1, we encountered these events much as they happened, detailing some of the shadings and inflections that make any particular incident of this kind unique in the history of a village or a family or, in the final account, in the life of a person. Motivations at this level focus on the relatively immediate events and emotions surrounding the murder. In part 2, we were able to place these particulars in the somewhat broader context of the political and social institutions of one village. This shift in focus had the effect of generalizing what had been specific individuals, places, and events into such institutional frames as social roles, political corporations, and judicial procedures characteristic of Sala'ilua. The particular or special case had become the village itself rather than any of its members. Again we might ask what "caused" the murder, and from this somewhat more abstract perspective, the motivations appeared more social, political, and economic, as we probed the tensions in that particularly dynamic village and uncovered a long-standing political rivalry between two powerful families in the village, two senior titles, and two ambitious teachers. From this distance, not only were motivations more general and diffuse, but they involved a longer time span, carrying our investigation to events well removed in time from the rifle shot and the events immediately surrounding it.

But we have not yet closed the case and must take yet another look at these events. In this chapter we will explore social conflict as if it proceeded not from a breakdown in social order, but from the very nature of that order itself. This is not to say that the murder of Tuatō Fatu was fully predictable or even fully illuminated by its culturally typical features, but rather to suggest that contributing to both the genesis of the incident and the way in which it was interpreted by villagers is a distinctively Samoan understanding of social relations. In this sense and from this perspective, I hope to demonstrate that Tuatō Fatu's murder was simultaneously a violation of explicit norms and laws at one level of understanding and an affirmation of Samoan normative categories at another. Bateson (1936,

1973) has suggested the extent to which cultural factors enter into the genesis and unfolding of warfare and other forms of violence. We shall have recourse in this chapter to Bateson's concept of "schismogenesis" in examining the distinctive Samoan contexts of aggression and social control. Finally, against the backdrop of these Samoan understandings of social relations and their link with conflict, I can hope to give a clearer and analytically sophisticated shape to my initial "intuition" that Sala'ilua was an unusually vigorous village among Samoan villages, and that this quality was linked to culturally distinctive features of the village's social structure.

The Coding of Social Contexts

If social structure is to be a viable concept through which to comprehend Samoa, a major aspect of this structure must be a kind of grammar of social contexts, ordering situations as they are understood by Samoan actors. It is to the structure of social situations that Samoan perceptions are turned in social action, and this structure renders action socially meaningful as *aga,* distinguishing it from *āmio,* or behavior. At the heart of a Samoan vision of social order lies a well-defined field for interaction. If I am right about these priorities in structuring social action, then the ethnographer's task becomes one of elucidating in detail how the context of social interaction is marked and what actors associate with each of these contexts.

Context suggests for Samoa two distinct layers or levels of analysis. On the one hand there is the context of social relations, and on the other, the context of symbolically charged settings or occasions in which these social relations are realized. These two levels, analytically distinct, are also interdependent. In this chapter I shall focus on important ways in which Samoans *teu le vā* (order social relations). Implicit in Samoan statements, proverbs, and other manifestations of social thought is a typology of social relationships. This typology may be thought of as a kind of cultural template that helps to order perceptions of situations of social interaction, and in response to which a similarly coded set of behaviors and cultural conceptions is matched. Without such a template or code, the notion of contextual "appropriateness" of social action would be meaningless.

The analytical framework I shall present for the explication of these relationship classes employs what I understand to be Samoan ways of thinking about Samoan relationships. Since it is the anthropologist and not the Samoan actor who is interested in formalizing such typologies, these relationship types are rarely if ever rationalized by Samoans to the extent that they appear here. More often, they are merely implicit in Samoans' statements and other culturally significant behavior. It remains the job of the anthropologist to wrest the abstractions from the concrete data in which they are embedded. This translation job, like all such undertakings, risks misinterpretation and misrepresentation. The anthropologist constantly risks interference from his own idiom, and the resulting translation may lack the graceful fluency of an original text innocent of the demands of analytical rigor or explicitness. Analytically motivated translations always suffer somewhat from their "accent," yet ultimately must retain an essential fidelity to the statements and acts of the performers from whom they are derived. The following account does, in fact, seem to make sense to Samoans to whom I have shown it, despite the fact that it appears in that analytical language of the observer rather than in the natural language of the actor. It is thus both an observer's model and a reconstructed native-model of the structure of social relations in Samoa.

Relational Thinking

While social anthropologists such as Radcliffe-Brown (1950:39) or Warner (1936) have dealt with social relations and terminological systems as inherently *relational* in character, the focus on social relations as distinct from the terms or persons related is in some sense foreign to Western atomistic thinking.[1] Social roles such as "mother" or "sister" or "teacher" are, for the Western thinker, easily grasped as particular persons and only secondarily comprehended as relationships. In chapter 9, I have suggested what I understand to be the major philosophical biases behind this Western focus on things in themselves rather than on things in their relations.

Samoans, by contrast, appear to be intellectually predisposed to comprehend social relations *as relations,* focusing on their world with a thoroughgoing sociocentric logic. Clues to this kind of relational thinking are built into the Samoan language. A kin term such as *uso* (sibling of the same sex), unlike English sibling terms, gives relatively little information about the intrinsic character (e.g., gender) of either sibling, but correspondingly more information about the nature of the relationship between those linked through the term (same sex). While the term by which a brother calls his sister (*tuafafine*) is distinct from that by which a sister calls her brother (*tuagane*), the brother–sister *relationship* is comprehended by a more general term *feagaiga,* a term to which we shall return.

A further linguistic indication of this relational bias in Samoan thought is in the use of plural pronouns. I have already discussed the importance of distinguishing inclusive forms of "we" (*tā'ua:* we-two; *tatou:* we-plural) which encompass the listener in the reference, from the exclusive forms (*mā'ua; matou*) which exclude the listener from the implied grouping. Linked to this linguistic sensitivity to group boundaries is the form in which the Samoan language casts references to aggregates of persons as subjects or objects. Forms that are cast in English as "My father and I" or "You and the girls" are rendered respectively in Samoan as "We-two (exclusive) with my father" (Mā'ua ma lo'u tamā) and "You-plural with the girls" ('Outou ma teine). The English forms require the social unit to be expressed as an aggregate of constituent parts; the Samoan forms require the social unit to be expressed as a primary encompassing whole with the (optional) sec-

ondary specification of a contextually unmarked element. A direct translation of a conceptually analytic form such as "My father and I" (Lo'u tamā
ma a'u) would constitute not only a grammatical error to a Samoan listener
but a semantic one as well.

Having noted the stress in Samoan thought on the quality of relationships
rather than on the intrinsic qualities of the units related, I turn to examine
the general distinctions Samoans make between different kinds of relationship. I have shown in part 2 of the study that Samoan social life is highly
formalized institutionally. Samoans have a flair for elaborating social schemata through which social life is regulated, schemata comprising social
groups, politically and economically specialized roles, and social categories
for classifying people. Another way of putting it is that Samoan social life
is highly differentiated and Samoan perceptions are finely attuned to this
complex social field and to the discriminations it requires. While these
discriminations operate at the level of particular roles such as those between
ali'i and tulāfale, village and subvillage, pastor and matai, or brother and
sister, Samoans also share a broader, more general set of categories, which
underlie these particular differences.

Status and Rank

Samoans categorize social relations by reference to two dimensions of
differentiation, dimensions that I shall call those of *status* and *rank*. I use the
term "status" in the restricted sense that Linton (1936:113) defined it, as
a "position in a particular pattern." Such a position normally refers to
what we commonly call a social role, a distinct social position in a set of
positions with associated rights, duties, and often symbolizations.[2] "Father," "Chief," "*Ali'i*," and "Pastor" are examples of different statuses.
In my usage, status can also refer to a collectivity or social category such
that village, district, Women's Committee, and church congregation are
also forms of status in Samoa. The important points for our analysis are
that status defines qualitatively (functionally or logically) distinct positions,
and statuses are often arranged in sets, such that the members of a set are
complementary, which is to say logically or functionally interdependent.
In Samoa, such sets are exemplified by *matai/taule'ale'a* (chief/untitled person), *ali'i/tulāfale* (high chief/orator), *nu'u/pitonu'u* (village/subvillage), and
tuagane/tuafafine (brother/sister), a relationship also defined by the single
term *feagaiga*.[3]

While relations of status difference define qualitative distinctions, those
of rank suggest quantitative or graded distinctions within any single status.
Rank differences are thus differences of degree of some quality (strength,
power, honor, wealth, size, etc.) along a *single* continuum, either functionally
or logically defined. In an American context, what I call rank differences
may involve differences in wealth (as in income groups or "economic
classes"), differences in degree of authority over others (such as the ranking
of privates, sergeants, and captains in the military), differences in the

"amount" of education received (such as define the difference between B.A., M.A., and Ph.D. academic degrees or the set freshman/sophomore/junior/senior/graduate student), or (more ambiguously) a rank scale may imply differences in general prestige or honor (such as characterizes the scale janitor/mail clerk/executive secretary/junior executive/corporation president). In Samoa, older brother/younger brother, high-ranking *ali'i*/low-ranking *ali'i,* and *tu'ua* (senior orator)/junior orator are examples of statuses with internal ranking.

In reality, the distinction between a difference of rank and one of status can become equivocal. For instance, on an airplane the relationship between pilot and navigator defines two levels of status insofar as they perform different though interdependent technical functions. In terms of "authority" or degree of "command," however, they represent two distinct ranks within the status-group "cockpit crew." In Samoa, the same ambiguity applies to relations among chiefs. When status differences between an orator and a high chief are relevant, such as in any large public political arena, the one is called *tulāfale* and the other *ali'i.* In reference to their common *pule* or authority over their own households, or over a member of the village in which they hold their titles, status differences become irrelevant and both chiefs are called *matai.* As *matai,* they may be differentiated by rank, which is to say by degree of general prestige or extent of authority.

While the analytical power of rank/status distinction may appear to be weakened by the inevitable ambiguities it entails, it is precisely where these definitional ambiguities are most apparent that conflicts are most likely to occur. Thus, for instance, the relationship between a village and a subvillage is particularly problematical in relation to the rank/status distinction. In some sense a subvillage is encompassed by a village, the relation being one of rank difference. In this understanding, a village is "the same" as a subvillage, only bigger and possessing proportionally more authority. Members of a subvillage, however, may claim that they have their own distinct functions and sphere of authority, either as a separate "part" of the village or as a unit fully equivalent to a village. In either case, the claim is to autonomous status rather than to hierarchical linkage.

As will be seen later in this chapter, the ambiguity contributes to the inherent instability of relations among constituent sections of any village, much as it does to the similarly ambiguous relations between district and village. These anomalies notwithstanding, status distinctions and rank distinctions suggest quite different principles of organization, with rather different implications for the genesis of conflict. I shall examine each of these dimensions separately before looking further into their interconnections.

Status: Symmetrical and Complementary Relations

Since social levels of status become meaningful through their membership in sets, I begin by looking into the kinds of relations possible between levels within a set. At first glance, it appears that three kinds of relations are

possible. First, statuses may be different from each other, and not interdependent. The set chief/father/subvillage is a case of such a noninterde-
pendent set. A second possibility is that statuses might be logically or
functionally different, but interdependent. Examples of such *complementary*
sets are parent/child, or chief/untitled man. Finally, there is a set defined
by more than one token of a single status, such as the set of several brothers,
a body of chiefs, a collection of villages, or the constituent subvillages
within a single village. These statuses are linked because they are logically
or functionally identical: they are linked metaphorically. I shall refer to
them as *symmetrical sets* or *relations*.

While I have defined three possible kinds of set, in fact only the last two,
complementary and symmetrical sets, have any analytical utility. Indeed,
since the concept of status set implies some kind of functional or logical
coherence among its members, the first type of set is really a contradiction
in terms as well as ethnographically insignificant.

Symmetrical Relations

Important Samoan examples of what I have called symmetrical sets or
symmetrical relations are the following.

1. Two or more brothers (*'auuso*)
2. Two or more sisters (*'auuso*)
3. A group of politically linked orators sometimes called in oratorical
   discourse *fale'upolu*
4. A group of politically linked *ali'i,* sometimes called in oratorical
   discourse *usoali'i* (a brotherhood of chiefs)
5. All of the chiefs of a single village (subvillage, district, etc.)
6. Two or more villages with political ties (*nu'u/nu'u*)
7. A village and its constituent subvillages (*nu'u/pitonu'u*)
8. Two or more untitled men (*taule'ale'a/taule'ale'a*)
9. Two or more girls (*teine/teine*)
10. Two or more dancers in the center of a dance floor dancing the
    graceful *siva*. (See chapter 13 for more on these dance styles.)
11. Two or more maximal branches of a descent group (*fuaifale/
    fuaifale*)
12. Two or more dancers at the periphery of the dance floor dancing
    the clowning *'aiuli* dance
13. Relations between any two rival military districts

Being in some important way "identical" to each other, symmetrical
levels of status are hard to distinguish from one another. There is a tendency
for boundaries within such symmetrical sets to become fuzzy, and for
relations among the linked units to become correspondingly unstable. In
Samoan terms, symmetrically linked statuses may "replace" or "stand in"
(*sui*) for one another.

In Samoan thought, the fact that such symmetrically related levels of status may replace or stand in for one another is of great importance. One village may stand in for another in district affairs, or may represent its entire district (i.e., all the other villages) on ceremonial occasions. One brother is logically and culturally equivalent to another, and a younger brother is normally expected to replace an elder as chief on the death of the latter (*toe 'o le uso:* right of succession for the remaining brothers). Potential leviritic rights are also recognized as logical, though actual unions between a man and his deceased brother's wife are rare. The same equivalence holds among sisters. The kinship term *uso* (same-sex sibling) gives formal recognition to the importance that symmetricality has in the Samoan classification of relationships. In fact, the term "symmetrical sibling" would be an apt gloss for the Samoan term *uso.*

Largely because of their functional equivalence, symmetrically related units are not simply logical representatives for each other, but also the proper alternatives to each other. Such symmetrical relationships are therefore inherently competitive and conflict-ridden. Competition, one-upmanship, and various forms of mutual aggression such as sports competitions, war, or competition for political titles, are recognized by Samoans as characteristic of symmetrical relations. For instance, the proberb "Ua fa'afeagai sega 'ula" (The red *sega* (vini) birds face each other) suggests, according to one knowledgeable informant, that "the persons who are confronting each other are equals—the same." When those of the same sort of status face one another in competition, the appropriateness of the opposition may be expressed formally by the statement "E lē tīoa" (It is no surprise). This would be the reaction to two *ali'i* facing each other in a meeting, or to two orators engaged in an oratorical contest. But when those of different status face each other competitively, the applicable proverbial expression is " 'O le fa'afagatua e lē tutusa" (Those locked in wrestling combat are not the same), indicating the inappropriateness of the relationship. My informant gave us a specific example of such inappropriateness, an *ali'i* engaged in a contest with a *tulāfale.*

Symmetrical relations structurally suggest competition and fission, and overt expressions of aggression are expected in such relationships. Symmetry suggests "climbing up" or unrestrained expression of feelings or desires. Thus it is hardly surprising that while the relations among brothers or among sisters may suggest a certain amount of mutual love and cooperation, particularly in the face of other families, fraternal relations are frequently areas of conflict, strain, and potential fission within a family. Brothers who may stand in for one another politically may also replace one another and competition among brothers (or sisters) is not uncommon. It is between brothers and their descendants that titles normally split and from which competing *itū paepae* (title-division segments) and *fuaifale* (maximal descent-group branches) originate. The kind of tension characterizing the relations among *uso* in Samoa is suggested by the comments of a New Zealand industrial relations expert, discussing relations among Samoan workers in his factory.

If, say, two brothers were playing [cards], one a winner and the other a consistent loser, the successful brother would support the loser for a time then tell him to stop gambling. The loser would withdraw but yell advice to his brother—good advice on how to win as only a loser can give. After a time the brother or one of the other players might tire of the commentary and forcibly eject the loser from the room and this would often cause bad feelings between the brothers for days.

This same competitiveness and aggressiveness is characteristic of relations among young men, or among young women. Most fights in a village take place between young men or women, and hardly ever between sexes, or between men or women of different age groups. Those most nearly alike are also the most likely competitors.[4]

The aggressive and divisive tendencies inherent in certain relationships in Samoa have frequently been noted by observers. Lemert (1972:229) noted the "deep substratum" of aggression evident in behavior among *taulele'a* in Samoa, and commented that "their aggressiveness is in part culturally inculcated, and . . . is encouraged in *certain kinds of structured situations*" (emphasis added). In attempting to account for the failure of Samoa ever to achieve a centralization of power in the traditional polity as was done in Tahiti, Hawaii, and Tonga, observers have often noted fissive tendencies inherent in Samoan society. Davidson, for instance, as quoted in Freeman (1964:556) referred to "the fundamental facts of genealogy" as "the most important key to an understanding of the balance of power in village politics" and then added that the character of Samoan social structure must be understood in relation to processes of progressive segmentation and consolidation through the creation of new family linkages." What Davidson does not indicate, however, is that the segmentation most commonly occurs between units linked symmetrically, while, as shall be seen, it is complementary links that work to maintain the units of the kin group.

Mead (1968:260) asserts that "Rivalry attitudes were highest between districts."

Man'ua claimed to be more sacred than any other part of the Samoan Islands. . . . But such claims were also accompanied by a great deal of mutual vituperation and abuse, by abusive songs about the other islands or districts and by insulting proverbs.

Further, she notes that "Standardized competitive situations between two villages in the same district might be set up and ceremonially recognized" (261). Mead was hard put to explain this rivalry, particularly since it contradicted certain of her assumptions about Samoa. She noted significantly, "this intervillage rivalry and ceremonial—and occasionally real—hostility lacked any basis in material circumstance" (ibid.).

The Keesings (1956:21) echoed Mead's observations about district organization, remarking that "Such groupings . . . have had in them divisive tendencies of factionalism, rivalry, intrigue and, until the enforced peace of recent decades, quite destructive war." Stanner (1953:269) generalized this structurally related instability to characterize the whole of the Samoan polity as "highly, because inherently unstable. Intervillage cooperation in large-scale political matters was possible only under a despotic *mālō*. Failing that, fission was the condition of life."

While observers have been quick to point out these aggressive and divisive tendencies in the relations between certain groups or in certain "structural situations," no attempt was ever made to characterize the precise structure of situations or relations in which these fissive tendencies manifested themselves. Fission was not, as Stanner suggested, "the consideration of life" in Samoa, but rather a condition of social structure, in particular of symmetrical relationships. It was a condition that was not only recognized by Samoans as part of an encompassing system of relationships, but also, as Lemert suggested, actually encouraged by the associations Samoans have with such relationships.

Complementary Relations

Complementary status levels are in some important sense qualitatively different from each other. Not only are they of dissimilar functional or logical types, but the paired functions or meanings are complementary to each other, suggesting some sort of significant interdependence. Important Samoan examples of such complementary relationships are the following.

    sister/brother (*feagaiga*)
    ali'i/tulāfale
    tamafafine/tamatane
    pastor/congregation
    female/male
    matai/untitled person
    husband/wife
    itūau/alataua (warrior district/passive worshipers)
    exchanges between *tōga* and *'oloa* goods
    siva dancers/*'aiuli* dancers

Symmetrically related statuses may stand for each other in the sense of replacing or displacing each other; units linked in complementary bonds may merely "represent" each other because of their functional interdependence. A wife represents her husband's title in the Women's Committee by virtue of the complementary functional link between them, and in the same way the orator "speaks for" his *ali'i*. Representation does not imply replacement or potential displacement, but rather reinforces the interdependence between the linked roles. *Replacing* such as characterizes symmetrical relationships is a metaphoric function predicated on the functional or cognitive similarity between statuses; *representation*, however, is based on cognitive or functional differentiation between complementary units. A brother may take the place of another brother, but an orator may only speak on behalf of or represent the thoughts of the *ali'i*, who cannot do his own speaking on important occasions. It is the dissimilarity between the two that allows the *tulāfale* to represent the *ali'i*, while it is precisely their similarities that allow one brother, village, or family to replace another.

While symmetrical relations are in general fully reciprocal in that either status may replace the other, complementary relations are more frequently directional and nonmutual. This distinction between mutual reciprocity of symmetrical units and the directed nature of complementary relations is reflected in Samoan kin terms. As we have seen, there is but a single term for symmetrical (i.e., same-sex) siblings—*uso*. But cross-sex sibling relations (complementary siblings) are expressed by two terms: *tuafafine* for males addressing sisters, *tuagane* for females addressing brothers. The linguistic relations between symmetrical siblings who use the same term reciprocally in referring to one another and those between cross-sex siblings who use different terms depending on the direction of the reference, parallel exactly the structural relations inherent in the two kinds of relationship. In symmetrical relations, whatever *A* does for or to *B*, *B* may also do for or to *A*. In complementary relations, however, whatever *A* (by virtue of being *A*) may do for *B*, *B* must not do in return to *A*. Similarly, whatever *B* is or does for *A* is precluded reciprocally.

Whereas symmetrically linked status levels are associated with competition, conflict, impulse expression, and fission, Samoans associate complementary relationships with deference, impulse control, love (*alofa*), and respect (*fa'aaloalo*). Social order and stability rather than conflict and fission characterize these relationships. These complementary relationships will be examined in detail in chapters 12 and 13.

Bateson's Theory of Schismogenesis

I have deliberately chosen the terms symmetrical and complementary as labels for these two general patterns of relationship Samoans recognize not only because they are appropriately descriptive, but also because they echo Bateson's important distinctions between complementary and symmetrical schismogenesis (1936, 1973). For Bateson, the genesis of conflict and its control are closely associated with the dynamics of interactions, and particularly with distinctive patterns of feedback between potential antagonists. The emergence of a conflict is also the creation of a difference or more accurately the process of progressive differentiation (hence the term *schismogenesis*). Bateson argues that interactions between potential antagonists tend to follow distinctive patterns, in which messages about the quality of the interaction are exchanged.

In one kind of process, that which Bateson calls *symmetrical schismogenesis*, there is a pattern of parallelism, a kind of behavioral one-upmanship in which an action by one party is matched—and intensified—by the other. Symmetrical interchanges of this sort are inherently competitive and structurally unstable, leading to progressive escalation in hostility. Here the genesis of a difference between the competitors leads to an attempt simultaneously to "close the gap"—since the antagonists are, in some sense, "the same"—and to create a difference. A second kind of interaction, *complementary schismogenesis,* is characterized by nonmutuality in exchanged behaviors, such that an aggressive action by one partner is reciprocated by a deferential action on the part of the other. The exchange is asymmetrical rather than direct, and reinforces a progressive differentiation in a relationship rather than attempting to deny it. Complementary relations tend toward stability and mutual control, though Bateson's emphasis is on the distinctive distortions such relations are liable to undergo in the form of complementary schismogenesis.

Bateson first made use of these conflicts in exploring the process by which an aggressive male ethos was learned by Iatmul youths of New Guinea (1936). He later applied the same concepts to characterize distinctive national (cultural) patterns of warfare (1973:62–79). These processes have obvious broad applicability and may suggest general types of regulators for human interactions, parallel to the well-known signal systems that regulate aggression and deference among lower animals. In Samoa, what Bateson characterizes as implicit patterns of interaction are explicitly built into the cultural structuring of social relations.

The Social Structure of Exchange

I have already noted the Samoan associations of aggression and expressive competition within symmetrical sets, and control, deference, and stability within complementary sets. The general patterns distinguishing symmetrical and complementary relations are evident in the kinds of formal gift-exchanges characteristic of each. Thus, where complementary status forms are involved in an exchange, the exchange tends to be asymmetrical, focusing on complementary goods, each moving in only one direction. Symmetrical relations are symbolized by symmetrical reciprocity.

The Samoan model for complementary reciprocity is the formal exchange between the two classes of gift, *tōga* and *'oloa. Tōga* (taken from the term *'ie tōga,* finely woven decorative mats) is a kind of female wealth, comprising fine mats and, rarely, other kinds of fine decorative handwork made by women.[5] The value of *tōga* is decorative rather than utilitarian, and is associated with the investment of labor in their production, a very fine mat taking up to a year or more to weave. *'Oloa* constitutes a kind of male wealth. Traditionally *'oloa* included boats, unprocessed foods, and work implements made by male labor. Nowadays, cash has largely replaced these goods as *'oloa* in complementary exchanges. Whereas the value of *tōga* lies in labor invested in its manufacture and in its decorative capacity, *'oloa* derives its symbolic value from its usefulness, its direct economic productive capacity. Gilson (1970) has noted this difference between *tōga* and *'oloa.*

In general, *'oloa* articles have utilitarian as well as symbolic value, as suggested by the application of the term *'oloa* to European trade goods. Articles of *tōga,* in contrast, have little direct utilitarian value. They do, however, represent large expenditures of time and labour, and are the only traditional goods which can be readily stored away and used in the manner of currency and coin, to pay off obligations, such as those incurred in the building of a house. The oldest fine mats, distinguished by special names, are very highly valued. (45:note)

Tōga have value only insofar as they are exchanged and circulated. They are in fact never publicly displayed except on occasions when they are given away, so that their decorative function is realized only in the context of an exchange. Otherwise, they are folded and hidden away in the rafters of houses or kept locked in wooden chests. Thus in comparing the uses of *tōga* and *'oloa,* it may be said that the value of *tōga* is to circulate between groups, while itself remaining untransformed in the process. The age of a fine mat is an index of its value for linking groups in much the same way as a woman moves about linking groups in this largely virilocal society. *'Oloa,* by contrast, is always *consumed* in some sense after an initial exchange. Its value is not to circulate so much as to be transformed directly into something else that is useful. Boats are used to produce fish, implements for crops and raw foods are transformed into cooked consumable nourishment. These broad distinctions are manifestations of a general Samoan dualistic ideology, which will be explored further in the next chapter.

Important for our purposes is the fact that this formal exchange of *tōga* and *'oloa* takes place on marriage to symbolize the relations between *pāolo* or affines. Here, *tōga* constitutes a kind of dowry, moving with the bride from her group to that of the groom. *'Oloa* represents a kind of bride price, given by the groom's family to that of the bride. In the case of important marriages involving politically prominent families, the exchanges at the wedding ceremony initiate ongoing complementary exchange relationships between whole descent groups.

The formal exchange relationship persists for the duration of the marriage, being activated on a smaller scale when a child is born and when the affines tend to contribute to one another's ceremonial functions. In the past, the two sides also approached one another with exchange goods when canvassing for help in war. Marriage itself conveyed no absolute right to political support; but once a child was born of a union, bridging the two lineages by virtue of his dual descent, conditions for the formation of an interlineage alliance were especially favourable. (Gilson 1970:45)

This reference to the children of such a union as stabilizers of the alliance begun by the marriage is important. From the perspective of the couple, the two allied descent groups exchanging *tōga* and *'oloa* are "bride's side" and "groom's side"—sometimes called *itū vaivai* (weak side) and *itū mālosi* (strong side), respectively. From the point of view of the children, however, the political linkage to their maternal descent group is as *tamafafine,* while that to their paternal *'āiga* is *tamatane*. Thus from the point of view of the off-spring, the continued exchanges of *tōga* and *'oloa* between the groups after the birth of children symbolize the political linkages between their own *tamatane* and *tamafafine* affiliations.[6] Both kinds of linkage are fundamental Samoan complementary sets based on the male/female complementarity realized as husband/wife or as brother/sister.

Tōga and *'oloa* exchanges symbolize what I have called complementary sets and thus are not supposed to involve overt competition or one-upmanship. The focus is on balanced reciprocity and the stabilization of relations between exchange partners through the reinforcement of differentiation, in the manner of Bateson's complementary schismogenesis. Competition, which is always at least latent in public presentations, is deliberately minimized. Gilson also discuses this point.

Since the extent of intra-lineage participation in marriage ceremonies is a function of rank, a balance is achieved in the number of participants and in the amount of goods exchanged only if the bride and groom are of similar rank. For this reason, among others, wide discrepancy of rank between the parties is most undesirable; to avoid it, the most important marriages are arranged by *tulāfale* among whose first concerns is the equivalence of affinal relationships. (*Ibid.*)

The apparently conscious attempt to minimize competition in these exchanges suggests the tension in affinal relations between the demands for balanced reciprocity in affinal relations (or in the relations between *tamatane* and *tamafafine* segments of a descent group), and a countervailing tendency for these relationships to become antagonistic and competitive. The reason for this tension has to do with a crucial ambiguity in the perception of these relations as either symmetrical or complementary. This structural ambiguity with be explored later in this chapter.

Complementary sets engage in complementary exchanges. The *tōga/'oloa* Exchange associated with the establishment and maintenance of affinal ties between descent groups is also associated with other complementary sets. Mead, for instance, refers to the customary exchange between *ali'i* and associated *tulāfale* as analogous to that between the "sides" of bride and groom at a wedding. "The families of chiefs," she says, "stand in a *tōga*-giving relationship to the families of talking chiefs who must reciprocate with *'oloa*" (1930:75–76). While such formal exchanges between families of *ali'i* and *tulāfale* are relatively rare in modern Samoa, the complementarity of the chief/orator relationship continues to be symbolized by asymmetrical exchanges of other sorts. The orator, for instance, is obliged to place his oratorical and political skills at the service of the chief who, in turn, provides his orator with a "payment" of fine mats and tapa cloth. Samoans recognize this kind of asymmetrical relationship in the proverb "'o mea a le ali'i e pala i le tulāfale" (things of the *ali'i* decay into the hands of the *tulāfale*). A similar complementary exchange characterizes the relationship between the pastor and his congregation. The pastor provides the congregation with moral guidance and "the good word" while the congregation in turn supplies the pastor with money, food, and a place to live. Finally, the bond between brother and sister may be understood in terms of a complementary exchange. A brother is understood to be responsible for providing food through his labor for his sister who, in turn, through her good name and chaste reputation, provides her brothers with their own respectability. This somewhat more abstracted exchange is characteristic of the *feagaiga* or bond between brother and sister and will be explored further later in this chapter and especially in the next.

In contrast to these asymmetrical exchanges characteristic of complementary relationships are the competitive symmetrical exchanges that take place between groups or individuals linked in symmetrical sets. The particular media of exchange are not formalized in these cases in the way they are for the more formalized complementary exchange. Thus—depending on the circumstances—money, food, mats, or tapa cloth may find their way into competitive giving. Two kinds of symmetrical exchange are possible. The first is the direct competitive exchange between groups or individuals in which each tries to return to the other exactly what they had been given, but in greater quantities. Whereas great pains are often taken in complementary exchanges to ensure quantitative equality between those perceived as qualitatively distinct, symmetrical exchanges encourage the maintenance of a quantitative difference between antagonists perceived as qualitatively identical. In Levi-Strauss' terms, complementary exchanges constitute *rituals* while symmetrical exchanges are more like *games*.

Games . . . appear to have a *disjunctive* effect: they end in the establishment of a difference between individual players or teams where originally there was no indication of inequality. And at the end of the game they are distinguished into winners and losers. Ritual, on the other hand, is the exact inverse; it *conjoins*, for it brings about a union (one might even say communion in this context) or in any case an organic relation between two initially separate groups. . . . In the case of games the symmetry is therefore preordained and it is of a structural kind since it follows from the principle that the rules are the same for both sides. Asymmetry is engendered: it follows inevitably from the contingent nature of events, themselves due to intention, chance or talent. The reverse is true of ritual. There is an asymmetry which is postulated in advance . . . and the 'game' consists in making all the participants pass to the winning side by means of events, the nature and ordering of which is genuinely structural. (1966:32)

Direct symmetrical exchanges operate in Samoa on a number of levels. For instance, individuals or groups who contribute money, mats, or food to a family during a funeral, wedding, entitlement ceremony, or other life crisis expect their gifts to be reciprocated, largely in kind. Prestige accrues both through the ostentatious presentation of one's gifts and also through the equally public receipt of the return gift. All such initial donations are carefully recorded by the host family in a book, and the amount originally donated is one of the criteria for determining the extent of the return gift.

The competitive nature of such exchanges is evident in the highly charged atmosphere of the redistribution, where tempers are sometimes short and memories always long. Accusations of ingratitude, reminders of past debts, and other expressions of dissatisfaction may be exchanged along with the goods, but usually the presiding orators are careful, in calculating the redistributions of food, mats, and money, to balance considerations of public face against private gain.

Direct competitive exchanges take place during parties between any two groups such as villages, teams, or schools. Each group takes an *itū* or "side" of the house, with the dance floor between them. The festivities then include a competitive alternation of presentations—dances, songs, or comedy "items." These presentations are given as a gift to the other side, and include good-natured clowning and satire as well as more serious entertainment. Each side takes turns being audience to the other, singing its appreciation for each item performed with a conventional chant of thanks. Then, after several presentations by one side, the entertainers formally "pass the fire" to the other side, by another conventional chant. The "fire" may be accepted by a satisfied group, who then present their own performance in turn; or it may be rejected by a dissatisfied audience who ask for more from the other side before they will reciprocate. While all is done in the spirit of fun, the competition between sides is real, and always potentially serious.

A final example of a direct competitive exchange is the *fa'atau*, a "battle" between orators. This oratorical duel comprises a set of exchanged speeches where the desire for one-upmanship in oratorical power is paramount. *Fa'atau* may take place within a *fale'upolu*, that is, within a group of orators from any single village or district who compete for the right to represent the group in speaking. When two or more villages or districts meet for any reason, however, there may be *fa'atau* initially within each local group, and then a more serious and, depending on the business at hand, sometimes more substantive battle between orators from different groups. Here again, what begins as a ritual often ends up as a game, sometimes a very serious game.

Not all competitive exchanges characteristic of symmetrical sets are of the direct type illustrated in the foregoing analysis. Direct competitive exchange is often avoided in Samoa by transforming it into a less direct and therefore less dangerous form of competition. Indirect competitive exchange occurs when each of several potential antagonists makes a public gift or offering to the same party and competition is masked as a series of parallel donations. This common form of competitive giving characterizes situations in which the appearance of antagonism or rivalry between parties would be unseemly or otherwise inappropriate, such as church collections or gifts to a family during a life-crisis celebration. Meticulous records are kept of each gift and, in the case of donations to the church, contributions of each family are read out publicly each month, inviting comparisons and highlighting the competitive impulse behind the donations.

The distinction between symmetrical and complementary sets is, for a theory of social control in Samoa, the most important dimension along which social relations are organized. Implicit in this model of social relations is a theory of exchange, complementary relations suggesting asymmetrical and noncompetitive exchange and symmetrical relations manifesting forms of exchange that are fully reciprocal and more or less explicitly competitive. We have noted the tendency for complementary exchanges to be rather more formalized and ceremonious than those characteristic of symmetrical sets, the former exchanges suggesting the qualities of ritual, the latter approaching the qualities of games. Another way to express this difference is that for complementary relationships exchanges tend to symbolize a preexisting bond, while for symmetrical relationships exchanges define or create a bond. This difference is part of what we have referred to as the relative instability of symmetrical relations, their tendency toward conflict and fission, and the relative stability of relationships characterized by complementarity.

While this model takes us much further into the implicit structuring of social relations in Samoa, it is incomplete. There is a second important dimension of differentiation that underlies Samoan perceptions and evaluations of social relations—that of rank. We turn now to examine Samoan concepts of hierarchy.

Ranked and Unranked Relationships

The dimension of ranking in Samoan evaluations of social relations is based on a continuum of distinctions in power, authority, or prestige. Logically, rank thus deals with graded or gradual differences rather than the categorical distinctions of status differentiation. Not surprisingly, rank evaluations in Samoa lack the precision of evaluations of status difference and are not supported by the same kind of elaborate symbolization. This difference between rank and status discrimination is partly inherent in the nature of these evaluations, but it is also due to a particular characteristic of Samoan thought, which is to keep rank differences as fluid, and therefore as ambiguous, as possible.[7]

The elaborate Samoan etiquette of social relations distinguishes those who may deal with each other as rank equals from those of unequal rank. On public occasions, only those of equal rank may "face each other" in oratorical or other kinds of exchange. The more formal the occasion, the more the encounter is likely to be ritualized, and rank equality to be enjoined. The less formal the occasion, the more likely an exchange is to become a kind of game, leading to reevaluations of rank and the possibility of unequals facing each other. This concern in ritual exchanges with rank equality or equivalence is distinct from considerations of status, as I have defined it. Considerations of status, it will be remembered, deal with categorical similarity (symmetricality) or distinction (complementarity) between linked status forms. By contrast, relations are judged as ranked or unranked in reference to quantitative evaluations within a single scale of evaluation. Apples and oranges are not rankable, in this sense, unless they can be treated as members of the same class, such as "fruits." In the same way, brothers and sisters in Samoa are rankable only if treated as "siblings," and *ali'i* and *tulāfale* may be compared on the rank dimension only when they are treated as *matai*. These kinds of rankings do indeed occur, but only in certain contexts. The implicit criteria in terms of which these otherwise distinct status forms may be contextually treated as members of a common—and therefore rankable—class must be made explicit. Such criteria may include graded concepts like *mana* or *pule* (forms of power, wealth, or chronological seniority).

Unranked Relationships

Unranked relationships describe bonds between social units (persons, organizations, residential corporations, etc.) that are structurally parallel and equal in relation to a specified quality. Unranked relations occur between symmetrical status levels such as two or more brothers, sisters, siblings (gender irrelevant), parents (gender irrelevant), chiefs (type of chief irrelevant), villages, districts, or families. However, in situations where chronological seniority becomes important (rarely in Samoa), relations among brothers, sisters, or siblings are transformed into ranked relationships. It is also possible to consider a class of unranked relationships between complementary status forms, such as brother/sister, *ali'i/tulāfale*, or husband/wife in cases where qualitative distinctions are maintained, but no gradations are relevant or permitted. We have seen, for instance, that in politically significant marriages, orators are careful to permit no significant "inequality" in the *tōga/'oloa* exchange, and consequently maintain an impression of rank equality.

Technically, however, the concept of rank equality or inequality between complementary status forms is logically nonsensical. Insofar as status distinctions are concerned, they may only be nonranked rather than unranked. Ranking always implies a single scale of evaluation, while status distinction implies multiple scales. What we have in cases where brothers and sisters or bride's and groom's sides are judged as equal is apparently a complex evaluation in which status dimensions and rank dimensions are considered simultaneously. Such evaluations, logically incompatible, are in fact empirically common, and the inconsistency of making a judgment that implies both essential comparability and incomparability of two things is simply glossed over. In the case of the marriage, for instance, the insistence on the equality of essentially different kinds of transactions requires an impressionistic reduction of both *tōga* and *'oloa* to some common denominator, an implied common value scale. In so doing, a perceptual distinction between irreducible classes of valuables is maintained, while a conceptual and

Table 11.1
Unranked and Nonranked Relationships

Unranked Relationships *(Equal)*	*Nonranked Relationships* *(Equivalent)*
brother/brother sister/sister	brother/sister
paramount *ali'i*/paramount (*ali'i*) senior orator/senior orator *matai/matai*	senior *ali'i*/senior orator
balanced reciprocity in fine mats balanced reciprocity in food	exchange of *tōga* and *'oloa*
two *'aumaga* (young men's groups from different villages) two *aualuma* (girls' organizations from different villages)	*'aumaga/aualama*

covert equivalence is calculated. The same kind of implicit double-dealing with distinct kinds of evaluations goes on when a sister is declared to "outrank" her brother. Since, as we shall see in the next chapter, the status levels of sister and brother are based on distinct qualities and judged in relation to different scales (a "double standard"), the statement that one "outranks" the other must involve the implicit introduction of a third scale of judgment in relation to which brother and sister are members of the same class. Seniority, wealth, physical size, or intelligence are all criteria with the capacity to reduce brother and sister to "siblings" and render them rankable. But in these cases, they are significantly no longer being judged specifically as brother or sister. Where such complex rank evaluations are made of complementary status forms, it is perhaps better to speak of rank equivalence than of rank equality. Failure to make these distinctions, nice as they may appear, leads to fundamental misapprehension of the structure of Samoan social relations. This distinction between unranked (equal) and nonranked (equivalent) relationships in Samoa may be clarified somewhat by contrasting examples. Several examples of each type of relationship appear in table 11.1

Ranked Relations: Hierarchy

When two units of the same status are recognized to possess different degrees or quantities of some significant quality, then they are ranked in relation to the focal quality. Rank discriminations may be based on any gradable concept, and are thus both culturally and contextually conditioned. What we call in English "deference" may imply either of two forms of subordination: deference to rank difference (as when a junior sibling obeys a senior) or deference to status distinction (as when a wife obeys her husband or a brother obeys his sister). As has been noted, rank differences are, in Samoa, more ambiguous and equivocal than distinctions of status; and there is, characteristically, no single term in Samoan signifying specifically rank deference. The term *fa'aaloalo* (to respectfully defer to) is more commonly used to specify status differentiation than rank. Ethnographically important examples of ranked relationships in Samoa include the following.

> senior *ali'i*/junior *ali'i*
> village/subvillage
> elder sister/younger sister
> firstborn child/subsequently born child
> district title/village title
> *tama'āiga* (paramount) title/district title
> *tu'ua* (elder orator)/junior orator

Four Types of Social Relationships

If the distinction between complementary and symmetrical relations is combined and cross-cut with the secondary dichotomy between ranked and unranked relationships, then we have an analytical matrix, each of whose quadrants describes a distinct structural type of relationship for Samoa. This matrix is represented in table 11.2. Each of the quadrants represents a relationship type defined by the intersection of one term from each axis. Referring to the diagram in table 11.2, each of the four relationship types will be discussed separately.[8]

Incorporation

Relationships defined as both ranked and symmetrical are relations between units that are seen as functionally or conceptually alike but hierarchically ordered. The difference between them lies in the degree of power or extent of authority but not in the type of function or power involved. I have called these bonds *relationships of Incorporation*, since the subordinate unit is encompassed or incorporated by the larger, superordinate unit. Examples of such incorporative relationships in Samoa are village/subvillage, district/village, senior *tulāfale*/junior *tulāfale*, elder sibling/junior sibling, and senior *matai*/junior *matai*.

One of the characteristics of such incorporative relations in Samoa is that the boundaries between the related units tend to be ambiguous or otherwise unclear. The ambiguity between boundaries in these relationships is paralleled by a linguistic masking of these distinctions. While no direct or causative relationship among linguistic, social, and cultural forms can be assumed, it is suggested that this linguistic masking of certain kinds of relationship, and the clear differentiation of others, are significant.

Table 11.2
A Matrix of Samoan Relationship Types

	Ranked	*Unranked*

Symmetrical	Incorporation
	Part-to-whole
	Encompassing/encompassed
	Cooperation and deference
	Underlying conflict and manipulation
	Unstable
	Lack of linguistic and other symbolic
	  differentiation
	Cognitive ambiguity
	
	Examples
	village/subvillage
	district/village
	chief/subordinate chief
	senior orator/minor orator
		Competition
		Equals of the same logical/functional type
		May face each other in competition
		May replace each other
		Overtly recognized competition and
		  sometimes hostility
		Intimacy, lack of social distance
		
		Examples
		village/village
		rugby team/rugby team
		two orators
		two girls dancing the *siva*
		two orators dancing *'aiuli*
		two traditionally competitive villages

	Competitive Unstable Relations: Use of Overt Formal Controls for Conflict	

Complementary	Authority
	Hierarchical relations between logically
	  different types
	Pule: control, authority
	High degree of code redundancy in
	  differentiation
	Respect and deference
	External control
	Stable authority and control
	
	Examples
	chief's council/village
	titled person/untitled person
	parent/child
		Mutual Respect
		Shame, avoidance
		Self-control
		Externalized super-ego
		Mutuality of control
		Complementary meanings/functions
		Unlikes who face each other
		Formality and distance
		Love and harmony overtly stressed
		
		Examples
		brother/sister
		tamatane/tamafafine
		ali'i/tūlāfale
		ituau/alatuaa villages

	Non-competitive and Stable Relations: Possibility of Conflict Denied, Overt Conflict Resolution	

This assumed significance of such covert classes of relationships is further suggested and supported by the fact that distinct conflict types are suggested by these covert relationship types. Thus, for instance, the term *nu'u* does not distinguish districts, villages, and subvillages, and although the term *pitonu'u* may be used, its use is relational and contextual rather than absolute. Similarly, there is no set of terms to differentiate clearly in Samoan among chiefs of the same status but different rank. One may qualify the terms *ali'i* or *tulāfale* with *sili* (best). Similarly, there are specialized terms such as *sa'o, matua,* and *ma'upū* to distinguish oratorically particular high titles for *ali'i* and, for *tulāfale, tū'ua* and *failāuga.* But in general, there is a paucity of terms to distinguish the fine rank gradations between *matai* that, everyone admits, do exist. As one chief put it: "All *ali'i* are not the same; there are *ali'i* and *ali'i,* and the one should not be confused with the other."

Finally, there is a parallel linguistic masking of relative seniority among siblings. The Samoan kinship terminology has no basic terms for senior or junior siblings. The term *tei* is sometimes used with smaller children as a term of reference to junior siblings who must be looked after. In reference to political succession, the term *ulumatua* may be used to specify the eldest of a group of siblings. But in general usage, there is no specification made of seniority among siblings. One could, if desired, specify *lo'u uso la'ititi* (my younger symmetrical sibling) or *lo'u tuafafine matua* (my elder sister— male speaking), but in fact such specification is rarely made.

This linguistic masking of relationships of Incorporation reflects, in large part, the fact that rank differences in Samoa are tentative and open to alteration and frequent dispute. Rank is also sometimes context bound: for example one particular holder of a split title may be recognized as senior in intra-*'āiga* affairs, but have equal rank with all other holders within the context of the village *fono*. Such a senior holder of a split title is thus in an ambiguous position in relation to the other titleholders. He is *primus inter pares*. Rare is the holder of a split title who will openly admit to an outsider that one of the holders ranks above him. For a culture so concerned with rank distinctions, there is a remarkable paucity of explicit terms for rank distinction. There is, among Samoans, unanimity of opinion that rank differences occur, but little agreement as to what those ranks actually are in any specific instance.

The norms associated with relationships of Incorporation are cooperation and some degree of deference of subordinate to superior units, but also a good deal of competition and potential hostility between the units. There is in such relationships acute attention paid to the proper delineation of spheres of authority, so that a senior chief does not interfere in the household affairs of a subordinate chief. Although Manono, for example, recognizes itself as a family of Malietoa, it is doubtful that a Malietoa would ever try to assert preeminent authority over the senior chiefs of any Manono village in local affairs. Similarly, a district would meddle in the affairs of a local village, or a village in those of one of its subvillages, only with extreme caution.

Since boundaries and lines of authority as well as rank distinctions are frequently ambiguous in Incorporation relations, and the very distinctions implied by the relations are commonly masked linguistically, they are often marked by tension and instability. Subvillages may gradually deny their incorporated status and claim that they are autonomous villages, thereby redefining a subordinate relationship with a village into one of openly competitive equality.

This is precisely what we saw happening in Sala'ilua in the relationship between Si'utu and the rest of Sala'ilua village. In the same way, a village may deny the superordinate authority of a district over its internal affairs. Finally, chiefs who once acknowledged their subordination to those of higher rank may suddenly or gradually assert their equality or even superiority in rank. Such mobility in ranking is encouraged in Samoa by the lack of formal, external indications of rank differentiation, of which the linguistic lack is only one example. Anyone who has entered a Samoan village ignorant of the local hierarchy can attest to the difficulties that proceed from the relative poverty of distinguishing features for rank differentiation, despite the avowed importance placed on such distinctions.

In relationships of Incorporation, the stressed norms of deference and cooperation are undercut by a tendency of subordinate units to challenge superordinates, and by ambiguity, blurring, and even denial of the rank distinctions. Further, competition and conflict are always close to the surface, giving these relationships a pervasive instability.

Authority

Ranked complementary relationships are unequal relationships between logically or functionally dissimilar units. These inequalities are actually nonequivalent relationships, embodying a complex evaluation of both status and rank. Differences are thus asserted at *two* levels. In these relationships the notion of *pule* or authority is important, so I have labeled these relationships relationships of Authority. Other Samoan concepts relevant in such Authority relationships are *usita'i* (obedience), *fefe* (fear), *fa'aalaolo* (respect/deference), and *puipuiga* (protection/walling in). The relationships between chief and untitled man, parent and child, *fono*/village, and *matai*/ *'āiga* are important examples of Authority relationships. In such relationships, where the hierarchical distinctions of rank are combined with categorical distinctions of status, the lines of authority are clearly delineated, boundaries are explicit, control is unambiguously externalized, and power relations are structurally stable. Authority relationships reveal a heavy emphasis on explicit symbolic differentiation between subordinate and superordinate, an emphasis in striking contrast to the blurring of such distinctions in relationships of Incorporation. Serious conflict within such bonds is never expected; it is structurally discouraged and rarely admitted when it does occur.

Overt Competition

Defined by the intersection of unranked and symmetrical axes, Competition relationships link units perceived as both qualitatively identical and quantitatively equal. Two units of like logical or functional type and equal rank face each other in a relationship that is characteristically competitive, unstable, and aggressive. Young men vying for recognition on the dance floor as *'aiuli* dancers, two young ladies dancing the graceful *siva* in the middle of the dance floor, two competing rugby teams, a group of orators, two *ali'i* within the same descent group, and two maximal branches of a descent group are all important examples of such competitive relations. Aggression and one-upmanship amount to near-explicit norms for such relations. These are the relationships that are frequently characterized in Samoan by the "climbing up" or aggression of those linked by them.

Not surprisingly, overt markers of differentiation between such competitive units are minimal. There is an extreme blurring of distinctions, and a correspondingly intense instability in such relations. These are the relations that appear to have caught the attention of many observers of Samoa who have noted the divisive and unstable tendencies within the Samoan polity.

Covenants of Mutual Respect

This important class of Samoan relationships is defined by the matrix as horizontal and complementary. Such relations suggest the linking of those who are of equivalent rank or position in parallel hierarchies but possess a complementary relationship. Lacking rank distinctions, they are exemplified by *tulāfale/ali'i*, brother/sister, *itūau/alataua* villages, *tamatame/tamafafine*, and *'aiuli/siva*. More problematical is the inclusion here of the relation of pastor/congregation, which also strongly suggests authoritarian relations.

A word commonly associated with many of the relationships of this type is *feagaiga*, which derives from the term *aga* (social conduct), the reciprocal form *fe-i*, and the nominative suffix *-ga*. *Feagai* means "to face one another," with the additional meaning of "covenant" or "bond." *Feagaiga* connotes in particular a covenant of peace. The relationship between brother and sister is known formally in Samoan as a *feagaiga*. This relationship is, I suspect, the primary model for all such covenant bonds, but the term may also be used to refer to the covenants between husband and wife, *ali'i* and *tulāfale* (see Schultz 1911:46) and (in the shape of the pastor, who is called the *feagaiga* in respectful address) between God and man.

The complementarity symbolically realized in these "covenant" relationships is of a special sort, which is the fundamental ideological underpinning to the Samoan system of social control. Typically, these relationships oppose a member interpreted as embodying form, dignity, passivity, and order with his complement, characterized by action, change, disorder, energy, and utility. The linking of these pairs suggests the radical separation and interdependent union of the complementary principles of form and growth. Attitudes associated with such social bonds of respect are *alofa* (love, kindness), *fa'aaloalo* (respect), and *mā* (shame) in certain situations, along with avoidance. Confronting a covenant partner, one will "naturally" *teu le āmio* (hold in/control one's behavior). Chapters 12 and 13 will comprise an extended treatment of this complementary dualism in Samoan social thought and social structure.

These covenant relationships suggest the antithesis of the competition and aggressiveness associated with relations of Competition. From table 11.2, the formal relations between the two relationship types may be seen

Table 11.3
Symbolic Attributes of *Ali'i* and *Tulāfale* Statuses

Ali'i	Tulāfale
Wears *tuiga* "headdress"	Carries flywhisk and staff
Ulāfala garland	Sits in *talaluma* of house
Bestows *taupou* title	Receives leg/thigh of pig
Bestows *mānaia* title	Eats and drinks from metal plates/mugs
Sits at *matua tala* of house	Tea poured from communal pot
Receives backbone/ribs of pig	Dances *'aiuli* at periphery of a dance floor
Eats from china plate	Stands and speaks in formal *fono* on the
Drinks from china teacup	*malae*
Tea served in own pot	Entitled to be addressed as *tōfā*
Dances *siva* in center of dance floor	Received fine mats from *ali'i*
Sits, does not speak	Appropriately speaks in intimate
Has kava title and is called *afioga* or *susuga*	k-pronunciation
Appropriately speaks in formal	Sits with legs folded in male style[a]
pronunciation	
May sit with legs folded in "female" style	

[a] I am grateful to George Milner for this observation of the different sitting postures of *ali'i* and *tulāfale*.

clearly. The two classes of relationship are divided along the axis of symmetry/complementarity, but are both unranked. While Competition relations, as I have shown, are characterized by a lack of emphasis on formal distinguishing features of the related units (such as brothers, sisters, orators, or *ali'i*), there is a sharply contrasting stress on the distinguishing attributes of members of complementary covenant pairs. For example, I have listed in table 11.3 the most important symbolic attributes of the status forms of *ali'i* and *tulāfale*.

As we shall see in the following chapter, there is a similar elaboration of distinguishing features between the members of other important covenant relationships such as brother/sister, husband/wife, male/female, and *tamatane/tamafafine*.

Hierarchical Structuring of Relationship Types

Another structural feature of these complementary covenant relationships is that they frequently crosscut certain allied symmetrical bonds of Competition. The structural framework that I have been outlining is a fundamental cultural template in Samoa for ordering contexts. As such, the symmetrical and especially complementary forms of relationship are powerful ordering models that "work" simultaneously at several levels of abstraction. Thus, not only may pairs of individual units be linked in complementary or symmetrical sets, but these sets may themselves be linked with other related groups in "metarelationships," which again may be either complementary or symmetrical. In a hypothetical example, at level 1, symmetrical relationships may obtain among various boys in a village all belonging to the same *'aumaga* or, among village girls, all belonging to the same *aualuma* organization. Complementary relations (of the brother/sister type) hold between particular village girls and particular village boys. These primary level 1 relationships may then be embedded in level 2 relationships at a higher level of integration. Thus, using the examples just suggested, level 2 relations may on the one hand be symmetrical, opposing two groups of males in sports competitions in a rivalry between two schools or villages, or different groups of females such as two weaving houses, or two Women's Committees. On the other hand, level 2 relations may be complementary: for instance, a dance or *pōula* between an *'aumaga* of one village and an *aualuma* of another is an example of a complementary level 2 relation between two level 1 units, each organized symmetrically.

Obviously even higher-level relations are possible in this scheme. For instance ethnographically, military alliances in Samoa appear to have been organized at several levels of integration according to the complementary/symmetrical dichotomy. Certain groups of men from particular villages in a military alliance were considered the advance guard in the fighting. These larger groupings of warrior villages were called *itūau*. Other villages in the alliance were given the status of *alataua*, a sacred position of *tapua'i* (worshiping) for a favorable outcome of the battle. These men of the *alataua* villages were forbidden to fight. Remaining in their houses, blinds lowered, *alataua* members sat in quiet support of the warriors. Under the direction of the *taula* (priests), they would attempt to invoke the aid of certain important deities of war, especially the goddess *Nāfanua*.

Structurally, we may describe these *itūau/alataua* relationships as level 3, in which groups of men (level 1 symmetrical relations) from each of several villages were united with other similarly organized groups of men in level 2 symmetrical alliances (groups of *itūau* villages and groups of *alataua* villages). These two level 2 groups were then related to each other in a level 3 complementary relationship as *itūau* to *alataua*. In the battle itself, *itūau* groups would presumably confront each other, an example of a level 3 symmetrical relationship (see Gilson 1970:56).

This division between "male" localities associated with war and "female" localities associated with peace is a common feature of Samoan social organization. Aside from the *itūau/alataua* distinction, for instance, there was a parallel division within the Tuamasaga district of Upolu. If the district were called together to discuss a peaceful matter, the meeting would be held in Malie, a village associated with Malietoa, being one of his "homes." The name Malie itself means "harmony" or "concord." If, however, the subject matter were war, the district meeting would be convened at Afega village, home of powerful orator groups.

Entire districts could even be categorized in their relations with other districts, such as the division of the island of Savai'i in the nineteenth century into *Itū-o-Tane* (Side of Men) on the north and *Itū-o-Fafine* (Side of Women) in the south, the result of the defeat of the southern part of the island by warriors from the north (Gilson 1970: especially 55 and 90). This comple-

mentary division would constitute a level 4 relation. These progressive
levels of relationships are represented in figure 11.1, using as an example the
structuring of traditional military alliances discussed above. Complementary relations are represented by a *C* and a double line suggesting asym-
metical exchange. Symmetrical relations are symbolized by an *S*, with a
two-way arrow suggesting symmetrical reciprocity.

This diagram represents only one possible (and ethnographically accurate)
example of the hierarchical structuring that relations may have in Samoa.
It suggests the organizing power of the complementary/symmetrical model.

In figure 11.1, the complementarity in the functions or meanings of symmetrical and complementary relations is apparent. Symmetrical relations
suggest activity and aggression. The aggression may be directed outward
to a unit at a higher level, in which case it is an aggressive alliance; or it
may be directed inward, between the linked groups, in which case the bond
is an aggressive rivalry. These two types of aggressive relationship, alliance
and rivalry, are highly unstable. A military alliance is always a potential
military rivalry. The complementary relationships, by contrast, tend to be
far more stable structurally, and are associated with various forms of control
on aggression.

Looking at relationships from the perspective of hierarchical structuring,
it might be hypothesized that the greater the number of symmetrical links
between levels, the more the unit would be unstable, aggressive, and overtly
associated with disruption and conflict. Large military alliances are an example of high-level relations that include a number of symmetrical links
among males; and indeed, they have proved to be highly unstable in Samoa.
The way of controlling the aggression of these symmetrically related units
without totally destroying their useful energies is to harness that energy by
crosscutting crucial symmetrical relations with stabilizing complementary

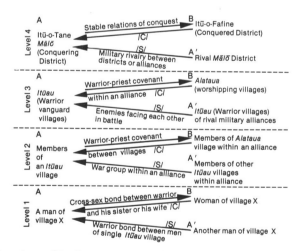

**Figure 11.1. Hierarchical Structuring of Symmetrical and Complementary
Relations.**

relations of control. This "solution" to a problem inherent in the logic of Samoan relations is itself implicit in that same logic. And ethnographically, that logic is exemplified in Samoan social organization. The most significant of these crosscutting relations of mutual control are set out in table 11.4.

This Samoan tendency to crosscut competitive symmetrical relations with stabilizing complementary bonds of control may be thought of equally well as the interposition of a dignified focus of respect, a *feagaiga*-type figure, between two symmetrical competitors. This image of an interrupted symmetrical relationship is not only an abstraction. This "model" of controlled relations was, for example, particularly vivid during the *fono tauati* or general village meeting convened in Sala'ilua to deal with Tautō's murder. The physical organization of this meeting placed the house of the *tapua'i* (worshipers), also called the house of the *feagaiga*, or pastors, midway between the two houses occupied by the *Sā Tuatō* and *Sā Tolova'ā*, the competing disputants in the murder (see figure 2.1). A similar pattern is evident in the general seating plan of the *fono*, where rival orators face each other at the front and rear of the house while *ali'i* sitting at either end of the house form the end points of a line that crosscuts that of the orators (figure 5.1).

Lest too passive a role be assumed for Samoan actors in relation to this general paradigm of relationship ordering, it should be emphasized that the template proposed as a Samoan model of social relations is not simply a received, prescriptive model of social action. It is also an important model *for* the active manipulation and restructuring of ambiguous relationships and situations. The dynamics of social conflict in Samoa frequently involve a more or less conscious attempt on the part of groups or individuals to redefine a relationship of one structural type into another sort of relationship

Table 11.4
Crosscutting Complementary Relations in Samoan Social Organization

Symmetrical Set	*Crosscutting Complementary Set*
Brother/brother (*uso*)	Brother/sister (*feagaiga*)
Tamatane/tamatane (descendants of title holders or their brothers; often rival claimants)	*Tamatane/tamafafine* (*tamatane* and descendants of a sister of an original or former title holder)
Fale'upolu (body of orators in a village)	*Fale'upolu/'āiga ali'i* (or *faletui*) (*fale'upolu* and groups of related *ali'i* in the village)
'Āiga ali'i (body of noblemen—*ali'i*)	*'Āiga ali'i/fale'upolu*
'aiuli dancers (source of overt competition on dance floor)	*'Aiuli/siva* (*'aiuli* and graceful *siva* dancers)
Mythical relations among three Upolu districts, each founded by one of Pili's sons	Upolu/Manono Island (the one sister of Pili's sons was placed on Manono and told to settle disputes among her three brothers)
Itūau village/*Itūau* village (as in military alliance)	*Itūau* village/*alataua* village (Passive worshippers/Fighters)
Alataua village/*alataua* village	*Alataua* village/*itūau* village

more to the advantage of the manipulator. Thus, for instance, a subordinate chief may attempt to raise the rank of his title, and assert its equality with that of a chief who had been recognized as his rank superior. In the terms defined in this chapter, a relationship of Incorporation, suggesting differences in rank but not in status, is asserted to be a Competition relationship of identical rank and status. Similarly, a subvillage may, like Si'utu in Sala'ilua, attempt to assert its structural equivalence to the village in which it had once been incorporated as part of a whole. In fact, in the case of Si'utu, which had once been incorporated in Ga'utaivai village to the south, it has undergone several changes in formal relationship in recent history. This most recent attempt of the subvillage to assert full independence from and equivalence to the rest of Sala'ilua threatened the overarching authority of the Sala'ilua *fono* over Si'utu and created a structurally predictable conflict. In yet another example of shifting relationship types, the case of a fight between two village youths I once observed in Sala'ilua, the arrival at the fight scene of the sister of one adversary provided a crosscutting complementary control on the fight, and the sister attempted to intervene in the fight and stop it. When the sister of her brother's adversary also arrived, however, the girl had a structurally appropriate competitive partner and the two girls began to fight, paralleling the conflict between their brothers. Here is an example of potentially conflicting demands of crosscutting symmetrical and complementary relationships. In this case, a relation of control, defined as a complementary convenant bond of respect, is "upstaged" by a competitive symmetrical link, as the latter is chosen as the more appropriate relationship for the circumstances.

Frequently, attempts to defuse hostilities involve the redefinition of relationship types from those suggesting aggression to those precluding it. Thus, whenever I expressed open annoyance or anger to a Samoan, suggesting competitive aggressiveness and hostile display, the response was usually a torrent of deferential respect speech, employing both phonological and lexical levels of respect address (chapter 13). Usually, my positions as *pālagi* guest, and teacher precluded my participation in openly hostile displays, and thus my presumptive "adversaries" attempted linguistically to reinforce the complementarity of the relationship, and thus the inappropriateness of my aggressive behavior.

Recognition of the active relationship people have with their own understandings of the nature of social relations saves this account from being a simple mechanistic vision of social relations in Samoa. While I believe that the complex set of understandings about social relations outlined in this chapter does provide the general boundaries within which Samoans understand their social world, this does not, I think, necessitate a simple deterministic view of things. Samoans delight in variety and in their ability to take an active role in fashioning social relations. What we have in this chapter is the suggestion that such manipulation of social life proceeds from a widely shared set of understandings about the nature of social ties.

CHAPTER TWELVE

The Symbolism of Power: Dual Organization and Social Order

To say that the relations between *ali'i* and *tulāfale* in Sala'ilua represent in some important sense a reversal of a characteristic political configuration is to imply a more general ideology of power in Samoa. That the unexpected preeminence of orators in Sala'ilua could be held even partially accountable for the general ethos of the village attributes to the formal structuring of power relations a very great significance. Before we can grasp just how significant this particular reversal is, we must explore the general ideology of power of which the *ali'i/tulāfale* relationship is but one example.

In the preceding chapter, the *ali'i/tulāfale* bond was comprehended in a general model of social relations in Samoa. This model distinguished not only ranked relations from unranked but, more significantly, differentiated symmetrical links from a set that was called complementary. In this context, the link between *ali'i* and *tulāfale* was defined as an ethnographically important example of a complementary relationship with significant implications for the distribution and control of political power. These final two chapters take a closer look at the symbolic and philosophical implications of complementary relations, for they represent to Samoans at the most general level a model for culture itself.

Culture As Control

In relations of symmetry there is, for Samoans, expansive competition and potential conflict, explicitly realized. In complementarity there is control, deference, and dignity. A popular song, played frequently on the radio station in Western Samoa, includes a chorus that ends with the significant line, "'O le aganu'u o le fa'aaloalo" (Culture is respect). When Samoans speak or sing about *aganu'u* (culture), they stress those aspects of social life associated with dignity and respectful deference. In the Samoan sense of the term, then, "culture," derived from the term *aga,* excludes aggression, competition, and the unrestrained expression of personal impulses. These impulses are aspects of *āmio* rather than *aga,* part of a natural order of things rather than cultural facts. In its Samoan sense, "culture" is closely linked with control and the social institutions and understandings that are associated with control. It is, therefore, not surprising that in the extraordinary elaboration of sociocultural institutions, their meanings, and the symbols through which they are understood—a complex that constitutes to Samoans their *aganu'u*, their *fa'a Samoa*—great emphasis is placed on a complementary dual organization that has power to order experience and guide behavior.

This equation of culture with complementary and noncompetitive relations is true only in the most restricted and refined Samoan sense of their culture. It suggests something similar to our use of "culture" in reference to the opera but not television soap operas, or to classical music but not hard rock. I have already alluded earlier to the fact that Samoan culture viewed more broadly does include conventionalized visions of competition and even disorder and suggests an attempt to encompass and restrict *āmio* by *aga*.

This cultural emphasis on complementary dualism has already been noted in the preceding chapter in the high degree of symbolic redundancy in distinctions between formal and complementary relations on the one hand (such as brother/sister, male/female, or *ali'i/tulāfale*) and, on the other, the poor symbolization of distinctions between symmetrically related units (such as village/subvillage, brother/brother, *ali'i/ali'i*, junior orator/senior orator). In this chapter I shall examine more broadly the concept of complementarity in social and cultural relationships in Samoa, and its pervasive manifestations and implications in the structure of Samoan social control. More particularly, a certain kind of complementarity will be discussed, a symbolic structure that I propose as a fundamental cultural model for Samoans in terms of which social order is conceived, and by means of which social control in particular is linked to social order in general. It is through this template that a collection of observed "texts"—social, cultural, and natural—becomes articulated into a set of significant social contexts.

Conceptually, this complementary relation in its most general aspect deals with the relationship between form and function. It suggests a Samoan political philosophy that separates and then links power in its most active and dynamic aspect, and stable forms that provide a sense of continuity over time with political life.[1] This is the sort of distinction that in many Western polities connects the transient government to the (ideally) enduring State. In Samoan thought the distinction involves the counterposition of qualities such as movement, energy, change, and diversity with others such as stasis, form, permanence, and accord. In chapter 8 I showed how this opposition manifested itself in Samoan creation stories, particularly in the existence of two cosmic *malae*, one for concord and the other for confusion and discord. In a special sense, we can understand this fundamental duality in Samoan world as an attempt to recognize the importance of both events in all their variability and forms or "structures" that give to historical events their enduring cultural meanings.[2]

In the following pages I shall argue that this dichotomy provides a powerful affective and cognitive model by means of which Samoans structure the contexts of social interaction, and in terms of which a potentially infinite

number of distinct situations is reduced to a limited set of culturally meaningful contexts. Because this paradigm structures concrete behaviors, formal
relationships, and social settings, it provides a general code in terms of
which behaviors are appropriated to contexts. Without some means of
collapsing and organizing the undifferentiated stream of experience into
conventional contexts, the concept of contextual appropriateness of behavior as used in this study would be meaningless.

The general human need for structuring paradigms by means of which
perceptions and associated behaviors are organized and rendered meaningful
is widely recognized in the works of those concerned with the sociology
of knowledge, and with social and perceptual psychology (see, for example,
Berger and Luckmann 1966, Schutz 1970, and Douglas 1973). Walter Mischel, a social psychologist, has discussed this ordering function in relation
to personality constructs.

The naive observer usually simplifies his observations both about himself and about
other people, by applying labels and constructs from a culturally shared trait theory.
(1968:41)

The data provided by judgments of others are restricted by the categories and
organizational limits of the judge. Constraints on the number of categories available
to a perceiver may help to account for the constant coding of diffuse perceptual
data into simpler forms: categorization of events into fewer and simpler units places
them within the limited scope of memory. . . . Without simplification of incoming
data by assignment of labels and category codings, it would be impossible to deal
with the virtually endless flood of perceptions that impinge from the environment.
Thus the construction of consistency, by relegating diverse events into broader
categories that subsume them, may be highly adaptive for many purposes and may
be dictated by limitations on the observer's organizing capacity. (1968:54)

While Mischel stresses this cognitive simplification and ordering function
in relation to the construction of personality types out of diverse behaviors,
such structuring in the Samoan case would focus on the organization of
settings for interaction rather than on the actors themselves. This structuring
would support the discrimination of contexts and behaviors, relegating
specific instances to general types, rather than the collapsing of a whole
range of the specific behaviors of a single actor into a single self-consistent
personality type. In Mischel's account, the organizing focus of the structuring is the person, while in the Samoan case it is the context or situation
of action.

In the preceding chapter, I examined complementary structures as part
of a broader framework of relationship types that helps to organize Samoan
perceptions of social relations. The following pages focus on the complementary relation in some of its important manifestations in the Samoan
sociocultural system, including political, kinship, and linguistically focused
institutions, as well as cultural conceptions of relations in time and space.
Because I shall be looking at complementary relations rather than any of
the relata themselves as the essential elements in Samoan context structur-

ing, the kind of meaning with which we will deal is strictly "relational meaning." Thus the significance of a particular term or unit emerges only in terms of its relations to other units, and particularly in its dual oppositions. Relational meaning is thus extrinsic rather than intrinsic, pointing to relations rather than to essences. Charles Taylor suggests that the term "relational meaning" is actually a tautology, since all meaning presupposes relationship.

Things only have meaning in a field, that is, in relation to the meanings of other things. This means that there is no such thing as a single, unrelated meaningful element; and it means that changes in the other meanings in the field can involve changes in the given element. Meanings can't be identified except in relation to others, and in this way resemble words. The meaning of a word depends, for instance, on those words with which it contrasts. (Taylor 1971:11)

Because we are interested in "relational meaning," which is to say, the context of meaning, a given institution or element cannot be said to have significance "in itself." Thus *tulāfale* or *ali'i* each has, as part of its meaning, the implicit complementary relation to the other, while the term *uso* (sibling of the same sex) points to a reciprocal, symmetrical relationship. In fact, it is significant that many of the Samoan kinship terms refer to bonds or relationships rather than to individuals. For instance, the term *feagaiga,* as a kinship term, refers not to brother or sister primarily (although it can refer to either secondarily), but to the relationship between the two, which defines both. Similarly, the term *ilāmutu,* which Mead (1930) gives as a kinship term for father's elder sister (and which appears in many Polynesian languages as either a term for sister's child, sibling's children, or, as in Samoa, father's sister), was defined by a Samoan as a bond including respect, fear, and obedience on one part, and solicitude and an advisorial role on the other. It is, possibly, the relationship among father's sister, brother's child, and brother and sister that is the primary meaning of the term, rather than any single related person. We have also seen that Samoan place terminology, such as *tai/uta* and *nu'u/pitonu'u,* follows the same pattern as kinship terms in defining positional relationships rather than intrinsic characteristics of places.

While *ali'i* and *tulāfale* each has as part of its implicit meaning the contrasted other term, the term *matai* (chief) is used when the contrast between high chief and orator is irrelevant. Yet the term *matai* has its own implicit relational context, opposed as it is to *taule'ale'a* (untitled person).

With a few exceptions, each term, such as *ali'i, tuagane* (brother—female speaking), or *teine* (girl) always suggests a particular side of an active/formal dichotomy, since the relationship is implicit in the term itself. Thus to refer to someone as a *tuafafine* (sister—male speaking) or an *ali'i* suggests the formal, dignified, controlled aspect of a two-place relationship. Conversely, referring to a *tulāfale, taule'ale'a,* or *tamatane* suggests the more active, dynamic, and utilitarian aspect of the relationship.

While these "sides" remain consistently linked to one or the other pole of the dual structure, the persons who bear these sides (roles) have no self-consistent identity. As brother, orator, or *tamatane,* a single male represents the functional and dynamic half of a set of relationships, while the same person may also possess "sides" that are the formalized and restrained part of a relationship, such as the roles of *ali'i, tamafafine,* and *matai.* These latter roles suggest behavioral orientations opposed to the former set of roles, but because each of the sides is normally bounded by a specific context, and care is taken in Samoan relationships that contexts be clearly specified and separated, there is no logical problem for Samoans in dealing with "contradictory" behaviors of an individual over time. For Samoans, paradox suggests violated context boundaries rather than temporal inconsistency.

The following sections comprise a detailed explication of this Samoan dichotomy between form and function, or formal and intimate behavioral styles as manifested in a large number of institutions and cultural conceptions. By now, many of these symbolic dual structures will be familiar, requiring only amplification and exemplification. A few complementary pairs will be newly introduced, requiring more elaborate discussion.

Male/Female

While gender distinctions are implicit in a number of different Samoan institutions, Samoans do not readily offer general characterizations of maleness and femaleness. When the questions are rephrased, however, from differences between male and female character to those distinctions between male and female behaviors or jobs, then the question becomes for Samoan informants much more meaningful, eliciting detailed response.

There is in Samoa an explicit sexual division of labor. In its most general aspect, this division attributes to women work that is *māmā* (light), *mamā* (clean), and focused on the central village and household areas. By contrast, work that is *mamāfa* (heavy), *palapalā* (dirty), or associated with the bush or other areas peripheral to the central village area (*'a'ai*), such as the cookhouse, the back part of the village, or the deep sea, is more clearly men's work. The specific tasks associated with each sex are outlined in table 12.1.

The light/heavy and clean/dirty dichotomies are clear from this list. The life of women appears to be focused in the centers of relative social order: the household, the residential core of the village, the shallow lagoon. By contrast, males are held to work more in the bush, in the back area of the village or compound, and in the open sea, areas that are conceived to be relatively unsubdued by social order. Moreover, male work is associated generally with wresting from these more or less hostile environments natural energy and nourishment for sustaining human life and producing growth. Fish, staple crops, and animal protein are won from the bush and sea through an expenditure of male energies and the application of male skills. Women are more concerned with the maintenance of a received order

Table 12.1
Samoan Sexual Division of Labor

Men's Work	Women's Work
Doing plantation work	Working on projects focused in village center
Planting taro and other root crops	Weeding plantations
Deep-sea trolling	Collecting shellfish in lagoon
Hunting wild pig and pigeon (rare today)	Weaving, sewing (mats, blinds, clothes)
Preparing of heavy starch food staples in ground oven	Preparing of "good" high protein foods, canned foods, European foods cooked within main house
House building	Cleaning of house and compound
Canoe building	Tending to village sanitation
Tattooing	Taking care of children
Participating in village and inter-village political affairs	Hosting village guests

and with sanitation and cleanliness. Whereas men are the agents of change and growth in the plantations, planting taro and *ta'amū* with their digging sticks, women are charged with keeping the plantations clean by removing the weeds that grow up. "Totō le tiapula" (to plant the taro shoot) is a common euphemism for the male role in sexual intercourse. Women, through their labor, impose or preserve order through negatively directed activity (weeding) while men harness natural energy through energies more positively directed (planting).

This general association of female work with a negatively conceived ordering is evident in the women's role in the village and district as sanitation and health specialists. Women's Committees inspect household compounds to make sure that they are kept neat and presentable for outsiders, with lawns trimmed, gardens free of weeds, and grounds free of rubbish. Women also ensure that the outhouse facilities are properly maintained and cleaned. One male informant summarized these women's roles in sanitation in a revealing way when he said: "They visit [households] to inspect things connected with the land. They check to see that no bush has grown up. They make sure that everything is clean and nice, especially the toilets." Moreover, while men's work is emphatically utilitarian, there is evident in many female roles a function more clearly decorative and aesthetic than practical. As we noted in the preceding chapter, fine mats (*'ie tōga*), the most valued product of female handiwork, have virtually no utility, and even the more functional baskets and mats woven by women often have a decorativeness rarely matched or expected in men's handiwork. To decorate (*teuteu*) is the reduplicated form of *teu* (to put in order), suggesting this containment of disorder. Furthermore the word *teu* is frequently associated with women's work, such as ordering the household compound or the houses themselves.

Mea lelei (the good food), cooked normally by women within the main living residence rather than in the cookhouse, is the most appropriate food for outside guests and important insiders. Such food is normally referred to as *kuka* (cooking) in preparation, a term associating it with pots, pans, kerosene stoves, *pālagi* houses, guests, and with the *pālagi* world in general. These associations in turn echo a more encompassing association of women with light and clean work on the one hand, and with the role of hostess on the other.

The association of maleness with positively defined activity and female-ness with activities defined negatively in terms of cleaning, ordering, weed-ing, and public presentability is pervasive in Samoan thought. As Samoans frequently say, girls *nofonofo* (stay put) and work generally near the places where they live (*nofo*). Males travel or move (*gāioioi*) both to their work and in their work, an activity that is seen to involve greater expenditures of energy and more activity than women's work.[3] These associations of stasis and movement with women and men respectively are fundamental facts of Samoan ideology about gender, and thus describe only partially the actual differences in men's and women's work as observed. Nonetheless, such associations tend to emerge in the ways Samoans talk about men and women. For instance, a middle-aged woman from Savai'i gave the follow-ing characterization of the differences between males and females.

If I have two children, a boy and a girl, they will be different. If, say, the mother is sick, the girl will have great love [*alofa*] but the boy—well, he will also be loving but he still will go off to roam about [*tafao*]. It's as if he didn't worry about his mother. The girl, however, can't go off roaming about like that, for she will stay [*nofo*] to look after her parents because of her great love. She will help.

The following two statements are excerpts from interviews with youths from Apia.

Girls are different; they rarely go roaming about like boys. For boys, it's easy to protect them. Nobody worries about them. But the parents worry about the girl lest she go out and do something stupid and they don't know about it. Because the girls are not strong enough to resist the boys. That's why the parents worry.

There are differences [between girls and boys]. The girl, in Samoan belief, she stays put in the house to help her mother, and the boy helps the father outside. There are also differences in games. The girls like *lape* [children's game like rounders] while the boys like rough games like rugby. Though you see some pretty rough girls too [laughs]. In Samoa, the girl should do clean, light work, while the boy does the heavy chores in the cookhouse. The girl does the *kuka* while the boy makes the heavy [starchy] foods. The girl makes the "good foods" [*mea lelei*], the *kuka*, stews, soups, things like that, and this food goes together with the heavy foods of the boys.

Girls learn early that they are expected to stay put, remaining near the village and near their household. Boys learn that they are freer to move about at will. This contrast of relative freedom and restraint for boys and

girls has other important manifestations. Prepubescent children frequently
go about naked. For boys, this period of freedom from the constraints of
bodily modesty may last until the seventh or eighth year, but girls are
generally dressed in shorts or underpants by the time they are five or six.
An elderly woman, living on Savai'i commented vividly on these sex-based
differences in modesty constraints.

A young child should not run around naked. It's bad. The child should have a cloth
around her. Girls, that is. But the boys, they run about naked. The girl, however,
should have her pants on when she goes out to play. The girl should be covered
up. The boys, they roam about at will. If they run on stones, that's fine for them.
If they roll about in the sand, well, that's the nature of boys' behavior. But for
girls, it's very unsightly [*matagā*] in Samoa to go about with no panties on.

The explicit association of nakedness and uninhibited expression in dress
with a general failure of control is evident in this account. While quite
young, girls learn to associate a complex set of attitudes and behaviors,
including staying put, control of impulse expression and movements, and
bodily modesty in relation to their brothers and, by association, to all boys.
Boys, in contrast, associate relative freedom of movement, lack of an-
choring to the household or the village center, relative lack of modesty
controls (except in the presence of their sisters), and the encouragement of
impulse expression.

Cross-Sex Relationships

In some sense, the basic model for all complementary relations is the
gender dichotomy between male and female, a fact that is no way surprising.
But despite its primacy, the basic cross-sex relation in Samoa is extremely
complex and problematical. The attitudes associated with all complementary bonds are probably derived from the cross-sex bond, which first commands the attention of the Samoan child and continues to be a model for
cross-sex relations throughout his life. This bond is that between brother
and sister. *Alofa* (love), *fa'aaloalo* (respect), *mā* (shame), and *āmio teuina* (self-
control of behavior) are the primary affective and behavioral associations
of the brother–sister relation. With certain crucial exceptions, to be discussed in the following chapter, the relationship of brother and sister is
passive, marked by avoidance of intimate contacts, shyness, and lack of any
aggressive displays. These associations are generalized in Samoan thought
to encompass all complementary relations.

Sexual drives and acts are considered the quintessential example of aggression and impulse gratification. Many of the terms used to refer colloquially
to sexual intimacy suggest this aggressiveness: *pi'i* (wrestle), *fai mea leaga*
(do evil things), *fai le āmio* (do the behavior). Others are merely neutral in
this respect: *ta'aalo* (play), *totō le tiapula* (plant the taro shoot). The English
expression "make love" would suggest the very opposite of sexual relations

to a Samoan, for *alofa* is frequently given as the very reason for avoiding sexual relations, at least before marriage. Even sexual relations between married couples, while obviously not disapproved of, are described in their functional aspect. They are, in their most polite euphemism, *fai 'āiga* (making a family).

All of these cultural associations with sexual relations are precisely the opposite associations that a male has in relating to a sister, and are commonly invoked as the justifications for the prohibition of incest. I asked one informant why he thought it was bad for a boy to have sexual intimacies with his sister.

Because I love [*alofa*] my sister. Sex is not something you do to people for whom you have love. It is bad for a person to go [sexually] to his own sister. For a sister is someone who was born together with me, and we have been doing things together. So that if I go to her, then I demonstrate to her that I don't love her.

Unlike parts of eastern Polynesia, particularly the Marquesas, the Society Islands, and parts of the Cook Islands, it appears that premarital sexual relations were never casual or "free" for Samoans. The *teine muli* or virgin was an ideal status for all Samoan girls before marriage, even prior to the Christianization of the archipelago. The fact that the chastity ideal for unmarried girls frequently remains merely an unrealized ideal, and that *de facto* casual premarital sex is not uncommon, in no way negates the ideological fact that such casual relations are considered wrong in Samoa. The *taupou* institution in which a village maiden (village virgin) represents formally all the girls of the village was one way of symbolically asserting the cultural value placed on premarital chastity, and at the same time of reconciling that value with the perceived realities of human passion and weakness.

Given the association of passivity, respect, and control with complementary bonds in general, and specifically with the primary male/female bond of brother/sister, there is an inherent problem for Samoans in dealing openly with the sexuality of cross-sex relationships in the sense that they embody a kind of structural contradiction and suggest what De Vos (1976) has called "affective dissonance." If the sexual complementarity of brother/sister precludes any suggestion of sexuality, there is no structural reason why the same attitude toward sex should not characterize all cross-sex relations. This, in fact, seems to be the case. When Samoans talk about sexual relations, they will often condemn sexual relations with an unrelated partner for precisely the reasons that they condemn sexuality with their own sisters. Sex, particularly premarital sex, is *āmio leaga* (evil behavior), *lē fa'aaloalo* (disrespectful), *fa'aleaga teine* (doing bad things to girls), and it demonstrates one's lack of *alofa* for the partner. Sometimes, informants will also argue that these girls also have brothers, and that when you think of their brothers, then you have love and pity for the girls, and you know that sex with them is bad. That is, it is the status of girls as sisters that suggests the inappropriateness and wrongness of sexual relations.

Structurally, the relationships between brother/sister and boyfriend/girl-friend are nearly identical. The only distinguishing feature is the concept that one is your relative, your own flesh and blood, while the other is not. Except for the primary relations between true biological brother and sister, however, this distinction in Samoa is one of degree and not of kind. There are, in Samoa, no categorical distinctions in kin terminology or classification between marriageable and nonmarriageable women and no distinction between norms of incest avoidance and those of exogamy.

When lovers are discovered to be related as '*āiga,* they are likely to invoke the conventional justification for their relationship that "children do not know their relations." The distinguishing behavioral feature of sibling and nonsibling cross-sex relations is that sexuality is absolutely proscribed in the one but not in the other. If not actually proscribed in relations between non-siblings, however, sexual relations are not exactly permitted either. The structural form of the cross-sex relationship even between non-kin denies, in a sense, the appropriateness of the very sexuality it suggests. The aggressiveness and impulse expression associated by Samoans with sexuality would better characterize symmetrical relations than complementary ones. One wrestles and plays, to use Samoan idioms, not with an individual in a complementary relationship, but with a symmetrically related partner. Sexual relations thus become for Samoans a residual problem of structural incongruity. Such relations are at least partially denied by culture much as they are suggested by nature.

The kind of relations that sexual intimacy suggests for Samoans are the sort that would be structurally suggested by symmetrical bonds. In public, casual homoerotic affection, wrestling, and play-fighting are commonly displayed among members of the same sex, particularly in youth and early adulthood.[4] Publicly, cross-sex physical intimacy is strictly denied, and confined to the secrecy of dark times and places. One may attribute this denial of cross-sex sexual expression to such factors as values or sentiments, but it is at least equally well accounted for in terms of the structuring of Samoan social relations. Relations of sexual complementarity suggest a more general relationship type that "logically" precludes the sort of behavior associated culturally with intimacy. Culturally, then, openly expressed sexuality is a problem that is resolved, if awkwardly, by the strict public denial of its legitimacy and frequently by the denial of its existence among the unmarried. Such premarital cross-sex sexuality is relegated to the subterfuges of night, the bush, or is otherwise denied.

'Aumaga/Aualuma

As we have seen, the young men and women of a village are formally organized into sex-based groups, the '*aumaga* for men, the *aualuma* for women. The membership criteria for the two organizations are not fully parallel, membership in the '*aumaga* being determined by the untitled status of a village male, while requirements for the *aualuma* include village birth, and sometimes considerations of residence and marital status. The *'aumaga* and *aualuma* organizations in Sala'ilua were described in part 2. Symbolically, these associations represent an extension of the Samoans' conceptions of male and female functions and meanings as described in the foregoing section of this chapter.

The *'aumaga*—literally, the "kava chewers"—is, in great part, defined functionally. Its members are known as the "strength of the village" ('o le mālosi o le nu'u), and carry out the orders of the chiefs' council, particularly in relation to the work (*galuega*) in the plantation or the village. Traditionally, the leader of the *'aumaga* was the *mānaia,* a titled son of a high chief. Today, the *mānaia* institution is largely moribund, and *'aumaga* leadership is normally in the hands of selected senior *taulele'a,* most frequently the sons of orators rather than *ali'i.* This association of *'aumaga* leadership with sons of orators is symbolically appropriate, given the generally "male" and utilitarian nature of the young men's organization. The *'aumaga* has relatively little part in village ceremonial life, except for the function of making and serving the kava.

The proper arena for *'aumaga* activity is the plantation or the back part of the village center where the ground ovens are located. On important occasions, groups of *'aumaga* members will be seen congregating about the cookhouses or the small sleeping huts (*fale o'o*) at the back of the compound. The term "strength of the village" suggests the qualities of toughness and energy associated with the village *taulele'a* and, more generally, with masculinity. Stair (1897:81) referred to an older version of the *'aumaga,* comprising a group of attendants to the district king or *tupu.* These attendants accompanied the king on journeys through the district.

During his royal progress, the *tupu* was accompanied by a large number of attendants and followers who were called O le Aumānga [sic], who were accustomed in a very arbitrary manner, to damaging the plantations through which they passed, and laying violent hands upon whatever they chose to take, whether pigs, poultry, or vegetables.

In this account, the *'aumaga* is associated with impulsiveness and aggression, features that are not realized in most *'aumaga* behavior but are nevertheless implicit in the meaning of the institution.

The *aualuma* is generally defined as comprising all the women and girls who were born and/or who grew up in the village. An out-residing village "girl" always retains potential membership in the *aualuma* for those occasions when she returns to the village. Leadership in the *aualuma* is traditionally provided by one or more *taupou,* generally daughters of ranking *ali'i* who possess a formal title associated with the *ali'i* title. Thus the *aualuma* is symbolically linked to the institution of the *ali'i* in much the same way that the *'aumaga* appears to be associated with *tulāfale* status. The significance of the *aualuma* in village life is as thoroughly ceremonial as that of the *'aumaga* is utilitarian. The *aualuma* has attached to it no functions other than the decorative one of acting as village hostesses for visitors, presiding over the care of any important guests in the village. In other words, the *aualuma* is charged with the responsibility of making the village publicly presentable to outsiders. Just as the *'aumaga*'s sphere of activity is at the peripheries of the village, that of the *aualuma* is the village center and the front part of the settlement, particularly in the *fale tele* or great meeting houses, where village ceremonial and "formal" life is carried out.

Functionally, the *aualuma* is more decorative than utilitarian. The *taupou* is a kind of summarizing symbol for the *aualuma* as a whole, a symbol of the grace, control, and negative activity seen as appropriate for females. She is sometimes referred to as the *taupou fa'anofonofo* (the sitting/immobile virgin). *Taupou* includes "virgin" as one of its meanings. It is upon the *taupou* that the respectful focus of the village is placed. The *taupou* is also normally one of the important figures held in reserve during dance parties, so that she dances the final *taualuga*, her focal and graceful *siva* style of dance contrasted by the wild *'aiuli* clowning on the periphery of the dance floor.

Traditionally, the *taupou* was also the focus of the value placed on premarital chastity for women, a value that increased in importance with the rank and prestige of the girl's family. Chastity was the ideal for all women before marriage, an expectation quite rigidly upheld for the holder of a *taupou* title. At her wedding celebration, the virginity of the *taupou* is said to have been publicly assayed by an orator, and the blood-stained piece of tapa constituting proof of chastity publicly displayed.

The value placed on premarital chastity for women is one aspect of the control and constraint associated symbolically with female status in general. Much as the male is encouraged tacitly to sexual activity and impulse expression, women gain their prestige from control, from what they manage *not* to do sexually. The defining attributes of the *taupou* are characteristically negatively articulated: she is frequently distinguished in terms of actions she does *not* perform. The following descriptions are typical.

The boy must show respect to the girls. For the girl, that is the one to whom the word *taupou* properly belongs, we say that she is a *taupou fa'anofonofo*. She doesn't do any chores. She just sits in the house and eats.

The *taupou* should act "*taupou* style" [*fa'ataupou*]. That means that she shouldn't walk about too much if she walks. She should walk about with a graceful sway [*fa'amāliuliu, fa'amāfulifuli*]. She sits, stays put in her dignity [*mamalu*]. She is like the *ali'i*. She doesn't speak too much. She doesn't laugh all the time.

The fact that the *mānaia* institution disappeared much earlier in post-contact history than did that of the *taupou*, and never appears to have had the same importance in Samoan ceremonial life, is not simply a fact of history, but also a fact of social structure and culture. Like the *tamatane/ tamafafine* institution, the *mānaia* title, attached to an *ali'i* title like its female counterpart, embodied a structural paradox, which the *taupou* title did not. The *mānaia* as an institution had a largely ceremonial function, for a group whose meaning was primarily utilitarian rather than ceremonial. Further, as son of an *ali'i*, the *mānaia* was an "illogical" choice for leadership of an organization that in its functional and symbolic aspects was more allied to the *tulāfale* status. Thus, the eclipse of the *mānaia* institution in favor of other *'aumaga* leaders chosen on the basis of criteria such as ability, age, experience, and commonly relation to a senior orator of the village, is a logical transformation, predictable from the Samoan logic of power.[5]

Brother/Sister

The brother/sister relationship, already discussed at length in several parts of this study, is a special—perhaps the most significant—instance of the male/female dualism in Samoan sociocultural organization. Because it is generally the first important cross-sex relationship between generation equals, the *feagaiga* or covenant bond between brothers and sisters is a powerful paradigm for all male/female relations.

As in all complementary bonds, the relationship between *tuagane* and *tuafafine* is asymmetrical. The sister is *mamalu* (dignified) in relation to her brother, who shows her *alofa* (loving concern) and *fa'aaloalo* (respect) through positive concern for her welfare and avoidance of intimate contacts, particularly contacts suggesting any aspect of sexuality. The respect owed the sister by her brothers is supported by a fear of a sister's power to curse a disrespectful or inconsiderate brother. One young male informant gave me the following remarks.

The brother must respect the sister; he can say no harsh words to her. If the sister should ever apologize to her brother for something, I would feel afraid. We begin to feel that we are cursed [*mālaia*]. No sister ever apologizes to a brother. I am afraid of being cursed by my sister. She would say, "You will have an unfortunate life because of me." That's what would make me feel crazy [*valea*]. I've heard many stories about sisters cursing their brothers.

A brother does not indicate his respect for his sister in any direct contact between them, since brothers and sisters generally avoid intimate contacts and are commonly *mā* (ashamed) in each other's presence. This is true even today, and testifies to the power of this traditional avoidance in Samoan culture. Rather, a brother must dignify (*fa'amamaluina*) his sister and honor (*fa'aaloalo*) her in the service or care (*tautua*) that he performs for her welfare. The brother moves about (*gāioioi*) for the sister, while the proper posture for the sister is to stay put/sit (*nofonofo*) and be served.

The sister is endeared by the brother. No matter what good thing the brother has, even if he has his own wife, his sister cannot do any hard work. She just "sits" while the brother "moves" to get her food.

The boy does chores. He "moves" for the girl. He brings the food, serves her, in order to show his respect and endearment for his sister.

The brother should dignify the sister. . . . The brother guards the sister. This is the respectful relationship within the family.

Girls in the family normally sleep in the front house closest to the village road or the *malae*. Traditionally, this house was inevitably the *fale tele* or great meeting house reserved for important ceremonial occasions and the housing of dignified guests. This sleeping arrangement is both functional and symbolically significant, placing the sister and her chastity under the watchful eyes of her parents or chief (who also slept in the *fale tele*) as well as placing her in the most public part of the household compound. At the same time, the symbolic value of the sister's position was underscored by her place in the frontmost part of the compound, that part most closely associated with dignity and formality. The brothers, by contrast, sleep in the *fale o'o* or sleeping huts at the rear of the compound, a physical position suiting their symbolic and functional status in the family. In relation to his sisters, a boy's status is primarily utilitarian. He "moves about" and "works" for the good of his sisters most particularly, and the rest of his family more generally. Through expending his own energy, the nourishes her. For her part, the sister does some chores for the brother. Though some of these chores, particularly the laundry, are in fact highly labor intensive, the sister's chores are conceived to be light and clean, at least in terms of their significance if not in terms of actual work. Indeed, they are generally associated with cleaning, laundering, ironing—with the public presentability of themselves and the other members of the family.

The relationship between brother and sister is thus one of asymmetrical exchange, the sister providing the bond with dignity and public presentability, the brother supplying the energy, strength, and movement. In political terms, informants expressed this same complementarity in brother–sister relations: "The *pule,* the [secular] power, is in the hands of the brother. But the dignity of the family, that is the sister." This same informant went on to describe the asymmetry implicit in the brother/sister bond. "The relationship between the brother and sister is very sacred [*sātaputapu*]. It applies to things like clothing. They cannot exchange clothing, especially the *lavalava* which is worn about the body."

The complementarity of the relationship in symbolic terms is reflected in the nature of the norms governing brother/sister interaction.

[The girl has to respect her brother too] but it is a different kind of respect. The girl shows her respect to the boy in the words she tells him and in the clothes she wears. The boy shows his respect in the care he shows the girl. The brother is unwilling to let his sister go to any boys and do any [sexually] bad things. He watches over her. . . . The sister also watches over the brother in the matter of starting fights. . . . She gets mad if he doesn't do things [i.e., chores].

The sister's chastity—or apparent chastity—is the focus of brotherly concern. Her dignity, and thus his, lies in her control over her body, in what she does *not* do. The sister's proper concern, however, is with what the brother *does* do, in making sure that he works properly. The concern is to keep him productively active, and to see that his energies are not improperly directed and squandered.

In light of this complementarity of function and meaning, we can better understand the privileged instances of legitimate norm-reversal in brother/sister relations. Normally shy and careful to avoid any intimate contact with his sisters, a brother will nonetheless react violently if a sister is caught with a lover. I have witnessed several instances where unfortunate girls have been severely beaten by outraged brothers who have discovered them in compromising situations with lovers. Conversely, and more frequently, sisters will loudly berate a brother either for lack of energy, calling him *paiē* (lazy) or *'augatā* (slow to work), or for misdirected or squandered energies, in which case he is accused of *tafao vale* (wandering aimlessly) or *ta'a* (playing around). The implication is that the brother should be channeling his energies productively for his sisters and, more generally, for the common good of the family, rather than squandering them on personal impulse gratification.

The complementarity that characterizes the brother/sister covenant relationship does not simply produce a sexual division of labor. In terms defined in the last chapter, it produces control of a very special and important kind in Samoa. The control, like the character of the bond itself, is complementary. A brother, in the face of his sisters, "holds himself in," controls himself, and "is shy/ashamed." These are postures that are alien to, indeed, the very reverse of, those generally associated with males in symmetrical relations with other males. Confronted with her brothers, a girl is never uninhibited or expansive, but she does tend to be far more assertive and demonstrative, particularly of anger, than are the boys.

By far the most striking behavioral reversal is that of the boy as brother. In the presence of, or even when thinking of, his sister, the normally assertive, "strong" male becomes relatively passive and shy. The structural asymmetry of the brother/sister tie, requiring elaborate deference of brothers to sisters, gives the sister (particularly an elder sister) considerable power and influence over her brothers. This power, enforced both by love and fear, especially fear of being cursed, creates an asymmetry in behavioral postures between brothers and sisters that would seem to deny their symbolic relations.

Thus, while the sister may stand symbolically for dignity and passivity, it is the brother who is clearly the more passive of the pair in brother–sister encounters. It is through a generalization of their dignified role as sisters that Samoan women seem to gain a remarkable energy and assertiveness, which appears to contradict their symbolic significance. Likewise, it is the experience of men as brothers that renders them shy and deferential in certain situations. The shyness that a male feels in respect of his sisters appears to underlie all relations of deferential respect for a male, especially cross-sex relations within the same generation that come to have an overtly sexual significance.

The norms of brother/sister relations thus undercut as much as they support the symbolic postures of males and females, which are otherwise encouraged in relations to outsiders. Through his direct relations with his sisters, a brother provides energy and utility, and receives in return dignity and public presentability. Conversely, a sister, in her relations with brothers, provides them with their dignity and public acceptability, and receives in return a measure of their energy and their strength. The resulting functional and logical bond of control through exchange and balance is, however, a delicate one. A sister may express a measure of assertiveness in relation to her brothers, but it is an assertiveness marked by restraint and distance. Similarly, a brother may be shy in front of his sisters, but it is a shyness proceeding from energy contained rather than weakness expressed. Such shyness and deference in the Samoan scheme of things are unstable, unsteady states born of their opposite potentials.

Tamatane/Tamafafine: Brother and Sister Relations Over Time

The *feagaiga* bond between brother and sister structures intra-*'āiga* political relations at levels beyond domestic ties. The most general and important of these extensions of the brother/sister tie is the *tamatane/tamafafine* relationship, which has already received considerable analytical attention in these pages. Based on descent from original or any former title holders and their brothers, on the one hand, and sisters of these men on the other hand, the *tamatane/tamafafine* descent categories reflect the symbolic relationship that is the direct parallel of the relationship between brother and sister.

Ideally, the *tamatane* members of a descent group wield secular power in relation to the title or set of ranked titles. This *pule* is recognized in the norm that only those claiming *tamatane* status in relation to a title have the right to an active voice in the discussions over succession to a vacant title. Moreover, the successor should come ideally from among the ranks of the *tamatane.* Those claiming *tamafafine* status in relation to the titles represent the dignity and respectability of the descent group. As such, they sit as dignified onlookers, praying for a harmonious conclusion to the *tamatane* discussions. Such harmony was frequently an exception rather than the rule, for different *fuaifale* (branches) of the descent group commonly support competing candidates for entitlement. Such competition in traditional times frequently resulted in open hostilities between these competing branches, or in a splitting of a title into two or more "pieces" in an effort to satisfy all claims. Competing *fuaifale* are generally traceable back to splits between brothers, sometimes many generations distant. Sometimes these branches originate from half-siblings, most commonly sharing a common father. In this case, the branches are called *faletama* (house of children) rather than *fuaifale* or *itū 'āiga* (but see Weston 1972 and Tiffany 1971 and n.d. for a more general and misleading use of the term *faletama*).

In relation to the competing (fraternal) branches constituting the *tamatane,* the *tamafafine* have a function of control and counsel. Specifically, the counsel tends to be of a negative sort, a kind of veto power over unacceptable candidates offered by and from the *tamatane* side of the descent group. Possessing no active voice in the selection of a new chief, and normally excluded from consideration for the office, the *tamafafine,* and particularly its senior members, have the function of adviser in the selection. More specifically, the advisory capacity of the *tamafafine* members suggests the *ilāmutu* function that Mead attributed to the elder sister in Samoa. The equation is supported by the belief among Samoans that the senior members of the *tamafafine* possess the power to curse (*fetu'u* or *fa'amālaia*) the *tamatane* members should the *tamafafine*'s advice not be heeded. Structurally, the relations between *tamatane* and *tamafafine* are identical to those between brother and sister, the one holding the utilitarian authority to effect change and exert power, the other maintaining a negatively defined dignity and power to nullify or otherwise channel and control the actions of the former. Employing an apt and suggestive metaphor, the sisters' side has a cleansing or "weeding" function to promote harmony and order by nullifying the potential sources of disorder that arise in the course of the often complex negotiations within the descent group. The *tamafafine* are associated with the maintenance or creation of harmonious relations between the competing fraternal branches of the descent group, a role essentially parallel to that played within the domestic arena by sisters in relation to brothers.

The brother/sister relationship not only structures the internal relationship of the descent group, but also provides a model for interrelating different titles. I have already dealt at several points with the *ali'i/tulāfale* opposition, and it will again be treated below. So powerful is the complementary relationship I have been discussing that it structures not simply the relations between *ali'i* and *tulāfale,* but also those between certain important *ali'i* titles. Not only do individuals bear genetic relations to one another, but titles also have their formal interrelations. For example, a set of high titles within a district may trace its origins to a set of siblings. In this way, titles come to have family-like relations to one another, and more specifically, come to be seen as bearing brother/sister ties. Two examples will serve to illustrate these brother/sister relations between senior titles.

To'oā, an *ali'i* title originally from the Falelatai district in western Upolu, has a *tamafafine* status in relation to the paramount title Malietoa. One of the prominent former holders of the To'oā title, Sualauvī, was the son of an elder sister to Malietoa Vainupō, both holding their titles in the midnineteenth century. Sualauvī was thus in a *tamafafine* relationship to Malietoa, a relationship that, when it concerns important titles, is called a *tama sā* (sacred child).[6] (Cf. *tamahā* in Tongan, the elder sister of the Tuitonga or Tuikanokupolu, the present royal line of Tonga.) The To'oā title, originally of *ali'i* status or *tamafafine* relationship to the Malietoa title, is today the *taupou* title associated with the Malietoa descent group and is presently held by Salamasina, the elder sister of the current Malietoa (Tanumafili II). For details on this relationship between Malietoa and To'oā, see Gilson (1970:117n) and Kraemer (1902: 1:302).

A title group or its associated descent line that bears a *tamafafine* relation to one or more important title lines or groups is sometimes given the formal designation of *ma'upū* in relation to the *tamatane* titles. An important example of a *ma'upū* relationship is the internal structuring of the huge political family of titles descended from Tuala and known jointly as the Sā Tuala. The associated titles and their original relations are represented in figure 12.1.[7]

These descendents of the original Tuala were the early settlers of the villages that are now Le'auva'a, Lefaga, Satapuala, Fasito'outa, and Nofoali'i in northern and western Upolu, and Lealatele and Amoa-i-Sisifo settlements in Savai'i (Le'auva'a being the resettlement community that was originally Lealatele in Savai'i). Together they comprise the 'Āiga Sā Tuala. Falenāoti was the daughter of the sole sister of six brothers, and her name is preserved in a title that has become the *taupou* title of the descent group called Sā Tuala. She and her descendants, moreover, have a sacred *ma'upū* or *tamafafine* relationship to the holders of all male titles in the Sā Tuala descent group. The present holder of the Falenāoti title is a distinguished and highly educated woman who is a former wife of Malietoa Tanumafili.

In addition to these relations, Falenāoti bears a formal relationship to the I'iga title, originated by a brother of Falenāoti. In recognition of its sister's status within the larger Sā Tuala descent group, the I'iga title uses the name of Falenāoti as an *ao* (honorific address) appended to the main name. Thus in formal address, I'iga is known as Falenāoti I'iga. The relativity of the *tamatane/tamafafine* status is clearly evident in this example. In relation to the descendants of Falenāoti, I'iga has a *tamatane* status, while he is *tamafafine* in the broader relationship to the 'Āiga Sā Tuala as a whole.

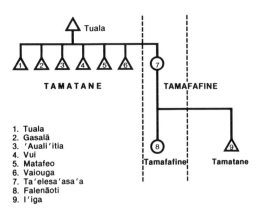

Figure 12.1. *Ma'upū* (*Tamafafine*) **Relations Within the 'Āiga Sā Tuala.**

My informant for this example, who himself holds a high title in the Sā Tuala, a title descended from one of the original male titleholders, described the significance of the *ma'upū* relationship in terms that are conventional in Samoan thought.

The title I'iga belongs to my brother. The sister of the I'iga title is the Falenāoti. The Falenāoti is the girl, while Pesetā [the informant's title] is the boy. So that their relationship is that of brother to sister. So we say that the Falenāoti is the *feagaiga* to the Pesetā. If we have some food in our family, the first food is served to the I'iga. Why? For that is the girl, the *feagaiga*. Pesetā is served last.

It is interesting that in this particular case, the I'iga title is held by a younger brother of Pesetā. The relation of the titles remains, however, that of brother to sister, despite the brother/brother relation between the holders. In contexts involving formal intra-group political matters, it is the conceptual relation between the titles that takes precedence over the biological relation between the holders.

The structuring power of the relational logic is clear in this example, for it works simultaneously on several levels. The logic is contextual in that a *tamatane* in one relation is *tamafafine* in another just as a brother/brother relationship in one context becomes translated into a brother/sister bond in another.

Yet another example of a complementary ordering of groups of titles employs the male/female idiom without brother/sister specification. In the nineteenth century, before the evolution of the present political system of *tama 'āiga* paramount titles, political supremacy in Western Samoa was symbolized in four older supreme titles called *pāpā*. Two of these supreme *pāpā* titles, Tui A'ana, king of the A'ana district, and Tui Atua, king of the Atua district, belonged to a widespread network of lineages in the A'ana and Atua districts known jointly as the 'Āiga Sā Tupuā. The other two *pāpā* titles, Gato'aitele and Tamasoāli'i, were said to be descended from the war goddess Nāfanua, and were associated with the other great political and kinship alliance in Western Samoa, the Sā Malietoā. These latter two titles were not associated directly with regency of a district as were the former two. The bestowal of the Tamasoāli'i title was the prerogative of orator groups from Safata in the southern Tuamasaga district of Upolu, while the Gato'aitele title was under the control of orators from Afega village in the northern part of the district.

Because they were "female" titles descended from a goddess, the Gato'aitele and the Tamasoāli'i were conceptually related to the Tui A'ana and Tui Atua titles as female to male. Thus, symbolically, the 'Āiga Sā Malietoā was the "female" part of the political organization of Western Samoa in relation to the "male" Sā Tupuā. The political ideal was the union of all four titles in a single holder or king called *Tāfa'ifā*, an unstable arrangement effected through intermarriage, war, and political cunning. The status of Tāfa'ifā has been realized only three times in the history of

Samoa, suggesting its extreme instability. Symbolically, the union of the four titles may be seen as the union of the Sā Tupuā and the Sā Malietoā, the female and male sides of Upolu. This idiom of union probably precluded the use of the brother/sister metaphor (i.e., *Ma'upū*) in expressing the relation between the Sā Tupuā and the Sā Malietoā.

The Weakness of the *Tamatane/Tamafafine* Distinction

In chapter 6, in relation to the Tuatō title of Sala'ilua, it was seen that the actual composition of the descent categories *tamatane* and *tamafafine* was variable and structurally ambiguous, depending in part on the particular generation from which membership was based. In fact, the categories of *tamatane* and *tamafafine* have proven in historical times to be relatively weak as a complementary bond between different classes of descendants from title holders. Ideally, *tamafafine* are supposed to advise *tamatane* on matters relating to title succession and political authority. But actual *pule* is supposed to be held by *tamatane*. Ideally, no one of *tamafafine* status is supposed to hold or even claim succession to a title. In fact, however, many titleholders in modern Samoa have made successful *tamafafine* claims to a title, even though such a claim is generally weaker than that of a *tamatane*.

This relative weakness of the *tamatane/tamafafine* model in structuring actual behavior is not, I believe, merely adventitious. The complementarity in the relationship between *tamatane* and *tamafafine* is a conceptual reality, the nature of which is not manifest in the concrete realization of those categories. That is, conceptually *tamatane–tamafafine* relations suggest a complementary brother/sister or male/female dichotomy; but it is a dichotomy whose concrete reality lies in genealogical history, rather than in immediate experience. Thus, while *tamatane* and *tamafafine* are conceptually distinct complementary categories, in any actual title fight they are both realized in mixed groups of women and men. The sexual dimorphism is nowhere evident, and the complementarity has no engaging symbolic manifestations as does the actual brother–sister or *ali'i–tulāfale* relationship.

Tamatane and *tamafafine* may stand conceptually for complementary functions and meanings, but perceptually that complementarity is denied, and groups of contending males dominate both "sides." The symmetricality in concrete *tamatane–tamafafine* groupings, suggesting competitive relations, undercuts the complementarity that is attributed to the relationship.[8] As we have seen in relationships of incorporation and competition, where redundancy in symbolic distinctions between related terms is low, the relationship itself is structurally unstable.

This hypothesis is not only supported ethnographically by the large numbers of title holders of *tamafafine* status, but is also confirmed by negative evidence. The norm that brothers and their descendants hold political titles is based on a more fundamental norm that titles are to be held by males rather than females. Females, particularly important ones, sometimes do hold titles; but in ethnographic fact, numbers of female *matai* are statistically insignificant. The fact that the complementarity of male–female relations in regard to title tenure has been largely maintained, while that between *tamatane* and *tamafafine* has tended to break down, is connected, I believe, with the fact that the external symbols of the male/female distinction are so vivid in relation to concrete persons and the distinction is notably absent in the relatively ineffective *tamatane/tamafafine* bond.

Tulāfale/Ali'i

The focus has now shifted from consideration of links that are primarily ties of kinship and descent to those that are phrased more emphatically in the idiom of supralocal power relations, and are thus political in character. It is, of course, just these political links that are at the heart of this analysis of Sala'ilua. As has been seen, every Samoan village is conceptually divided into a male side and a female side, suggesting the complementary sets of gender-based village corporations. This political division of the village corporations has its ideological parallel in descent constructs in the Samoan distinction between the "strong side" (*itū mālosi*) suggesting agnatic descent links and the "weak side" (*itū vaivai*) suggesting uterine links.

In addition to these two gender-based distinctions, there is a third division more clearly political in character. The political character of a village comprises several formal relationships, such as those between men and women and between the titled and the untitled. Within the group of chiefs, the titleholders within a village, there is a formal distinction made between those holding *ali'i* titles and those holding *tulāfale* titles. In ceremonial address, the village *ali'i* are referred to as *'āiga ali'i* (*ali'i* families), or simply as *'āiga*. They are also known in dignified oratory as *tamāli'i* (noblemen), a term that itself means "child of *ali'i*." Senior orators who speak on behalf of *ali'i* on important occasions are called *failāuga* (speakers) or *to'oto'o*, a synecdochic reference to orators as "orator staffs." The body of orators in a village is ceremonially addressed as *fale'upolu* (the house of Upolu), and in particular village or district greetings a reference to a group as a "house" such as "house of three," or "house of seven" may be normally assumed to refer to a body of orators rather than *ali'i*. While the *ali'i* may be seen as the repository of *pule* or authority, orators are commonly referred to as *faipule* (the activators of the *pule*), suggesting the distinction in power between its potential and kinetic aspects. The political core of a village, its *matai*, may thus be referred to formally as its *ali'i* and *faipule*.

A political unit such as a village or district is thus made up of descent groups whose senior titles are either of *ali'i* or *tulāfale* status. Originally, the distinction may not have been so clearly formalized as it is now, and the *tulāfale* were simply the privileged attendants and ministers of the king or *tupu*.[9] The relation of *tulāfale* to *ali'i* is that of function to form, or of the execution of authority to the origin or seat of that authority. The orator is a prime minister to the *ali'i*, carrying into effect his orders. One knowledgeable informant, an elderly *ali'i* with a particularly acute analytical capacity, described the distinction in the following way.

The separation between the *tulāfale* and the *ali'i* happened like this. This is my opinion on the matter. There are two things within each person: the power to command [*fa'atonuga*] and the power to execute those commands [*fa'ataunu'uga*]. *Each person has both of these potential powers.* This is how that class, the *tulāfale*, became important. They were not, in the old days, called *tulāfale*. But that title began with the Tui Manu'a when he said to those bearers, "I shall call you *tulāfale* and I shall assign to you the job of realizing or executing my dignity [*la'u afio*]. So that the Tui Manu'a held on to the *pule* [authority/secular power], but the realization of that *pule* was given to these other men. . . . [Originally] the King and the chief did alone the two things: the giving of the commandments [*fa'atonuga*] and the moving about [*gāioioiga*] to execute those commandments. Today we have this group of people called *tulāfale* who are like slaves, because of what happened in Manu'a. We have the class of *tulāfale*. These men carried the dignity of the Tui Manu'a. Things have changed since those days, but that is how we have today people who give the orders, and people who carry them out. [Emphasis added.]

On important occasions, the *ali'i* merely "sits" (*nofonofo*) whether in the fono house or on the *malae*, while the orator speaks for him and "moves about" doing his bidding. The *ali'i* is considered too dignified to move for himself. "The *ali'i*," an informant told me, "is dignified while the *tulāfale* does everything. The *ali'i* doesn't do many things, so you know that he is dignified."

Characteristically, the proper behavioral posture of the *ali'i* is defined negatively, by what he *doesn't* do. To protect his dignity, according to one informant, an *ali'i* must be "extremely cautious" (*fa'aeteete*).

A person is dignified by remaining very cautious. The loss of dignity in a chief results from his lack of wisdom and watchfulness. My habit is that I never eat in the house of another person from [the village of Lalomalava, where the speaker holds his *ali'i* title]. If I am invited into a house, I go. If they bring me some chicken soup, then I respond, "No, thank you; we have finished eating in my family." I do not eat even though my stomach growls with hunger. This is how many chiefs lose their dignity. People say, "Hey, look at who is feeding that *ali'i*, and look, he has finished all the soup he was served. That's why I never eat in the village. . . . I do not eat at any gathering of the village. The eating of the *ali'i* is watched over by everyone. Everyone wants to see whether he eats a lot, just like a commoner. No matter what is done, I am watched. Which is why I never eat on these occasions. Which is what I have been saying to you. The dignity of the *ali'i* lies in his cautiousness and wariness—in his holding back (*tāofiofi*).

The other thing about the *ali'i*—if he makes a promise, it is kept. He must never fail to do that. If a *tulāfale* goes to an *ali'i* and begs for a fine mat, and the *ali'i* promises one, or maybe even four or five, and then none are ever forthcoming, do you think that a *tulāfale* will ever have any regard for that *ali'i*? Never! That, they will say, is a poor *ali'i*! I have just given away a fine mat which I have had for five years. I never have to go to the orators of my own village and borrow a fine mat for them [laughter]. I always consider my dignity. Like if I go and command that this or that thing be exchanged—well, you know that Samoa is the land of bartering [*fefa'atautaua'i*]. Say, one night a plate of food arrives along with a cooked chicken at my house. Then I hold out a dollar and say: "Take this to the orator over there for him to buy his sugar with. Take it tonight. Don't wait until to-morrow." Then, on another night, I might ask: "Where did this plat of food come from? From the son of Pai? Oh well, what can I send him in exchange? Here, take this tapa cloth to him. Take this to cancel out that." I am explaining the sorts of things that one must do to keep firm the dignity of the *ali'i*. This is the sort of thing that goes on all the time between the *ali'i* and the *tulāfale*.

For the orator, no such extreme cautiousness is necessary. The orator is associated not with impulse denial and control, but with impulse gratification, exuberance, and aggressiveness: "It doesn't matter for the orator if he overdoes things. For he is the *tulāfale*. But for me [an *ali'i*], I must be extremely careful in my dealings with people."

In this general opposition between impulse denial or control and impulse expression, the distinction between the *ali'i* and *tulāfale* is a precise symbolic parallel of the relationship between sister and brother, and more generally between female and male in Samoan conception. While the *ali'i* increases his store of dignity by impulse denial, and by giving away items of value and utility such as mats or money to his orators and others, the orator eschews dignity for utilitarian power and wealth. The more highly ranked *ali'i* are known as *sa'o*, which literally means "the straight one" or "the correct one," while orators are described (although never formally or publicly) as *pi'opi'o* (devious/meandering) and *kuluku* (from the English "crooked"). As one informant volunteered, "If a *tulāfale* isn't crooked, he isn't a good orator." By "crooked" is meant cunning or skillfully manipulative; orators are generally held to be not simply the repositories of genealogical and historical knowledge, but *par excellence* the professional manipulators of tradition with an eye to local or self-interest. The Keesings describe this aspect of the orator role in their study *Elite Communication in Samoa*.

A great temptation exists for the elite person to impose idiosyncratic interpretations deliberately upon "messages" in the interest of facilitating communication or advancing other goals and values. . . . Deliberate manipulation by orators, for example, of information to the advantage of their chiefs and adherent groups approaches the character of being a norm. (1956:102)

In his dual role as repository and manipulator/creator of lore and history, the *tulāfale* energizes Samoan political life and is the source of much of the vitality and complexity of Samoan social organization. It is, after all, the orators and their penchant for the idiosyncratic and involuted aspects of tradition who are central in the elaboration of *fa'alavelave* (cultural entanglements/complications). As orator rather than simply as chief, a *tulāfale* has little dignity of his own. Rather, his dignity, like that of the "boy," the *tamatane*, or the "brother," lies in his bond, in this case the bond that links him to the dignified *ali'i*. If ideally *ali'i* preside over structure, clearly it is the orators who mastermind events in Samoa.

Orators pride themselves on their cunning and cleverness. If he wishes to accrue fame, power, and goods, an orator must be continually "on the move," seeking arenas for political and oratorical encounters. His work is seen as a manifestation of the particular relationship he bears to the *ali'i*. One orator described the *tulāfale* role as follows.

The *tulāfale* really suffers in his service to the *ali'i*. The *ali'i* just sits, and the only hardship he suffers is the giving of money and mats to the orator. But the orator— if he hears that guests have arrived, he is off in a flash to greet them. Like F., he is very clever. He hears that guests have arrived and he races off. The same with T. If there is a welcoming ceremony for visitors, T. never misses getting a fine mat out of it. He comes back with the *ālaga* [leg joint of pork reserved for senior orators]. If there is a visit of affines [*pāolo*] to the village, and they have their *taualuga* [final dance], their *taupou* will get up and dance. But our orator will clown about her, and collect his handouts. Perhaps money or mats. It's the hard work that wins the handout [*lafoga*]. That thing called an *ali'i*, we really have pity for him, for he gets only poverty. The *ali'i*—he gives away and gives away, but the orator gets every-thing for free. He gets his money, fine mats, tapa cloths. The *ali'i*, he just stays put, sits still, and suffers for giving everything to the orator.

The *ali'i* gains his dignity at the expense of his perceived utility. So constrained is he by considerations of respect and honor (called in other Polynesian societies *tapu*) that there is little of value that he can possess or do as *ali'i*. Utility, whether in the form of political knowledge, valuables, or nourishing foods, accrues to the orator. A negatively conceived dignity and formal presentability are the attributes of *ali'i* status.

Structural Anomalies in Ali'i–Tulāfale Relations

While ideally the *ali'i* and *tulāfale* are linked by a complementary rather than a competitive (symmetrical) bond, the asymmetry in their relationship does create a tension between them that can be understood structurally. While most brothers do, in fact, have sisters with whom they normally reside in their youth, the concrete ties between *ali'i* and *tulāfale* are not always so clear. Some high-ranking *ali'i* have particular orators who speak for them conventionally, but this formal relation between an *ali'i* and *tulāfale* is far from universal. Within village affairs, the *fale'upolu* (body of orators) has interests that are remote from any specific tie with *ali'i*. The balance between the active, functional role of the orators and the more passive dignity of the *ali'i* is often unstable. As has been seen, orators tend, by virtue of their status, to accrue wealth and political power, while *ali'i* are constrained from such activity by the dignity associated with their office.

Samoan history reflects a pervasive accumulation of power in the hands of orator groups, often at the expense of the *ali'i*. Savai'i, in particular, has been the home of powerful families of orators based in six *pule* (power) centers. Progressively, the *faipule*—the "execution of power"—which has been the traditional role of the orators, has tended to overshadow the formal possession of that power in the hands of the *ali'i*, until today the term *pule* has become symbolically identified with orators rather than with *ali'i*. This same tendency for the executors of an authority whose source lay elsewhere to come to view themselves as the source and seat of that authority is evident in the political history of Tonga, especially in the relations between the Tui Tonga lineage and that of the Kanokupolus (see Kaeppler 1971; Marcus 1980).

Occasionally, the balance between the orator and *ali'i* functions is upset. The drain of valuables from *ali'i* to *tulāfale* creates a disequilibrium for which abstract prestige or dignity cannot always compensate. Further, the power to speak for an *ali'i*'s interests is also the potential power to enhance one's own interests. In several villages, the problems inherent in the asymmetry of the *ali'i-tulāfale* relationship have been partially reconciled by the creation of a joint *tulāfale-ali'i* status. The *tulāfale-ali'i* has the functions and perquisites of both statuses. He may speak on his own behalf, holding flywhisk and staff as any senior orator would. He also has certain rights associated with *ali'i* status, such as a special kava name, a *taupou* title, the right to sit at the *matua tala* (front post) of the meeting house or to wear a *tuiga* (headdress). The *tulāfale-ali'i* may give away fine mats and money as an *ali'i*, but he may also receive them in his capacity as orator. The dual status enables the chief to keep a tighter control over his political and economic affairs.

The dissonances, both cognitive and functional, suggested by the *tulāfale-ali'i* institution, are partially avoided by the appropriation of the *ali'i* and *tulāfale* roles to distinct contexts. One never acts as both *ali'i* and *tulāfale* at the same moment. The *tulāfale-ali'i* is generally treated as *ali'i*, which is his unmarked or normal status. When he wishes to act as orator, he sits at the position in the meeting house normally reserved for important orators, carries the flywhisk and speaker's staff, and it is publicly announced, "O le'ā to'oto'o-ali'i lo tatou aso" (We shall have a *tulāfale-ali'i* for this day). Thus the bearers of the *tulāfale-ali'i* title, whose numbers are in fact small (I was able to confirm only three titles of this dual status), are little different from any other *matai*, who may possess both *ali'i* and *tulāfale* status by virtue of different titles, and thus of different descent and/or village relationships. Context orders their activation, just as it does for the *tulāfale-ali'i*. The main difference is that the *tulāfale-ali'i* possesses his two status forms by virtue of a single title and relationship and thus acts as an orator for his own *ali'i* "side."

The other major anomaly in *ali'i/tulāfale* relations occurs when orators come openly to possess the supreme authority in a village, and in this sense, outrank the *ali'i*. Normally the senior political status of a village belongs to an *ali'i,* who is considered more *tāua* (important) and *maualuga* (higher) than the orator by virtue of the ideological and functional aspects of the *ali'i/tulāfale* distinction. But through accidents of history (as in Sala'ilua, where the first settlers were the families of orators), orators may come to rule a village in the sense of being recognized as the preeminent political authorities in the settlement, commanding ceremonial deference from other chiefs. As with the *tulāfale-ali'i,* this situation represents a distortion of the normal relationship between the *ali'i* and the *tulāfale,* a structural anomaly.

The inversion of the relationship between orator and *ali'i* is, in part, inherent in the instability of the asymmetrical bond whereby orators accrue power, contacts, wealth, and knowledge in a manner denied to their more constrained and dignified counterparts. But normally a balance between the two sorts of status is maintained, although tenuously. Where it is not, as in Sala'ilua or in parts of the Aleipata district in eastern Upolu, political and social stress is predictable. While no unilateral "cause" of the stress and conflict-prone character of Sala'ilua village is suggested, such a character is at least consistent with the preeminent position accorded to orators within the village political and ceremonial organization. This preeminence of orators is reflected not only by the seniority of the titles Tolova'a and Tuatō in the village political structure, but also by the relation of the Sala'ilua general body of orators, the Sālemuliaga, to the rest of the village polity. Precisely this imbalance between *ali'i* and *tulāfale,* it will be remembered, constituted the subject of the heated debate between *ali'i* and members of the Sālemuliaga during the meeting convened to deal with the murder of Tuatō Fatu. According to several outspoken *ali'i,* the murder was the result of the "pretentiousness" of Fatu and Aleki and, by implication, of the body of village orators as a whole. Further, the political structure of the village was seen as significantly "out of balance," with the dignity of the *ali'i* being eclipsed by the very active authority of the village *tulāfale,* who were seen to pay little heed to the village nobility.

Pule and *Mana*: Structural Instabilities in Power Relations

In the foregoing analyses of relation sets between brother and sister, *tamatane* and *tamafafine,* and between *tulāfale* and *ali'i,* I noted a pervasive instability, a tendency for the dynamic and active power inherent in the instrumental member of the set to "spill over" into the formal member. These institutional sets each suggest the same opposition between instrumental and formal power, an opposition that also suggests distinctions between action and stasis and between movement and form.

For each of these sets there has been noted a tendency for the relationship to break down in the same way. In a very suggestive paper, Lévi-Strauss (1967) distinguishes between two structurally distinct types of dual organization. Moiety organizations of opposed clans or lineage segments ex-emplify what Lévi-Strauss calls "diametric dualism," in that the village area is divided into opposing sides with an implicit boundary drawn diametri-cally through the village. While this kind of opposition has geometrical manifestations, its basis, according to Lévi-Strauss, was in opposed social groups. In contrast, "concentric dualism" is for Lévi-Strauss uniquely spa-tial in character, being based on an opposition between center and periphery. As I have shown in the Samoan ethnography, the Samoan village is indeed conceived to be divided in terms of this concentric dualism between center (*'a'ai*)—or, more focally, the *malae*—and the village periphery. I have also noted that this same kind of concentric dualism is symbolically manifested in opposed complementary social categories, such as those in table 12.1. Lévi-Strauss goes on to make the important suggestion that in some sense the two kinds of dual organization are basically distinct. The diametric dualism, defined in terms of two points or parallel line segments, is static and unable "to transcend its own limitations" (1967:149). Concentric dual-ism, by contrast, defined in terms of a point and a line, is because of its structure inherently dynamic. More generally, Lévi-Strauss associates this concentric structure with symbolic oppositions, "drawn between terms which are logically heterogeneous, such as stability and change, state (or act) and process, being and becoming. . . . All these forms of opposition can be subsumed under a single category—the opposition between continuous and discontinuous" (ibid.).

Here, Lévi-Strauss suggests a symbolized distinction very close to that between formal and instrumental power, a distinction that I have discussed as implicit in the dual organization pervasive in Samoan institutions. While, for Lévi-Strauss, the dynamism in this concentric dualism is associated with implicit triadic structures, for the Samoan case the important feature is a pervasive instability. For instrumental power (such as that enjoyed by or-ators, brothers, and *tamatane* members) to effect change, increase itself, and move on, tends to accumulate at the expense of, rather than in coordination with, its complementary formal opposite. Ethnographically, this instability has been recognized in the tendency for orator power to increase at the expense of *ali'i* power, as in the case of the powerful orator groups who control the disposition of the paramount *ali'i* titles of Upolu or, on a smaller scale, the case of the dominant orators of Sala'ilua village. In fact, the institution of the joint *tulāfale-ali'i* status appears to be an *ali'i* response to this encroachment. As Samoans say, "Things of the *ali'i* rot away (into the hands of) the orators."

The sanctity and sensitivity of the relations between brother and sister, orator and high chief, *tamatane* and *tamafafine*, reflect this inherent tension. One senses in the sanctity surrounding the *ali'i* (particularly those of high rank), the respect mingled with fear enjoined upon brothers in relation to their sisters, and upon *tamatane* in relation to *tamafafine*, an attempt to protect the center of dignity and stability from the aggressive encroachments of instrumental power.

In terms of power, it is notable that the term *pule* (secular authority) is associated both with *ali'i*, who are held to possess (though not employ) it, and with the *tamatane*, who are said to exercise *pule* over the disposition of a vacant political title. This link between *ali'i* and *tamatane* seems hard to understand in terms of the symbolic dual organization, since it is with *tamafafine* and not with *tamatane* that *ali'i* have been linked.

Mead (1969:27) noted the tendency for *tulāfale* sometimes to assume *tamatane* obligations as the recipients of fine mats, and at other times to assume the *tamafafine* obligations as bestowers of the mats, depending largely on the social occasion. Mead is in error, however, in asserting that the orators "have abrogated to themselves the veto power normally exercised by a *tamafafine* group" (1969:26) in relation to the paramount titles of Western Samoa. In relation to the paramount titles of Upolu (Malietoa, Tuimaleali'ifano, Mata'afa, and Tamasese), the orators, associated with certain important villages, appear to possess actual *pule* of direct control over the disposal of a title. This kind of *pule* is in fact a *tamatane* function rather than one properly belonging to the *tamafafine*.

The use of the term *pule* in association with chiefs in general (in relation to a village, to untitled men, or to a household group), with *ali'i* specifically (in relation to the seat of ultimate authority in the *ali'i/tulāfale* relationship) and with *tamatane* in relation to the direct authority over disposition of political titles, is confusing and seems to link units that I have suggested are distinct.

The problem in the use of the term *pule* is the virtual disappearance of an explicit Samoan distinction between *mana* (sacred power), a kind of static attribute of nobility, and *pule*, a more secular authority to act. *Mana* today is used almost exclusively in relation to God. Rarely is the term ever used to refer to the power of men. It is my guess that the term *pule* has become the Samoan term for power in general, and in fact covers the distinction between sacred and secular power once common in Samoa. While the distinction has been largely masked, there is some evidence of the older division between *mana* and *pule* in contemporary Samoan. Thus, for instance, while *ali'i* are said to possess *pule*, orators are referred to as *fai pule,* the activators of power. In this sense, what I have been referring to as two kinds of power may be better understood as two *states* of power, a potential and a kinetic aspect.

The same linguistic shifts have not occurred in relation to *tamatane* and *tamafafine* status forms. *Tamatane*, to the extent that the institution is still meaningful in modern Samoa, are still associated with the *pule*, while the *mana* of the *tamafafine*, the static aspect of power of those who "sit" (*nofonofo*), is today rendered as *fa'aaloalo* (respect). This same term defines the power of sisters in relation to their brothers. This lack of parallelism between the related sets of *ali'i/tulāfale* and *tamafafine/tamatane* in relation to power may well be associated with the relative lack of emphasis in modern Samoa on the *tamafafine/tamatane* dichotomy in the allocation of titles. The point is that while the confusion is apparent at a linguistic level in the application of term *pule* to *tamatane* and to *ali'i*, the actual nature of the power relations and the distinction between sacred and secular power has remained. The *tamatane* are symbolically associated with the orator role in the sense of embodying an active, expansive, and utilitarian sort of power. The *ali'i* and the *tamafafine* retain their symbolic associations as embodiments of a formal, more static aspect of power. As we have seen, maintenance of the symbolic distinctions is difficult in light of instability in the relations between the two aspects of power, but this instability in no way denies the distinction of and the importance of these two sorts of power.

Chiefly Status: Symbolic Attributes

Associated with political titles is a set of important symbolic distinctions that conforms to the pervasive dual structure outlined thus far in this chapter. The most important of these symbolic attributes of *matai* status will be discussed here.

Title/Titleholder

It is considered polite in Samoan to address a chief using the dual pronoun, asking for instance, "Po'o fea lua te susī iai?" (Where are you-two going?).[10] Every chief, I was told, is really two "parts," a common or bodily part and an office or dignified part, called an *āfio*. It is the person who embodies and carries this dignity into action, realizing its potential, providing it with movement, energy, and utility. The *āfio* or office, by contrast, infuses this common aspect with its meaning and its dignity. The distinction between person and office is held to be universal, applying to all people regardless of political status. For *matai,* however, the duality is reflected in the use of two names, a chiefly title and a common or personal name.[11]

The distinction between the officeholder and the dignity of the office itself is fundamental to Samoan conceptions of political and social order, and both "parts" of a person are seen as necessary and interdependent. The distinction transcends the title/titleholder distinction, and applies to any individual who is seen to possess an *āfio* and a common aspect carrying that dignity into action.

Ceremonial Division of Food

In the context of the chief/untitled person distinction, the *matai* are served the *mea lelei* (good foods), particularly European-style food, foods high in protein, and foods that are light and require careful preparation. Here, the important distinction is between *mea lelei* and *mea 'a'ano* (starchy/heavy foods), those that consist mainly of root tubers such as taro and yams, and the large, starchy breadfruit that is roasted for food. In addition to this general distinction between types of food, there is a further set of distinctions made between foods and serving utensils appropriate for *ali'i* and those appropriate for *tulāfale*. The same distinction applies, though with less force, to the distinction between sisters and brothers. We have seen that ideally, at least, the eating habits of the *ali'i* are characterized by restraint, caution, and denial while those of the orator are associated with gratification, nutritiousness, and excess. One elderly informant explained: "The *ali'i* doesn't eat too much. He is brought his eating mat and is quickly finished. Two or three mouthfuls and he is done. He doesn't eat much because he thinks about what he does and he knows that he must eat little."

The "good food" association with the *ali'i*, and also with sisters, *pālagi*, pastors, and guests, is served on china plates (*ipu ō mea*). The *ali'i*'s tea is served in a china teapot, and is drunk from small, fine china teacups complete with saucers. By contrast, the tea for orators, brothers, and untitled people is served from a large metal teapot into capacious metal mugs. Their food is likewise served into heavy metal plates. I was told by informants that china plates, being delicate, fragile, and breakable, are more suited to the status of *ali'i* or sister. The roughly manufactured, sturdy metal dishes are more suitable for the orator and the untitled men. Not only are they tougher and larger, but they are more utilitarian, since they hold greater quantities of food. As one orator commented, with a bemused smile: "Oh, the cup and the plate of the *ali'i* are very fine indeed! They are made of china. But those of the orator are only made of metal. But there's plenty to eat and drink" (laughter).

Similarly, the division of the pig for ceremonial distribution during feasts allocates the *tualā*, the back, including the backbone and rib cage, for high *ali'i*. If there are two *ali'i* of rank, and only one pig, then the one gets the *tualā* and the other gets the *ō'ō,* a part behind the shoulder, including the ribcage from the *tualā*. For their part, the orators get a section called the *ālaga,* which includes the leg and thigh of the pig. Repeatedly I was told that the *ali'i*'s share of the pig is *tāua* (important) and the "good part" of the pig. Moreover, it is important precisely because it is fatty and bony, and because it includes the backbone and the ribs. Here, the words "good" and "important" refer not to the nutritional quality and edibility of the meat, but to the dignity attached to them precisely because of the relative lack of utility of these parts. The value of the *ālaga*, however, is precisely its utility rather than any decorative value. These differences in associations with *ālaga* and *tualā* were clear in one interview I held with an elderly senior orator. An excerpt from this conversation is reproduced below.

The *ali'i*, he gets the *tualā*.

(Is it a good thing to eat?)
Oh, it's nice because it goes to the *ali'i*.

(Is it good for eating?)
Yes, it's good.

(How about the meat?)
Oh, no! The *ālaga* is the fleshiest part [Laughs]. The thin part goes to the *ali'i*; the meaty part is for the orator!

Another informant, an elderly lady from Savai'i, chuckled as she told me: "The part that has all the meat, that goes to the *tulāfale*. The bone, the *tualā*, that's very thin and hardly has any meat on it. But we take it to the *ali'i*."

This distribution of pork symbolizes vividly the cultural attributes of *ali'i* and *tulāfale* status forms. The value of the orator's share of the pig lies in its utility. From the point of view of the consumer, the *ālaga* provides energy, nourishment, and movement. In relation to the pig, the leg/thigh joint provides the animal with movement. The *tualā* has its value in its lack of utility, much as the fine mat or *'ie tōga* does. Further, the value of the backbone is precisely that it provides the pig with shape or form rather than with movement, a distinction that clearly suggests the general symbolic status of the *ali'i*. One elderly *ali'i* made the following association between the cuts of meat appropriate to *ali'i* and *tulāfale* and their status: "The work of the *tulāfale* is much harder and takes more energy than that of the *ali'i*, which is why he gets such meaty foods. That's also why there's so much food for the *tulāfale*." The division of pork is thus not simply functional, but also logical, symbolizing as it does the conceptualized relations between *ali'i* and *tulāfale* status forms and, more generally, the relationship between form and movement.

In chapter 10, I examined the structure of Samoan social relations with particular emphasis on the connections between particular types of relationship and the genesis and control of aggression. While considerations of rank, which are the usual focus in analyses of social control, turned out to be important, I was led to see the even greater importance of what I have called symmetricality and complementarity in structuring social ties. Symmetrical relations, those linking similar units, were shown to be structurally unstable and associated with impulse expression and competition. In Samoan terms, symmetrical relations are the social structural realization of *āmio*, and are thus an important structural aspect of conflict in Samoa. As an institutionalized vision and disorder, such relations simultaneously present chaos and indirectly control it. Symmetrical relationships of this sort may ultimately be part of Samoan culture, but they do not represent for Samoans the fullest flowering of what they mean by their culture—their *aganu'u*.

In this chapter, I turned my attention to the kind of relations I have called complementary. These relations are associated with *aga*; that is, with culture in its refined sense, and thereby with direct control of aggression. While the focus in the preceding chapter was on the implications of the abstract form of these relations for social control, it has also become clear that those relations embody a general set of meanings for Samoans. By looking at the general associations Samoans have with such apparently distinct relations as brother/sister, *tamatane/tamafafine*, *tulāfale/ali'i*, a more general vision of two sorts of linked power emerges, which I assume to be an important part of Samoan world view and basic to Samoan institutions. This philosophy of power relations is not, for Samoans, a fully conscious set of principles; but neither is it unconscious. Rather, like all world views, this dual vision of the nature of existence is embedded in the forms that constitute the world for Samoans. The meanings are tacit meanings, which follow the shape of experience, and are thus lived-in meanings rather than speculations about the world.

In the following chapter we will pursue this Samoan world view by examining some of the more intimate forms that complementarity takes in Samoan life. The qualities of tacitness and embeddedness of this vision of experience suggest that daily life is saturated with its forms. These forms shape not only the tone and meanings of social relations, but come to dwell in the bodies of Samoans in the shapes of sound and movement that are taken for granted.

Plate 12. Village girls learn the art of weaving fine mats in the village weaving house (*fale lalaga*).

Plate 13. Village chief sounds the evening curfew with a blast of the conch.

Plate 14. Village children surround a house in which the Women's Committee is meeting. Note the contrast between the ordered center and the more chaotic periphery of the scene.

Plate 15. An orator, bearing the traditional symbols of his status, a fly whisk, and a staff, delivers an oration.

CHAPTER THIRTEEN

The Esthetics of Social Context: Dual Organization and Expressive Culture

Through a careful look at the esthetics of social relations, I think it is possible to show that even the most casual of interactions in Samoa is structured by the same dual categories as have been explored in relation to social roles. What I would like to examine here is the patterning of the emotional tone of interactions. Social contexts are always negotiated to some extent in the course of social interaction, but the range of possibilities for the tone of these contexts is sharply delimited by the logic of the culture from which they take their meaning.

The distinction between *āmio* and *aga,* so central to Samoan understandings of human nature, has been elaborated in this study into a theory of social structure viewed as a kind of dual organization, comprising sets of social roles linked through complementary opposition and mutual control. More diffusely, this dual organization suggests two distinct kinds of ethos, one refined and dignified, the other crude but powerful. These two styles define an esthetic arc through which the emotional tone of social life in Samoa swings. This tone is intimately linked to the structure of social relations, as shown above in chapter 11, where the arc was defined by symmetrical and complementary relationships. It is also tied to particular social roles. The *ali'i* and *taupou,* for instance, are held up as models of restraint and dignity, while the *tulāfale* and the untitled man embody the cruder and more dynamic forms of power.

I turn, in the end, to the esthetics of social relations, because I think it is possible to account in this way for the distinctive ethos of Sala'ilua. The preeminence of orator power in this village is not simply a political fact but an esthetic one as well, with important implications for the quality of the village's social life. Viewed in this way, I take the village itself to be a kind of large-scale context, different in scale but not in kind from the micro-contexts that will be examined in this chapter. If I am right, then I have arrived at the last set of clues for the solution of this Samoan mystery.

Dance Styles: Siva and 'Aiuli

The role of dance in Samoan society has frequently been the focus of commentary by observers. Lemert (1972), echoing a view made famous by

Mead, stressed the role of dance as a nearly unique outlet for personal expression among children.

> There are two outlets for the child who is placed under excessive pressures. One is to run away under the guise of a "visit" and to live with other relatives, who gladly welcome the child. The other *outlet for the child's unintegrated impulses and feelings* is the dance, in which all ages and sexes *participate on the basis of equality*. (204, emphasis added)

For her part, Mead stressed dance as a ritual of reversal in the life of the Samoan child.

> If the Samoan emphases are summed up as the subordination of the individual to the pattern, as the subordination of the younger to the older, of the commoner to the chief . . . then we find in one Samoan activity—the dance—a reversal of all these attitudes. . . . In a Samoan dance the whole usual order of the society is reversed. (1968:273)

While the dance does suggest for Samoa aspects of antistructure and an outlet for frustrated desires to "show off," a focus on this function masks the equally important part that dance plays in directly confirming and reinforcing certain distinctive cultural patterns rather than compensating for them. Instead of serving as an outlet for a child's unintegrated impulses and feelings, as Lemert suggests, the dance in Samoa may be profitably understood as an important arena where those feelings and impulses are structured and where appropriation of style to context is learned and reinforced.

The problem with the status attributed to dance in Samoa is that dancing has been viewed as largely homogeneous. As a cultural performance, however, dance is structured and differentiated in ways that support rather than contradict the normal sociocultural order. In this section, I shall consider some important dimensions of this structuring of dance forms.

In pre-contact Samoa, dancing was contextually differentiated into *pōula* (night dancing) and *ao siva* (day dancing). The *pōula* was characterized by a gradual acceleration of tempo and movement until the dancers and singers reached a feverish pace, the dancers' movements becoming less constrained and more overtly erotic. The *pōula* had a complementary counterpart, the *ao siva,* linguistically associated with the graceful *siva* rather than with *ula* (mischief). Stair gives the following account of an *ao siva*: "*O le ao siva,* as its name implies, was a day dance and much less objectionable than the *pōula*. This dance was practiced exclusively by the higher ranks, and unlike most of the other dances, consisted of a variety of graceful motions and gestures" (1897:134).

The formal distinction between the day dance and the night dance did not survive the Christianization of the archipelago, and is mentioned here as historical evidence of the conservatism and continuity of a characteristic Samoan dichotomy. The importance of traditional dancing has, however, survived the missionization of Samoa, and moreover has survived in a form that maintains the conceptual and stylistic dichotomy suggested by the opposition of *pōula/ao siva*. This dichotomy has become focused on a stylistic distinction between *siva* (dancing proper) and *'aiuli* (clowning), a distinction crucial to understanding the organization of the dance floor, but largely ignored by earlier observers of Samoan dancing.

I have already discussed the graceful, controlled *siva* of the center floor and the expressive, uninhibited, and relatively unconstrained *'aiuli* that surrounds it on the periphery. To Samoans, these alternative dance styles have vivid symbolic associations. These associations link the dance floor to a more general distinction between center and periphery which, as has been seen, has important associations for social control in a village. Some of the more suggestive associations that informants made with the two dance styles are translated here.

The *ali'i* dances inside [*'i totonu*], and he dances well [*e siva lelei*]. He dances gracefully [*onomea*]. But the *'aiuli*, the clown he doesn't dance gracefully like that. The *'aiuli* is really pretending to dance from the sidelines [*'autafa*]. We say in Samoan that they plead to the main dancers inside to dance nicely. The *'aiuli* really means to jump about wildly. They jump about on the sidelines so that the dancers inside will be seen to dance nicely, in a superior way.

The *'aiuli* is the dance of the *tulāfale,* and the *taulele'a*—the sons of the *tulāfale.* And if the *taupou* is dancing, the daughters of the *tulāfale* should *'aiuli* to her. Similarly, the wives of the *'aiuli* should dance *'aiuli* to those of the *ali'i*. When the *tulāfale* dances, he often jumps up, climbs up a pole, falls down—any possible sudden movement to shock those at the night dance. In some cases you'll find the *tulāfale* rushing up and striking down the houseblinds, and then picking up a pail of water and dumping it on the heads of the other singers. All these sorts of thing are characteristic of the *'aiuli*.

In Samoan custom, even if the house breaks apart, you still do the *'aiuli*. The *'aiuli* is the strong tough person. As if you are a bear or something. You jump in there and really kill them. The *'aiuli* is something like the bodyguard of the *ali'i*.

If you are dancing in the center, then I, as a *tulāfale,* will come up and help make your dance nice. I'll dance about crazily in the back. The *ali'i* does the *siva,* while the *tulāfale* clowns about. A high chief, for instance, one called a *sa'o* [senior *ali'i*, literally "the straight one"], dances the *siva*.

If there is a celebration of the *aualuma,* let's say there is a visiting party of affines to the village, then the *aualuma* will hold a greeting ceremony [*tau o le alafaga*]. There is a girl to whom the members of the *aualuma* give their respect, and she is addressed as Lau Āfioga a le Iligānoa [*taupou* title of the Savai'inaea *ali'i* title, Sala'ilua]. Another one is Lau Āfioga a le Samalaulu [*taupou* title attached to the Leala'itafea title, Sala'ilua]. These two are accorded the respect of the women. At night there is a dance party [*fiafia*]. At the finale [*taualuga*] the affines will take one side of the house, and the *aualuma* will take the other. And the time comes when her highness Iligānoa will take the floor to dance, and to grace our evening. And when she dances, the *tulāfale*—the girls, I mean—will go and roll about wildly, rolling their eyes way back in their heads. They put on old hats and clown around. That's the *fa'a Samoa*. They dance *'aiuli* to her highness Iligānoa.

The *taupou* dances slowly, sweetly, gracefully. She never tumbles about. But the orators, they roll all about there, jump about here.

The *ali'i* doesn't move around too much. He dances slowly. Only the *tulāfale* dances about all over the place. While the *taupou* is dancing, the *tulāfale* will be jumping wildly around on the sidelines, while Samalaulu [Sala'ilua *taupou*] is graceful, contained, and neat [*teu*] in the center. And then the dance is over. And the people who dance the *'aiuli*, the *tulāfale*, whether boys or women, will be given handouts of money or clothes by the *taupou* for having clowned. That's what's done for the *tulāfale*.

The classifying power of the *ali'i/tulāfale* distinction, and its relation to other dual structures in Samoan social organization, is evident in these comments, where those doing the *'aiuli*, whether male or female, titled or not, are called *tulāfale*. By this reference is meant that, in performing the *'aiuli*, these dancers fill an expressively appropriate *tulāfale* function.

The patterns expressed in the above statements are highly conventional for Samoans, and reflect a set of symbolized associations opposing on the one hand center, focus, grace, inhibition, and control, and on the other periphery, aggression, power, expansiveness, and disorder. The dance floor, mediating between these two aspects of the dance, is a kind of microcosm of the larger village arena, where an almost identical set of associations is made between village center (*'a'ai* or *malae*) and periphery (bush or the "back" of the village). These geographical associations were seen to have important implications for the village legal and moral system. On the dance floor, the periphery is associated with the orator or those representing the orator, the males, the untitled, and those showing respect. The center is left for the *ali'i*, the *taupou,* or, more generally, for anyone commanding respect and deference.

In the dance, it is the complementarity between restraint and impulse expression that is given supreme importance. The stress is on the maintenance and elaboration of a code distinction between controlled form and uncontrolled power, a distinction that is ubiquitous in Samoan sociocultural institutions. Behaviors that, in other contexts, might be considered disrespectful and deplorable—acts such as waving one's hand wildly above one's head, or emitting bellicose war yelps, or even the extreme measure of dropping one's waistcloth in a grotesque denial of norms of public modesty—are not merely permitted on the periphery of the dance floor; they are applauded as demonstrations of respect for those in the center. The wilder and more disordered the periphery, the more graceful and ordered the center appears by contrast. The code distinction is clarified and reinforced. It is in this sense that Mead was accurate in characterizing the dance as a social outlet, but it is an outlet that emphatically confirms rather than contradicts Samoan social order. In the face of one's complementary partner in the dance, actions that command respect (i.e., those associated with the *siva*) are the complementary opposite of those that confer respect (i.e., those associated with the clown).

Mead and Lemert were thus correct in attributing a special importance to the dance floor in Samoan socialization. The special significance of the dance floor appears to lie in its value as a testing ground for learned patterns of appropriate behavior. As a quintessential arena of social interaction, the dance floor provides a microcosm in which, contrary to Lemert's assertion, behaviors and impulses become organized and appropriated to contexts, and where the complex business of reading and assessing relationship types is learned, tested, and reinforced.

Lemert and Mead notwithstanding, it would seem that the dance floor in Samoa is far from an egalitarian and undifferentiated arena. It is a stage on which a dancer measures his or her ability to assess relationships, to judge social contexts and test his competence in the important skills of discrimination and of adjustment to shifting contexts. The following comments by informants suggest precisely these aspects of the dancer's perceptions of the dance floor.

On some occasions, a girl must dance *sa'o* [correctly/straight]. On respectable and dignified occasions she dances the *siva*, but then in others she must change the *'aiuli* style.

It is not dignified for a *taupou* to *'aiuli* or for the *tulāfale* to dance *sa'o*. If I dance, and it's just me alone, then I dance straight, but if there's a *taupou* also dancing, then I must *'aiuli* to her. It's very wrong for you to go into the center while a *taupou* is dancing *sa'o* and for you to dance *sa'o* at that time. If I am a *taule'ale'a* and there are *matai* in the center, they dance *sa'o* while I dance *'aiuli*.

The *tulāfale* should *'aiuli* to the *ali'i* if there is one present, but if there is a traveling party in which there is only one *matai*, a *tulāfale*, then the *tulāfale* should be shown the respect and others must dance *'aiuli* to him.

The girl's dance is good [*lelei*]. There are also times when the boy must dance well. If the *taupou* is dancing the *siva*, and you are an *'aiuli* to her, and you don't see that a *matai* has started to dance, and you continue to dance about the girl, with your back to the *matai*'s *siva*, that's one of the things we call "poor judgment" [*lē māfaufau*]. There are situations when you must dance properly, and then there comes a time when you must show respect. If you dance in the center when a chief is dancing, we say that that shows poor judgment. If a Samoan is really smart [*poto*], smart in a Samoan sense, then he will use his good judgment all the time and other people won't have to tell him what to do.

But such good judgment, being "smart" in a Samoan sense, is not inborn. Nor does it simply blossom naturally with age. It is learned—painfully, at times—through testing, trial and error. Life, for a Samoan child, presents many occasions for learning the discriminative abilities that make one "smart." These abilities involve learning to map gesture to occasion. But no occasion is more important for learning these skills, and none is more laden with clearly marked distinctive features of relationship types, than is the dance floor. Good judgment comes with difficulty and with practice. It is born of imitation, mistakes, mockery, and at times painful beatings. If the process of coming of age in Samoa is a song and a dance, it is, at least, a song not quite in rhythm and a dance ever threatened with finding itself out of phase with an occasion.

Linguistic Dimensions of Context Definition

The dance floor is one of several arenas of Samoan life where contexts are marked with great clarity. In such contexts, relationships are "built into" the situation, and stylistic appropriation of behaviors to context is relatively easy. These elaborated arenas of formal social interaction are ideal for teaching and reinforcing discriminatory skills, as we have seen in relation to the dance. But most occasions of social interaction are not so clearly marked, and relationships are inherently ambiguous. In such everyday encounters—on the street, between strangers, on first entering a house in an unexpected visit—contexts are not so much read as they are written. The skills required in such context composition involve negotiation and manipulation of context over and above the simpler perceptions of context type. Such context negotiation demands a fairly elaborate set of cues and rules for using and interpreting these cues. As with the learning of any sign system, receptive competence generally precedes productive competence, so that a Samoan may well learn to recognize cues for classifying situations and behaviors before he is able to manipulate those cues and create desired contexts.

Where context markers are not inherent in the external setting of interaction (as they are, say, in kava ceremonies, dancing, parties, church services, and most ceremonial occasions), it is the voice and body that carry the main burden of signing in the establishment of a formal or intimate context to which behaviors in an encounter are appropriated. The bodily signs are sometimes realized in decoration, marking status (such as the proliferation of uniforms for sports teams, schools, women's committees, pastors), and in the distinct styles of tying the *lavalava* for men, women, pastors, and transvestites. Other bodily signs of status and context definition are tattoos for *taulele'a* and chiefs, fly whisks and staffs for orators, and headdresses for the *taupou* and *ali'i*. In other cases, gesture carries the main burden of signing through distinctions in posture, physical proximity, suddenness or constraint of movement, all suggesting different degrees of dynamism or formality (i.e., symmetricality or complementarity) in a given relationship.

Vocal cues may be paralinguistic, such as the imploded whistle for calling dogs, children, and intimates. Intonation and pitch also mark context in Samoan speech, generally higher pitches signaling more formal contexts. Formality is also suggested by slowness and deliberateness of speech. Many of the important context signals are fully linguistic. For instance, I have already discussed the use of inclusive and exclusive we-pronoun form in signaling situationally defined degrees of intimacy and distance in social relations. The Polynesian pronominal system seems to be particularly suited for marking degrees of inclusion and distance in social situations.

In this section of the chapter, I shall deal with two kinds of linguistic distinction that reflect and also create contexts for social interaction in Samoa. They both register distinctions in speech and, while they share general features of structure, they are sociologically and culturally distinct from each other in important ways and require separate treatment.

"Respect" Vocabulary: An Overt Marker of Context

Samoan shares with Korean, Japanese, Javanese, Tongan, and Futunan a relatively elaborate division within its lexicon between common or ordinary and polite vocabulary. Samoans generally claim that there are two levels of vocabulary in their language, common words (the unmarked category, having no special distinguishing name) and "respect" vocabulary (*'upu fa'aaloalo*) or "chiefly" vocabulary (*'upu matai*).[1] Frequently it is said that common words are employed for commoners, while respect language is reserved for the chiefs and other dignitaries. This, for instance, appears to be the case for Tongan, where the chiefly language is literally that, a level of arcane discourse reserved for communications among members of the royal family (Garth Rogers, personal communication). In Samoa, despite the use of the term "chiefly language" to refer to the polite lexical forms, common or polite forms are appropriated more clearly to levels of discourse and interaction than to levels of persons. With the exception of young children, polite forms can be employed by and with anyone when the intention is to signal or support a formal interaction. Conversely, the use of everyday vocabulary signals intimacy and commonness in encounters, not so much in persons.

Only the most important and frequently used words have counterparts in polite speech, the most common being those terms that are the most likely to arise in formal interactions. In a few cases, there are several polite forms corresponding to a single common word. A sample list of common vocabulary items and the formal equivalents appears in table 13.1.

In addition to a positive signaling of respect by the use of respect terms in Samoan, there are several forms that indicate respect by humbling the speaker. Such forms of self-abasement are rare at the lexical level, and are more common in terms of proverbial expressions. But terms of self-abasement do appear, such as *'ua gaogao* for *ma'i* (sick). One could thus express respect either by referring to oneself as *'ua gaogao* or by using the polite form *gasegase* to another.

So far, the terms of respect discussed have been general, applying to encounters between individuals in which formality of deference is required. There are also specific terms of respect appropriate for different chiefly status levels. In table 13.2 is a list of respect forms in which there are different terms for use to *ali'i* and *tulāfale*.

It is clear from scanning the two tables that several possible relationships between common and polite vocabulary forms are found. Commonly, there is a simple one-to-one relation between common and polite forms. However, there are many cases in which semantic collapsing is evident. Polite forms may collapse several common terms into one respect term. Conversely, a single common term may be elaborated into a number of distinct polite forms. It is possible to generalize that, where one polite form realizes several distinct common forms, the condensation is semantic, in that the polite form is a more general term encompassing the denotations of the several common forms. Thus *vae* (leg/foot) and *lima* (arm/hand) are collapsed in formal vocabulary into the form *'a'ao* (limb). By contrast, where the common form is expanded into several distinct polite forms, the elaboration is connotative in terms of different degrees of deference or formality, rather than denotative. Thus *'ai* (eat) is realized in polite speech as either

Table 13.1
Common and Polite Forms in the Samoan Lexicon

English Form	Samoan Common Form	Samoan Polite Form
		taumafa
drink	inu	tausami
eat	'ai	taute
sit		saofa'i
live	nofo	fa'amautū
sleep	moe	tōfā
sick	ma'i	gasegase
full/sated	mā'ona	laulelei
village	nu'u	alaalafaga
want/desire	mana'o	finagalo
feelings	loto	
see	va'ai	silasila
know	iloa	silafia
hear	fa'alogo	fa'afofoga
head	ulu	ao
hand/arm	lima	'a'ao
leg/foot	vae	
beard	ava	soesā
face	foliga	
eye	mata	fofoga
		tu'umālō
die (human)	oti	maliu
		usufono
live/life	ola(ga)	soifua(ga)
blood	toto	palapala[a]
child (of woman)	tama	
son (of man)	atali'i	alo
daughter (of man)	afafine	
girl	teine	
woman	fafaine	tama'ita'i
speak	tautala	saunoa
		fetalai

[a] *Palapala* is used for blood only in cases where blood flows uncontrolled from the body. In common usage, *palapala* means "dirt."

Table 13.2
Special Polite Forms for *Ali'i* and *Tulāfale* Statuses

English Term	Common Term	Ali'i Term	Tulāfale Term	General Respect
come	sau	āfio mai / susū mai	māliu mai / sosopo mai	susū mai[a]
sir	(none)	āfioga	tōfā	susuga
house	fale	māota	laoa	māota
wife	āvā	faletua	tausi	faletua
wisdom/judgement	māfaufau	utaga	moe/tōfā	(none)
speech	lāuga	malelega	fetalaiga	saunoaga

[a] Malietoa, a paramount chiefly title, and titles related to the Malietoa descent group, are addressed conventionally as *susuga* rather than *āfioga*. According to Samoan history, Malietoa Vaiinupō, the first Samoan Christian convert, gave the right to be called *āfioga* to the Christian God in deference to a power greater than his own.

taumafa, tausami, or *taute,* with slight gradations of formality indicated, but no denotative distinctions.

As for general structural differences between common and polite forms, several general distinctions are apparent. In moving from common to polite forms, shorter elements are replaced by longer ones. Specifically, a movement from shorter to longer words is evident, as is a shift from single words to phrases. Such increase in the "volume" of speech forms corresponds to the Polynesian association of importance with quantity or size. Further, the effect of longer forms is to render the message less direct, a further feature of polite interaction. This indirectness of polite interchange is also suggested by the tendency for polite forms to refer to their referents metaphorically or metonymically, so that the reference becomes less direct. Thus while the common form for wife (*āvā*) refers directly to cohabitation, the chiefly forms refer to the back of the house (*faletua*) and to caring (*tausi*). Finally, several of the polite forms suggest older archaic forms, such as *finagalo* (feelings/desire).

The more formal the level of interaction, the greater the stress on elaborate forms and on style, rather than on directness of expression. Prestige and status are as much the "messages" of the communication as any of the subjects under discussion. It is interesting to note that in a chiefly council, the weightier matters are generally discussed in more formal and less direct terms. An exception is a serious and urgent crisis, during which time polite discourse tends to give way to direct and semantically explicit forms.

The important general use rules for lexically polite speech are as follows: polite speech is used to rank equals or superiors, but not always to subordinates; prestige and honor accompany both the giving and receiving of polite address, such that a chief may show respect by using polite forms to an untitled person, while he is shown respect by those who employ respect forms to him; polite forms are never used in reference to oneself except when referring to one's own title or position (Duranti, n.d.); forms of self-abasement confer honor on both the user and the person addressed;

and speech styles reflect situations, and thus "sides" of persons, rather than an absolute type of person.

In an informal context, an untitled youth may address a chief in familiar, everyday discourse. When contexts become more formal, and rank and status distinctions are relevant, the two may slip into formal discourse, with the untitled person more likely to use formal speech than the titled. The relationship and context have shifted into ones where rank and status differences are activated.

A common and important use of respectful address is to defuse a volatile situation. Open expression of hostility or anger between people is generally discouraged in public settings in Samoa. If one does openly express interpersonal hostility, particularly in an inappropriate (i.e., complementary) relationship, the response of the party addressed will commonly be to slip into a deferential posture and to erect a wall of polite speech, thereby buffering the anger and creating a context suggesting constraint and dignity. In cases of openly expressed hostility between symmetrically linked individuals or groups, the response is more likely to be an escalation of the violence, often into open conflict. In relation to conflict between formally linked units, this distinction between symmetrical and complementary reactions to aggression suggests Bateson's complementary and symmetrical schismogenesis (1936; 1973:35). See table 13.3 for a summary of social contexts associated with lexical levels of discourse.

One of the most significant associations that Samoans have with the lexical differentiation in their language is that between the titled and the untitled. Although polite vocabulary is not used exclusively either by or for *matai*, it is significant that such polite forms are most commonly associated by Samoans with chiefs, and more specifically with the oratory of the *fono*. Traditional Samoan "high culture" is associated with the *fono* and its *matai*. The chiefs are, for Samoans, the epitome of "cultured" people, and social interaction within the *fono* is a quintessential expression of *aga*. This association of lexical stratification in Samoan with chiefs and the *fono* is an important aspect of language stratification, and is essential for understanding the differences in lexical and phonological speech levels.

Table 13.3
Social Contexts Associated with Lexical Levels

Polite Contexts (respect vocabulary)	Informal Contexts (common vocabulary)
Display of deference to another	Suggests equality between speakers
Display of one's own humility	Intimacy
Speech to titled person	Speaking down, as to children
Speech to older person	Everyday talk
Formal oratory	Chiefly status irrelevant or absent
Welcoming guests	Speech competence of children
Chiefs' council	References to oneself
Diffusing hostility	

In summary, the more important rank is in any encounter, the more likely speech is to be liberally punctuated with formal words and phrases. Formal talk is quintessentially chiefly speech, whether or not *matai* are actually involved. Formal discourse is therefore an indication of the complementarity that marks the relations between chiefs and commoners. When chiefs speak as chiefs among themselves, they are likely to employ chiefly terms. When chiefs are addressed by non-chiefs, chiefly forms are also appropriate. Even when *matai* debate among themselves in their meetings— an apparently symmetrical exchange—the discourse is marked by formal vocabulary. The context is implicitly asymmetrical, however, since the use of chiefly language always distinguishes chiefly from common speech.

Phonological Stratification: Covert Context Marking

The existence of context-bound vocabulary levels is explicitly recognized by speakers of Samoan, and the lexical distinction between chiefly and ordinary speech is an important part of both native and observer's models of the language. Cross-cutting the distinction between common and polite vocabularies is a second linguistic distinction as important as the first in marking social context, but less explicitly formulated in Samoan conception.

Samoan speech is characterized by two phonological styles, or what Milner (1966) calls two phonological systems.[2] Milner associates these systems with "formal" and "colloquial" pronunciation (xiv). Phonetically, the differences between these two pronunciation styles are not marked, although the listener unaccustomed to Samoan may get the impression of two distinct languages being spoken. The phonetic system of each style is outlined in table 13.4.

The colloquial phonological system (henceforth, following common Sa-

Table 13.4
Formal and Intimate Phonological Systems in Samoan

	Consonental Phonemes				*Vocalic Phonemes*			
Formal pronunciation	p	t (k) ?			i	u ī	ū	
		s (h)			e	o ē	ō	
	f				a	ā		
	v							
	m	n ng						
	(r) 1							
Intimate pronunciation	p	k ?			i	u ī	ū	
		s (h)			e	o ē	ō	
	f				a	ā		
	v							
	m	ng						
	(r) 1							

( ) indicates in loan-words only.

moan usage, referred to as "k-pronunciation" or, using my own analytical terms, "intimate-style pronunciation") consists of an articulatory lateral shift to the rear of the vocal tract in the pronunciation of the phonemes /t/ and /n/. Thus [t], in formal-style pronunciation an apico-velar (or, in extreme polite usage, an apico-dental) stop, is realized in intimate pronunciation as lamino-velar stop. There is in addition a parallel shift from [n], in formal usage an apico-alveolar (or, in extremely polite speech, an apico-dental) continuant, to [ng] (written as "g" in Samoan orthography) in intimate style, a lamino-velar continuant. These shifts are represented schematically in table 13.4.

These parallel sound shifts [t] → [k] and [n] → [ng] are often accompanied by contextually conditioned allophonic variation in vowel pronunciation, such that the shift from formal to intimate pronunciation styles is characterized by a shift from acute to grave vowel qualities, giving intimate pronunciation a generally deeper and heavier quality than formal style.

The analysis of these sound shifts is complicated somewhat by the existence in the formal-style phonological system of both /k/ and /ng/ phonemes, phonetically identical with those of intimate-style pronunciation but with a different phonemic distribution. Thus in intimate-style pronunciation there are words such as [nganganga] (language), which is rendered in formal-style speech as [ngangana] and spelled "gagana," only one of the /ng/ phonemes being realized as [n]. Similarly, the colloquial form [anga] masks an "underlying" distinction between [anga] (social conduct) and [ana] (cave), a distinction that becomes phonetically realized only in formal pronunciation. Furthermore, formal-style pronunciation also includes the phoneme /k/, which is in distinct distribution either to the [k] resulting from the lateral shift from [t] in formal-style speech, or from the [k] found commonly in Polynesian languages in the position where Samoan has the [?] or glottal stop, written as an apostrophe in Samoan orthography. The formal-style [k] in Samoan appears only in loan words such as *suka* (sugar), Kaisa (Kaiser), or *kale* (curry). Of these loan words, only the word *saka* appears to predate European contact, and Milner (1966) suggests that *saka* (boiled food) may well be a loan word from Fiji, cognate with the Fijian word *saqa*.

This distinction between [t] and [k] in formal-style pronunciation is also marked in intimate-style speech, where both are realized as [k]. Thus, Samoans unskilled at handling the much less frequently used formal-style pronunciation tend to overcorrect their intimate-style pronunciation in formal encounters, creating phonologically hybrid forms like [suta] instead of [suka] and [tanata] instead of [tangata]. Such mistaken overcorrections are noted with amusement by Samoan speakers conscious of proper stylistic variations. These phonetically masked phonemic distinctions, which give rise to such overcorrections and to confusions for the student of Samoan language, are represented below in table 13.5.

The origin of the dual phonological structure is obscure. Samoans themselves are almost unanimous in asserting that the formal system is histor-

Table 13.5
Phonetic Shifts from Formal to Intimate Pronunciation:
Phonemic Distinctions, Phonetically Masked

Phonetic Shifts		*Examples*	
Formal	*Intimate*	*Formal*	*Intimate*
[t] ⟶ [k]		[tusi] ⟶ [kusi]	
[n] ⟶ [ng]		[puna] ⟶ [punga]	
/k/ /t/ ⟶ [k]		[kale] "curry" [tale] "cough" ⟶ [kale]	
/n/ /ng/ ⟶ [n]		[ana] "cave" [aga] "conduct" ⟶ [anga]	

ically prior to the intimate k-style. Pratt (1911), who was in Samoa soon after the arrival of the first missionaries to Samoa, confirms this opinion, although his characterization of the Samoan sound shift as parallel to that which took place in Hawaiian is inaccurate: "In Hawaiian they have changed from t into k, and ng into n. Thus tangata has become kanaka. Samoans are doing the same thing, to the great injury of the language" (Preface to the second edition). Samoans sometimes claim that formal pronunciation style is still common in those areas where Samoan culture is least affected by European contact, an observation that appears almost ironic in light of the actual distribution of social contexts in which both styles are used. The island of Savai'i, particularly the remote village of Faleālupo at the north-western tip of the island, is held to be a bastion of "proper" (i.e., formal-style) pronunciation. My own visits there, however, did not confirm this assertion. Milner (1966) claims to have found the formal pronunciation generally used only by some older residents of Fitiuta village on Manu'a.

In the experience of the present writer (which goes no later than 1959) the only occasion when he heard the formal pronunciation used normally (i.e., not delib-erately) was in the village of Fitiuta in the extreme east of Manu'a. Even there, however, this applied only to adults of local origin. (xiv, footnote)

My best guess is that the dual phonological system in Samoan was the product of a phonological drift that had already begun by the time the first missionaries arrived in 1830. When they orthographized the Samoan lan-guage as the initial step in translating the Bible, the missionaries selected the older and culturally preferred forms, thereby "freezing" the [t] and [n] into the written language. Moreover, this written form, with its older-style phonological system, was the vehicle for the translation of the *Tusi Pa'ia* (Holy Book) and the recounting of the *tala lelei* (good news), or the word of God. While the shift in everyday conversational speech proceeded, pro-ducing the intimate-style pronunciation spoken presently in casual or in-timate situations—which constitute the great majority of speech contexts—the formal style had become institutionalized and appropriated to its own contexts, primarily those associated directly or indirectly with the Church and the missionaries who brought it to Samoa. It is, of course, an open question what would have happened to this older form had the missionaries never arrived, or had they arrived one hundred years later than they did.

Our concern is properly not with the problematical issue of origins but rather with the contemporary meanings of the two phonological styles, and specifically with their synchronic significance as context markers in relation to dual organization. In the introduction to his *Samoan Dictionary* (1966:xiv–xv), Milner provides a brief characterization of the sociolinguistic dimensions of the two systems.

Formal pronunciation is held out to children, students and foreign visitors as a model to follow and is regarded by an overwhelming majority of Samoans as representing an older and purer state of the language than that which, alas, exists today. Formal pronunciation is used regularly by ministers of religion and by certain teachers in their official (though not necessarily in their private) capacity, by all Samoans while addressing God, and also frequently when speaking to foreigners.

Colloquial pronunciation is used by the great majority of Samoans both in public and private relations (except as specified above). Far from being incongruous in association with terms of respect or with the oratorical style, colloquial pronunciation is in fact frequently heard even on semi-formal and formal occasions. Yet for reasons which it is difficult to grasp fully, irrespective of their own speech behaviour in practice, Samoans regard formal pronunciation as the hallmark of good education and of good breeding and colloquial pronunciation as being uncouth and vulgar. Well intentioned attempts on the part of foreigners to adopt the colloquial pronunciation (unless those attempts are so successful as to pass unnoticed) are usually met with disapproval and discouraged by every means.

Kernan (1974), in a study that focuses on stages of phonological acquisition for Samoan children in American Samoa, gives a brief characterization of the sociolinguistic dimensions of the two systems, which he calls "formal" and "colloquial," following Milner's usage. On the basis of his observations of speech interactions in American Samoa, Kernan asserts that the colloquial style "is almost always used when speaking affectionately with children, spouse or close friends" (108). The formal style, however, "is always used in the *fono* . . . when making speeches, when delivering a sermon, when speaking to distinguished guests, when acting in the capacity of talking chief, and so forth" (*ibid.*).

Kernan's characterization of the sociological dimensions of the two speech styles appears to collapse the lexical level of chiefly/intimate speech discussed above, with the two phonological styles discussed here. Unless speech stylistics are significantly different in the village of Faleasao in American Samoa than elsewhere, Kernan is mistaken in associating the formal phonological style with the formal contexts of *fono* and oratory. This apparent anomaly in the association of chiefly vocabulary and colloquial phonology in oratory and *fono* speeches will be discussed further below.

I have been able to isolate an explicit distribution of contexts to which formal and intimate pronunciations are appropriated. These contexts are outlined in table 13.6.

The general contrast implicit in this enumeration of formal and intimate speech contexts with relation to phonological styles is that between institutions seen as indigenous aspects of the *fa'a Samoa* (and thus suggesting the symmetrical relation of Samoan/Samoan) that are associated with the k-pronunciation and, in contrast, institutions associated with the world of the *pālagi* or European, and its influences on Samoan life, that correspond with the formal t-pronunciation. The distinction is more complex than this, however, as suggested by the anomalous inclusion of "song-lyrics" as a category associated with formal pronunciation. One could conceive of "logical" explanations for including almost any institution in either category, depending on which aspects of the situation are defined as relevant. The use of formal pronunciation in Samoan singing suggests not *pālagi* origins but rather, I would guess, the coincidence of associating singing with church hymns, hymnals, and the historically older form of pronunciation passed on orally in lyrics. Further, to the extent that such songs have a hortatatory aspect, expressing public morality, formal rather than intimate pronunciation is appropriate.

Another apparent anomaly in this account is the association of indigenous forms with what is historically a more recently evolved phonological pattern, while the historically older form is associated with the European-introduced institutions. This contradiction is only apparent, however, since it confuses objective historical identity with subjective reality. The "indigenous" character of the k-pronunciation refers not to any historical or objective antiquity of the form, but rather to a sense of Samoanness, or an ideology of ethnic integrity felt subjectively. While the formal t-pronunciation may be seen as historically "purer" and prior to the k-pronunciation,

Table 13.6
Contextual Variation in Phonological Style

Formal Contexts/Phonology	*Intimate Contexts/Phonology*
School	General conversations among intimates
Church	Samoan-to-Samoan encounters
Encounters with pastor	Traditional formal orators
Song lyrics	Orators' speech
Radio broadcasts	Expression of extreme intimacy
Official government proclamations	Personal (as opposed to official voice)
Conversation with and by *pālagis*	Expressions of anger
Advice on proper behavior	Symmetrical response to hostility
Complementary response to aggression: difusing aggression	Gossip
	Swearing
Reading/writing	*Taulele'a* speech; young men
Encounters with strangers	
Speech for *ali'i*, girls	

its preservation is linked to European-based institutions (church, schools, pastor, the Bible, books) rather than to subjectively felt experience. If the "t" is more purely Samoan than the "k" it is nonetheless the purity of a museum piece wrenched from its original context, rather than an intimately-experienced reality.

Aside from these specific settings in which the two phonological styles are appropriated, there is a complex of associations that Samoans have about formal and intimate pronunciation. These associations are suggested by the common terms by which Samoans refer to the two pronunciation styles. The formal style is *tautala lelei* (good/proper speech) while the intimate style is *tautala leaga* (bad speech). The following series of excerpts from interviews suggests vividly some of the more specific concepts that Samoans associate with the two styles.

In some ways the "k" is more dignified. Many chiefs don't really speak in the "t."

Say if you meet a new person whom you don't know, you try to use the "t." If you are very well acquainted with someone, then you use the "k." If you go home and see that there is a stranger there, you use the "t." If the words you say are heavy ones, then usually you will speak in the "k." If you use the "t" when you are mad, it is as if you are speaking with weak words. When you are angry, you turn to the "k." But if you want to show respect to a person, then that's the time when you must use the "t."

In Samoan custom, it is respectful to speak in the "k." But in reference to Christianity, you know good behavior when somebody speaks in the "t." In Samoan custom, respectful behavior is the "k." But otherwise, good behavior [*āmio lelei*] means that you speak in the "t."

If someone speaks to you in the "t," it is nice and light. But if someone comes and speaks to you in the "k" it is as if they are angry with you.

"K" is proper when you speak with someone you know very well. But when you meet with someone you are not familiar with, and you think that that person is very dignified [*mamalu*], and you want to show him respect, then it is nice for you to use the "t."

When you speak the "t" to other people, it means that you want to show them your good side and your willingness to help them. If I speak to you in the "k," however, it shows that I answer you, but not with my full feelings [of cooperation].

You speak the "k" when your head is "out"—when you lose control.

When you're mad, you speak the "k." If I'm mad, and I say [in formal style] "Toeitīti 'oute alu e po lou gutu" [In a minute I'll smash your mouth], it doesn't sound right. It's not heavy like the "k."

Using the "t" means that a person is better off; he's a person of good behavior [*agalelei*], dignified and respectful. People who have a strong temper, are easily angered [*itāgofie*], enraged [*fa'ali'i*], speak badly and do bad things, speak in the "k."

Sometimes people speak to the "t" but when they go home to their families, they speak in the "k." If I am speaking to someone who has just come from a distance, then I speak the "t."

The "t" is harder to speak than the "k." It is not natural because it comes from the front of the mouth. You can't speak quickly in the "t." The words take longer to get to the front of the mouth. You have to think before you speak the "t" but in the "k" it just comes out naturally, without thinking about it.[3]

You use the "k" all the time when you are with your relatives and with your intimate friends. But the time that you want to show respect, to use respectful behavior, that's the time you switch to the "t."

Someone who is bad, but wants to be good, but then still wants to show his bad side too, he can speak with both the "t" and the "k"—the good and the bad.

"T" means that you want to appear angelic [*fia āgelu*].

The "k" is very natural, and it's what we speak in all the time. While the "t" means that we are well behaved. But then we go back and fall again to the "k." My name, for instance, is Tina, but I always know when my mother is angry with me when she says [kinga]. Also, some people grow up speaking with the "t" but when they are mad, then they go back to the "natural" way and speak in the "k."

If you are a *pālagi,* and you speak Samoan with a "k," it is as if you are a Samoan to them. Or a halfcaste with a *pālagi* part. They like that.

You know a halfcaste, because he always speaks the "k."

The associations mentioned in the interview excerpts between the intimate k-pronunciation and the halfcaste are interesting. One would not expect such an association, since the halfcaste is distinguished from the "full Samoan" precisely by his *pālagi* side, a side that would suggest the formal t-pronunciation. In his dealings with other Samoans, the Samoan halfcaste is frequently conscious of his lack of full Samoan status, and of the fact that he is often viewed by others as not quite Samoan. In Samoa, where a conscious pride in Samoan identity is everywhere apparent, this diminished status is in many ways more of a disadvantage socially than an advantage. The observed tendency for Samoan halfcastes to speak in the colloquial pronunciation exclusively may be understood as an attempt on the part of halfcaste speakers to confirm linguistically their Samoan identity, where speaking formal Samoan would underscore their Europeaness. Ironically, of course, it is precisely this tendency of halfcastes not to adopt the t-pronunciation that marks them as different from other Samoans. What is represented symbolically by the formal pronunciation for most Samoan speakers, in contradistinction to the intimate pronunciation, is suggested for the halfcastes by their use of English, since many are fully bilingual.

Speech Styles and Social Context

In relation to the social and political order, the t- and k-pronunciation styles are associated with certain roles that should by now be fairly predictable. The proper speech of the *taupou,* or more generally of girls, or sisters, is the formal-style phonology. This does not mean, of course, that women will always speak in the "t" but that they do so more frequently than their complementary counterparts, and that the formal style is seen as suitable for their roles when those roles become important. Boys, *tau-lele'a,* and brothers are associated with the informal k-pronunciation. The intimate pronunciation is seen as more natural and fitting for them and is also associated with their normal arenas of activity—the bush, the sea, the cookhouse, and the sleeping hut.

The matter becomes considerably more complicated, however, in relation to chiefs' roles and their linguistic correlates. Given the association of the informal k-pronunciation with contexts that are distinctly Samoan and independent of the effects of European contacts, it is not surprising that the chiefs per se and their traditional activities such as oratory and chiefly deliberation in the *fono* should be associated with intimate pronunciation rather than with the formal style. Rare is the speech in a *fono* that is made in the t-style of speech, and a chief who does speak in formal phonology is often a person closely associated with the church or with another European-introduced institution such as the school system or the European-style national government.

However, when the relevant semantic context is that of the internal differentiation between *ali'i* and *tulāfale,* the symbolic associations shift. In this case the intimate style of pronunciation is closely associated with the orator and his oratory, while the *ali'i* has come to be associated with formal style. This distinction was formulated vividly by an articulate elderly *ali'i.*

In my opinion, the "k" language is the language of the *tulāfale,* while the "t" language is the *ali'i* language. The church arrived and wrote the Bible in the language of Malietoa, for, as an *ali'i,* Malietoa spoke in the "t." In my opinion, this is a distinction from ancient times. Well, you have your own street language, your own "slang," though it is in words rather than in sounds that you know the differences among your people. Well, with us, the *tulāfale* chooses for himself whatever "careless talk" [English word used] he wishes to speak. This is why he speaks the "k."

But the ali'i, if he speaks, he speaks with caution because of his dignity. He does not speak too much, and when he does, it is never too quickly. That's why he speaks in the "t," because it is a nice and graceful way of speaking. It is not appropriate for an *ali'i* to speak quickly; that's for the *tulāfale* to do. And it is for the *tulāfale* to use the "k" because he is careless and speaks too quickly and too much. We call it speaking badly because it is the talk of the *tulāfale,* careless speaking. You realize that if an orator speaks the "t" when making a speech, it doesn't sound very nice. It's the sort of thing that people make fun of. If the orator speaks in the "k," however, he's the *tulāfale* and so that's very nice for him.

This view was reiterated by an elderly orator.

If the orator speaks in the "t," he'll speak the wrong way. That's because it's "good speaking" and doesn't suit the *tulāfale.* To mix "t" and "k" is not appropriate or pleasing to hear. If the orator speaks, he speaks in the "k," for anything he wishes to say. But if the orator speaks in the "t," you will hear all kinds of mistakes like *suta* [for *suka*]. The use of the "t" slows down his talk too much. You hear many orators nowadays trying to speak the "t," and you can hear how slow their speech is, and then they slip back into the "k." It just isn't fitting.

But not all *ali'i* speak in the "t," while there are some few orators who do attempt to speak in the "t." The apparent confusion in these styles is a result not simply of personality or biographical variation, but of an important contradiction in the definition of the context. As *matai,* a chief is led to speak the "k," particularly in traditional oratory, but when the *matai* happens to be of *ali'i* status, there is a contradiction between his status of *matai* in general and of *ali'i* in particular. This contradiction is apparent to many Samoans.

The linguistic dimensions of context definition discussed thus far, phonological and lexical, are important mechanisms for marking and supporting context definition. A summary of these two speech levels appears in figure 13.1. These levels are structurally problematical in several important ways. The stratification in the Samoan lexicon between formal and casual vocabularies might be expected to parallel directly the phonological distinction between formal and intimate pronunciations. This is not the case, however, since the two dimensions intersect one another rather than simply overlap. The relationships between the contextual aspects of lexical and phonological stratification in Samoan are represented in tables 13.7 and 13.8.

The fact that the two types of speech stratification intersect rather than overlap creates confusion among observers of Samoan language and speech. This confusion was clearly evident in Milner's account (1966) where he expressed an inability to understand how "k" pronunciation could be associated with "terms of respect or with oratorical style" and at the same time be considered "uncouth and vulgar" (xiv).

Again we have an example of what strikes Western sensibilities as illogic or contradiction or paradoxical reasoning. And yet, the association of intimate pronunciation with the darker impulses and cruder aspects of experience (*āmio*) and also with the most dignified aspects of chiefly culture (*aga*) is not illogical to Samoans. Samoan logic, as we have seen, is by Western standards highly diffracted and context bound, and embedded in semantic fields or contexts that are themselves sometimes embedded in

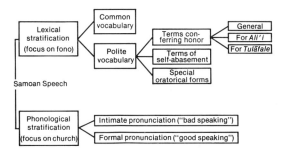

Figure 13.1. Forms of Speech Stratification in Samoan.

Table 13.7
Lexical and Phonological Stratification in Samoan Speech

	Polite Vocabulary	*Common Vocabulary*
Phonological Levels	Intimate pronunciation I. Polite Vocabulary + Intimate Pronunciation Chiefs, especially orators Traditional Samoan dignified occasions.	II. Common Vocabulary + Intimate Pronunciation Insult Anger Intimacy Affection Symmetrical relations Samoan occasions, intimate Household, intra-'āiga
	Formal pronunciation III. Polite Vocabulary + Formal Pronunciation Addressing pastors Pastor's sermons Deference to *pālagi* Radio broadcasts Addressing teachers on formal occasions	IV. Common Vocabulary + Formal Pronunciation Pastors addressing children Teachers addressing intimates Addressing Palagi intimates

other contexts more broadly conceived. Thus, what appears to an observer as inconsistency or illogic is commonly only a series of statements that are embedded in different semantic fields, contexts that are implicitly understood by other Samoans. Thus, to resolve the apparent contradiction in Samoan speech stratification, it will be necessary to take an excursus into two domains of the Samoan conceptual system.

Samoan Identity in Relations of Time and Space

The existence of two distinct and intersecting dimensions of linguistic stratification in Samoan, both important in defining contexts of intimacy and formality, reflects the fact that Samoans relate themselves to the formal/intimate dichotomy in two quite distinct ways. These associations are embedded in two separate semantic fields: the one suggesting the distinction *fa'a Samoa/fa'a pālagi* and the other suggesting a distinction internal to the *fa'a Samoa*, one between the formal and intimate aspects of Samoan life in itself.[4] The second semantic field, consisting of relations internal to the *fa'a Samoa*, has been the major subject of this chapter. It is the ways in which Samoans have organized their experience in relation to Europeans that will be discussed here.

The Samoan experience during the past two centuries with the world of the *pālagi* has left an unmistakable mark on the archipelago. The experience has produced a profound ambivalence on the part of the Samoans, not only

Table 13.8
Samoan Identity in Two Contrasting Historical Contexts

	AGA *Formal, Dignified*	*ĀMIO* *Intimate, Undignified*
Tradition as order	*Fa'a-Samoa* respect constraint law socio-centric tradition and culture neat dress, polite manner	*Fa'a-Pālagi* lack of respect freedom personal desire egocentric no tradition or culture sloppy dress, rudeness
Tradition as heathen	*Fa'a-Pālagi* clean life manual labor worker church consistency, straightness weak female educated controlled	*Fa'a-Samoa* dirty life clerical labor boss heathen life inconsistency, crookedness strong male uneducated uncontrolled

A. Samoan: Pālagi :: Formal Pronunciation: Intimate Pronunciation _____ Association of formal lexicon with chiefly culture and traditional occasions.
Fono as model setting
Matai as model speaker

B. Pālagi: Samoan :: Formal Pronunciation: Intimate Pronunciation _____ Association of formal pronunciation with Europeans, through whose institutions it was institutionalized.
Church as model setting
Pālagi and *pastor* as model speakers

toward the *pālagi,* but toward themselves as well. When a Samoan talks about himself as Samoan, his associations appear to operate in two totally distinct contexts, directing his thoughts in opposite directions. These implicit contexts relate him to the *pālagi* in two different ways. One defines Samoan culture by implicit reference to its chiefly culture, opposing it to the less formal and dignified qualities of European culture understood as modern culture. The other perspective defines Samoan identity as "heathen" in implicit opposition to European culture. Here, European culture suggests the Church and enlightenment.

In the first of these contexts, the Samoan is apt to see himself and the past of his people in a golden light as contrasted with the disruptive influence of a European society that lacks politeness, dignity, respect for social relations in particular, and for the elderly and high-ranking in specific. In the second of these two contexts, Samoa is characterized as a heathen place that lay in darkness and ignorance until the Church brought light, understanding, and social order.

The darker impulses and behaviors associated with *aso anamua* (ancient times) are seen as survivals in Samoa of untamed aspects of life that are at once condemned as wild and uncivilized, but also prized as lending power and energy to Samoan life, power lacking in the softer and more tamed, "enlightened" ways of the European.

The tendency for Samoans to characterize themselves in relation to Europeans in terms suggesting lack of control, disorder, dirtiness, energy, and motion appears to be longstanding. In the early 1830s the missionary John Wiliams met a young Savai'i chief from Sāfotulafai village who, speaking rudimentary English, warned Williams, not without a suggestion of pride: "Oh, my countryman, the Samoa man too much fool, plenty wicked; you don't know, Samoa great fool, he kill the man, he fights the tree. Breadfruit tree, coconut tree, no fight us. Oh the Samoa man too fool, too much wicked" (Williams 1838:389).

Much the same attitude of Samoans toward themselves, in relation to the *fa'a pālagi* and toward the Church in particular, is evident in the following interview excerpts.

Some people want to talk and dress like the *pālagi*. Some people don't want to touch any chores, but just sit around [*nofonofo*] just like the *pālagi* does. For the Samoan, he does dirty work. If this lady here doesn't want to do any dirty work or any heavy work, but only clean and light work, if she hates heavy work and dirt, then she is just like the *pālagi* who does only clean and light work. . . . The *pālagi,* he grows up with cleanliness, with clean things. The Samoan, he grows up with two things, the clean, the dirty, the good and the bad.

The *pālagi,* he doesn't have to do any chores. He only sits in the house, he wears only good and clean clothes. He doesn't wear any old rags like these. He tries to comb his hair nicely. He doesn't have his hair all disarranged and disordered like this. You know that in Samoan life you wake up, wash up, and then put on an old piece of cloth, grab your knife to work on the plantation. You're always dirty. But the *pālagi,* he rises in the morning, gets dressed, drinks his tea, and then grabs his pen to write in books. The Samoan has a special time when he bathes, and then he puts on his nice *lavalava.*

There's the dirt that the *pālagi* mechanic has when he works on the engines. It's really dirty, more dirty than the dirt of the Samoan. But you can wash that dirt off. . . . Well, there are times for dirty things and for clean things. In Samoa, we always go from dirty things to clean things, but then back to dirt again. Like when I do my laundry, but first I have to make my boiled taro [*saka*]. First you do the dirty thing, and then the clean thing.

You know that nowadays we Samoans call the *pālagi fale* the permanent house [*fale tū mau*]. The Samoan house is called the "easily knocked-down house."

Fia pālagi [having *pālagi* pretensions] means that you sit and relax all the time, and don't do any work, for we think that the *pālagi* always sits nicely and doesn't do any work. So if a Samoan is like that, we call him *fia pālagi*. And it's a bad thing too, for you don't help out, but only sit. You don't move around and work.

It's okay if [a girl and I] talk straight and cleanly to each other, and if we don't have any of those dark, Samoan thoughts, but just sit and talk straight in the light and don't do anything. But if we sit and whisper in the darkness, that's bad.

Popular songs and verse are a revealing source of these attitudes of Samoans about their own identity in relation to the Christian aspects of the *pālagi*'s world. One *solo* (chant) published in the *Samoa Times,* for instance, complained about the behavior of the modern generation of Samoans. Several of the most revealing passages appear below in translations.

> Strange Behavior
> Yes, the behavior is strange indeed
> Of these modern youth.
> Especially the boys of the younger generation
> Who wear long beards and long hair.
> From where has this behavior come
> That the youths have all adopted?
> Boys all want to be girls
> And the girls want to be boys.
> It is as if Samoa has returned to darkness
> In these unrestrained actions.
> There's no proper education,
> But only revolt in these behaviors.
> I don't know if any of these youth
> Have looked at themselves in the mirror.
> Whether they are happy with their hair
> Whether they think that it is fitting for our culture.
> This appearance is disgusting
> Just like the people from the mountains
> Or like the Papuans
> Or Samoans from the ancient times.

There is an ironic aspect to this poem in that the disordered appearance and manner of many of the young people in the eyes of the older generation of Samoans is attributed normally to the decay of traditional Samoan values rather than the reversion to them. A similar view to the one expressed in the above poem, but with a different mood, is suggested in the following excerpt from a popular song, which I have translated.

> The life from the ancient days of our ancestors
> In the days of darkness, was very harsh.
> But the morning came with the good news
> Which brought us to where we are.
> Samoa is enlightened, and now people all love one another. . . .
> Work for the welfare of our country.
>
> We pity our ancestors from the ancient days.
> We did not witness the transformations
> Which brought us to where we are,
> And the many new things which helped us out.

When the past is viewed as pre-Christian or heathen, Samoans tend to see themselves as associated with darkness, aggression, disorder, and energy. It is these qualities that they most frequently use to distinguish themselves from *pālagi* in these contexts. But to say that Samoans often associate their identity with the "darker" side of the conceptual duality, which in another place I have associated with that between *āmio* and *aga,* is not to say that they disapprove of themselves. The attitude is clearly ambivalent, for there is as much admiration and pride expressed about the power and strength that Samoans attribute to themselves as a people as there is disapproval.

The other semantic context in which Samoans define themselves as a people poses a golden age of the past, when things were ordered and dignified, against a post-contact Samoa that is disordered and chaotic, due to the destructive influences of a *pālagi* culture that is free, knowing no proper social distinctions or boundaries, and thus no respect.

There is a genre of popular songs that praise Samoan culture and particularly the culture as it revealed itself in ancient times, when everything was dignified. Many of the hortatory songs, urging the youth to abandon their disruptive and chaotic ways, blame the influence of *pālagi* culture for the general decay of order and dignity in Samoan life, and exhort the youth to return to their dignified culture and its respectful *aga.* One of these songs, for instance, praises the traditional order of Samoa, but laments "I doubt that we will ever be able to eradicate these *pālagi* ways that have infested Samoa," employing terms normally used for disease.

A song published in a school song book—part of which is quoted here— is called "In Praise of Samoa" and expresses the pride that Samoans have in themselves and in their dignified culture.

> Samoa is different from other lands;
> People are not oppressed as in other countries.
> The *matai* rules alone, and people look to their ancient customs.
> Just like the ancient Israelites,
> They have chiefs whom they serve.
> This is why Samoa is so dignified,
> Because people cannot do whatever they like.

Another song, of the same genre, praises the control and dignity of ancient Samoan custom.

> Kings and noblemen of our country—Samoa,
> Your culture is famed.
> Respect, forgiveness and politeness and love to all.
> You are proud in everything you do: your gait,
>   your speech and your appearance,
> Samoans, don't forget, remember every day
> Your culture is your respectfulness.
> Think what you will, but remember my advice.

> Your culture may well disappear.
> Remember Samoans from ancient days,
> Their culture and ways,
> Embodied in stories and practices. . . .
> Keep in mind the living, Samoa
> That is your crown.

One girl, who had associated Samoa with dirtiness and disorder in the implicit context of Samoan tradition/Christianity, made the following statement in a different context of discourse.

In the olden days, everything was very dignified [*mamalu*] but nowadays there is not really much use in having curfews. Well, actually, there is a use, but the trouble is that the kids have grown up in the *fa'a-pālagi,* and the *matai* can't control them. . . . Kids will just beat up the police nowadays, if they try to stop the kids from doing what they want.

In this context, where the traditional *fa'a-Samoa* is contrasted to the decay and disorder of modern life, Samoan identity stands as a reminder of dignity, respectfulness, and control. Here, then, Samoans stress the dignified and controlled aspects of Samoan associations about experience, those related more to *aga* than to *āmio,* rather than the darker, stronger aspect that is associated with the Samoan/Christian opposition.

Given this embedding of Samoans' associations about themselves in different semantic fields, it is possible to understand the relationship between two types of linguistic stratification we have examined. The lexical dichotomy between the respectful and common vocabularies suggests a distinction between the cruder and more dignified aspects of the *fa'a-Samoa* itself, independent of any relations between the *fa'a-Samoa* and the *fa'a-Pālagi.* Here dignity and control focus on the figure of the chief, and the paradigmatic situation is the *fono,* the informing source of order and dignity in traditional Samoan life. This focus on chiefly institutions as models for the polite/common distinction in this context is underscored by the fact that Samoans often refer to the polite language as "chiefly language" even though respectful vocabulary is neither used exclusively to or by chiefs. As I suggested above, it is perhaps structurally appropriate that the linguistic symbolization of the formal/intimate distinction in the context of chiefly/common is a vocabulary stratification that permits an infinite gradation in degree of respect, since the qualities of formality and intimacy suggested by these levels are derived from a system of chiefly titles that are themselves finely ranked.

The phonological dichotomy between the formal "t" and the intimate k-styles operates within a different context, one defined by the opposition of Samoan culture as a whole with the introduced European sector of Samoan institutions, particularly those institutions related to technology and the Church. Here the focus of dignity and control is both the *pālagi* and, even more important, the pastor, rather than the chief. The *pālagi* is the representative of the society that brought enlightenment to Samoa in the form of education, the Church, and a labor-saving technology. In this context, the internal intimate/formal distinctions within the Samoan culture are ignored in favor of an encompassing relationship between *fa'a-Samoa* as "heathen" and *fa'a-pālagi* as "enlightened." Here the former is associated with motion, energy, power, dirt, and moral disorder while the latter is associated with a kind of passivity that Samoans associate with dignity and cleanliness.

These contrasting associations find their realization in Samoan phonology. Intimate pronunciation is reserved almost uniquely for the expression of "Samoan thoughts" in "Samoan situations." As such, it is the speech of symmetrical relations, and thus a powerful though vulgar and spontaneous form of expression in Samoan conception. The intimate "k" style of pronunciation is simultaneously an object of public disapproval, since it is spontaneous, personal, and "heavy" and associated with *āmio,* but is also viewed with pride. In this context, the distinction between chiefly and non-chiefly is largely irrelevant, since both are equally Samoan status levels sharing in a distinctly Samoan identity.

The incomplete mapping of the phonological stratification onto the *ali'i/ tulāfale* distinction appears to be an attempt to adapt a relatively recent (phonological) distinction to an older (political) one. The association of the formal "t" pronunciation with the *ali'i* and the intimate "k" pronunciation with the orator is more an intellectual or logical equation than an empirically observable one, since *matai,* as chiefs, continue to use the k-pronunciation almost exclusively when dealing with matters internal to the *fa'a-Samoa.* Finally it is significant in contrast to the lexical stratification that the phonological distinctions, structurally suggesting an absolute binary opposition in which one may speak either one style or the other, but no combination of them, has been appropriated to support a symbolic distinction between absolutely opposed rather than graded principles of *fa'a-Samoa* and *fa'a-pālagi.* The distinctions between implicit contexts in which lexical and phonological stratification are embedded are schematically represented in table 13.8.

Thus we have seen that the contrast between intimate and formal aspects of experience suggests a more general, possibly universal, duality. But in Samoa, it has a special place because of its extensive elaboration throughout social and cultural organization. These manifestations and their associations are summarized in appendix B. As a kind of template for social order and a way of translating the continuum of experience into significant and articulable cultural forms, thus rendering a collection of texts as social contexts charged with shared significance, the model proposed for Samoan social order is relatively simple in its dual structure. Characteristically, however, it is also extremely complex in its elaborate manifestations.

The general model I have suggested is also the model I believe Samoans use to interpret and order their own experiences. As such it provides a way of comprehending Samoan social control and, more generally, social order. Because this dual organization is a general conceptual model at a high level of abstraction, it must not be mistaken for any particular Samoan reality. This is not to say that the model has no empirical manifestations, but rather to assert its proper relation to observable realities of Samoan life. The rigorously logical nature of the model, part of its abstractness, suggests for Samoan culture an attempt to articulate a coherent and sophisticated theory of power relations. Life, of course, is never as coherent or logical as any theory, and should not be confused with what is after all only a model for life. But this dual organization is, nonetheless, a very powerful model, I believe, and one that has a kind of shadowy reality behind the complex skein of particular events that make up life in Samoa. It serves simultaneously as a cognitive model for action, part of the structure of motivations for Samoans, and also as a model of action, influencing the interpretations that Samoans will make of their own experience.

The question has often been asked by Samoans and *pālagi* alike, what constitutes the elusive yet persistent *fa'a Samoa,* its brothers and sisters, its *matai* and *taulele'a,* its *ali'i* and *tulāfale,* and its complex political and ceremonial institutions. The *fa'a Samoa* is not simply its historically "traditional" elements, however, but also the Church, its pastors, the "k" and "t" slipping into distinct voices. It is the division of pigs between *ali'i* and *tulāfale,* but also the division of tin and china dishes. If we take the Samoan cue and "look to the relations" rather than to things in themselves, the *fa'a-Samoa* may be seen to lie precisely in the structuring of the relationships between cultural artifacts rather than in those artifacts themselves.

If it is relations rather than objects or isolated practices that structure "tradition" and define continuity for Samoans in time and space, then it is possible to account for a structure of tradition distinct from the enumeration or history of particular traditions. And if this view is correct, the Samoan way in its profoundest aspect is not, as some have warned, doomed to extinction—not as long as Samoans continue to look to their relations, and to look to them, moreover, with a double vision in terms of which they make themselves whole.

CHAPTER FOURTEEN

Conclusions: Structure and Event in Sala'ilua

Via a long and sometimes complex maze of back roads, I return for the last time to the village of Sala'ilua for a final look. As a set of events, the mystery was solved almost as it occurred. Within days of the murder, life in the village resumed something approaching its former order, only with the lives of several of its prominent members transformed radically by the events of an hour. Presumably, Tuatō's vacant title will one day be filled, perhaps by his brother or one of his sons. His empty place in the *fono* will be occupied again by an appropriate replacement. As for Tolova'a Aleki and his family, their "eternal" banishment will no doubt endure for several years, while the bitter memories of death and disorder gradually find their place in the minds of the villagers as bits of history and, eventually, as aspects of village lore. Already, I have been told, Aleki has established himself with a title in another village, perhaps awaiting the day he will be permitted to return to Sala'ilua and reestablish his political power there. Such is the power of structure in Samoa to order events, that even the most cataclysmic of disturbances soon finds its place in the larger scheme of things.

But what of this particular social order in Sala'ilua? To what extent can we take facts of a structural order as clues for the resolution of a mystery defined by historical events? Insofar as we see the mystery as simply events, in this case as the murder of one man by another in the heat of aroused passions at a particular time and place, then the anthropologist can shed little light on the matter. But while particular events can never be fully illuminated in the structural terms of which anthropologists are fond, it is possible, I believe, to demonstrate here that part of the mystery of Tuatō Fatu's murder can be accounted for through appreciation of the social and cultural forms outlined in this study. More specifically, by taking the events of the moment and placing them back in the context of the village in which they occurred, one can approach a distinctively anthropological solution to the mystery. This is not to claim that Fatu's murder could have been predicted, nor even that any particular conflict in Sala'ilua was structurally inevitable. In relation to particular events, the anthropologist works largely from hindsight, and can demonstrate only the probable implications of the structures he posits in the events he records.

In these final pages I return for a last look at the events surrounding the murder of Tuatō Fatu in Sala'ilua. This time, however, these events will be viewed from the perspective of the general structures I have suggested make up a distinctively Samoan vision of the social world. In this, the final step toward a solution to our Samoan mystery, I shall reconstitute the events surrounding Fatu's death as *cultural facts*, clues to a distinctively anthropological mystery.

Genesis: Relations Between Tuatō Fatu and Agafili Ioane

The two primary antagonists involved in the murder, Tuatō Fatu and Agafili Ioane, had a long history of conflict and rivalry. Fatu, several years before his death, had been formally and temporarily banished from Sala'ilua village following a fight between him and Ioane over public insults that he had hurled at Ioane. The two also had recently clashed in a land dispute over the precise boundaries between their adjacent taro plantations. Further, something of the rivalry between the two was evident in their relations as teaching colleagues at the local primary school, each clearly trying to outshine the other at faculty meetings.

From a Samoan point of view, Fatu and Ioane were almost perfect competitors. Their rivalry was as comprehensible structurally as it was from their particular aggressive temperaments. The conjunction of the two factors constitutes a kind of "overdetermination" of the events that led to Fatu's death. In terms of the scheme outlined in chapter 11, Fatu and Ioane are a fairly clear example of a relationship of overt Competition. In relation to several key status forms, the two were linked by symmetrical and unranked or at least equivocally ranked bonds. These ambiguous areas of rank prove to be significant as well. Both men were teachers at the same primary school. Fatu had once been the head teacher (principal) at the school but had been demoted several years earlier due to some problems he had had with the Department of Education in Apia. Any claims to "rank" superiority over his rival Ioane in the context of their job were thus nullified, or at least diminished. Both men had, by local standards, fairly distinguished educations, having graduated from two of the better high schools in the country.

Politically, the personal rivalry was sustained by the parallel prominence of their families in Sala'ilua. Both men possessed important orator titles. Here a distinction between the men was to become important, however. Fatu, as we have seen, held one of the two ranking orator titles in Sala'ilua. This kind of statement about the relations among titles is often made privately by interested parties, but to say it publicly is clearly inflammatory, and the fight that had resulted in Fatu's earlier banishment from Sala'ilua was the result, I had been told, of his publicly calling Agafili "the lapdog of the Tuatō and Tolova'a."

Ordinarily, this relatively clear rank difference between the titles of the

men would have muted their rivalry and stabilized their relationship. However, rank relations within any one status are always somewhat clouded,
we have seen, and this ambiguity is underscored by a general lack of cultural
symbolism of rank differentiation. In this case, what transformed an equivocally ranked relationship into one more clearly unranked and symmetrical
was the fact that Ioane was the oldest son of Tolova'a Aleki, a leading
holder of the powerful Tuitolova'a orator title, along with the Tuatō, the
senior title in Sala'ilua. The titles Tuatō and Tolova'a are paired in the
Sala'ilua *fa'alupega* in such a way as to suggest their competitive symmetrical
status. Where a village polity is reducible to a set of two titles (a kind of
dual organization); where, moreover, these two titles have symmetrical
(orator/orator) rather than complementary (orator/*ali'i*) status; and where,
finally, the titles share no significant descent links and are thus genealogically
irreducible, there exist the structural preconditions for perpetual rivalry.
That such a rivalry between the "families" of the two titles existed was
clear from the beginning, and the history of conflicts between members of
the two families was made apparent just days before Fatu's death when the
village was preoccupied with settling the fight that had erupted between
two young girls from the Sā Tuatō and the Sā Tolova'ā.

In addition to representing two parallel and opposed political families in
Sala'ilua, Fatu and Ioane also represented the major religious rivalry in
Sala'ilua. Fatu's father had been a famous pastor and seminary teacher for
the Congregational church. While Fatu himself was not particularly devout,
the large Congregational church in Sala'ilua, as well as the impressive pastor's residence, stood on land donated by his family to the church, and Fatu
was very closely associated with the Congregational church. Ioane's family,
by contrast, were prominent members of the local Methodist church. Indeed, at the time of the murder Ioane's father, Tolova'a Aleki, was representing the local Methodist congregation as a church elder at the annual
meetings of the Methodist congregations in Apia.

When looked at from the perspective of the broader political relations
between their *'āiga* and the associated titles, the rivalry between Fatu and
Ioane becomes associated with what I have called relationships of overt
Competition and, thus, structurally significant.

Judicial Consequences of the Murder

As has been seen, the elaborate judicial process brought into play within
Sala'ilua to deal with the murder and its consequences focused largely on
the immediate political and social implications of the crime, rather than on
its causes. This stress is understandable, I believe, in terms of Samoan
epistemology, and the related tendency to evaluate acts in relation to their
consequences rather than in terms of "underlying" causes. This kind of
epistemology leads to a pragmatic and situational ethics sensitive to political
contingency.

The immediate concern of the assembled *matai* and pastors was to "order" (*teu*) the situation and particularly to forestall any attempt at retaliation by the offended family of Tuatō. An important aspect of this ordering process is to clarify publicly an appropriate social definition of the situation at hand. A particular fight between two individuals must be reconstituted as a socially meaningful conflict between groups, since this is the only way in which a traditional village tribunal is prepared to treat a disturbance. Several alternative social definitions of the conflict were possible, employing any of the several significant social statuses of the antagonists. Fatu himself, it will be remembered, had two Sala'ilua titles, Tuatō and Tualevao, representing distinct (though genealogically related) descent groups. Agafili also had two political links, the one, Sā Agafilī, through his own title, and the other, Sā Tolova'ā, through his father's title.

From the point of view of the senior orators of Sala'ilua who met in secret session the night before the general village meeting to plan strategy, there was little doubt as to how to constitute the conflict socially. Appropriately, the conflict was phrased between groups which were of the highest political rank, articulated at the most inclusive social range, and structurally symmetrical and unranked. The Sā Tuatō, the descent group of Tuatō's own title, was set against the Sā Tolova'ā, the title group of Ioane's father. A *de facto* conflict between individuals was culturally constituted by the chiefs as one between groups linked in a relationship structurally appropriate for such a conflict. Hence the focus was on symmetrical status forms. Moreover, the conflict involving murder was of the highest degree of seriousness, and thus necessitated the definition of the situation at an appropriately high level of rank and political inclusiveness. Hence the conflict was understood to involve the two senior descent groups of the village.

Although it may appear inevitable *post hoc* that the conflict would be phrased as one between the Sā Tuatō and the Sā Tolova'ā, the process characteristically permitted a certain amount of negotiation in the definition of situation. For instance Tolova'a Aleki, who, though he was not even in Sala'ilua at the time of the crime, would be the main object of punishment should the conflict involve the Sā Tolova'ā, attempted to claim that his title and its decent group had nothing to do with the crime. The conflict, he insisted, was one between the Sā Tuatō and the Sā Agafilī, the descent group defined by his son's own title. Here is a clear instance of an active manipulation of the structure of Samoan social relations by a canny and interested politician. In making the claim, Aleki was careful to refer to Ioane only as Agafili, never as his own son, in an attempt structurally to distinguish himself from the crime. The *fono* of Sala'ilua, however, chose to focus implicitly on this very father–son connection. In Samoan custom, parents (and chiefs) are usually held legally responsible for misdeeds committed by their children. The overt stress, however, was not placed on the kinship link of father to son, but rather on the political link between the two titles possessed by father and son. Thus, the crime committed by a holder of the subordinate Agafili title was translated into one by a holder of the superordinate Tolova'a title. Aleki's claim fell on deaf ears.

In the general village meeting the definition of situation was symbolically reflected in the physical placement of the involved parties. Characteristically, neither the family of the murdered man (Fatu) nor that of the accused (at this point, Tolova'a Aleki) was directly involved. Rather, structurally appropriate representatives (*sui*) stood in for the parties. A cousin of Aleki who resided normally in Apia but who also possessed the Tolova'a title, Tolova'a Musumusu, represented the Sā Tolova'ā at a house on one end of the *malae*. Tuatō Sāpati, a cousin of Fatu, represented the Sā Tuatō in a house directly opposite to that containing the Sā Tolova'ā representatives, at the other end of the *malae*. Directly between these two houses of the antagonists was the house for prayer, containing several pastors. Here we see vividly an explicit attempt to mediate a symmetrical competitive relationship with a complementary link, represented in this case by the *feagaiga*—the pastor. The assembled chiefs and orators of Sala'ilua (excluding those directly involved in the conflict) gathered in a fourth house in another part of the *malae*.

Banishment

The punishment announced by the assembled chiefs was banishment, not only for Tolova'a Aleki but, in the words of the proclamation, "for his sons, and his son's sons, and the sons of those sons, eternally excluded from Sala'ilua village." Banishment is the most severe sanction a village has in enforcing its laws. It is at once a punitive measure, depriving a family of its political rights and its livelihood from lands under the jurisdiction of the village *fono*, and a self-protective measure, excluding physically from the village a source of past conflict and a likely object of future vendettas by the victim's family. This banishment order, however, raised serious jurisdictional and legal problems for the chiefs. No one questions the right of the village chiefs to "exclude" an offender and his family from active political and social membership in village affairs. Exclusion of this sort (*fa'ate'a*) constitutes a kind of social death, and is itself a serious step for a village to take. But actual physical removal of the offenders from their own lands and houses (*tō 'ese mai le nu'u*), the additional step necessary at times for maintaining the peace of the village, is far more serious. It is also problematical legally, since it involves a complex issue of relative autonomy and jurisdiction among village, descent group, and national government.[1]

While a full treatment of this problem of jurisdiction is not possible in this context, certain social structural features of the problem are illuminated by the model of social relations developed in this study. I have implied elsewhere that pervasive ambiguities or instabilities in Samoan relationships may be demonstrated to be manifestations of the problematical categorization of those relationships in relation to Samoan understandings of social structure. The issue of banishment is a key example of precisely this kind of cognitive ambiguity. The ambiguities in this case involve two distinct relationships: that between a village and its constituent descent groups, and that between the village and the national government.

Two conflicting Samoan models of the descent group/village relationship are evident. One model focuses on the village as an organic whole, incorporating its various descent groups in a clearly hierarchical manner. The *fono* in this vision is a village-based corporation, while the village greeting is a statement of organic relations. The other model sees the village as little more than a mechanical aggregate of essentially autonomous and equivalent descent groups, each of which is given its prominent place within the greeting (taken as a kind of list of associates) and within the *fono* (viewed as an assembly of descent-group heads). Where a village is made up of one genealogically connected network, focused on a single dominant descent group, the organic unity of the village is underscored and made easier to enforce. Where, as in Sala'ilua, the village is itself a rather more loose association among descent groups—each of which claims genealogical and political autonomy and maintains various other alliances beyond the local level—the organic nature of the village is undercut and descent groups are likely to assert their autonomous rights. It is in this context that we can understand Tolova'a Aleki's claim to the village council and later to the national Lands and Titles Court that the *fono* of Sala'ilua had no legal right physically to exclude a family from its own (rather than "village") land and buildings.[2]

In formal terms, the ambiguity in local jurisdiction involves a conflict between viewing a village as a corporation of descent groups linked by a hierarchical relationship of Incorporation, and viewing it as a mechanical aggregate of autonomous descent groups linked in symmetrical and un-ranked relationships of overt Competition. The same kind of ambiguity underlies the problematical relations between any one village and the national government, the former claiming "traditional" jurisdiction over its "own" lands, the latter hesitantly claiming a legal right of jurisdiction in conflicts between villages and constituent descent groups. Lest one too quickly conclude that this conflict is simply a product of modern Samoan history, it should be pointed out that the problem is one built into the structure of Samoan understandings of social relations. It is essentially the same ambiguity that characterizes the relations between subvillage and village, or between village and encompassing district.

Conflict and the Structure of Political Relations in Sala'ilua

Finally at this point I can attempt to place this particular conflict in Sala'ilua in a broader context of Sala'ilua village life. In part 1 of the study I noted that Sala'ilua appeared to be distinctively conflict-prone among Samoan villages, and that this tendency appeared to be part of a general vigorous and ambitious "spirit" pervading life in the village. In part 2 I noted that this aggressive character was given more or less formal recognition by the villagers, who liked to refer to their village as a "second Apia," and to characterize themselves as distinctively vigorous and assertive

people, people "who know how to get things done" (e iloa fai mea mafai).
Part of the explanation for this aggressiveness and effervescence may be
traced to historical factors. I have noted, for instance, Sala'ilua's prominence
during the German colonization of the islands as an administrative center
for western Savai'i, and a local trading center with its own small harbor
and wharf and several larger trading shops. But historical explanations deal
with events. Anthropological mysteries, by contrast, are solved through
structures, or at least through the interplay of structures and events. I must
thus look to structure as well as to' event to understand something about
the distinctive qualities of this village, qualities that I think lie at the heart
of our mystery.

To understand what is at once characteristically Samoan and yet distinctive about Sala'ilua, it is necessary, I believe, to return to my initial observation that the political order of the village involved a reversal of the traditional Samoan relations between *tulāfale* and *ali'i*. In most Samoan villages,
public prominence and official power in the village are given to the *'āiga
ali'i* (families of high chiefs). These chiefs are the "nobility" (*tamāli'i*) of the
village, and their public prominence represents a symbol of village dignity.
The orators, no less powerful in their own right, nevertheless do not usually
represent publicly the formal authority of a village. In Sala'ilua, however,
they do. The preeminent titles of the village are those of orators—Tuatō
and Tolova'a, "strong men of Sala'ilua"—and the *'āiga ali'i* have taken
something of a back seat in the running of things. Their public voice has,
for historical reasons, been largely eclipsed by that of powerful orators.
Moreover, these two orator titles are linked in what we have seen as competitive relations. In the Samoan vision of power relations, this reversal of
tulāfale/ali'i relations has profound and pervasive implications.

Chapter 12 presented a detailed analysis of the implications of the *ali'i/
tulāfale* relationship in terms of a more general theory of power relations
in Samoa. It should be evident that the reversal of the normal relations
between the two kinds of chief in Sala'ilua constitutes for Samoans a basic
transformation in the cultural and social structuring of social control. The
apparently isolated prominence given to orator titles in Sala'ilua cannot help
but have significant implications for the delicate balance in the minds of
villagers between *āmio* and *aga* as it manifests itself in a system of social
controls. Indeed, most of the chiefs' meeting after the murder was taken
up with precisely this problem of power relations. The context-sensitive
theory of social control outlined in this study suggests the attentiveness of
Samoans to even subtle shifts of context and their implications for ordering
behavior. The subordination of the dignity of the *ali'i* of Sala'ilua to the
cruder kind of power represented by orators could be expected to leave its
profound mark on village life. This mark appeared evident from my first
visit to the village.

It is appropriate as this study ends to wonder, after all, to what extent
it has accounted for the distinctive nature of Sala'ilua, its striking effervescence, and its proneness to conflict. More generally one might ask how far

it is possible to go in attributing so-called structural significance to any particular events. To suggest that social and cultural structures fully determined the tragic events on that hot July afternoon in Sala'ilua would be to deny to the residents of that village their essential humanity—which is to say the fundamentally open-ended creativity of their lives. It would also preclude the real possibility of accidents and unique events. But it would be equally misleading to refuse to look beyond the actions of the moment, to deny for the lives and minds of Samoans the existence of the powerful models for experience that we recognize as their culture. It cannot ever be known to what extent a particular cultural form influenced an act, but certainly such influences are there and are as necessary for human existence as are the personal motives of which the observer is sometimes more fully aware.

I am not able to provide a full accounting for Tuatō Fatu's death. Human life remains too complex and multi-dimensional for such final accounts. That the tragic events of a moment could be convincingly illuminated as a cultural mystery and that this mystery could be resolved through the lens of Samoan culture and society is, for the moment, solution enough. The fact, however, that we could make intelligible the patterns that shape Samoan lives and even, perhaps, glimpse in them something of our own lives, points beyond Samoa to something else. But that is another, deeper, mystery.

Two Voices of Moral Judgment: An Analysis of Questionnaire Results

The complex opposition between the personal and the social dimensions of experience is reflected in some intriguing ways in the response patterns to several questions in the questionnaire that was administered to 140 school children on Savai'i. Among a set of true–false items were three dealing with self-control versus external control over one's behavior. These statements and the tabulated results of the responses given appear in table A.1.

Statements 1 and 2 in table A.1 pose the issue of self-control in the first person, while statement 3 poses the same question in the third person. The former two statements are thus judgments about one's own behavior while the third statement is a general statement about the behavior, which linguistically distances the respondent personally from its implications. The responses indicate a strong emphasis on self-control when respondents judged themselves (statements 1 and 2). This emphasis is particularly marked in the responses to the first question, where over 85 percent of the informants felt they could control their own behavior. However, when in response to statement 3, the issue is phrased in general rather than in personal terms, dealing with "everyone" rather than with oneself, the pattern is reversed, revealing a marked distrust of self-control, and a need for strong central authority.

The implications of these response patterns become even clearer when the responses are tabulated in pairs to show how respondents answered two of the three questions. I have set out the cross-tabulation results for each of the three possible pairings of the three statements. In table A.2 responses to statements 1 and 2 are paired.

The stress on self-control is clear in these pairings, in which both statements deal with one's own behavior. I have underlined the key word "I" in the summary statements to stress this personal focus to the statements. If we reduce each statement to a simple ratio using the summary terms "self-control" and "external control," it is clear the rank order of decreasing response frequency proceeds from a double stress on self-control to a double stress on external control (see table A.3). Tables A.4 and A.5 pair responses to statements 1 and 3, in the same manner as tables A.2 and A.3.

These cross-tabulation pairings match a statement about behavior of oneself with one about behavior in general. The most frequent pattern of response, by far, links self-control of one's own behavior with external

Table A.1
Response Frequencies to Three True–False Items Dealing with External versus Self-Control

Statement	True No.	%	False No.	%	No Response No.	%
1. "I can control my own behavior in anything I do."	121	85.8	13	9.2	7	5
2. "I am more diligent at my work and chores when watched than when alone."	58	41.4	76	53.9	7	5
3. "Everyone would be up to no good if other people didn't control them."	94	66.7	40	28.4	7	5

Note: A total of 141 questionnaires were completed.

control for behavior in general. Second most frequent was the association between self-control for both self and everyone in general, a pattern that appeared only two-fifths as frequently as the most popular response pattern. The other possible pattern had negligible response frequencies.

Finally, the cross-tabulations for responses to statements 2 and 3 appear in summary form in tables A.6 and A.7.

The general response pattern evident in this analysis is a consistent opposition of attitudes about personal behavior, all of which place clear emphasis on self-control, to attitudes about behavior in general, which stress the need for strong external control. General prescriptions about authority

Table A.2
Cross-Tabulation Results for Pairings of Responses 1 and 2 Dealing with External and Self-Control

Response Pairing 1/2	No. with Response Pair	% with Response Pair	Summary Statement of Implications
True/False	70	49.6	*I can control my own behavior at all times./ I work better when not watched by others.*
True/True	50	35.5	*I can control my own behavior at all times./ I work better when watched.*
False/True	7	5.0	*I cannot control my own behavior./ I work better when not watched by others.*
False/False	6	4.3	*I cannot control my own behavior./ I work better when watched by others.*

Table A.3
Response Pairings for Statements 1 and 2 Reduced to Summary Labels

Rank Order of Frequency	Response Pairing		
	Statement 1: One's Own Behavior	/	Statement 2: One's Own Behavior
1	Self-control		Self-control
2	Self-control		External control
3	External control		Self-control
4	External control		External control

and control of behavior thus appear to be expressed by a voice different from and opposite to that which expresses prescriptions about one's own behavior. Personal and general perspectives are, for this Samoan sample, distinct.

To check the conclusions emerging from this analysis, the questionnaire included a somewhat more complex test of the relation between general moral judgments and prescriptions, and those involving the informant personally. In the first section of the questionnaire, the following sentence-completion item was included: "When it is dark, and no one is looking, then I can. . . . " The Samoan word *mafai* (to be able) is, in general usage, ambiguous in much the same way as its English equivalent "can," suggesting both capacity to perform and moral right to perform an act. This ambiguity between a moral and utilitarian judgment is similar to that inherent in the terms *lelei* (good) and *leaga* (bad) as discussed earlier in this study. The responses to this sentence-completion item were categorized

Table A.4
Cross-Tabulation Results for Pairings of Statements 1 and 3 Dealing with External and Self-Control

Response Pairing 1/3	No. with Response Pair	% with Response Pair	Summary Statement of Implications
True/True	85	60.3	*I* can control my own behavior./ *Everyone* would act badly without external control.
True/False	35	24.8	*I* can control my own behavior./ *Everyone* would not act badly without external control.
False/True	9	6.4	*I* cannot control my own behavior./ *Everyone* would act badly without external control.
False/False	4	2.8	*I* cannot control my own behavior./ *Everyone* would not act badly without external control.

Table A.5
Response Pairings for Statements 1 and 3 Reduced to
Summary Labels

Rank Order of Frequency	Response Pairings	
	Statement 1 Own Behavior	Statement 3 Everyone's Behavior
1	Self-control	External control
2	Self-control	Self-control
3	External control	External control
4	External control	Self-control

into response classes, and these classes were arranged in order of decreasing frequency. The results appear in table A.8.

The generally morally negative character of these responses is not surprising, since the question was deliberately phrased in such a way as to elicit activities that were normally disapproved of. Also, as has been seen, darkness is associated in Samoan thought with illicit and antisocial activity. Further, the question was deliberately put in the first person, thereby eliciting a personal and intimate response rather than a general and formal one.

At the end of the long questionnaire, I presented respondents with two matrices, which they were requested to fill in. Both matrices dealt with various categories of physical and moral deviance that had, through interviews, been elicited from informants. The categories employed in the matrices were: deaf-mutes, cripples, blind persons, transvestites, mental defectives, thieves, those with bald heads, rapists, and murderers.

In the first matrix, respondents were asked to indicate for each of these person categories, which of seven attitudes they had. They were free to choose, for each deviance type, one, several, all, or none of the attitudes.

Table A.6
Cross-Tabulation Results for Pairings of Statements 2 and 3 Dealing with
External and Self-Control

Response Pairing 2/3	No. with Response Pair	% with Response Pair	Summary Statement of Implications
False/True	55	39.0	I work better when not watched./ Everyone would act badly when not controlled by others.
True/True	39	27.7	I work better when watched./ Everyone would act badly when not controlled by others.
False/False	21	14.9	I work better when not watched./ Everyone would not act badly when not controlled by others.

Table A.7
Response Pairings for Statements 2 and 3 Reduced to Summary Labels

Rank Order of Frequency	Response Pairing	
	Statement 1 Own Behavior	Statement 3 Everyone's Behavior
1	Self-control	External control
2	External control	External control
3	Self-control	Self-control
4	External control	External control

The listed attitudes paired with the deviance types were: pity, fear, mockery, person is dangerous, person is evil, person is sick, person is being punished by God for prior evil deeds.

The second matrix matched the same ten deviance types with nine possible reactions to them. Again, respondents were free to select for each of the deviance types any number of reactions, from none to all nine. These nine reaction categories were: must be well cared for by family; must be banished from village; must be watched by others; must be imprisoned; must be scolded; must be beaten; must be monetarily fined; must be hanged; must be hospitalized.

To test the relationship between responses to questions asking for a general moral evaluation, and responses to items about personal desires, the category of theft was chosen, since it figured importantly in the responses to the sentence-completion item about secret desires. Certain of the responses to the sentence-completion item tabulated in table A.8 were cross-

Table A.8
Frequency Table of Responses to Sentence-Completion Item Starting: "When it is dark and no one is looking, then I can. . ."

Response Class	# Responding	% Responding (Out of all responses to item)[a]
Steal.	32	22.7
Do whatever I wanted to do so.	22	15.6
Commit a (specific) bad act.	18	12.8
Other.	16	11.4
Steal or sneak food.	13	9.2
Escape to a forbidden place (Apia, another village, etc.)	13	9.2
Do (specified) virtuous act.	11	7.8
Surreptitious sexual activity.	5	3.5
Sleep.	4	2.8
Get into trouble./Get a beating.	2	1.4
No response.	16	11.4

[a] Since several informants gave complex answers that were included in more than one response class, the total percentage adds up to more than 100 percent.

tabulated with certain of the responses in the "thieves" sections of the two matrices. The most interesting and revealing of these correlations are set out in table A.9.

Column C contains the number of respondents who gave both responses in adjacent columns A and B. The percentage figure in column C indicates what percent of all responses made to items in column B, the figure in C under (#) represents. Thus, for example, a figure 10 in column C means that 10 respondents felt that both (a) they would be free to do their will if no one were watching them at night and (b) a thief is a dangerous person. Further, these 10 respondents represent 25 percent of all of those who indicated that "a thief is a dangerous person."

While it would be unwarranted to infer too much from these figures, there does seem to be a striking correlation between the personal desire to steal (a personal judgment in the first-person voice reflecting *āmio*) and a general moral judgment against thieves (a general judgment in the third-person voice reflecting *aga*). Further, this correlation is higher for the responses to stealing in general (an act strongly condemned) than for the less seriously regarded act of stealing food.

Table A.9
Cross-Tabulation Results of Sentence-Completion and Matrix Responses to Attitudes on Theft

Response to Sentence-Completion Item Starting: "When it is dark and no one can see me, then I can . . ."	Response to Matrix Item "A Thief"	A + B Correlation	
		# responding	% of all B responding
A	B	C	
be free to do my will.	is dangerous.	10	25.0
steal food.	is dangerous.	1	2.5
steal (generally).	is dangerous.	11	27.5
be free to do my will.	is evil person.	17	17.3
steal food.	is evil person.	7	8.8
steal (generally).	is evil person.	22	27.5
be free to do my will.	should be scolded.	6	16.7
steal food.	should be scolded.	4	11.1
steal (generally).	should be scolded.	11	30.6
be free to do my will.	should be banished.	10	23.8
steal food.	should be banished.	3	7.1
steal (generally).	should be banished.	10	23.8
be free to do my will.	should be fined.	11	7.8
steal food.	should be fined.	4	8.5
steal (generally).	should be fined.	12	25.5
be free to do my will.	should be jailed.	10	13.7
steal food.	should be jailed.	7	9.6
steal (generally).	should be jailed.	23	31.5

I have presented the results for only three of the sentence-completion response categories in column A, since these were the most relevant categories for the purposes of this study. It should be noted that the percentage figures 11, 22, 10, 12, and 23, which represent the correlations between personal desire to steal and general condemnation of stealing, are very high figures, indicating far higher correlations than most obtained for any other pairings, and the highest in their respective groups. The number of respondents, for example, who both condemned theft in general and who said they would do good deeds under the cover of darkness was much lower than any of these. If we are to trust cross-tabulation figures, there seems to be a close inverse correlation between the personal voice of desire, an expression of *āmio*, and the more social voice of moral prescription, an expression of *aga*.

Contrast Pairs: Formal and Intimate Styles

Social Context	Formal Member (*Aga*)	Intimate Member (*Āmio*)
Domestic, kinship, division of labor	Female	Male
	Sister	Brother
	Tamafafine	*Tamatane*
	Household chief	Household members
	Fale tele	*Fale o'o*
	Front of compound	Rear of compound
	Sleeping house	Cook house
	Light, clean work	Heavy, dirty work
	Lagoon fishing	Deep-sea fishing
	Shell-fish (immobile)	Mobile (finned) fish
	Village center	Village periphery
	Household	Plantation
	Weeding (cleaning)	Planting
Village, political system	Titled	Untitled
	Village center (*'a'ai*)	Periphery
	Ali'i	*Tulāfale*
	Front of village	Rear of village
	Seaward (*tai*)	Landward (*uta*)
	Malae	Residential area
	Metting house	Outside of house
	Front of *fono* house (*matua tala*)	Sides of *fono* house (*tala luma*)
	Government road	Family land
	Taupou	*Mānaia*
	Aualuma	*'Aumaga*
	Women's committee	*Matai* committees
	Title	Titleholder
	Title	Personal name
	Group of *ali'i*, *'āiga ali'i*, *uso ali'i*	Group of *tulāfale fale 'upolu*
	Taupou	*Aualuma*
	Mānaia	*'Aumaga*
Weaving house	*Lātū-o-faiva*, food distributer	*Matua u'u*, weaving expert
	Weaving leaders	*'Ause'efala*, workers, students
Fono house	*Māota* (for *ali'i*)	*Laoa* (for orator)
	Matua tala (front)	*Tala luma* (front)
	Seaward side	Landward side
	Seating space with post	Seating space without post
	Malae (*fono tauati*)	House (*fono fale*)
	fono tauati (day, open)	*Fono māitu* (night, closed)

Social Context	Formal Member (*Aga*)	Intimate Member (*Āmio*)
Attributes of rank and status		
Kava	Cup name (*ali'i*)	No cup name (*tulāfale*)
	Kava served from side, palm forward (*ali'i*)	Kava served directly, back of hand first (*tulāfale*)
	Short, contained call	Long, warbling call
Dress, ornament	*Tuiga* (headdress) (*ali'i*)	Staff, flywhisk (*tulāfale*)
	Clean clothes	Dirty clothes
	Hair neat	Hair disordered
	End of *lavalava* tucked in (women)	End of *lavalava* hanging out (men)
	'Ulāfala (neat garland of pandanus keys)	Necklace of wild leaves.
	Hair short, cropped (aboriginal female style)	Hair long (aboriginal male style)
	Skirt of fine mats	Skirt of tapa cloth
	Pālagi clothes	Samoan *lavalava*
	White clothes (church)	Colored clothes
	Leather sandals	Rubber sandals
	Tailored *lavalava*	Simple *lavalava*
Dance styles	*Siva*	*'Aiuli*
	Day dance (*ao siva*)	night dance (*pōula*)
	Taualuga (final dance)	Initial dance
	Center of floor	Periphery of floor
Political alliances	*Alataua* (priests)	*Itū au* (warriors)
	Itū-o-Fafine	Itū-o-Tane
	Malie village	Afega village
	Malae of Peace (Creation myth)	*Malae* of Confusion (Creation myth)
	Tamasoaali'i and Gato'aitele	Tui A'ana and Tui Atua
	Tamafafine titles (*Ma'upū*)	*Tamatane* titles
Language	Silence	Speech
	Chiefly vocabulary	Common vocabulary
	Indirect address	Direct address
	Formal pronunciation	Intimate pronunciation
Food, eating implements	*Mea lelei* (good, protein foods)	Heavy, starchy food
	Pālagi-style foods	Samoan-style foods
	Control of appetite	Gratification of appetite
Food, implements	Eat first	Eat last
	Tualā (backbone, ribs of pig)	*Ālaga* (leg, thigh of pig)
	China plate/cup breakable, small	Large metal plate/cup durable capacious
Kinesics	*Nofo* (sit, stay put)	*Gāioioi* (move)
	Controlled, deliberate movement	Spontaneous, rapid movement
	Stay at home	Roam about
	Sit with legs folded but not tucked in (for women, *ali'i*)	Sit with legs folded, feet tucked in (for men, orators)

Social Context	Formal Member (*Aga*)	Intimate Member (*Āmio*)
Perceptual qualities	Clean	Dirty
	Light	Heavy
	Fragile	Tough
	Passive	Active
	Neat	Disordered
	Impulse control	Impulse expression
	Smooth	Rough

Notes

Introduction

1. Department of Statistics, Government of Western Samoa, Apia, *Annual Statistical Abstract, 1971,* table 1.

2. Isolating discrete territorial units is frequently difficult in Samoa because of the ambiguous and shifting boundaries separating village, subvillage, and district.

3. For more detailed information on the geography, geology, and economy of Western Samoa, see Fox and Cumberland 1962.

4. See Pitt 1969 and Lockwood 1971 for socioeconomic studies of Western Samoa using similarly defined regional distinctions.

5. For further history and details of the political organization of Manono see Gilson 1970; Kraemer 1902 1:159–161; Ala'ilima and Ala'ilima 1966; Turner 1884:228; Steubel 1896:105.

6. See Gilson 1970: ch. 14, especially pp. 350–53.

7. The nature of this homogeneity and the variations within it is an important issue in understanding Samoa. By cultural homogeneity, I refer to a shared commitment to a large number of political and kinship institutions, a common consciousness among Samoans of their singular identity, origins, language, physical characteristics, and history, and finally a shared set of understandings and categories which serve as common premises for interpreting and orienting behavior. This sort of homogeneity does not preclude wide divergences in specific practices and beliefs between villages, members of different descent groups, and different individuals, or within the same individual on two different occasions. Such "subjective" variation is distinct from the shared understandings that make up a distinctly Samoan "intersubjectivity." See Taylor 1971 for a discussion of the notion of intersubjectivity.

8. In the preface to his *Samoan Dictionary*, Milner (1966) refers to the "dialectical nature" of Samoan culture and language (p. xii). His characterization of this quality suggests something more akin to idiolectic, individual variability in speech and cultural knowledge, than to genuine dialects. A more accurate description of this tendency in Samoa toward variability would have to focus on its contextual nature, defining social situations rather than individuals.

9. One Western Samoan I know claims he can distinguish regional accents in Samoan, but this is the only such claim I have ever heard from a Samoan.

10. A clear account of this "traditional" (nineteenth-century) political structure of the entire Samoan archipelago may be found in Keesing and Keesing 1956:18–24. See especially the map on page 22 of that volume.

1. A Death in the Family

1. Not only does the drinking together symbolize the solidarity of a gathering, but an implicit weighting or ranking of "voices" is clarified in the order of service. The kava ceremony thus serves to fine-tune the decision-making process of any group.

2. REPERCUSSIONS

1. On important occasions, it is customary for a chief from the village of Sālelesi to attend. The Sālelesi, as this figure is called, is known as "the lapdog of Malietoa," a peculiarly honorific description deriving from special services rendered by members of this village to the chief Malietoa in times past. A Sālelesi has the right to demand from his hosts any food or mat he fancies, and to refuse such a request is considered shameful. Bringing nothing, the Sālelesi returns home with anything he wishes, an apparent denial of the normal reciprocity characterizing social relations. The Sālelesi institution suggests the Tongan *fahu* and the Fijian *vasu*, the rights of sisters' sons to demand goods or aid from their mother's brothers. A similar privileged relationship called Sālele'a binds the village of Sāpapāli'i in Savai'i with those of Falealili district on southern Upolu.

2. Orators hold preeminent rank among chiefs in Aleipata district in eastern Upolu, and in the *pule* centers of Savai'i as well as the *Tūmua* centers of Upolu they enjoy particularly high rank in their villages. (The terms *pule* and *tūmua* are explained in note 4.)

3. *Malae* are located within a village, but their primary association is with a title and its descent group. Only important *ali'i* titles have *malae* associated with them. Lesser *ali'i* titles and all orator titles are never directly linked to a *malae*.

4. *Pule* refers to Savai'i's six political centers, bastions of orator power. *Tūmua* are centers of orator power on Upolu: the villages of Leulumoega, Solosolo, Afega, and Malie. *Ituau* are villages in each district designated as vanguards in war, while *Alataua* villages retained a priestly and passive function in wartime, functioning as *tapua'i*, communities of prayer. *'Āiga i le tai* (family by the sea) refers to the islands of Manono and Apolima, political allies of Malietoa and traditional naval powers. Finally, *va'a-o-Fonotī* (Fonotī's ship) is a reference to the village of Fagaloa, an isolated naval power on eastern Upolu.

3. SALA'ILUA VILLAGE

1. What constitutes a "typical" Samoan village is problematical. In the course of my research at the Turnbull Library in New Zealand I came across the complete Records of Evidence for the Commission on Village and District Government. In 1949 and 1950 the Commission made a detailed survey of the institutional organization of every village in Western Samoa. I coded and recorded all the answers to this extensive questionnaire and hope to analyze these records in detail one day. When this is done, we shall have some idea of the range and dimensions of variability in structure among villages at any one time in history.

2. This ambivalence of children toward centers of power and dignity was suggested by responses on a questionnaire I distributed to 141 schoolchildren on Savai'i. One of the sentences in a sentence-completion section of the questionnaire began, "In my village, I am afraid to go near the . . . " with the children left free to supply any answer they wished. By far the most common response (41 or 29 percent of all responses) indicated a fear of places where guests, pastors, chiefs, Europeans, or other dignitaries were gathered. The second most frequent response (19, or 13 percent of the total) indicated a fear of going near the house of another family. To a child, another family represents a concentration of alien authority. Fear of external authority and power is marked among the children sampled, as is their awareness of social boundaries.

Another of the sentence-completion items in the questionnaire began, "Samoan children would all be cheeky if. . . . " The most frequent response here was "When there are strangers, Europeans, and other important people nearby," a response given by 35 (25 percent) of all those responding. The next most common response was "When they are not properly taught/ guided" which was given by 29 (20 percent) of the children. Regretfully, I did not perform a computer cross-tabulation comparing responses to these two items, and thus do not know how many of these responses came from the same children. While ambivalence in attitudes toward outsiders and others with prestige and power is not clearly demonstrated here for particular individuals, such an ambivalence does characterize the sampled population as a whole.

3. Another term is *fuaiala*. *Fuai-* is a prefix meaning "sub" or "section" and appears to be related to *fua* "to bloom."

4. The term *'au'āiga* has caused some confusion in the anthropological literature since it appears to refer to several quite distinct kinship units. Tiffany (1971) and Weston (1972) both use *'au'āiga* to refer to the widest possible extension of the *'āiga*. While the term is sometimes used this way, *'āiga potopoto* is the more common term for the extended kindred. *'Au'āiga* refers to an actively cooperating group of kin, rather than a group of any particular genealogical configuration. Thus normally the *'au'āiga* would consist of a single co-residential extended family, under the primary authority of a household chief. On occasions, when a larger group of kin assembles for a celebration, the effective *'au'āiga* includes a much larger grouping than normal.

5. This census leaves out two households whose chiefs refused to give any census information. Using the average obtained for *'au'āiga* size, the addition of two other *'au'āiga* would add about thirty people to the village population, bringing the total to 858. The members of another household were temporarily residing in American Samoa; its members have not been counted in the census. Fifty-two households were actually surveyed.

6. Despite the clear criteria which have been outlined for the definition of an *'au'āiga*, there is inevitably a certain arbitrariness in distinguishing between related households. In some households, for instance, there is more than one chief resident, with the junior *matai* serving the senior. Generally, these multi-chief households count as a single household, and are frequently much larger than households which have sub-divided under autonomous chiefs. Where such multi-chief households have been specified by residents as a single jural and commensal unit I have listed them as a single *'au'āiga*, but specified the internal differentiation by the addition of letters to the numbers (e.g., 1a, 1b, 1c). Because Samoan households are defined in terms of authority and cooperative relations, there are naturally different degrees of *'au'āiga* corporateness. In some of the larger household compounds, therefore, the distinction between one and several *'au'āiga* may well become a matter of situation, and thus somewhat arbitrary for census purposes.

7. It is characteristic that the definition of a "true" member of a village as opposed to an outsider is frequently context-dependent. Any person who can trace through maternal or paternal links a connection to a village is potentially one of its members. This potential is activated through actual residence in the village, which may be permanent, intermittent, or only occasional. Still, on certain occasions and for certain purposes a person normally residing elsewhere may be considered a member of a village. Thus the precise reckoning of village membership is not always possible.

8. "It is . . . more satisfactory to think of Savai'i, east of Fa'asaleleaga, as composed of villages and 'subdistricts' linked nonlocally by formal lineage affiliations, and locally by exigencies of intermittent warfare, though at any given time there was never a great deal of difference between district organization in Savai'i and that in Upolu" (Gilson 1970:53). On territorial and kin-based political organization, see Panoff 1964.

9. The origin of the Sālemuliaga is linked closely to the founding of Savai'i itself. The immediate ancestors of the Muliaga family are the founders of Savai'i. The father of the first of the Muliaga was Lafai (called sometimes La'ifai or Laifai), who is held as the founding ancestor of the political organization of Savai'i, particularly of Fa'asaleleaga district. In traditional oratory, Savai'i is known as Sālafai (the family of Lafai). The Sālemuliaga spread throughout the southern half of Savai'i through a series of marriages of sons of Muliagalafai (see Kraemer 1902:1:87–88).

10. Alternatively, titles may spread beyond their original localities through the process of fission, whereby a title is subdivided and the associated descent group splits into two or more *itū paepae* (title-division branches). Over successive generations, the actual genealogical ties that are the foundation of the alliance come to have less importance than the ceremonial connections suggested by a common title in the formal greetings of several villages. Thus

villages and individuals may claim that they are related "through a title," rather than through specific genealogical links.

4. THE MATAI SYSTEM

1. According to the *Tusi Fa'alupega* (Book of Village Greetings), the Sā Amituana'ī also resided traditionally in Sataputu, having its house there, called 'Olo'itefu. While this name is still referred to in oratory, I was not able to discover where this *malae* actually is in the village, if anywhere.

2. It is interesting to compare these Samoan kin-group categories with their Tokelauan cognates *kaukaiga* and *puikaiga*. Huntsman (1971:1:326–327) defines the Tokelauan *puikaiga* on Nukunono Island as one of four large and unclearly bounded descent categories based on descent traced ambilaterally to one of four founding sibling sets, and to a territory associated with the founders. The *kaukaiga*, by contrast, is the primary functional corporate group, of shallow genealogical depth (two or three generations), temporary duration, and common property rights. *Puikaiga* are temporally stable but have little functional significance in modern Tokelauan society.

3. A *matai* holding more than one title in the same village will thereby participate in the affairs of two or more descent groups (usually related *'āiga*) in that village, and by virtue of the titles have authority over different tracts of land and distinct household compounds. It is also not unusual for a chief to hold titles in several villages, in which case he has a voice in affairs of a number of descent groups *and* also a number of village *fono*. Such dispersion of political affiliations accounts in part for the Samoan love of traveling. Periodic visits serve to activate and reinforce one's political and kinship ties throughout the islands.

4. A title's ranking suggests only a relative position of a title at one point in history, and in one *fono*. Thus some titles that do not enjoy especially high place in Sala'ilua have a high rank in other villages where they are also localized. For instance, the titles Su'a and Faumuinā, relatively undistinguished in Sala'ilua, enjoy great prestige and high rank in other villages. Other Sala'ilua titles such as La'ifai and Va'asili have a prominent place in the policitical history of Savai'i, but have been eclipsed in Sala'ilua by other names.

5. The term *taule'ale'a* may also be used for girls suggesting their adolescent status between childhood and full adulthood. Women may also hold chiefly titles, though female *matai* are statistically infrequent. Occasionally, a particularly distinguished woman will be selected by an *'āiga potopoto* in which she claims membership and will be given *matai* status. In recent times, many of the young women who have returned from schooling overseas have become *matai*. Nonetheless, *matai* status is customarily conferred upon men, women achieving political status in Samoa either by the possession of a *taupou* title, by leadership in a *tamafafine* branch of a descent group (by virtue of sisterly status), or by assuming authority and prestige in relation to village women by virtue of a father's or husband's title.

6. For a more detailed discussion of Samoan adoption practices and several detailed case studies of *tama si'i* adoptions, see Shore 1976a.

7. The government judicial system, adopted from a New Zealand model, did not follow the Samoan custom of attributing moral and legal responsibility to the offender's father or chief. Only Ioane himself was tried in court for Fatu's murder. The guilty verdict, upheld in two widely publicized appeals, meant that Ioane would receive the mandatory death sentence. This penalty was finally commuted by the head of state to one of life imprisonment.

5. FA'ALUPEGA AND FONO: THE FRAMEWORK OF A LOCAL POLITICAL ORDER

1. For an interesting and sophisticated structural analysis of Samoan political organization showing this distinction between political relations defined in terms of territory and kinship

relations defined in terms of descent, see Panoff 1964. See also Mead 1930/1969 and Goldman 1970.

2. The kinship aspect of the title seems to be primary. One may be a *matai* as household head and holder of a descent group's title without ever having fed the village or shared kava in the *fono*. Full chiefly status, however, implies the additional political role within a village. It is significant that, although a village may exlude a chief from participation in its *fono*, only the members of a descent group may remove a title from its holder. Thus, in banishing Tolova'a Aleki and his immediate family from Sala'ilua, the village council had clear authority to exclude the *matai* from participation in distinctly village matters. Less clear was the right of the Sala'ilua *fono* to remove Tolova's from his house or garden lands. Finally, there was no way in which the *fono* could claim any say in the continued right of Aleki to bear the Tolova'a title.

6. TITLES: THE ARTICULATION OF AN ARISTOCRACY

1. The reason for the common convergence of the *'augānofo* and *gafa* among the paramount titles is the common tendency in Polynesian societies for titles to pass in a patrilineal succession line among the highest-ranking chiefs. Most common is succession from father to son (*nofo soso'o*), while succession by the eldest remaining brother (*toe 'o le uso*) is also common. Patrilineal succession is not followed consistently even for these highest titles, however. The paramount Malietoa title, for instance, has today several competing contenders from different descent group branches.

2. This conceptual distinction between a person and his office as separable entities is the basis of the medieval European conception of the king's two bodies, a concept still reflected in the usage of the "royal we" (Kantorowicz 1957). For Samoans, the distinction suggests a more general one between passive dignity (the title) and the active embodiment for the dignity (the titleholder), a distinction that will be explored in its broader cultural context in chapter 12.

3. The status of the various forms of the Samoan *'āiga* as true descent groups has remained something of a problem in the anthropological literature. This problem has several dimensions. First is the classic problem in anthropology of the status of nonunilineal descent reckoning and its relation to the formation of discrete groups (Davenport 1959, Freeman 1961, Murdock 1960, Goodenough 1955, Leach 1962, Lévi-Strauss 1949, Fortes 1959, Radcliffe-Brown 1951).

At issue here are cognatic descent systems found primarily in Oceania and Southeast Asia, but also existing in parts of central Africa (Forde and Radcliffe-Brown 1950) and South Asia (Yalman 1961). By definition, the traditional wisdom has held that bilateral reckoning of descent, the universal basis for the reckoning of biological "kinship" (Fortes 1959), was incapable of defining discrete and thus nonoverlapping groups. It was only for these discrete groups with unambiguous boundaries that the term "descent group" could apply. Furthermore, it was asserted by British social anthropologists that the basis of descent-group solidarity had to be functionally derived from either jural authority (Fortes 1959) or rights of transmission over joint property (Goody 1961). Such conditions were taken to be logically satisfied only by unilineal descent reckoning. It is important to note the emphasis placed on the "logical" rather than the empirical basis for the restriction of descent group status to those groups formed by unilineal descent principles.

In addition to these more explicit assumptions, descent theorists have generally assumed that descent group structure logically implied the unambiguous allocation of a whole person to one and only one group (Schneider 1965). Simultaneous membership in different groups was held to be incompatible with the preconditions for organized social life. Cognatic descent such as characterizes Samoan descent concepts thus seemed an impossible paradox.

The whole issue of cognatic descent in anthropology has resulted from a number of basic fallacies that tell us more about our own assumptions about structure than about the nature of descent groups in the Pacific. In recent years, anthropologists have begun to refine their ideas about descent to make room for these otherwise anomalous systems. Scheffler (1966) helped by distinguishing descent constructs from actual concrete groups. Thus, following a Parsonian scheme, descent was seen to have both a cultural (ideational) and a concrete social status. The Samoan *'āiga*'s continuity should be defined on the conceptual level as a descent construct, while actual concrete groups might form occasionally as particular realizations of the descent construct. Such a notion is clearly consistent with the Samoans' own treatment of the *fono* or of chieftaincy, where a distinction is made between the position or structural form, which is eternal, and any particular realization or token of that form, which is taken to be transient and variable.

In 1963 Firth pointed out that bilateral reckoning of descent required further operational principles to limit the effective range of any particular cooperating group. Goodenough (1955) had already demonstrated that, for Malayo–Polynesian social organization, residence seems to have been the most important of these operational principles, carving concrete descent groups out of what we now recognize as descent constructs. Indeed residence, in the form of primary cooperation in the production and consumption of food, has been distinguished in these pages as the feature that separates the Samoan *'au'āiga* and the *pui'āiga*. Genealogical connection is not the basis for inclusion in an *'au'āiga*, while it is fundamental in the definition of one's *pui'āiga*.

In the end, cognatic descent remains a paradox only as long as the structure of society is held to consist of the distinction of discrete social groups, with an unambiguously defined membership that is stable over time. If, however, we allow for what Keesing (1968) has called "the contextual definition of status" in which an individual's loyalties are to a number of distinct descent groups, such that the individual is socially fragmented into a number of distinct "sides," the problem of the viability of cognatic descent disappears. The logic and social order of such a system requires a number of additional principles, such as the degree of cooperation or residence for sorting out the extent to which an individual is incorporated into a particular descent group. Further, attention is inevitably turned to the cultural definition of social boundaries in any particular context, thus contextually (and not absolutely) avoiding overlapping loyalties and thus social and political chaos.

A second serious misconception about Samoan descent stems from a claim made by Ember (1959, 1962) and by Sahlins (1964) that Samoa lacked a ramifying system of descent lines, articulated beyond the local level. For Ember, the basic Samoan descent group was what he termed the local sept. While correctly suggesting that Samoan descent groups were significantly localized and lacked the orderly ramifying structure of the lineages of some other Polynesian groups such as the Maoris or Tahitians, Ember was clearly incorrect in denying for the Samoan *'āiga* any significant supralocal articulations. Freeman (1964) was quick to point to the rather intricate network of associations of any single descent group beyond its local boundaries, and Panoff (1964), using the old "breed and border" distinction, demonstrated how territorial links are set against the significant supralocal networks of kinship in ancient Samoan social organization.

The present study of Sala'ilua should make it clear that despite the localization of the title-based descent groups in a village *fono*, these groups maintain a number of different kinds of supralocal linkage with related groups in other locations. Occasions such as the funeral of Tuatō Fatu are opportunities for representatives of related groups (such as members of the other branches of the Sālemuliaga, or members of Tuatō kindred residing elsewhere, or those who trace their connection to the Tuatō title rather than to Fatu personally) to validate their connections.

4. Upon gaining political independence in 1962, Western Samoa presented its people with a referendum to decide whether the new nation should adopt universal suffrage. By an overwhelming majority Samoans voted to give to their chiefs the sole right to elect representatives to their legislative assembly. This limitation of voting rights to the titled led to the wholesale creation of hundreds of new titles by senior chiefs with political ambitions. In effect, they could create their own constituency. Such minor titles gave relatively little actual power to their holders in village affairs and threatened to dilute *matai* authority. They quickly gained the name of *matai pālota* (ballot chiefs) and despite the government's attempt to curb their proliferation by tightening laws requiring registration of all titles with the Registrar of the

Land and Titles Court, the electoral system still appears to exert an influence on the creation and proliferation of political titles.

5. The classic Samoan instance of this kind of filial relationship is the story of the founding of Upolu political structure by Pili, a culture hero. Pili is said to have had four children. Three sons, 'Ana, Tua, and Saga, were each given a district of Upolu over which to preside, giving rise to the districts of Atua (Tua) in the east, 'A'ana ('Ana) in the northwest, and Tuamasaga (Saga) in central Upolu. A fourth child, Tolufale, claimed by some to have been a girl, was given as her dominion the island of Manono and was allocated the task of looking after the other three siblings and acting as a conciliator in any disputes. This pattern, the classic model for brother–sister relations, will be discussed in chapters 12 and 13.

6. A more direct analogy is the historical Tongan pattern of a king giving his secular authority to his son, or to a junior line, and retaining the sacred power for himself. See Kaeppler 1971 for specific cases.

7. In this relationship one is reminded of the common practice in parts of eastern Polynesia, such as the Society Islands or the Marquesas, of a chief giving up his power to his first-born son, the *matahiapo*, upon the birth of that child (Goldman 1970).

8. To make this information more useful, I organized it by means of a matrix, indicating the relationship of every titleholder in the village to every other *matai*. I have decided not to reproduce this matrix here for several reasons. Foremost is the fact that such display of another's genealogical ties constitutes for Samoans *talagafa*—reciting another's genealogy in public—which is strongly condemned and which would constitute a breach of trust on my part. A second reason for omitting the matrix is its extreme complexity. It is possible to summarize the important patterns evident in the matrix without subjecting the reader to a grid specked with hundreds of numbers.

9. It is also conceivable, of course, that this very ideology affected the memories of my informants such that they were far more likely to frame genealogical ties throughout the village in terms of the focal chiefs and thus provide detailed information for them. In constructing the matrix, I tried to complete the elaboration of the ties by filling in the relationships that were implied by informants' information but had not been explicitly stated. Thus, if I were told that *A* and *B* were brothers and that *B* and *C* were brothers, I inferred that *A* and *C* were at least half-brothers.

10. This distinction is also realized as *itū mālosi/itū vaivai* (strong side/weak side).

11. In recent years the distinction between *tamatane* and *tamafafine* has lost much of its traditional force in the decision-making process for political succession. *Tamafafine* have successfully pursued claims to titles for which they once had no customary right of succession, and both descent groups and the Land and Titles Court have frequently agreed to this breach of custom. The frequency with which claims are now settled by the court rather than within the descent group itself may have contributed to the weakening of the traditional role of *tamafafine* members of a descent group. Further, the rapid growth of population in Western Samoa has placed considerable pressure on agricultural lands that are under the direct control of titles. The ensuing competition for direct *pule* over the lands by descent group members has led *tamafafine* members to eschew their more traditional advisorial role in relation to titles in favor of a move toward direct control.

12. In a fascinating analysis of female rank and power in Tonga, Rogers (1977) illustrates the relations between the inheritance of male and female power in a diagram strikingly similar to figure 6.4. However, Rogers calls the line of genealogical connection through women a *matriline* (to be distinguished from a corporate matrilineage). This term strikes me as inappropriate and misleading. The connections between females in this line are, indeed, matrilineal, but the relevant status of these women is that of sister and not mother. Matrifiliation defines relations within the line, but the significant attachment of the line to a focal title or member of a descent group is the relation of a woman as a sister (or FZ, FFZ, etc.). In Tonga as well as Samoa, the status of *mother* of each female in this line is in relation to a different descent group or title, as illustrated in figure 6.4.

13. Rogers (1977) illustrates nicely a Tongan solution to this inherent ambiguity in tracing descent from a fraternal or sororal connection. In Tonga, descent classifications are structurally

and semantically parallel with the Samoan *tamatane/tamafafine* distinction, but somewhat more elaborate. Tongans classify collateral offspring as *'ilamutu* (sister's child), *tama a mehekitanga* (father's sister's child), or *tama a tuasina* (mother's brother's child). Rogers claims that for Tongan commoners a recent, and often the most direct link is employed in reckoning descent classification. Nobles, however, most frequently calculate their descent classifications in relation to a collateral relative through a more distant and conventionally accepted link, rather than through the most direct one. I have no information suggesting a similar Samoan distinction, perhaps because the line between commoner and nobility is considerably fuzzier for Samoans than for Tongans.

14. In addition to these four *pāpā* titles, there was the Tui Manu'a title of Manu'a, now part of American Samoa, and six *ao*, senior titles of the six *pule* centers of Savai'i. Tutuila Island, now the main population center of American Samoa, was, throughout the nineteenth century, politically allied to the Atua district of Upolu.

15. For more on the complexities of the traditional polity of Samoa see Keesing and Keesing (1956); Panoff (1964); Gilson (1970), especially ch. 2, and Kraemer (1902).

16. This maintenance of traditional flexibility in the operation of the Land and Titles Court is at a great cost in efficiency and speed of operation of the court. The impressive increase in the number of cases brought to the court in recent years has led the government of Western Samoa to establish a commission to examine the court's operation and make recommendations for its modification.

17. See Marsack (1958) for a detailed statement on the operation of the court by one of its former Chief Justices.

7. VILLAGE ORGANIZATION: STRUCTURES OF SOCIAL CONTROL

1. While the functions of the *pulenu'u* are restricted to the recording of village births and deaths, the office seems to be used by villagers as an index of official recognition of the autonomy of a village. For a subvillage to insist on having its own *pulenu'u* signals its intention to declare itself a distinct political unit. In this context it is significant that the village of Sala'ilua has two *pulenu'u*, one for Si'utu and the other for Sataputu and Sala'ilua subvillages. This indicates something of the ambiguous status of Si'utu as a subvillage within Sala'ilua.

8. PERSONS

1. The text of the Samoan creation story is drawn largely from Mead (1930) and is based on translations made at the turn of the century by Fraser and Pratt. Another version of the story by Steubel (1896), translated by Brother Hermann, will also be used. For another kind of analysis of Samoan creation stories see Shore 1980.

2. The usual translation of the name as Tagaloa the Creator is misleading in several important ways. The name does not refer directly to the creation of people, but of inhabited places (*nu'u*) such as villages, islands, etc. Even more important is the meaning of the word *fa'atupu*, which suggests not creation in the sense of mechanical construction but rather the causing of things to grow. The implication here seems to be that "creation" constituted a conjuring or inspiring of a potential force into activity. The Samoan terms for actual creation (used in the translation of Genesis) are *fai* (do or make), *gāosi* (fabricate), and *fao* (build by lashing or nailing things together). The distinction between the evolutionary implications of conjuring and the implications of mechanical creation is important for understanding the differences between Western and Samoan notions of creation.

3. It is this sort of ordering or assignment of proper activities, functions, and ranks to people, elements, or other aspects of existence that is suggested by the Samoan term *tofi* (calling/allotment) as it is used in proverbial and common speech.

4. The earth, to which the body returns after death, is referred to poetically as *'o le nu'u o*

ilo, the abode of maggots/worms). This is, of course, suggestive of the Christian concept of "ashes to ashes. . . . ," a return to a primordial form. The Christian influence is possible here, but it appears more likely that the notion of man being created from maggots and returning to them is truly Samoan.

5. These are two examples of the more general tendency in Samoan myth to attribute creation to the power of words. Origins are commonly traced back to the union of two concepts or elements both linguistically and materially, in what functions as a generative punning. The tendency for traditional Samoan explanations of origin to involve an account of the agglutination of morphemes into words, or of two separate words into one, is extremely common. As Mead has pointed out, the susceptibility of the phonologically limited Samoan language to punning and to the fragmentation of words into various combinations of aggregate elements, each variation with a distinct meaning, encourages manipulative and idiosyncratic validation of title or regional status through diverse explanations of origin. Thus, for example, the "origin" of Samoa is commonly interpreted in terms of the origin of the word Samoa, which is, in term, analyzed in terms of its component parts. Thus *Sā* may be (a) sacred; (b) a personal name; (c) a past tense verbal marker; or (d) a prefix indicating a title-based descent group. *Moa* may mean (a) hen; (b) center, as of a road or path; or (c) a personal name. Combinations of these words in various semantic realizations suggest a number of different meanings of "Samoa," and thereby distinct origins of the archipelago. Several of the more common interpretations are: (a) the sacred center of Polynesia; (b) the product of the union of a couple named Sā and Moa; and (c) the descent group of the Tui Manu'a, to whom the chicken (*moa*) was sacred.

6. The transformation from "shade-producing" vine to "people-producing" vine has some interesting implications for Samoan thought. The term *pāolo* (shade) is the most common term for affines. The equation of shade and the generation of people in the metaphor of the vine is thus logical in Samoan thought, for it is through the transition from *gafa* (a line of descent) to *pāolo* that new descent lines are generated.

7. For an interesting discussion of Western notions of self, character, and interiority and their absence in a Malay epic see Errington 1975:4–9.

8. The term *vā*, translated here as "relationship," has other senses of "space" or "between."

9. Relatively recent trends in information science, structuralism, and related schools of thought show a similar refocusing of our perceptions on things in their contexts, turning away from an older interest in reducing experiences to essential qualities. While the academic mind may be attuned to a new contextualization of knowledge, most of us continue to maintain assumptions in everyday experience grounded in the search for essences.

10. See Shore (1976a) for an extended discussion of the claims that an adopted child (*tama fai*) may make. The article also contains a detailed case study of a person who possesses two different kinds of claim to a particularly distinguished title: one by direct descent, the other by a high-level, politically motivated adoption.

11. The psychological significance of these fine distinctions in pronoun reference cannot be taken too lightly. For an English speaker learning a Polynesian language, the correct use of these pronouns constitutes one of the most difficult challenges, since it requires an unfamiliar skill in assessing the relative and shifting strengths of different ties.

12. The conception of appropriateness that seems to guide Samoan behavioral orientations is similar to the Tahitian notion of "meaning" as discussed by Levy (1973:262): "The ordinary term to designate the *meaning* of a word or situation is *au ra'a*. *Au ra'a* means the 'fitting together of matters', 'the relationship of things'; sometimes it implies a relationship which is fitting, comfortable, pleasant to the speaker. *Ra'a* indicates a process. *Au ra'a* used for kin designates their kin relationships. Thus the word for meaning designates the object's relationships, its contexts."

13. See Levy (1973:214) for a discussion of similar depersonalization of action in Tahiti.

14. Minimally, each Samoan recognizes four distinct *'āiga* as his primary social sides: those of his four grandparents. One may commonly speak of one's maternal or paternal sides, but usually the specification is clearer, distinguishing precisely one of the four grandparental connections. Although kin ties may be traced by Samoans as far back and as broadly collaterally

as knowledge and interest allow, a person's hope for titles is usually limited to his four primary *'āiga*, with some slight preference for patrilateral links.

9. ACTION

1. Levy's analysis (1973) of Tahitian personality is in marked contrast to the characterizations that have been drawn here of Samoans. According to Levy, Tahitians show little inclination to aggressive behavior, maintaining a constant stress on smooth and harmonious relations.

2. Tongans seem to make a similar distinction between *anga* and *amio*. Whereas in Tongan, *anga* is the normal term for behavior in general, *amio* refers to a sullenness or desultoriness in carrying out expected behavior due to personal disinclination. Thus, by implication, *amio* refers to the disruptive effects of personal drives on socially appropriate behavior.

3. The social patterning of such socially disapproved forms of conduct is a general phenomenon in human society. Linton (1936:431) refers to the "presence in all cultures of patterns for misconduct" that specify precisely how to go about breaking the rules correctly. Such "rules for breaking the rules" are very important in Samoan social life and are behind what I shall characterize as a double-socialization for the handling of both *aga* and *āmio*. On patterns for misconduct see also Devereux 1978:142.

4. The similarity of *āmio* and *aga* to Freudian conceptions of id and superego is striking.

5. Milner (1966) uses these translations for *agaga*, and suggests that the term is really a reduplicated form of *aga* which should be spelled *agaaga*. In my experience, however, the term *agaga* is distinct in pronunciation from *agaaga*, the former being pronounced with a shorter *a*. The term *fa'aagaaga*, however, pronounced with the reduplicated *a*, means "to intend" or "to prepare" something for a special use, and may be related to *aga*.

6. This Samoan vision of socialization bears striking resemblance to George Herbert Mead's notion of the "social self."

7. The significance of *aga* in understanding Samoan ethical categories is suggested by the possible derivation of the term *leaga* (bad) from the negation (*lē*: "not") of *aga*, suggesting not simply evil but rather a quality of an act which has lost all contact with social order.

10. KNOWLEDGE AND JUDGMENT

1. The anthropologist was not the first observer to be confused by an exotic Polynesian epistemology. Levy (1973) suggests that in their dealings with Tahitians the missionaries found similar difficulties. Levy writes: "To the Western mind this separation of surface emotional display from the inner 'truth' was to be a particular problem: it confronted the evangelical missionaries who appeared in strength in the early nineteenth century, looking for salvation for the inner man" (p. 98).

2. The difference between this Samoan equation of sight and knowledge and the Occidental dissociation of the two is suggested by Gloucester in Shakespeare's *King Lear* and by Oedipus in Euripides' plays. Both characters gain true knowledge of themselves and their condition, knowledge that we recognize as "insight," only on becoming blind. The wisom of the blind as a characteristic premise of Western epistemology is suggested by the sense of appropriateness rather than irony that greets the concept of a blind Milton or Homer.

3. This section has benefited from discussions with Robert Levy.

4. Such complexity is also implicit in the structure of Samoan kinship and political relations, which permit people to elaborate their connections to the maximum complexity that their abilities and resources will allow.

5. It is interesting to note at this point Sahlins' contention (personal communication) that insofar as Samoan genealogical reckoning stresses the tracing of an advantageous line of links from a stressed ancestor to an individual or group making a claim, it might be best described as "ascent" rather than "descent" reckoning.

6. It is interesting to recall that such sexual activity is also associated with the term *āmio*.

That the terms *āmio* and *leaga* are generally equivalent euphemisms for sexual activity raises the possibility, which we have already discussed, that *leaga* derives from the negation of *aga* (chapter 9, note 7), perhaps in the same sense that *āmio* implies the absence of *aga*.

7. The experience among Samoan children of culturally induced frustration of the desire to eat may have something to do with the famous Polynesian obsession with food, particularly with food in abundance.

8. This form of expressing excess may be heard in everyday Samoan conversation, though in colloquial terms, the word *ova*, borrowed from the English "over," is becoming frequent in statements such as "'Ua ova 'ai le tama" (The boy has overeaten).

9. By custom and choice, Samoans have always appointed a European as their Chief Justice, both in the Supreme Court and in the Land and Titles Court. Samoans readily admit they they cannot conceive of a Samoan judge who would take a neutral or objective perspective on important matters, especially where lands and titles are involved. In the Samoan view of things, objectivity would presume a lack of social relations, a vantage point that is amoral and, for any Samoan, nonexistent.

10. This discussion has benefited from Levy's work on shame and guilt (Levy 1972/74, 1973) and his theory of the differences between "steady-state" and dynamic societies in relation to social control. This theory is derived from Bateson's work on learning (1973) and on Russell and Whitehead's theory of logical types of language.

11. Conflict in the Context of Social Relations

1. See Leenhardt (1947) for a fascinating discussion of relational thinking in a Melanesian context.

2. In so defining status, I am using the term quite differently from Goldman (1970).

3. Sets with more than two members exist, as in the set *itū mālō/nu'u/pitonu'u* (district/village/subvillage), or a set of kin terms for members of a nuclear family. Generally, however, Samoans seem to stress simple dual reciprocals, a fact that will be discussed in chapter 12.

4. Thus in New Zealand, for instance, young Samoans are far more likely to get into conflicts with closely related Tongans than with any of the other ethnic groups with whom they have less in common.

5. Mead (1930:74) includes among *tōga* items: "tapa, coarser varieties of mats, grass skirts (*titi*), coconut oil, turmeric and other dyes." There is an interesting parallel here with women's exchange goods in the Trobriand Islands (Weiner 1978).

6. Of course in relation to any one political title, *tamatane* and *tamafafine* statuses operate within a descent group, specifically between descent lines of brother and sister, rather than between paternal and maternal groups. See the extended discussion of *tamatane* and *tamafafine* relations above, chapter 6.

7. This Samoan tendency to maintain flexibility and fluidity in ranking at the expense of precision distinguishes Samoan from contemporary Tongan culture. The Tongan system appears to have gone a long way toward transforming a system of graded rank into one of categorical levels of status. For interesting analyses of variation within traditional Polynesian social systems in terms of graded rank and categorical status, see Goldman (1970). On Tonga, see Kaeppler (1971) and Marcus (1980).

8. For a similar account of Tokelauan social relations see Huntsman 1971. Her account employs similar analytical terms, with the important exception that the Samoan stress on ranked relations is replaced in Tokelauan thought by a stress on chronological seniority.

12. The Symbolism of Power: Dual Organization and Social Order

1. This dual conception of power, distinguishing formal from executive powers and spiritual from secular authority, appears to be a common feature of Malayo-Polynesian social thought. Within Polynesia it is manifested in a pervasive general distinction between sacred and secular

political offices. The former type of power is suggested by the Polynesian terms *mana* and *tapu*, while the more secular form of power is commonly referred to as *pule* or some form of that term. Thus, for instance, there is the Tongan distinction between *eiki* and *matapule* (Gifford 1929, Kaeppler 1971, Marcus 1980); the Samoan distinction between *ali'i* and *faipule* (orators); the Tikopian distinction between the sacred chiefs (*ariki*) and the heads of genealogically senior households (*pure*) (Firth 1936); the traditional Tokelauan distinction between the sacred *aliki* or *tupu* in the person of the Tui Tokelau, and the *faipule* or *puseve*, his executive officer representing him at council meetings (MacGregor 1937, Goldman 1970); and the dual power structure of traditional Uvea distinguishing *aliki* and *matua* (heads of junior lineages).

Elsewhere in Polynesia, this dual power structure was perhaps less precise but nonetheless evident. Thus, for example, in Mangaia, the title of Temporal Lord (*mangaia*), originally a sacred priestly office, "became dislodged from the senior lineage of the Ngariki" (Goldman 1970:79) and instituted as a distinctly achieved secular office, separate from the sacred *ariki*. Traditional Easter Island society elaborated two complementary political orders parallel roughly to those on Mangaia. "one, traditional, organized around sacred ariki and their descent lines; the other, highly mobile and representing warrior chiefs and their separate descent lines" (Goldman 1970:109–110). This double-edged political system distinguished the sacred *ariki mau* from the largely achieved status of the Bird Man of the Rongo Cult. These patterns are mentioned here not to mask the significant distinctions among Polynesian societies in the elaboration of political structures, but rather to suggest a common Polynesian political philosophy, which attempted to stabilize political relations by dissociating the more instrumental and executive functions of political power from the more formal and sacred powers. Of those who have writen on Polynesian polities, Goldman (1970) appears especially aware of this religious bias in Polynesian thought and social structure, and has attempted to demonstrate as far as the available ethnographic material would permit, subtle but significant transformations of this structure throughout the region. For Micronesian analogies to this ideology of power see Labby (1976) on traditional Yap and Riesenberg (1968) on Ponape.

2. Panoff (1964) suggested the importance for Samoa of this complementarity in the structuring of Samoan political institutions, although he phrased the dichotomy more narrowly than is done here as one between the centrifugal tendencies of relations of kinship and the opposing centripetal tendencies of territorial relations. In another context, Panoff translated this dichotomy into the social control function of the *ali'i* as opposed to the economic functions of the *tulāfale*. Goldman (1970:267) also focused on the structural aspects of the *ali'i/tulāfale* relationship, noting that it represented a "bipolar relation between form and function," a relationship that suggested to him the connection between role and actor.

3. Huntsman (1971) has described for the Tokelau Islands a similar conceptual association of stasis for women and movement for men. In the Tokelauan case, however, the associations are understood in relation to a uxorilocal residence pattern. Women thus "stay put" (*nofonofo*) in their own households, while men move out to reside with their wives. Furthermore, males retain lifelong obligations to their sisters and their sisters' children to provide them with food and other forms of assistance. Men's lives are thus defined in terms of movements between natal households and those into which they have married.

4. For a psychoanalytic perspective on the associations between equality, symmetrical relations, and sexuality, see Devereux (1978:210).

5. The *Reports of Evidence* for the Davidson Commission on Local and District Government (1950) indicate that of the 179 localities surveyed (all the villages of Western Samoa), 69, or just under a quarter, indicated that their *'aumaga* were led by sons of orators. Of these, 49 specified that these youth leaders were to be sons of leading orators. Only 35 of the surveyed villages indicated that their *'aumaga* were led by sons of *ali'i*.

6. An articulate and knowledgeable informant provided the following explanation of the *tama sā*:

> That refers to the highest position. *Tamafafine* is the common word for it. Any heir of
> the female you can call the *tamafafine*. But if the Malietoa marries Galuega Pāpā, the *taupou*
> of the Tamasese (another paramount title), and they have a son, call him Laupepa, well
> if Laupepa goes to visit the family of his mother, then Tamasese will be his mother's

brother, and Laupepa is the *tama sā* of the Tamasese, his sister's child. Tamasese and Malietoa are both kings (*tupu*), so that the child of the king's sister is his *tama sā*.

Note that though the informant initially defines both the *tama sā* and *tamafafine* as "any heir of the female," it is only in relation to that woman's brother that the status is relevant. Female here thus implies sister.

7. Kraemer's genealogies contradict this account provided by my informant. According to Kraemer, the origin of the 'Āiga Sā Tuala is:

I do not know how to reconcile these discrepancies. Gasalā and 'Auali'itia may be the offspring of another union of Tautaiolefue, although this would not reconcile all the discrepencies between the two versions of the descent lines.

8. The same argument can also be made in relation to the bride's and groom's sides at a wedding exchange. As we have seen, there is a competitive tension underlying the overtly ritualized exchange of *tōga* and *'oloa*. This latent competition stems, I think, from the fact that despite the *conceptual* arrangement of the two families as complementary (bride and groom), they are *perceived* as symmetrically opposed families and villages.

9. One informant related the following account of the origin of the *tulāfale*.
Tulāfale is a word from Manu'a. The ancient legend says that the house of the Tui Manu'a was called the *fale 'ula*. That house was thatched with bright red [*'ula*] feathers taken from brilliantly colored parrots. . . . This house was stolen by the Atafu-mea, people from the Tokelau Islands of Atafu. It must be understood that these sorts of houses called *fale 'ula* could actually be stolen, because they were not actually houses in which people lived, but rather something thrown together for special events.

The entire body of the house was stolen. The Tui Manu'a ordered his men to go to Atafu to retrieve his house. They went and warred with the Atafu islanders and defeated them. Then they brought back the house. Each man had a pole to carry, and they all swam in the sea with the house resting on the poles which lay on the necks of the attendants. So that is the real origin of the word *tulāfale*: *tulaga-o-le fale* [resting place of the house]. This is your calling, he said, and I will spill over my strength to you and you will execute the power [*pule*] of my dignity [*āfio*].

10. But see Hocart (1927), where he denies the existence of the polite dual pronoun in Samoan.

11. In a legend from Manu'a associated with the Tui Manu'a and the origin of his title, a legend cited by Mead (1930:176–177), the conceptual distinction between person and office is suggested by a tapa turban that was held to embody the dignity and power of the chief Galeai. Instructed never to loosen this crown, Galeai arrives on earth and proceeds to the village of Lafaga on Upolu, where he takes upon himself the greater title of Tui Manu'a. Galeai's action brings the god Tagaloa to earth, and when Tagaloa removes this turban from Galeai's head, the latter becomes a common man once again.

13. THE ESTHETICS OF SOCIAL CONTEXT: DUAL ORGANIZATION AND EXPRESSIVE CULTURE

1. It would be more accurate to characterize the Samoan language as possessing three speech levels. The first is everyday or common speech used by everyone in intimate settings or by elites to nonelites in appropriate contexts. Second are the respect forms used by all adults and

some children to signal formal contexts and deferential relations. Third are the specialized and arcane forms of oratory that have their place mainly in meetings during oratorical debates.

2. The problem of whether these two systems are distinct phonemic systems with semantically complementary distribution or two realizations of a single phonemic system will not be discussed here.

3. This excerpt is actually a paraphrase of a statement that had once been made to me but which I never recorded verbatim. The other statements are all direct translations of transcriptions from interviews.

4. These two distinctions are appropriate in form to the nature of the opposition that each represents. Thus the lexical stratification associated with the formal/intimate dichotomy internal to the *fa'a Samoa* is a gradual opposition allowing many gradations in degree of formality or respect. The phonological opposition, by contrast, is an absolute and simple binary structure permitting no degrees. It is appropriate for expressing Samoan/European distinctions.

14. CONCLUSIONS: STRUCTURE AND EVENT IN SALA'ILUA

1. For a legal treatment of the complex issue of jurisdiction over the right to banish a family from a village see Powels 1973. See also Davidson et al. 1950a, 1950b, and Davidson 1967 for a consideration of historical and regional variations in the treatment of banishment in Samoa.

2. At the time I left Samoa this claim had not been settled by the courts. The banishment of Tolova'a Aleki and his family from Sala'ilua was being informally enforced by threats of physical violence by villagers against any of Aleki's family who dared set foot in the village. In fact members of Aleki's family twice attempted a return to their house but were forced to withdraw after their residence was stoned by irate villagers.

Glossary of Samoan Terms

'a'ai	village center; residential core
'āiga	kin; kinsman; kindred; descent group; family
'āiga ali'i	constituent families of a village possessing *ali'i* titles; the totality of *ali'i* in a village
'āiga potopoto	assembling kindred, focusing on ancestor, common relative or political title
'āiga sā–	descent group of–(followed by name of title)
āitu	spirit; ghost
aga	social conduct; behavior style
aganu'u	culture; formal culture; custom
agasala	sin; punishable behavior
'aiuli	clowning dance on periphery of dance floor
ālaga	leg and thigh of pig (orator's portion)
ali'i	high chief, nobleman
āmio	personal impulse and behavior
'au'āiga	primary cooperating kin/residential unit
aualuma	village girls' organization
'aumaga	village organization of untitled men
'ausese'e	body of girls and women in a weaving house
fa'alupega	village courtesy address
fa'a-pālagi	European culture; European language (i.e., English)
fa'a-Samoa	Samoan style; Samoan language; Samoan culture
faiā	relations, genealogical connections
faiāvā	man residing in his wife's household/village
fale	house; building
faletautū	formal, arranged marriage
fale'upolu	formal designation of the body of orators in a village
feagaiga	covenant of respect; brother/sister relationship
fono	meeting; chiefs' council; organization of chiefs
fono māitu	special, secret meeting at night, between orators to discuss an especially sensitive matter

fono tauati	general village meeting held on the *malae*
fuaiala	village segment; subvillage
fuaifale	descent group branch
gafa	descent line
ifoga	ceremonial humiliation in which chiefs representing the group of one who has seriously offended another group make amends by sitting outside the house of the offended group with fine mats over their heads
igoa	name
iloa	to know; to perceive; to see
itū paepae	literally, "the side of the foundation"; branch of a title group whose title has been split
laoa	formal term for the residence of an orator
lātū o faiva	senior woman in a weaving house, in charge of food distribution
leaga	evil; bad
lelei	good
loto	feelings; emotions
māota	formal term for the residence of an *ali'i*
mā	shame; ashamed; shy
māfaufau	to think; judgment
malae	village green; political center of a village
mālamalama	to shed light on; to understand
mamalu	dignity; dignified
mānaia	head of the young men's grop ('aumaga)
matagā	unseemly; bad to look at
matai	chief; title holder; houschold head
matua	parent; old; title which is a progenitor of another
matua u'u	senior weaver of a weaving house
monotaga	obligatory contributions of a chief or household member to the village; usually food
nofo	stay; sit; live
nofo soso'o	direct lineal succession to a title
nu'u	settlement; village
pālagi	European
pāolo	literally "shade"; affinal connections(s)
pitonu'u	village segment; same as *fuaiala*
pito vao	subsidiary title

pōula	night dance
pui'āiga	secondary cooperating kin group, residing nearby one's own, and related to it by blood
pule	secular authority
sā–	see *'aiga sā–*
sa'o	senior ali'i
saofa'i	entitlement ceremony for a new chief
sa'otama'ita'i	same as taupou
siva	dance; formal dance at the center of the dancefloor
suafa	title; respect term for *igoa*
suli moni	true heir (appropriate successor to a title)
tamafafine	"child of the female"; descent category comprising those descended from a sister to a chief or an original title-holder; more generally, sister to a male
tamatane	"child of the male"; descent category comprising those descended from a male titleholder or any of his brothers; more generally, a brother to a female
tapua'i	to pray; a passive participant in a war or other serious undertaking whose contribution is silent prayer
taualuga	"roof"; final dance of a party
taupou	village "princess"; leader of village *aualuma* (girls' association); virgin
tautala leaga	"bad speaking"; reference to intimate pronunciation style
tautala lelei	"good speaking"; reference to formal pronunciation style
tautua	to serve (a chief, village etc); a servant
teu	to put in order; hold in
taule'ale'a	untitled man; young person (pl. *taulele'a*)
tualā	ribs and bacbone of a cooked pig (*ali'i's* portion)
tulāfale	orator chief
tulāfono	rules, laws, regulations
tu'ua	elder statesman; senior orator known for wisdom
ulu matua	first-born child

Bibliography

Ala'ilima, F. and V. Ala'ilima. 1966. Consensus and Plurality in a Western Samoa Election Campaign. *Human Organization* 49:240–55.

Allport, G. W. 1929–30. The Study of Personality by the Intuitive Method. *Journal of Abnormal and Social Psychology*, vol. 24.

—— 1937. *Personality: A Psychological Interpretation*. New York: Holt.

—— 1966. Traits Revisited. *American Psychologist* 21:1–10.

Barth, F. 1975. *Ritual and Knowledge Among the Baktaman of New Guinea*. New Haven: Yale University Press.

Bateson, G. 1936/1958. *Naven*. Palo Alto: Stanford University Press.

—— 1973. *Steps to an Ecology of Mind*. St. Albans: Paladin.

Bateson, G. and M. Mead. 1942. *Balinese Character: A Photographic Analysis*. Special Publication of the New York Academy of Sciences, vol. 2. New York: New York Academy of Sciences.

Benedict, R. 1946. *Patterns of Culture*. Cambridge: Harvard University Press.

Berger, P. and T. Luckmann. 1966. *The Social Construction of Reality: A Treatise on the Sociology of Knowledge*. Garden City, N.Y.: Doubleday.

Burrows, E. 1936. The Ethnology of Futuna. *Bulletin*, Bernice P. Bishop Museum, vol. 138.

—— 1937. The Ethnology of Uvea. *Bulletin*, Bernice P. Bishop Museum, vol. 145.

Davenport, W. 1959. Non-Unilinear Descent and Descent Groups. *American Anthropologist* 61:557–72.

Davidson, J. et al. 1950a. *Reports and Evidence: Western Samoa Commission on Village and District Government*. Apia: Government Printer.

—— 1950b. *Final Report of the Commission to Enquire into and Report Upon the Organisation of District and Village Government in Western Samoa*. Apia: Government Printer.

Devereux, G. 1978. *Ethnopsychoanalysis*. Berkeley: University of California Press.

De Vos, G. 1976. Affective Dissonance and Primary Socialization. *Ethos* 1:165–81.

Douglas, M. 1966. *Purity and Danger: An Analysis of Conceptions of Pollution and Taboo*. Baltimore: Penguin Books.

—— 1973. *Rules and Meanings: The Anthropology of Everyday Knowledge*. Baltimore: Penguin Books.

Dumont, L. 1965. The Individual in Two Kinds of Society. *Contributions to Indian Sociology*, no. 8, pp. 7–61.

—— 1970. *Homo Hierarchicus*. Chicago: University of Chicago Press.

Duranti, A. n.d. The Samoan Respect Vocabulary: An Ethnographic Approach. Manuscript.

Ember, M. 1959. The Non-Unilinear Descent Groups in Samoa. *American Anthropologist* 61:573–77.

—— 1962. Political Authority and the Structure of Kinship in Samoa. *The American Anthropologist* 64:964–71.

Erikson, E. 1950/1964. *Childhood and Society*. Second Edition. New York: Norton.

—— 1964. The Nature of Clinical Evidence. In *Insight and Responsibility*, pp. 47–80. New York: Norton.

Errington, S. 1975. A Study of Genre: Meaning and Form in the Malay Hikayat Hung Tuah. Ph.D. dissertation, Cornell University.

Firth, R. 1936. *We the Tikopia*. New York: American Book Company.

—— 1957. A Note on Descent Groups in Polynesia. *Man* 57:4–8.

—— 1963. Bilateral Descent Groups: An Operational Viewpoint. Reprinted in A. Howard, ed., *Polynesia: Readings on a Culture Area*, pp. 22–37. Scranton: Chandler.

Forde, D. and A. R. Radcliffe-Brown, eds. 1950. *African Systems of Kinship and Marriage*. London: Oxford University Press.

Fortes, M. 1959. Descent, Filiation, and Affinity: A Rejoinder to Dr. Leach. *Man* 59:193–97, 206–12.

Fox, J. and K. Cumberland. 1962. *Western Samoa: Land, Life, and Agriculture in Tropical Polynesia*. Christchurch: Whitcomb and Tombes.

Freeman, J. D. 1961. On the Concept of the Kindred. *Journal of the Royal Anthropological Institute* 91:192–220.

—— 1964. Some Observations on Kinship and Political Authority in Samoa. *American Anthropologist* 66:553–68.

Freud, S. 1924–1950. *Collected Papers*. 5 vols. London: Hogarth Press.

Geertz, C. 1973. *Interpretation of Cultures*. New York: Basic Books.

—— 1975. On the Nature of Anthropological Understanding. *American Scientist* 63:47–53.

Gifford, E. W. 1929. Tongan Society. *Bulletin,* Bernice P. Bishop Museum, vol. 8.

Gilson, R. 1963. Samoan Descent Groups: A Structural Outline. *Journal of the Polynesian Society* 72:372–77.

—— 1970. *Samoa 1830–1900: The Politics of a Multi-Cultural Community*. Melbourne: Oxford University Press.

Goldenweiser, A. A. 1937. *Anthropology*. New York: F. S. Crofts.

Goldman, I. 1970. *Ancient Polynesian Society*. Chicago: University of Chicago Press.

Goodenough, W. 1955. A Problem in Malayo-Polynesian Social Organization. *American Anthropologist* 57:71–83.

Goody, J. 1961. The Classification of Double Descent Systems. *Current Anthropology* 2:3–25.

Hecht, J. 1977. The Culture of Gender in Pukapuka: Male, Female, and the *Mayakitanga* "Sacred Maid." *Journal of the Polynesian Society* 86:183–206.

Hocart, A. M. 1927. *Kingship*. London: Oxford University Press.

Hopper, A. and J. Huntsman. 1975. Male and Female in Tokelau Culture. *Journal of the Polynesian Society* 84(4):415–30.

Huntsman, J. 1971. Concepts of Kinship and Categories of Kinsmen in the Tokelau Islands. *Journal of the Polynesian Society* 80:317–54.

Kaeppler, A. 1971. Rank in Tonga. *Ethnology* 10:174–93.

Kantorowicz, E. 1957. *The King's Two Bodies: A Study in Medieval Political Theology*. Princeton: Princeton University Press.

Keesing, F. and M. Keesing. 1956. *Elite Communication in Samoa*. Palo Alto: Stanford University Press.

Keesing, R. 1968. Non-Unilineal Descent and the Contextual Definition of Status: The Kwaio Evidence. *American Anthropologist* 70:82–84.

Kernan, K. 1974. The Acquisition of Formal and Colloquial Styles of Speech by Samoan Children. *Anthropological Linguistics* 16:107–19.

Kraemer, A. 1902. *Die Samoa-Inseln*. 2 vols. Stuttgart: E. Naegele.

Labby, D. 1976. *The Demystification of Yap*. Chicago: University of Chicago Press.

Larkin, F. 1972. Review of the second edition of Mead's *The Social Organization of Manu'a*. *Journal of Pacific History* 7:219–22.

Leach, E. 1962. On Certain Unconsidered Aspects of Double Descent Systems. *Man* 62:214.

Leenhardt, M. 1947/1979. *Do Kamo: Person and Myth in the Melanesian World*. Chicago: University of Chicago Press.

Lemert, E. 1972. Forms and Pathology of Drinking in Three Polynesian Societies. In *Human Deviance, Social Problems, and Social Control*, pp. 218–33. Englewood Cliffs: Prentice-Hall.

Levine, R. 1973. *Culture, Personality, and Behavior*. Chicago: Aldine.

Lévi-Strauss, C. 1949/1963. *The Elementary Structures of Kinship*. Boston: Beacon Press.

—— 1967. Do Dual Organizations Exist? In *Structural Anthropology*. Garden City, N.Y.: Anchor Books, pp. 128–60.

—— 1966. *The Savage Mind*. Chicago: University of Chicago Press.

Levy, R. 1972/1974. Tahiti, Sin, and the Question of Integration Between Personality and Socio-Cultural System. Reprinted in R. LeVine, ed., *Culture and Personality: Contemporary Readings*, pp. 287–306. Chicago: Aldine.

—— 1973. *Tahitians: Mind and Experience in the Society Islands*. Chicago: University of Chicago Press.

Linton, R. 1936. *The Study of Man*. New York: Appleton-Century.

Lockwood, B. 1971. *Samoan Village Economy*. Oxford: Oxford University Press.

MacGregor, G. 1937. Ethnology of Tokelau. *Bulletin*, Bernice P. Bishop Museum, vol. 146.

MacKenzie, M. n.d. Personal communication.

Malinowski, B. 1932. *Argonauts of the Pacific*. New York: Dutton.

—— 1935. *Coral Gardens and Their Magic*. 2 vols. London: Allen and Unwin.

Marcus, G. 1980. *The Nobility and the Chiefly Tradition in the Modern Kingdom of Tonga*. Memoir no. 42. Wellington: Polynesian Society.

Marsack, C. C. 1958. *Notes and Practices of the Court and Principles Adopted in the Hearing of Cases*. Apia: Government of Western Samoa, Justice Department.

Maxwell, R. 1969. Samoan Temperament. Ph.D. dissertation, Cornell University.

Mead, M. 1928. The Role of the Individual in Samoan Society. *Journal of the Royal Anthropological Institute* 58:481–95.

—— 1929/1961. *The Coming of Age in Samoa.* London: Cape.

—— 1930/1969. The Social Organization of Manu'a. *Bulletin,* Bernice P. Bishop Museum, vol. 76. 2d ed. Honolulu: Bishop Museum Press 1969.

—— 1968. The Samoans. Reprinted in A. Vayda, ed., *People, and Cultures of the Pacific.* New York: Natural History Press.

—— 1970. *Blackberry Winter.* New York: Morrow.

Milner, G. 1966. *Samoan Dictionary.* Oxford: Oxford University Press.

Mischel, W. 1968. *Personality and Assessment.* New York: Wiley.

Murdock, G. P. 1960. Cognatic Forms of Social Organization. In *Social Organization in South-East Asia,* pp. 1–14. Chicago: Quadrangle Books.

Neffgen, E. n.d. The Samoan Race. The Alexander Turnbull Library, Wellington, New Zealand. Manuscript.

Panoff, M. 1964. L'ancien organisation ceremonielle et politique des Samoa occidentals. *L'Homme* 4:63–83.

Parsons, T. 1937. *The Structure of Social Action.* Glencoe: Free Press.

—— 1951. *The Social System.* Glencoe: Free Press.

Pitt, D. 1969. *Tradition and Economic Progress in Samoa.* Oxford: Clarendon Press.

Powles, C. G. 1973. The Status of Customary Law in Western Samoa. Masters thesis, Victoria University, Wellington.

Pratt, C. G. 1860/1911. *Dictionary and Grammar of the Samoan Language.* Malua: L. M. S. Church Press.

Radcliffe-Brown, A. R. 1950. Introduction. In D. Forde and A. R. Radcliffe-Brown, eds., *African Systems of Kinship and Marriage.* London: Oxford University Press.

—— 1951. *Structure and Function in Primitive Society.* London: Cohen and West.

Riesenberg, S. 1968. The Native Polity of Ponape. *Smithsonian Contributions to Anthropology,* vol. 10.

Rogers, G. 1977. The Sister Is Black. *Journal of the Polynesian Society,* 86:157–82.

—— n.d. Personal communication.

Sahlins, M. 1963. Poor Man, Rich Man, Big Man, Chief: Political Types in Melanesia and Polynesia. *Comparative Studies in History and Society* 5:285–303.

—— 1964. That's Not What I Said: Reply to Derek Freeman. Brief Communication. *American Anthropologist* 66:616–20.

—— n.d. Personal communication.

Scheffler, H. 1966. Ancestor-Worship in Anthropology or Observations on Descent and Descent Groups. *Current Anthropology* 7:541–51.

Schieffelin, E. 1976. *The Sorrow of the Lonely and the Burning of the Dancers.* New York: St. Martins Press.

Schneider, D. M. 1965. Some Muddles in the Models: Or How the System

Really Works. In M. Banton, ed., *The Relevance of Models for Social Anthropology*, pp. 25–85. ASA Monograph no. 1. London: Tavistock Publications.

—— 1968. *American Kinship: A Cultural Account*. Englewood Cliffs, N.J.: Prentice-Hall.

Schoeffel, P. 1978. Gender Status and Power in Samoa. *Canberra Anthropology* 1(2):69–81.

Schultz, E. 1911. The Most Important Principles of Samoan Family Law and the Laws of Inheritance. *Journal of the Polynesian Society* 20:43–53.

—— 1965. *Proverbial Expressions of the Samoan People*. Wellington: Polynesian Society.

Schutz, A. 1970. *On Phenomenology and Social Relations: Selected Readings*. Chicago: University of Chicago Press.

Shore, B. 1976a. Adoption, Alliance, and Political Mobility in Samoa. In I. Brady, ed., *Transactions in Kinship*, pp. 164–99. Honolulu: University of Hawaii Press.

—— 1976b. Incest Prohibitions, Brother-Sister Avoidance, and the Logic of Power in Samoa. *Journal of the Polynesian Society* 85(2):275–96.

—— 1979. Ghost and Government: A Structural Analysis of Alternative Institutions for Conflict Management in Samoa. *Man* n.s., 13:175–99.

—— 1980. World View, Literally: Images and Reflections. Manuscript.

—— 1981. Sexuality and Gender in Samoa: Conceptions and Missed Conceptions. In S. Ortner and H. Whitehead, eds., *Sexual Meanings*. Cambridge: Cambridge University Press.

Silverman, M. 1978. Maximize Your Options: A Study in Symbols, Values, and Social Structure. In R. F. Spencer, ed., *Forms of Symbolic Action*, pp. 97–115. Seattle: University of Washington Press.

Snell, B. 1960. *The Discovery of Mind*. New York: Harper and Row.

Stair, J. 1897. *Old Samoa, or Flotsam and Jetsam from the Pacific Ocean*. London: Religious Tract Society.

Stanner, W. E. H. 1953. *The South Seas in Transition*. Sidney: Australasian Publishing.

Stuebel, O. 1896. *Samoanische Texte; Unter Beihülfe von Einegeborenen Gesammelt und Übersetzt*. Berlin: Geographische Verlagshandlung Dietrich Reimer.

Taylor, C. 1971. Interpretation and the Sciences of Man. *Review of Metaphysics* 2:3–51.

Tiffany, W. 1971. Political Structure and Change: A Corporate Analysis of American Samoa. Ph.D. dissertation, University of California.

—— n.d. Manpower Mobilization in Ambilineal Descent Systems. Manuscript.

Trilling, L. 1971. *Sincerity and Authenticity*. Cambridge: Harvard University Press.

Truebetskoy, N. S. 1969. *Principles of Phonology*. Berkeley and Los Angeles: University of California Press.

Turner, G. 1884. *Samoa: A Hundred Years Ago and Long Before*. London: Macmillan.

Wagner, R. 1975. *The Invention of Culture*. Chicago: University of Chicago Press.

Warner, W. L. 1936. *A Black Civilization*. New York: Harper and Row.

Weiner, A. 1978. *Women of Value, Men of Reknown*. Austin: University of Texas Press.

Western Samoa, Government of. 1971. *Annual Statistical Abstract*. Apia: Government Printer.

Weston, S. 1972. Samoan Social Organization: Structural Implications of an Ambilineal Descent System. Ph.D. dissertation, University of California.

Williams, J. 1838. *A Narrative of Missionary Enterprises in the South Sea Islands*. London: John Snow.

Yalman, N. 1961. *Under the Bo Tree*. Berkeley and Los Angeles: University of California Press.

Index

Adoption: and *'āiga potopoto* (assembling kindred), 84; as a social link, 65, 66, 138, 306*n*6; and title bequests, 96, 311*n*10; *see also* Descent Groups; Genealogy; Kinship

Aga (social conduct): and *agaga* (soul), 155, 156; *agaga* as a socializing force, 156; ambivalence towards, 162, 186; as containing private experience, 185, 186; definition, 154, 251, 312*n*7; as distinguishing man from animal, 155; and respect vocabulary, 266; as virtuous behavior, 155, 171; and Samoan world view, 251, 252; *see also* 293–99; Behavior; Control; Relationship between *ali'i* and *tulāfale*

Agafili (orator title): conflict with *Tuatō*, 17, 64, 68, 285; definition, 15, 16; kinship links with *Tolova'a*, 90; translation of title, 287; *see also* Titles; *Tulāfale*

Aggression: and alcohol, 150, 151; constraint of, *see Aga*; expression of, *see Āmio*; as individual or unsocialized, 151–53; and inversion of *ali'i/tulāfale* relationship, 118; and untitled men, 150; *see also* Behavior; Control; Impulse expression

Ali'i (nobleman title): *'āiga ali'i* (families of *ali'i*), 25; census of, 62, 63; definition, 59; and food, 242, 250, 251; inversion of normal relationship with orators, 24, 25, 27, 246, 244, 245; link with *tamatane*, 248; as *matai*, 59; phonological style, 274, 275; position in greetings (*fa'alupega*), 76; resentment towards orators, 29, 30, 31; residence (*māota*), 61, 70; title succession, 61; *see also* Relationship between *ali'i* and *tulāfale*; *Tulāfale*

Alliances: dispersed, 57, 59; and marriage, 204, 205; political, 56, 57; *see also* Self, Samoan concept of; Titles

Āmio (personal behavior): and *āmioga* (acts typical of a group), 155, 156; *āmioga* as a socializing force, 156; as a conception of nature, 167; as controlled by *aga*, 185, 186; definition, 154; and evil (*leaga*), 171;

and human nature, 158; relation to laws, 157, 158; as socially disruptive, 155; suggesting animal behavior, 155; *see also* 293–99; *Aga*; Behavior; Control; Freedom; Self, Samoan concept of

Amituana'i (title), 87, 306*n*1

Aristocracy: *see Ali'i* (nobleman); *Matai* (chief); Titles; *Tulāfale* (orator title)

Aualuma (organization of village girls): definition, 104; function, 104, 105, 231, 232; leadership, 231; membership, 104, 231; proper area for activity, 232; recent changes, 105; structure as derived from *fono* (chiefly council), 77, 78; symbolic link with *ali'i*, 231; and the *taupou* (village "princess"), 231, 232; *see also 'Aumaga*; Village of men; Village of women

'Aumaga (untitled men's organization): definition, 101; function, 101, 102; leadership, 101, 231; membership, 101, 231; proper arena for activity, 231; as a socializing force, 102; structure as derived from *fono* (chiefly council), 77, 78; symbolic link with *Tulāfale*, 231; traditional leadership with *manaia* (titled son of a high chief), 231, 232; *see also Aualuma*; Village of men; Village of women

Authority (*pule*): ambivalence towards, 159, 304*n*; and church, 106, 107; definition, 65, 67, 159; as held by brothers, 234; and *malae* and *'a'ai*, 163; and *matai*, 107; *see also Matai* (chief); *Fono* (chiefly council); *Tulāfale*

Back (*tua*), as symbolic orientation, 50

Banishment: and ambiguity, 288; announced and actual, 120; definition, 114, 288; of *Tolova'a Aleki* and family, 28, 29, 31, 32, 288; *see also* Sanctions

Barth, F., 169

Bateson, G., 193, 194, 202, 203, 266, 313*n*

Behavior: and boundary testing, 51, 119; and evil, 171; and laws, 119, 120; on *malae*, 50, 109; and public knowledge,

Village orientation (*Continued*)
road, 50; seaward (*tai*), 49; as a structure of social control, 50, 162; and subvillages, 48, 51, 52; symbolism of *i tai* (towards the sea), 49, 50; symbolism of *i uta* (towards the land), 49, 50; *see also* Sala'ilua; Subvillage
Village plaza (*malae*), *see under* Village orientation

Wagner, R., xiii
Warner, W. L., 195
Weiner, A., 313*n*5

Weston, S., 35, 237, 305*n*4
Williams, J., 278
Women's Committee: definition, 102; membership, 102; and potential conflict with *matai*, 107; responsibilities, 11, 103, 226; structure as derived from *fono*, 77, 78; subcommittees, 103; *see also Aualuma*; Village of women
World view, Samoan: 251, 252, 277, 278; as dual 282, 283; *see also* Culture, Samoan; Self, Samoan concept of

Yalman, N., 307*n*3